Alexander Balmain Bruce

The Epistle to the Hebrews, the First Apology for Christianity

An exegetical study

Alexander Balmain Bruce

The Epistle to the Hebrews, the First Apology for Christianity
An exegetical study

ISBN/EAN: 9783337419646

Printed in Europe, USA, Canada, Australia, Japan

Cover: Foto ©Lupo / pixelio.de

More available books at **www.hansebooks.com**

THE
EPISTLE TO THE HEBREWS

THE FIRST APOLOGY FOR CHRISTIANITY

AN EXEGETICAL STUDY

BY

ALEXANDER BALMAIN BRUCE, D.D.

PROFESSOR OF APOLOGETICS AND NEW TESTAMENT EXEGESIS IN THE
FREE CHURCH COLLEGE, GLASGOW

AUTHOR OF
"THE KINGDOM OF GOD" "ST. PAUL'S CONCEPTION OF CHRISTIANITY"
"THE TRAINING OF THE TWELVE" "THE HUMILIATION OF CHRIST"
"APOLOGETICS; OR, CHRISTIANITY DEFENSIVELY STATED"
ETC. ETC.

CHARLES SCRIBNER'S SONS
153, 155, AND 157 FIFTH AVENUE
NEW YORK CITY
1899

TO

A. J. BUIST, Esq.

AND

OTHER SURVIVING MEMBERS OF EAST FREE CHURCH, BROUGHTY FERRY, WHO, NEARLY THIRTY YEARS AGO, HEARD LECTURES ON THE EPISTLE TO THE HEBREWS, CONTAINING THE GERMS OF THOUGHT OUT OF WHICH THIS BOOK HAS GROWN

PREFACE

This work is a companion to *The Kingdom of God* and *St. Paul's Conception of Christianity*, published respectively in 1889 and 1894.

The greater part of the contents appeared in the pages of *The Expositor* in 1888, 1889, 1890. All has been carefully revised, some portions have been re-written, and a chapter on the theological import of the Epistle, entirely new, has been added at the end of the book. The recent literature of the subject has been duly taken into account in footnotes on important points connected with the exposition.

Among the works referred to in these new notes, the chief are the Commentaries of Westcott (1889), Vaughan (1890), Weiss (in Meyer), and von Soden (in *Hand-commentar*). To these may be added the work of Ménégoz on the theology of the Epistle (*La Théologie de L'Épitre aux Hebreux*, 1894). It gives me pleasure to name here a book just published on the same subject by the Rev. George Milligan, son of the late Professor Milligan, some sheets of which I had an opportunity of reading while it was passing through the press.

I had expected, and even hoped, that recent publications on this important book of the New Testament would have made a new contribution to its interpretation superfluous. I cannot honestly say that I have found this to be the case. The last word has not yet been spoken. The interpretation of the letter has been carried to a high degree of perfection. But there is room and need for fresh work in the unveiling of the *soul* of this sacred writing, in the light of its author's aim, which I take to be to show the excellence of Christianity to a community possessing a very defective insight into its true nature. It is indeed *the first apology for Christianity*, as indicated in my sub-title. Readers will judge how far I have succeeded in placing this view of the book on a solid foundation.

I can at least claim for this effort that it is not the product of a brief and hasty consideration. It is the mature fruit of study carried on for a period of thirty years—a fact which I deemed it not unfitting to commemorate in the form of a dedication to friends to whom my thoughts were communicated in their earliest shape.

I owe thanks to my esteemed colleague, Professor Denney, D.D., for assisting me in reading the proof sheets, and for offering some valuable suggestions.

A. B. BRUCE.

GLASGOW, *March* 1899.

CONTENTS

CHAPTER I
INTRODUCTION .   PAGE 1–25

CHAPTER II
CHRIST AND THE PROPHETS: CHAP. I. 1–4   26–44

CHAPTER III
CHRIST AND THE ANGELS: CHAPS. I. 5–14—II. 1–4   45–64

CHAPTER IV
THE HUMILIATION OF CHRIST AND ITS RATIONALE: CHAP. II. 5–18   65–87

CHAPTER V
THE CAPTAIN OF SALVATION: CHAP. II. 10   88–105

CHAPTER VI
THE WAY OF SALVATION: CHAP. II. 11–18   106–128

CHAPTER VII
CHRIST AND MOSES: CHAP. III.   129–150

CHAPTER VIII
THE GOSPEL OF REST: CHAP. IV.   151–173

CHAPTER IX
CHRIST NOT A SELF-ELECTED, BUT A GOD-APPOINTED PRIEST: CHAP. V. 1–10 174–195

CHAPTER X
THE TEACHER'S COMPLAINT: CHAPS. V. 11-14—VI. 1-8   196-218

CHAPTER XI
THE TEACHER'S CHARITY: CHAP. VI. 9-20   219-239

CHAPTER XII
THE ORDER OF MELCHISEDEC: CHAP. VII. 1-10   240-261

CHAPTER XIII
THE PRIEST AFTER THE ORDER OF MELCHISEDEC: CHAP. VII. 11-28   262-287

CHAPTER XIV
CHRIST AND AARON: CHAP. VIII.   288-305

CHAPTER XV
THE ANCIENT TABERNACLE: CHAP. IX. 1-10   306-325

CHAPTER XVI
THE MORE EXCELLENT MINISTRY: CHAP. IX. 11-14   326-354

CHAPTER XVII
THE NEW COVENANT: CHAP. IX. 15-28   355-372

CHAPTER XVIII
SHADOW AND SUBSTANCE: CHAP. X. 1-18   373-392

CHAPTER XIX
DRAW NEAR!: CHAP. X. 19-31   393-409

CHAPTER XX
BE NOT OF THEM THAT DRAW BACK: CHAPS. X. 32—XII. 29   410-427

CHAPTER XXI
THE THEOLOGICAL IMPORT OF THE EPISTLE   428-451

THE EPISTLE TO THE HEBREWS

―――◆―――

CHAPTER I

INTRODUCTION

My purpose in this work is to expound the *Epistle to the Hebrews* in relation to its leading idea, or distinctive conception of the Christian religion. The main object of this introductory chapter will be to state what, in my view, that central idea is. But as this question is closely connected with another, namely, What was the religious condition of the first readers? and that again to a subordinate extent with a third, Who were the first readers? it may be advantageous to approach the main question by a brief preliminary discussion of the other two.

The question as to the first readers resolves itself into three distinct questions : (1) Were there, properly speaking, any first readers? *i.e.* was the writing designed for the benefit of any particular community? (2) Were they Jews or Gentiles? (3) Where were they located?

As to the first point: it is in favour of a special

definite destination that, throughout, the author not only employs the second person, but in exhortations expresses himself with a fervour and urgency that forcibly suggest a circle of readers whose spiritual needs are known and lie as a burden on his heart. "Wherefore, holy brethren, partakers of the heavenly calling, consider the Apostle and High Priest of our profession, Christ Jesus." "Take heed, brethren, lest there be in any of you an evil heart of unbelief, in departing from the living God." "Having therefore, brethren, boldness to enter into the holiest by the blood of Jesus . . . let us draw near with a true heart." Justice is not done to such hortatory intensity when it is treated as a mere oratorical device on the part of a writer who is all the time dealing with tendencies rather than with persons, though doubtless aware that many persons, unknown to him, in whom these tendencies reveal themselves, may be influenced by what he says.[1]

As to the second point, the nationality of the first readers: till recent times the generally accepted view was that the inscription *To the Hebrews*, though not original, correctly indicated the destination. But of late there has been a tendency, especially among German scholars, to set this traditional view aside, and to hold that the first readers must have been *Gentiles*, not Jews.[2] Among the grounds on which this hypothesis is made to rest are such as these: the fundamentals enumerated in

[1] So Reuss. Vide *La Bible*, vol. viii.; *L'Épitre aux Hébreux*, pp. 12, 14.

[2] Among those who hold this view may be named Schürer, Weizsäcker, and von Soden; and, among English writers, M'Giffert, in his *History of Christianity in the Apostolic Age*.

chap. vi. 1, 2 are such as were suitable only for catechumens of pagan antecedents; the expression "the living God," chaps. iii. 12, ix. 14, suggests an antithesis between the true God and pagan idols; the moral exhortations in the Epistle possess special appropriateness only when conceived as meant for Gentile Christians. Those who advocate a Gentile destination recognise, of course, that the writing, on the face of it, seems to connect its readers, in respect of religious traditions and sympathies, with the Jewish people. But the numerous phrases which seem to imply readers of Hebrew race are explained by the assumption that at the time when our Epistle was written the Gentile Church had served itself heir to the title and privileges of the elect people. To the question, What need for so elaborate a plea for Christianity as against Leviticalism in a work written for Gentile Christians? the answer given is: The type of Gentile Christianity the author had to deal with was an eclectic syncretistic system into which an amateur attachment to Levitical institutions entered as an element, and became so strong as to imperil the Christian faith with which it was associated in a time of persecution.[1]

That this hypothesis has been supported with an amount of ingenuity sufficient to lend it plausibility may be frankly admitted. But that the case has been even approximately proved cannot be allowed. After all has been said for it that can be said by such a scholar as von Soden,[2] one cannot but sympathise with the verdict

---

[1] So in effect Pfleiderer in *Urchristenthum*, p. 620. In his *Paulinismus* he assumed that the readers were *Jews*.

[2] *Vide* his commentary in *Hand-Commentar*.

of a distinguished English commentator who pronounces the theory, however ably supported, "an ingenious paradox."[1] Whatever impression arguments in its support may make on our minds for a moment, the old view soon reasserts itself with irresistible force. A recent French writer on the theology of the Epistle has well said: "What strikes us in this Epistle throughout is a Jewish taste of the soil, and an absence of allusion to pagan worship so complete, that we have difficulty in comprehending how anyone can discover in it the least indication of its being meant for readers of pagan antecedents."[2] Ostensibly, the first readers are certainly Hebrews, and Hebrews alone; the *onus probandi* lies on those who affirm that they were not really such. It requires a very extensive display of exegetical ingenuity to explain away the Jewish physiognomy and costume. If the readers were indeed Gentiles, they were Gentiles so completely disguised in Jewish dress, and wearing a mask with so pronounced Jewish features, that the true nationality has been successfully hidden for nineteen centuries.

In comparison with the question of nationality, that of locality is of quite subordinate importance. The home of the community addressed, according to the traditional opinion, was Jerusalem, or at least Palestine. The chief argument in support of this view, intrinsically probable, is one of which the full force cannot be felt till the question as to *spiritual* situation has been discussed. Here it can only be briefly stated. The Epistle in its

---

[1] Westcott, *The Epistle to the Hebrews.* Introduction, p. xxxv.
[2] Ménégoz, *La Théologie de L'Épitre aux Hébreux*, pp. 26, 27.

whole contents implies a very grave situation. Those to whom it is sent are in danger of apostasy, not merely through outward tribulation, but even more through a reactionary state of mind. The evidence of reaction is the pains taken to meet it by an exhibition of the nature and excellence of the Christian religion in comparison with the Levitical. Now this state of mind was more likely to be found in Palestine, in Jerusalem above all, than anywhere else; especially if, as has been inferred from some things in the Epistle, the temple was still standing and the temple worship still going on when it was written. Jerusalem was the home of Jewish conservatism, and all the influences there tended to develop and strengthen even in Christian circles a reactionary spirit. It is this consideration which tells in favour of Jerusalem as against *Alexandria*. In the neighbourhood of this Egyptian city, at Leontopolis, there was a temple where Jews resident in Egypt might worship, which outlasted the temple at Jerusalem by one or two years. In so far, therefore, as the Epistle implies the present practice of temple worship, that part of the problem might be met as well by Alexandria as by Jerusalem. But the religious atmosphere of Alexandria was less conservative than that of Jerusalem. There one might expect to find in the Christian community a type of thought more in sympathy with that of the writer of our Epistle. For such readers such a writing was not needed. To outward trial they might be exposed, but in absence of the more serious inward trial there was no demand for so elaborate an apology for the Christian faith.

Objections to the Jerusalem hypothesis have been stated, which to not a few modern scholars have appeared insuperable. The most formidable, perhaps, is the language in which the Epistle is written. If it was addressed to the Church in the Holy City, why was it not written in Aramaic, the language with which they were most, if not exclusively, familiar? In ancient times this difficulty was met by the suggestion that the Epistle was originally written in the Hebrew tongue, and then translated into Greek. This opinion, entertained by Clement of Alexandria, was merely a device to get over stylistic objections to Pauline authorship and linguistic objections to Palestinian readers. If the work was first written in Hebrew, it might be Paul's, though the Greek was not his; and it might be intended for Jews in Jerusalem as its first readers, though they understood Greek with difficulty, or not at all. The hypothesis has nothing else to commend it. For no one reading the Epistle, and noting the fluent style of the Greek, and the original cast both of thought and expression, will readily acquiesce in the view that what we have here is a translation out of another tongue, so entirely different in structure, of the thoughts of another mind. The simplest solution of the difficulty in question is that the writer used the language he had at command. A Hellenist, Jew by race, Greek in culture, he wrote in the Greek language, hoping to be understood by his readers sufficiently well, if not perfectly, through their knowledge of Greek, or with the aid of an interpreter.

Other objections are of so little weight as to be

hardly worth mentioning; and on the whole it may be said that, in spite of all that has been urged against it, the traditional view is still entitled to hold its ground. What has been advanced in favour of other places, such as Rome,[1] at most amounts to this, that they satisfy more or less the conditions of the problem, and are not improbable suggestions. None of them satisfy so well as Jerusalem or Palestine the main condition, namely, the moral and spiritual situation required by the contents of the Epistle. I care not, for my part, where the first readers are located, provided this fundamental requirement be duly secured. I am content to leave the question of locality unsettled—an attitude demanded by the state of the evidence—so long as the religious position is justly conceived. That the Epistle itself fully puts within our power.

The spiritual situation of the persons addressed was very serious, full of peril both from outward and from inward causes. They were in danger of apostatising from the faith, because of persecution endured on account of it, and also because of doubts concerning its truth. The former part of this description of their state rests on express statements in the Epistle. That they had in time past been a persecuted people is manifest from chapter x. 32: "Call to remembrance the former days, in which, after ye were illuminated, ye endured a great fight of afflictions." That they were subject to tribulation on account of their faith, still, is plain from the fact that they are exhorted to remember

[1] One of the ablest recent contributions in support of the Rome hypothesis may be found in Reville's *Origines de L'Episcopat*, 1894.

their former experiences and their heroic bearing under these as an aid to patience now. The fact is also apparent from the eloquent recital of pious deeds done by the fathers in ancient days, in the eleventh chapter. The noble army of martyrs is made to march past as in a military review, to inspire the living sufferers with martial fortitude. Then, when the main body of the army has marched past, the attention of the spectators is directed to the Great Captain, for the same end. Tried Christians are bid look at Jesus, that His example may keep them from growing weary and faint in their minds.

The inner spiritual condition of the Hebrews is not so plainly and explicitly described, but ominous hints occur here and there in the Epistle from which it can, with tolerable certainty, be inferred. They are in danger of slipping away from the Christian faith, as a boat is carried past the landing-place by the strong current of a stream (chap. ii. 1). They have become dull in hearing, and in all their spiritual senses; they are in their dotage or second childhood, and need again to be fed with milk, *i.e.* to be taught anew the rudiments of the Christian faith, instead of with the strong meat which befits spiritual manhood (chap. v. 11–14). Their state is such as to suggest to a faithful instructor, anxious for their welfare, thoughts of a final apostasy and malignant renunciation of Christ, and to call up before his mind the unwelcome picture of a land well tilled and rained upon, yet bringing forth only thorns and briers, and, so, nigh unto cursing (chap. vi. 6–8). Evidently those of whom such things can be said are men who have never had insight into the essential nature and distinctive features of the Christian religion; who, with the lapse of time, have fallen more and more out of sympathy with the faith they profess, and who are now held to it chiefly by a tie of custom, which, under the stress of outward trial, may be snapped at any moment; insomuch that their friend who writes to them feels it necessary to make a desperate effort to rescue them from the impending danger by trying to show to them what is so clear to his own mind, the incomparable excellence of the Christian religion.

That effort, in which the writer, stimulated by a supreme occasion, puts forth all his great intellectual and moral strength, is the best evidence that the foregoing account of the spiritual state of the Hebrew Church is not exaggerated. Such an effort was not made without urgent cause. The writers of the New Testament were not literary busybodies, or theologians by profession, who studied theological topics in a purely academic spirit. They wrote under the imperious constraint of urgent needs. When, *e.g.*, Paul writes epistles to prove that salvation is through faith alone, it is because there is a powerful party at work, endeavouring to subvert the gospel of grace by reintroducing a religion of legalism. In like manner, when some unknown doctor in the Church sets himself to commend Christianity as the perfect religion, it is because he finds many fellow-Christians clinging to Levitical rites, unable to see that, when the perfect has come, the rudely imperfect should be allowed to pass away. Some have thought that the book before us, which we have been accustomed to call an Epistle, is in reality a theological treatise, or a carefully studied discourse delivered by a superior man to a Christian congregation in a great centre of intellectual culture, like Rome.[1] It is, one would say, too long, and in part too abstruse, to be suitable for preaching, though portions of it, like the eloquent eulogium on faith in the eleventh chapter, may have formed the substance of congregational addresses. But if it be a sermon, it is a very unusual one, exceptional in its moral intensity not less than in its ability, spoken with peculiar solemnity to a congregation placed in very critical circumstances.

Be it treatise, sermon, or epistle, this writing is no mere collection of theological commonplaces. The writer is not repeating but *creating* theology. His readers or hearers are persons with whom nothing can be taken for granted, not even the most elementary ideas as to the significance of Christ's death. No greater mistake, I believe, can be committed (though it is a common fault of commentators) than to assume that the first readers were in the main in sympathy with the doctrinal views of the writer, and that the chief or sole occasion for writing was the need of consolation and strengthening under outward trial.[2] Such an assumption involves a virtual reflection on the judgment of the writer in ex-

---

[1] *Vide* von Soden in *Hand-Commentar*, p. 5.

[2] Professor A. B. Davidson expresses this view in these terms: "The writer evidently feels that, on the whole, he has his readers on his side." "The Epistle is written from the secondary position of theological reflection upon the facts. The fact that the Son is a High Priest is a commonplace to his readers."—Commentary, in *Handbooks for Bible Classes*, pp. 14, 106.

patiating at unnecessary length on accepted truths, and it must exercise a prejudicial influence on the exposition of the weightier, that is the doctrinal, part of the Epistle, taking the soul out of it for the expositor, and making the most strikingly original thoughts appear in his eyes trite formulas of an already familiar system. Thus the remarkable combination of the idea of a *forerunner* with that of a High Priest in chapter vi 20 will probably provoke no remark, but be quietly passed over as if it were as familiar to the first readers as it has become to us; whereas it must have appeared quite startling in their eyes, and not unnaturally, as the one word πρόδρομος expresses the whole essential difference between the Christian and the Levitical religions—between the religion that brings men nigh to God and the religion that kept or left men standing at a distance.

Observing the points which are emphasised in the Epistle, we gather that three things connected with Christianity were stumbling-blocks to the Hebrew Christians :—

(1) *The superseding of an ancient, divinely appointed religion by what appeared to be a novelty and an innovation.* The Levitical worship was of venerable antiquity, and not of man's devising but of God's ordering; and how a system which had lasted so long and had derived its origin from heaven could ever pass away, and how it could be legitimately replaced by a religion which was of yesterday, were matters which ill-instructed Hebrew believers were at a loss to comprehend. Nor can we wonder greatly at this, when we consider with what desperate tenacity many at all times cling to old

religious customs which can make no pretensions to Divine origin, but are merely human inventions.

(2) The Hebrew Christians found another stumbling-block in *the humiliation and sufferings of Jesus regarded as the Christ.* They were unable to reconcile the indignity of Christ's earthly experience with the dignity of His Person as the Son of God and promised Messiah. They did not see the glory of the Cross. They were unable to understand and appreciate the honour which was conferred upon Jesus in His being appointed to taste death as the Saviour and Sanctifier of sinners. They were unable to comprehend how it was consistent with the character of the First Cause and Last End of all things either to permit or to command His Son to pass through a curriculum of suffering and temptation as a qualification for office as the Captain of Salvation. In this respect they were like the apostles in the days of their discipleship, who, having confessed their faith in Jesus as the Christ, the Son of the living God, were utterly confounded when they heard their Master immediately after go on to tell "how that He must go unto Jerusalem, and suffer many things," and even be put to death. The pains taken and the ingenuity displayed by the writer in endeavouring to make it clear that suffering, or death, was *for one reason or another*[1] a necessary experience of one occupying Christ's position, show how much his readers stood in need of enlightenment on the subject.

(3) The third stumbling-block in Christianity to the

---

[1] On the various aspects under which the death of Jesus is presented in the Epistle, *vide* the last chapter of this work.

mind of the Hebrews was *the absence therefrom of a priesthood, and a sacrificial ritual.* For that Christ was at once a Priest and a Sacrifice they do not seem to have been able to comprehend, or even to imagine. Their ideas of priesthood and sacrifices were legal and technical. A priest was a man belonging to the tribe of Levi and to the family of Aaron, physically faultless, whose business it was to offer in behalf of the people the blood of bulls and goats as a sacrifice for sin. Of course Jesus could lay no claims to a priesthood of that sort. He was not of the tribe of Levi, or the house of Aaron, and He had nothing to offer—nothing, that is, which the legal mind could regard as a victim. And of any other priesthood than the legal, men accustomed to Levitical rites doubtless found it difficult to form any conception. A priest without priestly robes, and visible materials of sacrifice such as oxen, sheep, and goats, was to them a shadowy, unreal being. The author of the Epistle was well aware that such was the feeling of his readers; his whole manner of treating the subject betrays consciousness of the fact. Thus when he introduces a reference to the royal priesthood of Melchisedec to show them that a priesthood other than legal was recognised in Scripture, and to help them to rise up to the thought of the spiritual, eternal priesthood of Christ, he cannot refrain from giving expression to a feeling of irritation, as if conscious beforehand that he will not succeed in carrying their intelligence and sympathy along with him. He feels it to be a hard, thankless task to set forth such lofty truths to dull, mechanical, custom-ridden minds.

Such being the situation of the parties addressed, it is

easy to see what must be the character of a writing fitted and designed to conduct them through the perils of a transition time. It must combine argument and exhortation, now expounding a great spiritual truth, now pausing to utter a warning, or to speak a word of an inspiring, cheering nature to heavy-hearted men. Such, accordingly, is the writing before us. It is not a merely didactic theological treatise, though it begins in an abstract theological manner, without preface or salutation. It is what it is called in the superscription in our English Testament, an epistle or letter, in which the writer never loses sight of his readers and their perilous condition, but contrives to mingle argument and exhortation, theoretical and practical matter, so as to be at every point in contact with their hearts and consciences as well as their intellects. Theology and counsel are interwoven throughout so as to give to the whole the character of a "word of exhortation."

The theoretical sections of the Epistle, however, may be looked at apart, and the question asked, What do they teach, what conception of the Christian religion do they embody? That is the question to which we now, at last, turn our attention.

The theoretical matter may be viewed either abstractly and *per se*, or in relation to the occasion of its being written. Viewed in the former way, it shows us the author's own mode of conceiving Christianity; viewed in the latter, it shows us the method he pursued to bring others to his way of thinking. In the one aspect it is a dogmatic treatise, in the other it is an apologetic treatise. The question we propose to consider thus resolves itself into two: What is the author's own idea of Christianity? and, What is his method of insinuating it into minds prepossessed with beliefs more or less incompatible therewith?

The author's own idea. He regards Christianity as the *perfect*, and therefore the *final*, religion. It is perfect because it accomplishes the end of religion, and because it does this it can never be superseded. Nothing better can take its place. But what is the end of religion? To bring men nigh to God, to establish between man and God a fellowship as complete and intimate as if sin had never existed. This, accordingly, is what the writer of our Epistle emphasises. Christianity for him is the religion of *free, unrestricted access to God*; the religion of a new, everlasting covenant, under which sin is completely extinguished, and can act no longer as a separating influence. This thought runs like a refrain through the Epistle. It appears first distinctly in the place where Christ the High Priest of the New Testament is called a *forerunner* (vi. 20). Where the High Priest of the new era can go, we may follow, in contrast to the state of things under the old covenant, according to which the High Priest of Israel could alone go into the Most Holy Place. The thought recurs at vii. 19, where the Christian religion is in effect characterised as the religion of the better hope, because it is the religion through which we draw nigh to God. The same great idea lurks in the puzzle concerning the altar of incense, whose position in the tabernacle it is impossible to define (ix. 4). It belonged to the place within the veil in spirit and function, but it had to be without for daily use, in connection with the service carried on in the first compartment. The source of this anomaly was the veil, whose very existence was the emblem of a rude, imperfect religion, under which men could not get nigh to God. Finally, how prominent a place the idea of free access held in the writer's mind appears from the fact that when he has finished his theoretic statement he commences his last prolonged exhortation to his readers in these terms: "Having therefore, brethren, liberty to enter into the holiest by the blood of Jesus, by a new and living way, which He hath consecrated for us, through the veil, that is to say, His flesh; and having an High Priest over the house of God: *let us draw near* with a true heart in full assurance of faith" (x. 19–22).

This positive idea of the Christian religion contains an implicit contrast between it and the Levitical religion, which is conceived of as failing to accomplish the end of all religion—keeping or leaving men far off from God. Many things connected with Leviticalism were, in the writer's view, significant of this radical fatal defect, but chiefly the veil dividing the tabernacle into two compartments—an outer chamber, accessible to the priests for daily service, and an inner chamber, accessible to the high priest alone, and even to him only once a year and after the most careful precautions. That veil prohibitory and minatory was, to his mind, the emblem of a religion which taught a negative idea of Divine holiness, presenting God as saying: "Stand off, I am unapproachably holy"; and left the conscience of the worshipper unpurged, so that he feared to come near.

As such the veil was a prophecy of transiency in reference to the system with which it was connected. For no religion may or can endure that fails in the great end for which religion exists. Accordingly, in the Epistle the temporary character of the Levitical religion is proclaimed with emphasis and iteration. On the other hand, *permanency* is predicated of the Christian religion with, if possible, greater emphasis and iteration. The burden of the Epistle is: Leviticalism for a time, Christianity for aye. Of everything connected with Christianity eternity is predicated. The salvation it provides is *eternal*, its priesthood is *for ever*, the great High Priest of humanity possesses the power of an *endless life*, and by the offering of Himself through the *eternal* Spirit has obtained *eternal* redemption for men. Those who believe in Him have the promise of an *eternal* inheritance. The new covenant is *everlasting*.

This contrast between the two religions in the vital point naturally suggests the method of contrast generally as a good one for the apologetic purpose in hand. The central defect presumably implies defect at all points. Accordingly, the writer adopts this method, and institutes a series of comparisons so managed as, while duly and even generously recognising whatever was good in the old system, to mark it indelibly with a stamp of inferiority. The first point of comparison most readily suggesting itself is that of the priesthood. The Levitical religion had its high priest, with his gorgeous robes a very imposing figure. How about Christianity? can its superiority be demonstrated here? If not, the cause is lost, for the whole value of religion lies in its power to deal with the problem of sin. The vital question is: Can it perfect the worshipper as to conscience? Only where there is a perfect priest can there be a perfect religion. The writer will need all his skill to establish his case here. Not that there is any room for doubt to men possessing spiritual insight; but he is writing to men who lack that gift, and to whom it is difficult to make it clear that Christ was a Priest at all, not to speak of His being the perfect Priest, the very ideal of Priesthood realised.

A contrast between Christ and Moses might readily suggest itself. To institute this contrast might indeed seem to be raising questions not vital to the argument. But there was room for relevant comparison here also. For Moses was the leader of Israel during the memorable epoch of her redemption out of Egypt, and Jesus was the Captain of a still greater salvation. The general resemblance in the point of leadership might make plain some things incidental to the career of a captain. And if it could be shown that Jesus was greater than Moses, it would prevent the prestige of the lesser leader from shutting the mind to the claims of the greater.

Another contrast still was possible—one that would not readily occur to us, but which lay ready to the hand of one writing to Hebrews familiar with the current views of Jewish theology. In that theology angels figured prominently, and in particular they were believed to have been God's agents in the revelation of the law to Moses and Israel. This view gave to that revelation a very august and imposing character, through which the

Christian revelation might suffer eclipse. A comparison between Christ and angels was therefore forced on a writer who desired to deal exhaustively with the sources of anti-Christian prejudices. He must show that Christ was higher in dignity than angels, that the word spoken through Him might receive due attention.

These contrasts are all instituted in the Epistle, but in the reverse order. The most remote from the centre, and as we are apt to think the least important, comes first; and the most vital, last. First the agents of revelation under the two Testaments are compared; then their respective Captains of salvation, and then finally their High Priests. It is shown, first, that Christ is greater than angels as one who speaks to men in God's name; second, that He is greater than Moses as the leader of a redeemed host; third, that He is greater than Aaron as one who transacts for men in God's presence. The argument will unfold itself gradually, and need not be here outlined.

The opening sentences of the Epistle may be said to contain yet another comparison—between Christ and the *Prophets*, the human agents of the earlier revelation. This comparison is less developed and less emphasised, partly because the prophets were in the same line with Jesus, precursors rather than rivals, preaching the gospel of a Messiah and a Divine kingdom before the epoch of fulfilment, pointing on to that epoch and making no pretence to finality; partly because they were men, not angels, less likely to become the objects of an overweening idolatrous esteem. But there is a latent contrast here also, as we shall see. The revelation of the Son was the natural and needed complement of prophetic revelation.

We have thus in all *four* contrasts, forming together a full statement as to the comparative merits of the two religions. In the first two Jesus, as Revealer, is contrasted with the Old Testament agents of *Revelation*, prophets and angels. In the second couple Jesus, as Redeemer, is contrasted with the Old Testament agents of *Redemption*, Moses and Aaron. The position formally proved is that in both respects the new religion is *better* than the old. The real view of the writer is that Christianity is the best religion possible, the ideally perfect and therefore final religion.

Taken as a whole, the Epistle, in its apologetic aspect, is a masterpiece, meeting effectually a most urgent need of the early apostolic age, and in its general principles, if not in all its arguments, of perennial value to the Christian Church. At transition times, when an old world is passing away and a new world is taking its place, it is ever the fewest who enter with full intelligence and sympathy into the spirit of the new time. The majority, from timidity, reverence, or lower motives, go along with the new movement only with half their heart, and have an all but invincible hankering after old custom, and a strong reluctance to break with the past. Christ signalised and also kindly apologised for this conservative tendency when He said, "No man having drunk old wine desireth new; for he saith, The old is good." For such half-hearted ones, numerous in a transition time, a prophet is needed to interpret the new, and a literature of an apologetic character, vindicating the rights of the new while knowing how to recognise the worth of the past. Such a prophet was the writer of this Epistle, and such a literature is preserved for us therein. It is the only writing in the New Testament of a formally and systematically apologetic nature. Elsewhere may be found ideas helpful to Christians passing through a transition time, notably in the Pauline Epistles. But the stray apologetic thoughts in these Epistles, though of great value, were not sufficient. A more detailed and elaborate theology of mediation was required to make Jewish believers men who did not look back. Paul did not go sufficiently into particulars. He spoke of the law too much as a whole, as was natural for one who had passed through his experience. He had tried to make the law everything, and having failed, he swung to the opposite extreme and pronounced it nothing. That salvation could not come through legalism needed no further proof for him: it was axiomatically clear. It was enough to say oracularly, "By the works of the law shall no flesh be justified."

That might be enough for a Paul, but it was not enough for ordinary men who lacked Paul's intense experience, clear insight, and the intellectual thoroughness that can follow to their last consequences accepted principles. A more detailed, one may say a more patient, less impassioned apologetic was needed to carry the mass of Jewish Christians safely through the perils of a transitionary period. It was not sufficient to say, Christ is come, therefore the legal economy must end; it was necessary to point out carefully what men had got in Christ—not merely a Saviour in a general way, but the reality of Old Testament symbols, the substance whereof legal rites were adumbrations; to demonstrate, in short, that not *grace* alone, but *truth* came by Christ, truth in the sense of spiritual reality. Paul insisted mainly on the grace that came by Christ. It was reserved for the author of the Epistle to the Hebrews to insist on the *truth* that came by Christ. Paul, indeed, had not altogether overlooked this aspect. His epistles contain hints of the doctrine that Levitical rites were shadows of good things to come, as in the significant passage, " Christ our Passover is sacrificed for us" (1 Cor. v. 7). But these hints remain undeveloped. Of what splendid developments they were capable appears in our Epistle, where the Melchisedec Priesthood of Christ is unfolded with such subtlety of argument and elevation of thought as awaken the admiration of all.

If the view prevalent in the Eastern section of the early Church, that Paul was the author of our Epistle, were true, then we should have to say that in it he performed a service which he had not had leisure or occasion to render in any other epistle. But the Pauline authorship seems destitute of all probability. *A priori* it was unlikely that the man who wrote the recognised Pauline Epistles should be the man to achieve the task prescribed to the writer of this Epistle to the Hebrews. It is seldom given to one man to do for his age all that it needs. Paul surely did enough without claiming for him everything. Moreover, the style, the temperament, and the cast of thought characteristic of this Epistle are markedly different from those traceable in the letters to the Galatian, Corinthian, and Roman Churches. The difference in style has been often commented on, but the contrast in the other respects is even more arresting. The contrast has its source in diversity of mental constitution and of religious experience. Paul was of an impetuous, passionate, vehement nature; hence his thought rushes on like a mountain torrent leaping over the rocks. The writer of our Epistle is obviously a man of calm, contemplative, patient spirit, and hence the movement of his mind is like that of a stately river flowing through a plain. Their respective ways of looking at the law speak to an entirely different religious history. The law had been to Paul a source of the knowledge of sin, an irritant to sin, and a murderer of hope; therefore he ascribed to it the same functions in the moral education of mankind. The writer of our Epistle, on the other hand, appears to have gained his insight into the transient character of the Levitical religion and the glory of Christianity, not through a fruitless attempt at keeping the law with Pharisaic scrupulosity, but through a mental discipline enabling him to distinguish between shadow and substance, symbol and spiritual reality. In other words: while Paul was a moralist, he was a religious philosopher; while for Paul the organ of spiritual knowledge was conscience, for him it was devout reason.

One consideration which biassed the ancients in favour of Pauline authorship, and which is still not without influence on opinion, was the wish to have for so important a writing a worthy and, in view of the question of canonicity, an apostolic author. It is certainly remarkable that the writer of so important a book should have remained unknown. But there is no call for solicitude on that account. Canonicity is entirely independent of authorship. It depends on canonical *function*. That the Epistle to the Hebrews performs an important function in the organism of New Testament literature is evident if the views presented as to its character and aim in this chapter be correct. We may therefore rest content that the name of the writer should remain unknown, and even find a certain satisfaction in the reflection that anonymity is a not incongruous attribute of a writing which begins by virtually proclaiming God to be the only Speaker in Scripture and Jesus Christ to be the one Speaker of God's final revelation to men.

And yet it might be advantageous for the interpretation of the Epistle if we knew, if not the name, at least the thought-affinities of the writer. It always helps us to understand an author when we know the *school* he belongs to. Some are of opinion that this can be positively ascertained in the case before us, the evidence being found in the thought and style of the book itself. The writer's speech, it is held, bewrayeth him. He is thereby shown to be a disciple of *Philo*, an adherent of the Alexandrian school of religious philosophy. The fact is that there are words, phrases, and ideas in the Epistle which sound like an echo of the dialect and type of thought characteristic of that school, as these are made known to us in the pages of Philo. How far the acquaintance of the writer with Alexandrian philosophy extended cannot be determined, but there is that about his style of thought, expression, and argument which suggests an Alexandrian influence or atmosphere, and lends plausibility, if not probability, to the conjecture of Luther, which has since his time found wide acceptance, that he is to be identified with the Apollos mentioned in Acts xviii. 24–28, there described as "born at Alexandria, an eloquent man, and mighty in the Scriptures." While, however, keeping in view the Alexandrian culture of the writer as a possible factor, we must be careful not to exaggerate the extent of its influence on his thought. There is certainly, as we shall have occasion to point out, no trace of abject, helpless discipleship. We shall do wisely, indeed, not to make the writer a slavish follower of any school, whether Alexandrian, Pauline, or Rabbinical, but to recognise frankly the free independent activity of his mind, and to be ever on the outlook for originalities.

The date of the Epistle has been variously fixed. There are some things in it which suggest the impending destruction of the Jewish State in the year 70 A.D., and such an ominous situation harmonises well with the grave tone of the book throughout. All seems to say: a judgment day is approaching; a general overturn is at hand, when all that can be shaken will be shaken to make room for the kingdom that cannot be shaken. There is therefore a high degree of probability in the suggestion that the Epistle was written when the war which issued disastrously for the Jewish people was raging, and drawing near to its awful crisis.[1]

[1] *Vide* on this Rendall, *Epistle to the Hebrews*, Appendix, p. 65.

CHAPTER II

CHRIST AND THE PROPHETS

Chap. I. 1-4

The long sonorous sentence with which the Epistle opens serves as an introduction to all that is to follow. It is, so to speak, the portico of an august temple, its weighty clauses being a row of stately ornamental pillars supporting the roof. This temple front has an imposing aspect! It fills the mind with awe, and disposes one to enter the sacred edifice in religious silence rather than to undertake the interpreter's task. May a fitting spirit of reverence control and chasten throughout the train of expository thought!

The writer announces at once the theme of discourse, and introduces the leading thought on which he intends to expatiate. The rhetorical style of his work may explain in part why, being an Epistle, it does not begin with salutations, but rushes *in medias res*. Be this as it may, our author does, without a moment's delay, plunge into the heart of his subject: defining his Christological position; setting forth Christ as the supreme object of religious regard, superior to prophets, priests, and angels; the Apostle through whom God made His final revelation to men; the Priest who effectually and for ever made that purification of sins which Levitical sacrifices failed to accomplish; the Heir, Maker, and Sustainer of all things; not only above angels, but Divine, God's Eternal Son and perfect image.

While forming a suitable introduction to the whole writing, the opening paragraph is at the same time the first instalment of an apologetic argument designed to show the superiority of Christ, and by consequence of the Christian religion. Therein the writer institutes a contrast between Christ and the Hebrew prophets as agents of Divine revelation. "God, having spoken of old in many parts and in many modes, to the fathers in the prophets, at the end of these days spake to us in (His) Son."

By "the prophets" may be meant chiefly those strictly so called, the literary prophets—Hosea, Isaiah, Jeremiah, etc. In that case the contrast stated, though still valid, loses somewhat of its sharpness. For the men who uttered the oracles of the New Covenant, and of the suffering servant of Jehovah, and (including Psalmists among the prophets) such evangelic sentiments as "He hath not dealt with us after our sins," were, as already remarked, forerunners rather than rivals, preachers of the Gospel of Divine Grace before the time. Still, even in their case, there is a contrast at least in degree, if not in kind (as in the Pauline antithesis between law and gospel). The terms employed to discriminate between the earlier and the final revelations apply to the whole contents of the Old Testament. Hence the term "prophets" is probably intended to cover the whole body of Hebrew Scriptures, the "law," as well as the "prophets" in the narrower sense. It is not against this that the angels are recognised as the agents by whom the law was given (ii. 2), for such recognition may be regarded as a concession to Jewish opinion rather than as the serious expression of the writer's own view.

Before considering the terms in which the two revelations are contrasted, we may pause for a moment to note and comment on the manner in which the recipients of the earlier revelation are described. They are called "the fathers." The title implies that the Epistle is meant for the special benefit of Jewish readers. Does it imply further that the writer recognises only Jewish Christians, or recognises Gentile Christians only on condition of their consenting first to become Jews by submitting to the rite of circumcision? In that case we should have to say that the author was not merely not Paul, but not even a Paulinist, a man, that is, sympathising with the universalist position taken up by Paul in the great controversy between him and the Judaists. This I cannot believe. The Epistle, though apparently identifying Christendom with the Hebrew Church, is manifestly universalistic in spirit. No one who considers the freedom with which the writer speaks of Levitical institutions as weak, useless, doomed to pass away, can imagine him having any difficulty about recognising Gentile Christianity without regard to circumcision, any more than one who understands the spirit of Christ's teaching can think of Him as attaching religious importance to the Jewish national rite, although in the Gospels, as in this Epistle, there is no express indication of opinion on the subject. Then, on the principle that a man is known from the company he keeps, Pauline sympathies may be inferred from the writer's acquaintance with Timothy.[1] That acquaintanceship makes it all but certain that he could not be ignorant of the controversy, and therefore cannot be conceived of as one to whom the question between Paul and the Judaists had not occurred, and who was in the same state of mind as if he had written his book before the controversy arose. He must have had an opinion on the subject; and under whatever influences he had been reared, Palestinian or Alexandrian, we may be sure that his sympathies were on the side of universalism. While therefore he is not to be identified with Paul, he may be regarded as a Paulinist: not in the sense that he resembles or follows Paul in the details of his theology, which he certainly does not, but in the sense that for him, as for Paul, the Israel of God means all in every land that believe in Christ, and that in Christ for him, as for Paul, there is no distinction between Jew and Gentile.

Passing now to the terms of the contrast, we observe that the ancient revelation is characterised objectively by the ascription to it of certain attributes, whereas on the other hand the quality of the final revelation is indicated by a simple reference to the agent. The former is in effect described as a piecemeal, multiform, or multimodal revelation, the latter as one made through a *Son*.

[1] Chap. xiii. 23.

God spake to the fathers "in many parts and in many modes" (πολυμερῶς καὶ πολυτρόπως). These epithets are not employed for the purpose of merely literary description, to suggest, *e.g.*, the picturesque nature of the Hebrew sacred literature; still less for the purpose of pointing out its spiritual excellence. They are rather carefully selected to serve the end aimed at in the whole writing—to indicate the inferiority of the earlier revelation, that Hebrew Christians might not cling to it as something final. Each of them is serviceable to this purpose, both together adequately describe the situation. The first of the two words points to the obvious fact that there were many human speakers, each making his little contribution to the unfolding of the Divine will, the law being given by Moses, the story of Divine Providence in Israel's history by a series of chroniclers, the songs of the sanctuary by sacred poets, the wisdom of life by the sages, and the Messianic prophecies by Isaiah, Jeremiah, and their brethren. The mere fact that there were many speakers involved of course the partiality and fragmentariness of any one of the contributions. If the law was all God had to say, *e.g.*, why did the Hebrew Bible contain more than the Pentateuch? No intelligent person could dream of regarding any section of the ancient sacred literature as by itself a complete revelation. But perhaps taken altogether they might lay claim to that character? The writer's reply is a decided negative; for it is to exclude this idea that he adds the second epithet. The meaning of it is not so clear as that of the first, but the best guide to its interpretation is the end it is designed to serve—the exclusion of the notion of finality as attaching to the Hebrew Bible as a whole. The thought intended is that the sum of the parts could not make a complete, satisfactory revelation, because each part, besides being fragmentary, was disadvantageously qualified by the fact of the human agent knowing only in part. Each speaker or writer was an imperfectly enlightened man, and his contribution was coloured by his ignorance. The separate pieces of revelation were tinged with the subjectivity of the writer and the prevailing ideas of his time. Hence they could not be summed up in one uniform whole, because they were heterogeneous and even discrepant in religious tendency. They might be bound up in one volume, but that did not make them one coherent revelation. The one sacred book contained two types of religion—one legal, the other evangelic; two theories of Providence—one teaching an unvarying, exceptionless, retributive moral order, rendering to every man according to his works, the other having for its keynote, "He hath not dealt with us after our sins"; two conceptions of the Messianic kingdom—one particularistic, the other universal. How could such a book be God's full final message to men? How needful at the very least an authoritative interpreter who should tell us to which parts of the Holy Book we must attach most importance!

After centuries, during which the voice of prophecy was silent and the "night of legalism" prevailed, God at length sent One who was able to do that and more. In the end of the days He spake in or by *a Son*. This is all that is stated by way of characterising the new final revelation. No descriptive epithets are employed, as in the case of the earlier revelation, *because they are not needed*. The one expression "in a Son" (ἐν υἱῷ) involves in itself a full antithesis to the fragmentary modal revelation given to the fathers in the prophets. In the first place, there is only one agent of revelation instead of many, therefore the revelation is given in one gush instead of in many separate parts. Then the absence of the article in the phrase ἐν υἱῷ gives it this meaning, that one standing to God in the relation of Son can make a revelation which shall be perfect in its character, therefore complete and final in contents. The thought is substantially identical with that expressed in the Fourth Gospel: "No man hath seen God at any time; the only begotten Son, who is in the bosom of the Father, He hath declared Him." A Son dwelling in the bosom of God, His Father, and having access to His inmost thoughts, is fit to be the perfect exegete of His mind: such is the implicit argument of both Gospel and Epistle. This view implies that the Son must be the last speaker: no more remains to be said; it implies further that He is the only Speaker of the new era —apostles and apostolic men sinking into the subordinate position of witnesses, confirmers of what they have seen and heard of the Son, echoes of His voice, commenders of His teaching to the world.

Who the "Son" is does not immediately appear, but from the sequel we learn that He is Jesus Christ, who is called by His historical name, *Jesus*, for the first time, in chapter ii. 9. That ascertained, we know what is meant when it is stated that God hath spoken by the

Son. The reference, doubtless, is to the words spoken by the Son when He was in this world, and as a historical personage was known by the name of Jesus of Nazareth. And as God's speech through Him is placed in parallelism with His speech through the prophets, which took written form in a sacred literature, the presumption is that the author of our Epistle had in his mind a fixed, accessible, probably written, tradition of all that Jesus taught and did. That such an evangelic tradition, of definite contents, was in existence when our Epistle was written, and was known to the author, there can be little doubt; that he valued it highly, and desired his readers to value it, may be taken for granted. It is true, there is no very clear reference in the Epistle to a Gospel literature, unless we find one such in chapter ii. 3. It is also true that copious indications of acquaintance with evangelic facts are not forthcoming. There are, however, more traces of such acquaintance than we might at first imagine, and it is quite misleading to say that there are in the Epistle only two data with reference to the terrestrial life of Jesus, namely, that He was of the tribe of Judah, and that He offered up prayer with strong crying and tears.[1] In any case, paucity of reference to evangelic facts must be ascribed to lack of occasion, by no means to any supposed indifference to the teaching of Jesus as we find it recorded in the Gospels. Such indifference would be self-stultifying on the part of one who laid such stress on the revelation made through the Son: inconceivable

[1] Ménégoz, p. 77. For traces of acquaintance with evangelic facts in our Epistle, *vide* chapter iii. of this work.

in one who was so fully alive to the defects of the Old Testament, and the need there was for a further revelation in regard to the very fundamentals of religion—the ideas of God, man and their relations, the true nature of righteousness, and of the kingdom of heaven and the conditions of admission within its borders—that is to say, of just such a revelation as the recorded words of Jesus contain.

The speech of God through Jesus is represented in the first place as speech through a Son, to invest it with due authority. It may here be pointed out that in all the four contrasts the superiority of Jesus Christ is made to rest on the foundation of His *Sonship*. It is so here in the first contrast, that between Jesus and the prophets. It is so also in the contrast between Jesus and angels. He, as Son, is begotten; angels, like all creatures, are made. Therefore His word claims more attention than that spoken by angels, with whatever solemn accompaniments, on Sinai (chaps. i. 5, 10: ii. 1, 2). So, also, in the contrast between Jesus and Moses. Moses was great in God's house, but only as a servant; Christ is not only greater, but belongs to another category, that of Son (iii. 5, 6). So, finally, in the contrast between Jesus and Aaron. Aaron, though an important personage within the Levitical system, was but a sacerdotal drudge, ever performing ceremonies without real value, "daily ministering and offering oftentime the same sacrifices which can never take away sin" (x. 11). But the High Priest of Christendom is Jesus, *the Son of God* (iv. 14), who, as a Son, learned obedience through suffering (v. 8), and who, after His Passion, voluntarily endured, was, as the Son, "consecrated for evermore" (vii. 28).

Sonship being the basis of Christ's claim to supremacy, it was fitting that on the first mention of His filial standing occasion should be taken to unfold the full significance of the august title. This, accordingly, is done in the following clauses of the opening sentence, in a manner which shows how far our author was from understanding the title in a common or attenuated sense. He indeed takes it so much in earnest that the effect of his statement is to make Christ, to all intents and purposes, not the highest of creatures,[1] but absolutely Divine. His Christological position is not less advanced than that of the prologue of the Fourth Gospel. Whence he drew his lofty ideal of the Son we may try to guess, and the pages of Philo, with their constant eulogistic references to the Logos, the texts which follow relating to the excellent name inherited by the Messiah (i. 5-12), and logical analysis of the idea of Sonship, may be suggested as possible sources of inspiration. What we have to do with, however, is the ideal as here presented, and the interpretation of the phrases by which it is delineated. Our best guide in this task will be *to keep constantly in view the bearing of the attributes ascribed on the fitness of the Son to be the full and final Revealer of God's mind*.

The first attribute is *heirship*, which is immediately suggested by the idea of Sonship. This attribute has no remote bearing on fitness to be the final Revealer. Heirship of all things implies that all things exist for the heir. He is the moral aim of creation; the key to

---

[1] Ménégoz maintains that the Christology of the Epistle is *Arian*. *Vide* his work on the Theology of the Epistle, p. 100.

the religious significance of the universe is in His hands. Who, then, can better than He tell what it all means—this vast world—its *raison d'être*; give us a hint of the true theory of the universe, surely a most important subject of revelation?[1]

It is next said concerning the Son, that by Him also God made the worlds. This is not, like heirship, an immediate, obvious deduction from Sonship. The Logos idea perhaps lies behind this part of the account given of the Son's privileges and functions. In that case, *making* means not mechanical agency, but supplying the plan according to which a thing is made. The Son, as the Logos, is the Divine idea of the world, its rational basis. He is the ideal origin of the world, as well as the world-aim. And the former attribute, not less than the latter, qualifies Him for being the Revealer *par excellence*. In virtue thereof He can reveal the spiritual essence of the world, the great thoughts of God which find expression in the laws of nature and in the course of history. It is not His business, indeed, to discover the secrets of science, and play the part of a Newton. His work is higher: to tell us what we are to think of the Being who appointed the laws of the planetary system and set the sun to shine in the heavens. He was performing this work when He said, "A sparrow shall not fall on the ground without your Father" (Matt. x. 29), and, "He maketh His sun to rise on the evil and on the good" (Matt. v. 45).

Of special importance is the third clause in the

[1] The thought of our Epistle at this point has affinity with the Epistle to the *Colossians*.

eulogium on the Son, that in which He is declared to be the effulgence (ἀπαύγασμα) of God's glory, and the exact image (χαρακτήρ) of His essence. The terms employed had a place in the vocabulary of the Græco-Jewish religious philosophy. Philo called *man* a ray (*apaugasm*) of the Divine,[1] and in the Book of Wisdom the same term is used to express the relation of wisdom to the Eternal Light.[2] Philo calls the Logos the *character*, or image, on the seal of God,[3] and the higher spirit in man a certain type and character of Divine Power.[4] In view of such passages in the Alexandrian literature, possibly known to our author, we might give to the expressions he employs an alternative reference, either to the Son as man or to the Son as the Logos or Wisdom of God. Adopting the former alternative, we should find in his phrases the thought that the Son as man—God in human form—was in an eminent manner what all men are in their degree, a ray of Divine Light and an image or copy of the Divine Nature. But it is more probable that the mind of the writer does not at this point touch the earth, but moves in the high transcendental region of the Son's eternal relations, and that it is of the Son as Logos, or the Reason of God, that he makes the statement on which I now comment.

The two terms *apaugasma* and *character* are susceptible of a double interpretation. The former may mean either the effulgence or the refulgence of the Divine

[1] *De Opif.* M. 51.   [2] vii. 26.
[3] *De Plantat.* 5, σφραγῖδι θεοῦ ἧς ὁ χαρακτήρ ἐστιν ἀΐδιος λόγος.
[4] *Vide*, on these passages, Siegfried's *Philo von Alexandria*, p. 321.

Glory,[1] the direct outgoing radiance or the reflected image, as of the sun in water. The latter may mean either the figure carved on a seal, or the impression which it makes when stamped upon a soft receptive substance like wax. Taken in the former sense, in either case the two words would express the Son's relation to the world, setting Him forth as the Divine Light which illuminates the world, "the true Light which lighteth every man that cometh into the world," and as the Divine Figure on God's seal by which He puts His stamp on the whole creation, and especially on man. Taken in the latter sense, they would place the emphasis on the Son's relation to God—the Son the luminous image of God, a reflected sun, and resembling God as exactly as the copy in wax resembles the figure on the seal. It is not necessary to decide between the two alternative renderings and references, as both convey or imply the same view of the Son's Divine nature.

It was to be expected that these pregnant phrases would play their part in the history of theological controversy. Heretics and orthodox had each their own way of interpreting them. The Sabellians laid stress on the term *apaugasma* as suggesting the idea of a modal manifestation rather than of a distinct personality. The Arians emphasised the term *character* as implying a position of dependence and derivation belonging to the Son in relation to the Father. The orthodox, on their side, maintained that by the combination of the two both errors were excluded, the one phrase implying identity of nature—"Light from Light"—so excluding

[1] *Vide* Westcott, *ad loc.*

Arianism; the latter implying independent personality, so excluding Sabellianism. Strict exegesis cannot settle the controversy.

Whatever the precise theological import of the phrases, there can be no doubt that they serve well the purpose of evincing the fitness of the Son to be the full and final Revealer of God to men. It is for this end, not to furnish in a scholastic or speculative spirit a definition of the Son's Divinity, that they are here employed, and in that view they are happily chosen. Who so fit to make God known as one who is related to Him as the sun's rays to the sun, and who resembles Him as the image impressed on wax resembles that on the seal? His word must be as the bright light of day, than which nothing can be brighter, and He can say of Himself, "He that hath seen Me hath seen the Father."

One clause more completes the imposing description of the Son's nature and functions: "Bearing all things by the word of His power." It claims for the Son the functions of Providence, as a previous statement had claimed for Him the functions of Creation. He is the Sustainer of the world, as He is the Creator, Light, and Reason of the world. This attribute also bears on His fitness to be the full *final Revealer*. He who is the Providence of the world can interpret Providence, can tell us authoritatively what the course of nature and history means, what is the Divine Purpose running through the ages. The prophets tried to read the riddle of life, but they were as men groping in the dark. The Son came and spoke as one who was in the secret, finding a Gospel of Divine Grace even in sunshine and rain, and assigning beneficent redemptive virtue to the sufferings of the good which had so sorely perplexed a Jeremiah and a Job.

In view, now, of all these august attributes ascribed to the Son, what is the inevitable inference? Surely that here is One who when He speaks for God eclipses all previous speakers, and has a supreme claim to be listened to! And yet, is the argument not too conclusive, the logic too crushing? Does the writer not defeat his own purpose by making everything turn on status, dignity, rather than on intrinsic merit? The final Speaker is exhibited as *Divine*: would it not have been more serviceable to have exhibited Him rather as eminently *human*? Would it not have been better to have said, "Hath in these last days spoken to us by the meek, lowly Son of Man," thus giving the word spoken by Him a chance of appearing *winsome*, and not merely *awful*? Yes, if he had been writing for *us* and not for Hebrew Christians. But the melancholy fact was that he was arguing with men who had no power of appreciating the humiliation state of Jesus, and the pathos of the contrast between the incomparable sweetness and light of His speech and the lowly condition of the Speaker. Therefore there was no course open but to fall back on a celestial dignity which was not apparent in the earthly life, and to borrow therefrom a robe of external authority wherewith to invest words which, on their own merits, however exceptional, would fail to command attention. Whether by this means attention was secured, and what might be its moral value, are questions which may be left to private reflection.

The closing part of the sublime encomium on the Son remains to be noticed: "Who having made purification of sin, sat down on the right hand of the Majesty on High."

From the beginning of verse 3 the exaltation of Christ is in the view of the writer, as appears from the fact that all the clauses preceding that in which the session on the throne is spoken of are participial in form. "Who being, etc., having made purification, etc., sat down." The participial clauses indicate two grounds for the exaltation, a physical and an ethical. Being Godlike in nature, a celestial throne is the place that *fits* the Son; having made purification of sin, He *deserves* it.

The purification is antecedent to the exaltation, and belongs to the earthly state, the state of humiliation. From the slight parenthetical manner in which it is referred to, one might hastily infer that the earthly state and all that belonged to it was in the writer's eye something to be ashamed of. How very far that was from being the case we shall see hereafter. Meanwhile it is enough to point out that the author of our Epistle, like the Apostle Paul, evidently viewed the exaltation-state not only as congruous to the nature of the Son, but as the reward of His priestly performance. "He humbled Himself and became obedient unto death, therefore God exalted Him," said Paul. Our author means the same thing when he says: He made purification of sin and then sat down on the throne.

In the Textus Receptus the means of purification are specified: "When He had *by Himself* purged our sins." The words δι' ἑαυτοῦ, omitted in the best codices, were a natural, almost inevitable addition, slipping from the margin into the text; for that Christ's offering was HIMSELF is one of the great leading ideas of the Epistle, written, so to speak, in large capitals. Yet it was not at all likely to be introduced here. The writer was too skilful a master of the art of persuasion to bring in so distinctive, and for his readers so difficult, a truth before he could make more of it than was possible at the outset. Therefore he contents himself with stating Christ's priestly achievement in the barest terms, reserving developments for a later stage.

At this point alone the lofty encomium on the Apostle and High Priest of the Christian confession touches the earth. But for this brief reference to the purification of sins, we might almost doubt whether the august personage spoken of in the proem had ever been in this world of time and sense. It is indeed natural to assume that the Son, being placed on a line with the prophets as an agent of revelation, like them appeared as a man among men, and heroically witnessed for truth amidst the contradictions of the world. But when we read on, and observe the lofty, superhuman epithets attached to the name, we half suspect that we have been mistaken, till we come to the words, "when He had purged sins," whereby we are reassured. Some hold that the purification itself took place in heaven; but even in that case we touch the earth, at least inferentially. For purification implies blood shed, and bloodshedding implies death, and death bears witness to a previous incarnate life. Thus the priestly service, wherever performed, has a human history for its background—a history which when inquired into will doubtless turn out to be full of instruction, pathos, inspiration, and consolation. It may be said to have been the interest of one writing to tempted Hebrews to make as much use as possible of this history, to bid them look to the Man Jesus, and to show them this Man in His brotherly sympathy, heroic fidelity, and manifold experience of trial, so that they might see Him in a way fitted to nerve them to endurance. We expect therefore, and we desire, to find in this writing not a little relating to the earthly life of the Son. Our bias is not to relegate everything to heaven; it is decidedly the opposite,—we avow it at the outset,—to hold on firmly to the earth wherever we can, consistently with honest exegesis. That the priesthood of Christ is placed in the heavenly sanctuary is admitted, but it is a question how far this is due to the apologetic method of the Epistle. We must distinguish between the form and the substance of the writer's thought, between his essential idea and the mode in which he states it in an argument constructed for the benefit of others. But of this more hereafter.

The exaltation is described in terms taken from Psalm cx., amplified by a rhetorical circumlocution for the Divine name. In other places the language employed for the same purpose is simpler, except in chapter viii. 1, where the formula becomes even more solemn: "Sat down on the right hand of the throne of the Majesty in the heavens." There the session on the right hand seems to be referred to as the symbol and proof of the completeness, and therefore finality, of Christ's self-sacrifice. Here the aim rather is to make the exalted Christ completely eclipse the angels. For the long introductory sentence winds up with the declaration that in taking His seat on the right hand of the Majesty on high the Son became " by so much better than angels as He hath inherited a more excellent name than they." Thus, after the skilful manner of the writer, is the new theme woven into the old; for angels are to be the next subject of comparison with Christ. The preliminary statement here made has to our ears the effect of an anticlimax. It seems a small thing to say of One who sitteth at the right hand of God that He is higher in dignity than angels. So it is from the view-point of modern Christian thought, in which angels occupy a very subordinate place. But the high rank assigned to angels by Jewish theology at the beginning of our era imposed upon the writer of our Epistle the unwelcome necessity of making what appears to us this superfluous assertion of Christ's superiority.

CHAPTER III

CHRIST AND THE ANGELS

CHAP. I. 5-14; CHAP. II. 1-4

A MODERN interpreter would not be sorry to pass over in silence this section about angels. It is an unwelcome task to consider gravely a proof that Christ is greater than angels; the thing to be proved is so much a matter of course. For modern men the angels are very much a dead theological category. Everywhere in the old Jewish world, they are next to nowhere in our world. They have practically disappeared from the universe in thought and in fact. The "nature" angels, by whose agency, according to the Jewish theory of the universe, the phenomena of the physical world were produced, have been replaced in our scientific era by mechanical and chemical forces. The angels of Providence, though not so completely discarded, are now rare and strange visitants.

The subject was probably a weariness to the writer of our Epistle. A Jew, and well acquainted with Jewish opinion, and obliged to adjust his argument to it, he was tired, I imagine, of the angelic régime. Too much had been made of it in rabbinical teaching and in popular opinion. It must not be supposed that he was in sympathy with either. His state of mind was, doubtless, similar to that of all reformers living at periods of transition, who have lost interest in the traditional, old, and decadent, and are eagerly, enthusiastically open to the influences of the new time. He cared as little for angelology as for Leviticalism. Both for him belonged to the old world of Judaism, which was ready to vanish away, and whose disappearance he did his best to promote. This mood of his one can fully appreciate; it lends a pathetic interest even to his argument about the angels.

That argument possesses a certain religious grandeur. Overlooking for the moment critical and exegetical difficulties connected with this picturesque mosaic of Old Testament texts,[1] how impressive the sublime contrast drawn, how admirably it serves the purpose of making angels dwindle into insignificance in presence of Christ! He, the first-born of God, Himself Divine, performing creative functions, everlasting, sitting on a Divine throne, victorious over all foes, and exercising righteous rule; they, worshippers, servants, subjects, creatures, perishable like all created beings.

When studied in detail, however, the proof of the thesis maintained is much less plain than the thing proved. We have no difficulty in believing that Christ is greater than angels. But the citations by which this proposition is supported bristle with perplexities of

---

[1] Let it be here noted, once for all, that in quoting the Old Testament the writer relies entirely on the Septuagint. He uses a text closely resembling that of the Codex Alexandrinus.

all sorts. There is hardly a text in this Old Testament mosaic that does not present a problem, soluble perhaps, but by its presence weakening for us the religious impression which the whole passage can be conceived to have made on minds for which our difficulties did not exist.

These problems, critical and exegetical, I shall lightly touch, just sufficiently to indicate their nature and the direction in which solution lies. That done, we shall be in a better position for appreciating the broad effect of the contrast running through the quotations.

There are seven quotations in all, having for their general aim to show the surpassing excellence of Christ's *name*—His Messianic inheritance from Old Testament Psalms and Prophecies. Some divide them into two classes—those which relate to the more excellent name, and those which relate to the better dignity, including under the former head the three quotations in verses 5, 6, and under the latter the four in verses 7–13. Such a rigid distinction is uncalled for. The two topics run into each other. The ostensible aim throughout is to show the kind of titles given to the Messiah. But into the exhibition of the name the dignity intrudes, simply because each implies the other. Thus in one of the texts Christ is set forth as a Divine *King*. It is a name and also an office, or, if you will, an office and also a name.

Another solicitude of interpreters is to determine the relation of the citations to the "states" of Christ. Some think that they all refer exclusively to the state of exaltation. This, doubtless, must be the case if the writer of our Epistle held the theory concerning the position of angels in the old world which certain recent commentators ascribe to him. The theory is this: that angels were the rulers of the present visible world, that to their dominion men in general were subject, and Christ also when He was on earth. The contrast drawn between Christ and the angels is thus really a contrast between two worlds, the present world and the world to come, and between two universal administrations, that of angels in the world about to pass away, and that of Christ and men in the new world about to come in. It is only in the latter that Christ occupies a position of superiority, therefore the texts which assert His superiority must be relegated to the post-earthly state in which He *became* better than angels.

There is no evidence in the Epistle that the writer held this theory as to angelic rule. There is no evidence that he regarded it even as a tenet of contemporary Jewish theology. The statement in chapter ii. 5, "Unto the angels hath He not put in subjection *the world to come*," may indeed contain a hint that he was aware of such a view, based on Deuteronomy xxxii. 8, being entertained by Jews, but it would not follow that he himself held the opinion, or even that he thought it worth reckoning with, like the Jewish doctrine of the angelic function in connection with the lawgiving, which for argumentative purposes he assumed to be true.[1]

[1] *Vide* on this point Professor Davidson, who ascribes to the writer the above theory, and Bishop Westcott, in his Commentary, who thinks it possible the writer in chap. ii. 5 had the statement in Deut. xxxii. 8 (Sept. Version) in his mind, as expressing the belief that God had assigned the nations to the care of angels, while Israel was His own portion.

Turning now to the quotations, questions may be raised either as to their *relevancy* or as to their *legitimacy*. They are not relevant unless the passages quoted refer to the Messiah. The writer assumes that they do, and takes for granted that the assumption will not be disputed by his readers. Not only so: he assumes that these texts are directly and exclusively Messianic. He proceeds on the same assumption in reference to all his Messianic citations throughout the Epistle. His interest in the Old Testament is purely religious and Christian. He thinks, not of what meaning these holy writings might have for the contemporaries of the writers, but only of the meaning they have for his own generation. This need cause us no trouble. The limited, purely practical view taken of Old Testament prophecy by New Testament writers is no law for us, and ought not to be viewed as interdicting the scientific, historical interpretation of the prophetic writings. It were a more serious matter if it should be found that passages cited as Messianic had no reference whatever to the Messiah, either directly or indirectly. Now, on first view of at least some of these quotations, it certainly seems as if the writer thought himself at liberty to quote as Messianic any statement about either God or man that appeared to suit his purpose. Which of us, *e.g.*, would have thought the passage quoted from Psalm cii. in vers. 10–12 applicable to Messiah? Yet on second thoughts we discover that, consciously or instinctively, the writer proceeds on a principle, and does not quote at haphazard. Two principles appear to underlie the group of quotations: that all statements concerning men, say, kings of Israel,

4

which rise above the historical reality into the ideal are Messianic; and that statements concerning Jehovah viewed as the Saviour of the latter days are also to be regarded as Messianic. The former of these principles applies to the first two quotations in ver. 5, and to the fifth and seventh in vers. 8, 9, and 13. All these passages may be regarded as referring originally to a king of Israel, to Solomon, or some other; but in each case there is an ideal element which could not be applied to the historical reality without extravagance. "I have *begotten* thee," "Thy throne, O *God*," or even "thy throne of God," the words implying in either case Divine dignity, "Sit on My right hand," taken along with "thou art a priest *for ever*." The latter of the two principles above stated applies to the quotation from a Psalm (cii.) which speaks of a time coming when Jehovah shall build up Zion, and when the kingdoms of the world shall join with Israel in serving Him. It is possible that the writer regarded this text as Messianic, because in his view creation was the work of the pre-existent Christ. But it is equally possible that he ascribed creative agency to Christ out of regard to this and other similar texts, believed to be Messianic on other grounds.

The third quotation, in ver. 6, presents a complication of difficulties. The first is, whence is it taken? The thought is substantially found in Psalm xcvii. 7, "Worship Him, all ye gods" (angels in Sept.). But the "And" (καὶ) with which the quotation begins is against the Psalm being the source. The sentence, word for word, including the "and," occurs in the Septuagint Version of Deuteronomy, xxxii. 43, and there can be little doubt that it was from that place the writer made the citation. But just there the Septuagint diverges widely from the Hebrew original as we know it, the verse in Greek consisting of four clauses, only one of which, the third, has words answering to it in the Hebrew. It is the second clause which is quoted in our Epistle. The question thus arises: With what propriety could use be made, in an important argument, of words taken from the Greek version which have nothing answering to them in the Hebrew text? This is a question of legitimacy. Now it is possible that the Greek translators found Hebrew words corresponding to their version in the Codex they used, but as that is only a possibility the question cannot be evaded. The answer offered in an apologetic interest by commentators is, that the thought contained in the quotation is found elsewhere in Scripture, as, *e.g.*, in the above cited Psalm, and that therefore no wrong is done to the teaching of the sacred writings in the original tongues by quoting from the Septuagint a passage to which there is nothing corresponding in the Hebrew. This consideration is for *our* benefit. For the first readers there was no difficulty. For them, as for the writer, the Septuagint *was* Scripture; and hence throughout the book it is always quoted without hesitation, and apparently without reference to the question how far it corresponded with the Hebrew original. For us the Septuagint is nothing more than a translation, sometimes accurate, sometimes the reverse, based on a Codex which might have many defects. Hence the argument of the Epistle cannot always carry for us the weight it had for the first readers. Nor is it necessary it should. What we have mainly to do with is the essential teaching, the principles which the arguments are adduced to establish. Arguments are for an age; principles are for all time.

Why did the writer take the citation from Deuteronomy rather than from the Psalm? Possibly because it was the first place in Scripture where the thought occurred; possibly because he found the thought embedded there in a passage Messianic in its scope, on the second of the two principles above enunciated; for therein Jehovah is represented as appearing in the latter days for the deliverance of Israel by the judgment of her and His adversaries. If the Messianic reference be admitted, of course the use of the text in a eulogy on the Son is legitimate. But we observe that the writer calls the Son the "first-begotten," and speaks of Him as introduced into the inhabited world on the occasion to which the text refers. Whence the title? and what is meant by this introduction? As to the title, the writer possibly regarded it as implicitly contained in the texts quoted in ver. 5; or he may have had in his mind the words, "I will make Him My first-born" (Psalm lxxxix. 27), which, like the first two texts, refer to the promise made to David through Nathan. In the latter case the use of the title here is virtually the introduction of another quotation illustrative of the excellent name conferred on the Son. It is as if he had written, "Unto which of the angels said He at any time, 'Thou art My Son, this day have I begotten Thee'? And again, 'I will be to Him a Father, and He shall be to Me a Son'? and again, 'I will make Him My first-begotten'?"

By these texts the Son is placed in a position of peerless eminence, in a unique relation to God. The next text, that taken from Deuteronomy, assigns to angels, though also called sons of God in Scripture, the lowly position of worshippers: "Let all the angels of God worship Him." This order is conceived by our writer as given out by the Supreme Lord "when He bringeth in the First-begotten into the world." How are we to understand this statement? It seems to me simply an imaginative interpretation of the quotation to which it is attached. The summons to worship addressed to the angels suggests to the writer's mind, as a fit setting, the idea of a solemn introduction of the Son to the world which He has made, and of which He is the heir, that He may receive worshipful homage, as the heir, from its rational inhabitants, and especially from angels as the highest created intelligences, and as representing the universe of being (τὰ πάντα). The "introduction" is ideal, not historic: the conception is dramatic, as in chapter v. 10, where the Son entering heaven, perfected by suffering, is represented as hailed, saluted by His Father: "High Priest after the order of Melchisedec!" It is poetry, not history or dogmatic theology.[1]

[1] Some find in the text an implied antithesis between a first and a second introduction of the Son into the inhabited world (οἰκουμένη), and understand the writer as referring to the latter event, *i.e.* to the second coming of Christ accompanied by an angelic host. Their chief grounds are—(1) the place in Deuteronomy from which the words are taken speaks of judgment; (2) the position of πάλιν in the sentence requires us to render, not "and again when," but "and when again," and suggests connection with the nearest verb = and when He *again bringeth in*. Against this is the previous use of πάλιν, ver. 5, to introduce a second quotation, which makes

The quotation we have been considering refers indirectly to angels, assigning to them a place of subordination to the Son. The one which follows in ver. 7 refers to them directly. It is the only one of the seven quotations which does contain a direct statement concerning the angels, so that it is of great importance as revealing the writer's conception of their position in the universe. In reference to this quotation there is a preliminary question of legitimacy to be considered. The words are an exact reproduction of the Septuagint version of Psalm civ. 4, their sense in English being: "Who maketh His angels *winds* (not spirits, as in A.V.), and His ministers a flame of fire." But it has been doubted whether the Greek version is a correct rendering of the Hebrew. It is held by some commentators

it likely that it is here used a second time to introduce a third. If the writer had meant to hint at a second introduction, he would probably have used another word, say, δεύτερον. Further, how unlikely that he would in this abrupt way refer to a second coming without any mention of a first! It is therefore most probable that the "again" is to be taken with "He saith," *i.e.* as introducing another quotation, and that its transposition is to be regarded as a rhetorical negligence. (So von Soden: "Doubtless an inversion of πάλιν, as often found in Philo's citations." Westcott says, "Such a transposition is without parallel—yet see *Wisdom* xiv. 1.") The aorist εἰσαγάγῃ rendered as a present "bringeth in" in the Authorised and Revised Versions, strictly means "shall have brought in," but an incongruity thus arises with "He saith," which practically compels us to take εἰσαγάγῃ as a present. But granting it is future, from what point of view is futurity contemplated—from the writer's living in the end of the days, or from the day when the Son is begotten? We may conceive him placing himself back in the eternal "to-day" of the Son's generation, and looking forward into time. So viewed, the "when He shall have brought the First-begotten into the world" might refer to an event happening at any time in the world's history, if indeed it refer to any historical event at all.

of good name, including Calvin, that the proper translation is, "who maketh the winds His messengers, and flaming fire His ministers"; according to which the passage contains no reference whatever to angels. And it must be confessed that a reference to angels seems out of place in the connection of thought. The Psalm is a Hymn of Creation—a free poetic version of creation's story; and in the foregoing context the psalmist praises God as the Maker of the light, and of the visible heavens, and of the clouds, and of the waters; and one expects to read, in such a connection of wind and fire, but not of angels. Recent Hebrew scholarship, however, defends the Septuagint Version, and the opinion gains ground that it faithfully reflects the original. In that case there is no question of legitimacy, but while a doubt remains the question will intrude itself: Of what value is a statement concerning angels occurring merely in the Septuagint, and having nothing answering to it in the Hebrew text? And the reply must be similar to that given in connection with the previous quotation from Deuteronomy. The words express a scriptural idea, if not an idea to be found in that particular place. It occurs in the preceding Psalm, the one hundred and third. The words, "Bless the Lord, ye His angels, that excel in strength, that do His commandments, hearkening unto the voice of His word: bless ye the Lord, all ye His hosts, ye ministers of His that do His pleasure," suggest the idea of a multitude of ministering spirits who surround the throne of the Sovereign of the universe, and who are continually receiving commissions and being sent on errands in the administration of the

Divine King—essentially the same idea as that contained in the text quoted from Psalm civ.

With reference to angels, then, He saith, "Who maketh His angels winds, and His ministers a flame of fire." Is this a poetic comparison suggestive of movement and mighty power, or is it a matter-of-fact statement concerning the nature of angels, implying that angels are transformable into winds and flames—in short, that they are the elements and forces of nature under another name? It was poetry at first, but as time went on it became dogmatic prose. In the Jewish theory of the universe angelic agency occupied the same place that physical causation holds in ours. Angelology was the animistic philosophy of the later Judaism. It had as many angels in its world as there were things or events. "There is not a thing in the world," says the Talmud, "not even a tiny blade of grass, over which there is not an angel set." What the writer of our Epistle, however, was interested in was not the physical constitution of the angels, but their functions; not that they were fire-like or wind-like, but that they were *messengers* and *ministers*. This is what he finds stated about them in the one representative text he quotes concerning them. This is the name *they* have inherited: simply ministers, mere instruments like the will-less, unconscious elements. No word of rule, dominion; only of service. Why, having quoted Deuteronomy in reference to the First-begotten, not also quote from the same chapter these words concerning the angels: "He fixed the bounds of the nations according to the number of the angels of God," suggesting the idea that each nation had its angelic Prince? Because the notion of rule did not enter into his angelic idea.

Passing now from detailed criticism and comment, let us note the broad contrast which runs through the group of quotations. There is only one radical contrast, but it has three aspects: Son and servants, King and subjects, Creator and creatures. Christ is the Son of God, angels are the servants of God. They too are sons, but in comparison with the sonship of the First-begotten their sonship is not worthy to be mentioned, and is not mentioned. They simply appear as ministers of the Divine will. This is the contrast suggested in vers. 5–7. Then, secondly, Christ is a Divine King, sitting on a throne of omnipotence exercised in behalf of righteousness. The angels are His subjects. For the God who maketh His angels winds is none other than the God who sits on the throne of righteousness. Formally He is to be distinguished from the latter, inasmuch as He is represented as addressing the Son: "To the Son He saith." But the King is the Creator, and it is the Creator and Governor of the world who maketh His angels winds. This contrast between King and subjects is contained in vers. 8, 9. Finally, Christ is the Creator, and the angels are His creatures: He everlasting; they, like all created beings, perishable. Creatureliness is not expressly predicated of angels in the sixth quotation (vers. 10–12), but it is implied in the comparison of them to winds and flames, which connects them with the elements and involves them in their doom. The one statement concerning angels in ver. 7 stands in antithesis to the two following statements concerning the Son: "With regard to the angels, He saith," etc., but with regard to the Son, that He is a Divine King, and also that He is a Divine Creator. Even the Rabbis thought of the angels as perishable like all other creatures. "Day by day," they said, "the angels of service are created out of the fire-stream, and sing a song and disappear, as is said in Lamentations iii. 23, 'They are new every morning.'" This final contrast is contained in ver. 7 and vers. 10–12.

The writer concludes his argument with a final statement about the angels in interrogative form: "Are they not *all ministering* spirits?" (ver. 14). He brings the whole class under the category of service, not dominion, for the words "all" and "ministering" are emphatic. None are excepted, not even the highest in rank; not even the princes of the nations, who rule not, but act as tutelary spirits, guardian angels. The assertion that they all *serve* is absolute, not merely relative to the kingdom of redemption, concerning which a supplementary statement is made in the closing words: "Being sent forth for ministry for the sake of those who are about to inherit salvation." Service is not an incident in the history of angels; it is their whole history.

This category suits the nature of angels so far as we can know it from Scripture. They are associated with the elements and powers of nature—are these under another name. They are changeable in form, appearing now as winds, now as fire. They are perishable, transient as the pestilence and the storm, as tongues of flame, or clouds, or dew. They are one and many in turn, the one dividing into many, the many recombining into one. They are imperfectly personal, lacking will and self-consciousness; thinking, deliberating, resolving not their affair, but execution. "Ye ministers of His that do His pleasure." They are disqualified for rule by the simplicity of their nature. Angel princes cannot take a wide survey of a nation's character and desert, like the prophets. They are blind partisans, mere personifications of national spirit. Each angel prince takes his nation's side in a quarrel, as a thing of course. A human will is the meeting-place of many forces brought into harmony; an angelic will is a single force moving in a straight line towards a point. Angels are mere expressions of the will of God. To impute to them dominion were to infringe on the monarchy of God. It were to reinstate Paganism. Angel-worship is nature-worship under another name, not improved by the change of name. No wonder the author of our Epistle is so careful to connect angels with the idea of service. It is his protest against the angelolatry which had crept into Israel from Persian sources.

In chapter ii. 1–4 we have the first of those exhortations which come in at intervals throughout the Epistle, relieving the argument and applying it at each point. This exhortation reveals the purpose of the foregoing comparison between Christ and the angels. It is to establish Christ's superior claim to be heard when He speaks in God's name to men. As in Stephen's speech before the Sanhedrim, and in Paul's Epistle to the Galatians, angelic agency in Divine revelation is recognised, that is, in the revelation of the law on Sinai. How far the recognition expresses personal conviction in either of these instances, or is merely an accommodation to existing opinion, need not be discussed. It is enough in the present instance to say that the writer is aware of current modes of thought, and, if he does not sympathise with them, at least accommodates his reasoning to them so far as to regard the law as a "word spoken by angels."

Law and gospel might have been compared on their own merits, as is done by Paul in 2 Corinthians iii. 6–11 in a series of contrasts. But the power of appreciating the gospel being defective in the Hebrew Christians, it is the merits of the speakers that are insisted on, though the incomparable worth of the gospel is implicitly asserted in the phrase, "so great salvation." The admonition, delicately expressed in the first person, is to this effect: "I have shown how vastly greater Christ is than angels in name and dignity. In proportion to the august dignity of Him by whom God hath in the end of the days spoken to men ought to be the attention paid to His words. Let us then give due, even the most earnest possible, heed to the things which, directly or indirectly, we have heard from His lips, out of respect to Him, and also out of regard to our own spiritual interests, which are imperilled by negligence. Respecting as we do the word of angels, let us respect still more His word."

Why should there be any difficulty in acting on such reasonable counsel? Because the word of Christ is new, and the word of angels is old and has the force of venerable custom on its side. This difference the writer has in view when he adds: "Lest at any time (or haply) we drift away" (μή ποτε παραρυῶμεν¹). It is a most significant figure. It warns the Hebrews against being carried past the landing-place by the strong current of a river. It is a warning suitable for all times; for there are currents of thought, feeling, and action which, if not resisted, carry down to the sea of spiritual death—currents of irreligion, secularity, and the like. But the current by which the Hebrew Christians were in danger of being carried headlong was that of established religious custom, specially perilous in transition times. That current threatened to carry them away from Christianity to the Dead Sea of Judaism, and so to involve them in the dire calamities that were soon to overwhelm the Jewish people. How much is suggested by these two words—μήποτε παραρυῶμεν! They warn against national ruin, if not the eternal loss of the soul, through the force of use and wont, like a strong flood rushing away from the new Christian land of promise to the old world of Leviticalism, its very strength appearing to justify as well as compel surrender; for why go against an almost unanimous public opinion? How ready are men in the situation of the Hebrew Christians to say: "We follow the religious customs of our pious forefathers, we observe the word of God spoken to them by angels, on Sinai, millenniums ago; therefore we dread no evil, though we neglect the doctrine of Jesus, which requires us to break with the old and take up with something new and revolutionary."

---

¹ This verb occurs in this sense in Proverbs iii. 21 (Sept.) υἱὲ μὴ παραρυῇς, τήρησον δὲ ἐμὴν βουλήν = Son, do not drift away, but observe my counsel.

The exhortation to give heed to Christ's teaching is enforced by three reasons: It is the teaching of the Lord; the penalty of neglect is great; the teaching is well attested. The word of the great salvation began to be spoken *by the Lord*. The Lord means for the Hebrew readers Christ seated on His heavenly throne. The gospel is the word spoken by One who is now the exalted Lord, and the writer would have his readers view it in the light of that fact. It is a way of lending importance by external considerations to a doctrine not appreciated on its own merits. For himself the gospel stands on its own merits. It does not need to be invested with the glory of the Exaltation in order to receive his attention. It is welcome to him as the word of the man Jesus. The man Jesus is for him Lord, even in His humble earthly state. He does not need to think of Him as sitting on His heavenly throne that he may be enabled to resist the temptation to give less heed to His word than to that spoken through angels on Sinai. The temptation does not exist for him. In comparison with the words of Jesus recorded in the Gospels the law is as moonlight to sunlight. It is to be feared that those who are otherwise minded will get little help from the thought that He who spake these words is now glorified. It is not true faith which needs the Exaltation to open its eyes. To such faith the exalted One might say, " I was a stranger, and ye took Me not in."

The word spoken through angels may appear a very solemn matter. Yet, after all, it was a word at second-hand. The law was given by God to angels, then by angels to Moses, who in turn gave it to Israel. The gospel came from God immediately, for Jesus was God speaking to men in human form.

The greatness of the penalty of neglecting this final word of God is indicated by the question: "How shall we escape if we neglect?" The nature of that word enhances culpability. It is a word of *grace,* of "salvation." The Sinai-word was a word of *law.* It is more culpable far to sin against love than against law, to despise God's mercy than to break His commandments.

For those who scorn appeals to fear, considerations of a different order are suggested. The teaching of Christ, they are assured, is well attested; it is confirmed to "us" by men who heard it, their credibility in turn being guaranteed by signs, wonders, mighty works, and various gifts of the Holy Spirit. The writer means to say that he and those to whom he writes, though not enjoying the advantage of having heard Jesus Himself speak the words of salvation, are by this twofold attestation placed practically in as good a position as those who did hear Jesus. The doctrine does indeed come to them at second-hand through the companions of Jesus; but the teaching of apostles is simply an echo of the teaching of their Master. Their voice is His repeated. They simply report what they saw and heard.

The claim thus made to be virtually in the position of direct hearers of Jesus implies a knowledge of His teaching such as we possess through the Synoptical Gospels. It is not necessary to suppose that the author of this Epistle was acquainted with these Gospels, but the manner in which he expresses himself justifies the inference that he was familiar with the evangelic tradition whereof they contain the written record. A careful study of the Epistle bears out this view. The image of Christ which is presented therein rests on a solid basis of fact. The writer knows of the temptations of Jesus; of His life of faith, and the scope that His experience afforded for the exercise of faith; of His agony in the garden: of the contradictions He endured at the hands of ignorant, prejudiced, evil-minded men; of His gentle, compassionate bearing towards the erring; of the fact that He occupied Himself in preaching the gospel of the kingdom; and also of the fact that He was surrounded by a circle of friends and disciples, whose connection with Him was so close that they could be trusted to give a reliable account of His public ministry. Of course the man who knew so much had the means of knowing much more. It will be interesting and instructive to learn what conception of Christianity is entertained by one who is well acquainted with the historical data lying at the foundation. We observe that the word he employs to denote the subject of Christ's preaching is secondary, reminding us of the style of the apostolic Church rather than of Christ Himself. Christ spoke of the kingdom, our author speaks of "salvation." But let not that be to his prejudice. The word is universally current and convenient, and as good as any other, provided the right meaning be attached to it. We shall find that the thing so named is presented under various aspects, citizenship in the kingdom, though not prominent, being included among them.

CHAPTER IV

THE HUMILIATION OF CHRIST AND ITS RATIONALE

CHAP. II. 5-18

THIS supremely important section of our Epistle may have for its heading either *The Humiliation of Christ and its Rationale*, or, *The Great Salvation and how it has been obtained*. The former title is the more fitting from the point of view of the writer's apologetic aim; the latter, from the point of view of biblical theology. The two themes practically coincide, for the rationale of Christ's Humiliation just consists in this that the method of the Great Salvation demanded it, so that the boon could not be obtained without the drawback.

At this point the writer passes from the ideal dignity of the Son, which has hitherto been his theme, to the startlingly contrasted historic reality presented in the life of Jesus—the Son, now a human being with blood and flesh like other men, subject to temptation, suffering death. He cannot avoid the topic, for to his readers the ideal and the historic reality appear irreconcilable, present an absolute, insoluble antinomy. He has no wish to avoid it, no need even to state the facts in subdued terms; for to his mind the antinomy is not absolute. He sees a glory even in the humiliation, so that he can afford to let the humiliation appear in its most sombre colours.

The sum of the doctrine taught as to the Great Salvation is, that it consists in *Lordship in the world to be*, and that, because men were to share in that Lordship, it behoved the Captain of salvation to descend into their low estate in order to make them partakers of the coming glory. These thoughts are introduced in vers. 5–9. In vers. 10–18 the method of salvation by a suffering Captain is defended, developed, and illustrated. What is there written will be dealt with in the next two chapters.

Why does the writer not speak of the Great Salvation in the terms used by "the Lord," who, as he states, was its first preacher? The burden of Christ's message was "the kingdom of God is come." The conception of the *summum bonum* implied here is: lordship in the new world. It may be the same thing in different terms, the idea of Jesus modified. But why are the terms altered: what need for the modification?

Here, as so often throughout the Epistle, the explanation is to be sought in its apologetic aim. The conception of the highest good latent in ii. 5 is not the author's exclusive or even favourite view. It is one of several, taking its place in a series of *tableaux*, then making way for others. As indicated in the introductory chapter, nearness to God, unrestricted access to God, is his central conception—that to which in a purely positive and didactic theological statement he might have adhered throughout. But his apologetic aim requires him constantly to keep in view what will help his first readers. Therefore at this point he uses this mode of presentation, which fits well into his argument at its present stage, and enables him to meet one of the most urgent spiritual needs of the Hebrew Christians. He has, with ample Scripture authority, set Christ above angels; intrinsically, always, but especially in heaven. But beyond doubt He was lower too, on earth; not absolutely, but in certain respects constituting together the state of humiliation. That fact must be reckoned with and reconciled to his doctrine. The two he clearly sees to be perfectly compatible, but their compatibility is not apparent to his readers, and it now becomes his urgent task to make it plain to their apprehension. With this purpose in view he avails himself, with characteristic skill, of a passage from the Psalter. The value of the citation for him lies in the fact that *in it the ideas of humiliation and exaltation are combined.* The use of it determines the form under which the state of exaltation—salvation—must be presented, for in the Psalm it is made to consist in lordship over all.

The new section setting forth the nature and way of salvation opens thus: " For not to angels did He subject the world to come of which we are speaking." The references to angels here and in ver. 16 have misled some into the notion that from this point onwards to the end of the chapter we have a continuation of the discussion of the relative positions of Christ and the angels. It is a mistake carefully to be avoided, as exercising an unhappy bias on the exposition. The angels are not the theme of what follows; rather are they here respectfully bowed out, that they may give place to more important actors, in appearance less than angels in so far as human and subject to death, but destined to rise to higher heights, if doomed for a little while to descend to lower depths. Henceforth what we have to think of is the Great Salvation and the Great Saviour and the sublime career of suffering through which He passed to glory and prepared the way by which a host of redeemed men might follow Him. The contrast between Christ and angels exercises a certain influence on the form of thought, but the thought itself is not a further contribution to the argument about angels.

The " for " with which the new section begins shows that the writer has in view what he has just said in his first admonition to his readers. What is uppermost in his thoughts—the greatness of the salvation or the human agency by which it was proclaimed? Probably both. He means to justify the use of the epithet " great " in reference to the gospel, and he means also to emphasise the importance of man in connection with the gospel salvation, both as recipient of its benefits and as agent in its proclamation. The former end is served by identifying salvation with lordship in " the world to come," the latter by laying stress on the fact that not to angels does that world pertain, whether as inheritance or as theatre of activity. " Not to angels, but to men " he means to say, but the antithesis is completed not in this sentence but in the following quotation. Not to *angels*, but to *men*. Some think that the antithesis intended is one between the world to come, the new world of redemption, and the old world that is destined to pass away, and the thought suggested: the new world not subject to angelic sway, as the old one has been. This interpretation is not justified by the order of words in the sentence, in which "angels," not "the world to come," occupies the emphatic place. We cannot legitimately find in this text a recognition of the dogma that in the old world angels exercised dominion: not even acquaintance with it, still less acceptance of it. What it really contains is safe counsel to Hebrew Christians still hankering after the past, to this effect: "Open your hearts to the new world ushered in by Christ; in it lies man's highest hope." This new world belongs entirely to man, not to beings of angelic nature. Humanity determines its whole nature, and its manner of coming into being.[1]

The citation which forms the Scripture basis of this implicit admonition follows. It is introduced by the vague, indefinite phrase: "But one hath somewhere testified saying." The vagueness proceeds not from ignorance, but is simply a characteristic of the oratorical style which disdains pedantic accuracy in minutiæ.[2]

---

[1] Hofmann, who holds the view that we are not here to find a new argument to prove Christ's superiority to angels, adverting to the fact that ἀγγέλοις wants the article, renders: "God hath subjected the world to come to beings who are no angels, no mere spirits." The force of γάρ he thus brings out: The writer has spoken of a σωτηρία, but the bare idea of a salvation implies that its subjects are not angels, and what is implied he expresses in commencing a new paragraph. *Die Heilige Schrift*, vol. v. p. 104.

[2] Von Soden finds here a trace of Alexandrian influence: "The person of a Scripture writer is or the Alexandrian view of inspiration indifferent."

The words quoted, as they stand in the 8th Psalm, refer to mankind at large. This Psalm, like the 104th, is a hymn of creation. It celebrates first the Divine glory as seen in the visible world, and especially in the firmament at night; it then proceeds to speak of the signal favour shown to man, apparently insignificant as compared with the heavenly bodies, in constituting him creation's lord. In describing the honours conferred by God on the sons of men, the Psalmist appears to have in view what is written in the Book of Genesis concerning man when he was created. The first clause, "Thou hast made him little less than God," or, as it stands in the Septuagint and here, "than the angels," recalls the words spoken by the Creator when He contemplated creating the human race: "Let us make man in our image after our likeness"; and the other clauses seem to be a free poetic version of the charter by which the Creator conferred lordship over all other creatures on the being whom He had made in His own image. The reference to Genesis has indeed been questioned, but the resemblance between the Psalm and the history is so close that it is difficult to escape the inference that either the Psalmist drew inspiration from the historian, or the historian from the Psalmist. Which of the two alternatives is to be adopted depends on the critical question of priority in authorship. That the writer of our Epistle found in the Psalm reminiscences of the book of Origins I can hardly doubt, and for this reason, that all his representations of salvation in the early chapters rest on the accounts of man's primitive history contained in Genesis. Salvation is represented successively as lordship; as destruction of him that had the power of death, and consequent deliverance of man from the fear of death; and as a rest or Sabbatism; with obvious allusion to man's original position in the creation, to the curse which overtook him after the Fall, and to God's rest on the seventh day after He had finished His creative work.

The words quoted from the 8th Psalm have the same reference here as in their original place. The glorious things written there are quoted here as describing favours conferred by God on *men*. This some have failed to see. Because the passage is ultimately applied to Christ, it is assumed that it applies only to Him, and in consequence it has been maintained that the words as they stand, even in the Psalm itself, are purely and exclusively Messianic in import. This view misses the meaning of the writer, involves his argument in confusion, and is quite gratuitous. We are not precluded by the application made eventually to Christ, from applying the oracle in the first place to men in general. The two references are perfectly compatible, and, indeed, the one involves the other. Whatever is true of man as man must be pre-eminently true of Him who loved to call Himself "the Son of Man." Whatever is predicable of the first man as God made him, is in a still more eminent sense predicable of the Second Man. And, since the first man stood not in his integrity, whatever favour God continues to confer on men is conferred on them for the Second Man's sake; so that, while we read the 8th Psalm as really referring to the children of men, sin notwithstanding, we must think of them as included in and represented by the seed of the woman who was to bruise the serpent's head, remove the curse, and restore paradise lost to mankind.

It is just in this way that the writer of our Epistle views this Psalm. He regards the words, "Thou hast put all things in subjection under his feet," as applicable to the sons of men, but not to them apart from Christ. He attaches great importance to this comprehensive reference, because the very doctrine he means to teach is, that in speaking of the great salvation he is really speaking of that lordship whereof the Hebrew prophet sang; in other words, that nothing less than that inheritance is the glorious hope and prospect of Christians. As surely as he believes that the great salvation concerns man, does he believe that the prophetic oracle he quotes refers to man. But while this is so, he is not conscious of any inconsistency in proceeding to speak of Jesus, as if He were THE Person of whom it is said in the Psalm that God had made Him a little lower than the angels, and at the same time lord of all. For the other great doctrine he means to teach is, that the lordship spoken of in the Psalm comes to men through the Man Jesus Christ, and must therefore belong to Him personally and pre-eminently.

But now, these things admitted, a question arises here. Why does our author take occasion from his Psalm-text to call the sphere of lordship a *world to come*? The Psalmist seems to have in view this present visible and tangible world, for he names such substantial things as sheep, oxen, fowls, fishes as the subject of man's dominion. While not furnishing any direct answer to this question, the writer supplies materials out of which we can construct an answer for ourselves. First, like Paul in 1 Corinthians xv., he lays stress on the word "all" (ver. 8), and insists that it be taken in earnest, that man's rightful dominion be viewed as absolutely complete. Then he notes the actual state of matters patent to observation, which is that now, at this present time, all things are not put under man. Some, influenced by the theory of angelic dominion in the old world, think the reference is to angels, as if the idea intended were: the dominion promised is not yet complete—the angels are yet unsubjected. Surely this can hardly be what is meant! The supposed exception is not particularly open to observation. Neither is the alleged angelic reluctance to come under man's sway a very great grievance. If all were right in man's estate but that, there would be little to complain of. And surely it is not necessary to have recourse to this imaginary angelic obstinacy to prove that man's present state is not one of perfect lordship, as if all would be right if only the angels would surrender! Too many things show that man is as yet more slave than lord, a slave oftentimes in virtue of seeming lordship, at best lord with a very insecure tenure. The Hebrews were conscious of being under something more grievous than the yoke of angels—the grim iron yoke of *Rome*.

Man is not yet to all intents and purposes lord. What then? Is God's purpose towards men to be fulfilled? If it is, the fulfilment must be a thing in the future, the present state of things being such as we sec. And the fulfilment when it comes will be the world-to-come of our Epistle. For the world-to-come does not mean something entirely distinct from and having no relation to the present world. It rather means this world, where much is out of gear, put right, delivered from the curse, restored to a normal condition, death abolished, man made fit to be lord by temperance and sanctity and godliness, and no longer kept out of his inheritance by envious barriers, but actually exercising dominion, the meek inheriting the earth, and delighting themselves in the abundance of peace. Therefore it is not wholly future and transcendent, but in part present and immanent. "The hour cometh, yea, now is," said Jesus. In like manner, here and throughout the Epistle our author says in effect: "The new world of redemption is to come, and it is here. It is to come, for the ideal is not yet realised; it is here, for the work of realisation has commenced."

Such being the relation between the world-to-come and the present world, it is evident that the mention of the former in connection with the quotation from the Psalter is not to be justified on the ground that it is a *part* of the "all" which is declared subject to man. "The world-to-come" is not a part of the all, it *is* the all. When the all shall really, fully, permanently, and inalienably have become subject to man, then the world-to-come will be the present world. The justification of the reference to a world-to-come is simply that from the Scriptures it appears to be God's purpose that man should inherit all things, and that the fulfilment of that purpose is a thing we see not yet. The writer infers a world-to-come from the purpose of God and the present state of the world, just as further on he infers that a rest stands over for the people of God because a rest has been promised, and it has never yet come.

Having adverted to the present visible situation of the world, in its bearing on man's lordship, the writer next speaks of what may be seen in *Jesus* in reference to the same subject. "Looking around us we see not yet all things put under man; looking unto Jesus what see we there?" "We see," such is the reply in effect, "we see at once that which confirms the statement that man has not yet fully entered into his inheritance, and that which lays a sure foundation for the hope that the promise will ultimately be fulfilled." "But Him who hath been made a little lower than angels—even *Jesus*, we do see, with reference to the suffering of death crowned with glory and honour, that by the grace of God He might taste death for every one" (ver. 9).

In this remarkable sentence, by which transition is made from mankind in general to the man Christ Jesus, two things at once arrest attention. First, Jesus is spoken of as if He were the one man who had been made a little lower than angels. He stands out in the history of mankind as *the man made lower than angels*. That is for our author as much a distinctive name for Him as the Son of Man, or the Second Adam. Then, secondly, very noteworthy is the introduction of a reference to *death* in this application of the Hebrew oracle to Jesus. There is not a word about death in the Psalm. The thought of mortality or weakness may be latent in the question, What is man? and in the name *enosh*, but on the surface all is sunny, bright, cheerful. The one fact would seem to imply that for Jesus alone was the being made lower than angels in any emphatic sense a humiliation; the other may throw light on the nature of the humiliation.

Now as to the former of these two points. It is really the case that, in the Psalm, being lower than God or angels is not mentioned as a humiliating feature in man's estate. It rather forms an element in his state of exaltation. Man's privilege and glory consists in this, that he has been made a little lower than God, or Divine angelic beings—the Elohim—and appointed lord and head of creation. He is less than Divine, but the point emphasised is not that he is less than God, but that he is so little less, a kind of God on earth, as Jehovah is God in heaven. The inferiority to God does not stand in antithesis to the lordship; the two attributes are not incompatible or mutually exclusive, but harmonious and contemporaneous elements in one and the same condition. The question is whether our author, in quoting the Psalm, so understands the matter, or whether he does not rather regard the inferiority as detracting from the lordship, and therefore as an element that must be removed before the state of lordship can come to pass. The latter view has often been assumed to be the truth, as a matter of course, and that in connection with the interpretation of $\beta\rho\alpha\chi\acute{u}$ $\tau\iota$ as meaning "for a little while."[1] There is, however, no urgent reason for assigning to the phrase a temporal sense.

---

[1] On this view *vide* an ingenious article by the late Professor W. R. Smith in *The Expositor*, vol. i. 2nd Series, p. 138.

It may be taken throughout as an adverb of degree, not to the exclusion of the temporal sense, for the two senses are not incompatible. Why should not the meaning of the oracle, both in its original place in the Psalter and as quoted here, be: Thou hast made man only a little lower in nature and position than God or angelic beings?

If this be indeed the sense, then we can understand how the writer of our Epistle should regard Jesus as the only man to whom the predicate of inferiority to angels can be applied with emphasis, as a predicate of humiliation. For while Jesus as man was lower than angels in the same sense as other men, that is to say in so far as He was partaker of flesh and blood, and was no longer, like the angels, pure spirit,[1] there was for Him in that fact, apart from all other circumstances of His earthly experience, humiliation enough. Other men were never anything else or higher, and, so far from its being a signal humiliation to them that they are lower than angels, it is rather their glory to be little less than angels. But for the Son of God it was a descent to be made even *a* little lower than angels, by becoming *man*, partaker of flesh and blood. In the case of ordinary men we wonder to what all but angelic

---

[1] If the writer was imbued with the Alexandrian religious philosophy, which shared the Greek view of the flesh as the foe of the spirit, we can understand how intense would be his sense of the humiliation involved for Christ in taking flesh and blood. If, on the other hand, he held the Hebrew view of the flesh, according to which it was the symbol of *weakness* rather than the seat of sin, then his sense of the humiliation would be less acute. Jesus as man—spirit allied with flesh—would appear to him made only a *little* lower than angels.

heights of thought and worship those can arrive who began their being as "babes and sucklings," flesh born of flesh. In the case of the man Jesus we are astonished to hear of the Son of God being born, wrapt in swaddling clothes, laid in a manger, a helpless, speechless infant. Yet while astonished, we believe and gratefully acknowledge that out of the mouth of this babe and suckling God hath perfected His own praise, and by means of this Holy Child, Jesus, hath stilled the enemy and the avenger.

The assumption of human nature on its material side being what constitutes the humiliating inferiority to angels for Jesus, the phrase "made a little lower than angels" applied to Him becomes a synonym for the Incarnation. But to complete our view of its meaning, we must take into account the reference to the suffering of death. If the Incarnation alone constituted the humiliation, then permanent inferiority would be the consequence, and the exaltation of Christ would involve the laying aside of His humanity. We must conceive of the humiliation as consisting in the assumption of humanity subject to suffering in various forms, death the supreme suffering included. Thereby the "little" of degree becomes a "little" of time. The patristic commentators were right in thought, though wrong in grammar, when they connected the clause "made lower than angels" with the clause "for the suffering of death." The true construction of the sentence is to regard "Jesus" as closing up the subject—and all that follows as the predicate—reading "Him who was made lower than angels, namely, Jesus, we see so and so situated." But while the suffering of death belongs to the predicate, it influences the writer's thought of the subject, and it ought also to influence our interpretation of it. Death enters into his conception of Christ's humiliation, though he consistently avoids introducing it into the definition, because his aim is to set Christ's Passion in a new light—surrounded with a halo of glory.

"Made a little lower than angels"—such is the writer's formula for the humiliation of Christ as a partaker of humanity. It is not the way in which we would naturally speak of it. The phrase sounds to our ears artificial, and so tends to obscure rather than reveal the moral grandeur of the train of thought in vers. 5–18. We are inclined to ask, Would it not be better for us to forget the angels and translate the phrases referring to them into modern equivalents, throwing away the antiquated shell that we may get at the eternal kernel? Let those who thus feel do so, by all means. Only let us not forget that the shell was important to the Hebrews, and let us admire the sympathy and tact displayed by their teacher in adapting to their modes of thought his statement concerning the great Christian verities, speaking of these in terms which took up his readers at the point where he found them, and led them on to more perfect insight into the genius of the new religion.

And now at length we come to the *crux interpretum* —the *crowning of Jesus with glory and honour*. The *crux* lies in the thought rather than in the grammar. The plain meaning of the text seems to be, that Jesus was crowned with glory and honour, in reference to the (prospective) suffering of death, in order that by the favour of God (to Him) He might taste death for men. This rendering suggests a crowning *antecedent to death*, a fact occurring in the earthly life of Jesus, an exaltation in the humiliation, a higher even in the lower, a glory consummated in heaven but begun even on earth. But commentators almost with one consent regard such a view as inadmissible; or rather, to speak more correctly, hardly seem to have had it present to their minds as a possibility. Since one or two writers ventured modestly to propound it, the view in question has been disposed of by a jest as "a fine modern idea, but one to which Scripture has hardly yet advanced." It requires some courage to retain an opinion, long cherished,[1] thus treated by great authorities, but the recent history of exegesis is reassuring. Not that one can boast of many new adherents,[2] but that the embarrassments betrayed by supporters of the traditional view—that the crowning refers to the state of exaltation—have all the effect of a *reductio absurdum*.

---

[1] *Vide* my work, *The Humiliation of Christ*, p. 30, and for remarks on the view there advocated, *vide* Professor A. B. Davidson's work on the Epistle in the "Handbooks for Bible Classes" Series.

[2] Among the supporters of the view advocated in the text are Hofmann, Matheson (in the *Monthly Interpreter* for November 1884), and Rendall (*The Epistle to the Hebrews*, 1888). Rendall places the crowning in the preincarnate state, but the ethical effect is the same. "As the victim is crowned unto death, so it was purposed in the eternal counsels of heaven to exalt the Son that He might sacrifice the more, and exhibit the fulness of God's love to man by tasting for him the utmost bitterness of death."

The traditional view is beset with insuperable difficulties, especially with this difficulty, that it is not easy under it to assign a natural sense to the words in the last clause of verse 9. What clear satisfactory sense can one attach to the statement that Jesus was exalted to heaven in order that He might taste death for everyone? It is pathetic to observe the expedients to which interpreters have recourse to get over the difficulty. The most plausible solution is to assign to the verb γεύσηται a retrospective reference, and find in the last clause of the verse the doctrine that Christ's exaltation gave to His antecedent death redemptive efficacy. Some who adopt this expedient admit that the manner of expression lacks logical precision, and that the more correct way of putting the idea would have been: "In order that the death which He tasted might be for the good of all."[1] Bleek, still our greatest authority, regards the retrospective reference assigned to the verb as inadmissible, and gets out of the difficulty by supplying after τὸ πάθημα τοῦ θανάτου the words ὃ ἔπαθεν, and rendering: "Crowned for the suffering of death *which He endured* in order that He might by the grace of God taste death for every man." Two other suggestions have been more recently made. One is to take the particle ὅπως as connected, not with ἐστεφανωμένον alone, but as referring to all that precedes —"to the Passion crowned by the Ascension."[2] The other is to subject the sentence to violent dislocation so as to bring out this sense: "Him who had been made a little lower than the angels, even Jesus, for the sake of

[1] So Ebrard.   [2] So Westcott.

suffering death—in other words, that by the grace of God He might taste death for every man—Him we now behold crowned with glory and honour."[1] The scholar who makes this suggestion truly observes that "the chief objection to this arrangement of the construction is its interrupted and dislocated character," and he would apparently be glad to fall back on the retrospective sense of γεύσηται were it not that he sees in that direction an objection not less formidable, namely, that for the rendering "that He may have tasted" no clear parallel can be found.

Considering the forced, unnatural character of all these solutions, I am constrained to ask interpreters, "Why should it be thought a thing incredible with you" that the crowning referred to may be prior, not posterior, to death — an exaltation latent in the humiliation? If I am met with the sceptical question, With what glory and honour can the man Jesus be said to have been crowned on earth? I reply, With just such glory and honour as are spoken of in the third and fifth chapters of this same Epistle: with the glory of a Moses and the honour of an Aaron; the glory of being the leader of the people out of Egypt into the promised land, that is, of being the "Captain of Salvation"; the honour of being the High Priest of men, procuring for them, through the sacrifice of Himself, life and blessedness. The glory and honour spoken of as conferred on Jesus may thus quite well be those connected with His appointment to the honourable and glorious office of Apostle and High Priest of our profession.

[1] So Vaughan.

This, accordingly, is the thought I find in this text: Jesus, "crowned for death," to use the happy phrase of Dr. Matheson, by being appointed to an office whereby His death, instead of being a mere personal experience of the common lot, became a death for others, and a humiliation was transmuted into a signal mark of Divine favour. This crowning had a twofold aspect and relation; a subjective and an objective side, a relation to the will of Christ and a relation to the will of God. It would not have been complete unless there had been both an act of self-devotion on the part of Christ and an act of sovereign appointment on the part of God. The subjective aspect is in abeyance here, though it is not forgotten in the Epistle; it receives full recognition in those places where it is taught that Christ's priestly offering was *Himself*. Here it is the objective Godward aspect that is emphasised, as appears from the remarkable expression, "by the grace of God," and from the line of thought contained in the following verse, to be hereafter considered. There was a subjective grace in Christ which made Him willing to sacrifice His individual life for the good of the whole, but there was also conferred on Him by His Father the signal favour that His life, to be freely given in self-sacrifice, should have universal significance and value.[1]

[1] It is to the subjective aspect that Dr. Matheson gives prominence in the article previously referred to. Dr. Edwards' main objection to our interpretation of the crowning is based on an exclusive regard to the subjective aspect. "If," he argues, "the apostle means that voluntary humiliation for the sake of others is the glory, some men besides Jesus Christ might have been mentioned in whom the words of the Psalm find their accomplishment. The

By the expression "by the grace of God" (χάριτι θεοῦ) favour to us men has usually been supposed to be intended. Some modern commentators, *e.g.* Ebrard, instead of falling back on the interpretation here offered, have sought refuge in the ancient reading χωρὶς θεοῦ, "apart from God." The adoption of this desperate shift by so independent a theologian as the one just named shows what need there is for insisting on the thought that Jesus by the favour of God *to Him* tasted death for men, that His death, by being a death for others, was transmuted from a humiliation into a glory. From the common consent of interpreters to shun this view, one might conclude that it was indeed only a fine modern idea to which Scripture had hardly advanced. Strange that an idea of which the Greek Euripides had clear vision [1] should have been so completely hidden from the highest Hebrew minds, inspiration notwithstanding. But the fact was not so, as the following particulars will show.

Kindred to the thought I find in the text is the Beatitude pronouncing the persecuted blessed; [2] Paul's words to the Philippians: "Unto you it is given as a favour (ἐχαρίσθη) in the behalf of Christ not only to believe in Him, but also to suffer for His sake"; [3] and Peter's word to the Hebrew *Diaspora*: "If ye be reproached for the name of Christ, happy are ye; for the

---

difference between Jesus and other good men would only be a difference of degree." *Vide* his work on the Epistle in *The Expositor's Bible.*

[1] *Vide* Lecture on the Greek tragic poets in my *Gifford Lectures*, 2nd Series, soon to be published.

[2] Matt. v. 12.   [3] Phil. i. 29.

spirit of glory and of God resteth upon you."[1] Kindred also are the texts in John's Gospel in which Jesus refers to His approaching Passion as His glorification. Add to these the voices from heaven pronouncing Jesus God's beloved Son when He manifested at the Jordan and on the Mount of Transfiguration His readiness to endure suffering in connection with His Messianic vocation, and the reflection on the later event in 2 Peter: "He received from God the Father honour and glory, when there came such a voice to Him from the excellent glory, This is My beloved Son, in whom I am well pleased."[2] With these Divine voices stand in contrast the voices from hell uttered by Satan in the temptation. The God-sent voices say in effect, "Thou art My beloved Son because Thou devotest Thyself to the arduous career of a Saviour, and I show My favour unto Thee by solemnly setting Thee apart to Thy high and holy office." The Satanic voices say, "Thou art the Son of God, it seems; use Thy privilege, then, for Thine own advantage." God shows His grace unto His Son by appointing Him to an office in which He will have an opportunity of doing a signal service to men at a great cost of suffering to Himself. Satan cannot conceive of Jesus being the Son of God at all unless sonship carry along with it exemption from all arduous tasks and irksome hardships, privations and pains. God puts a stamp of Divinity on self-sacrifice, Satan associates Divinity with selfishness.

There can be little doubt, then, that the crowning, as I conceive it, is an idea familiar to the New Testament

[1] 1 Pet. iv. 14.   [2] 2 Pet. i. 17.

writers. The only question that may legitimately be asked is, whether this thought be relevant to the connection of thought in the passage, and serviceable to the purpose of the Epistle, that of instructing in Christian truth readers who needed to be again taught the merest elements of the Christian faith. To this question I can have little hesitation in giving an affirmative answer. Was it not desirable to show to men who stumbled at the humiliating circumstances of Christ's earthly lot, that there was not merely a glory coming after the humiliation, compensating for it, but a glory in the humiliation itself? This ethical instruction was more urgently needed than a merely theological instruction as to the purpose and effect of Christ's exaltation into heaven. The exaltation needed no apology, it spoke for itself; what was needed was to remove the stigma from the state of humiliation, and to do this was, I believe, one of the leading aims of the Epistle. The blinded Jew said, "How dishonourable and shameful that death of Jesus—how hard to believe that He who endured it could be Messiah and the Son of God!" The writer replies, "Not disgrace, but favour, honour, glory, do I see there: this career of suffering is one which it was honourable for Christ to pass through, and to which it was nowise unmeet that the Sovereign Lord should subject His Son. For while to taste death in itself was a humiliation, to taste it for others was glorious."

It is a point in favour of the interpretation here advocated, that it makes the crowning not subsequent to the being made lower than angels, but, as in the Psalm, contemporaneous with it. It is unnecessary to add that the glory in the humiliation is not exclusive of the glory after it. The full thesis of the Epistle on this topic is: "First lower, then higher, nay, a higher in the lower." Most interpreters find in its teaching only the former member of the thesis. I find in it both. The two truths, indeed, are complementary of each other. There could not be exaltation subsequent to the humiliation unless there were an exaltation in the humiliation. "Exalted because of" implies "exalted in." One who does not appreciate the latter truth cannot understand the former. The posthumous exaltation must be seen to be but the public recognition of the eternal fact, otherwise belief in it possesses no spiritual value. That is why, in his apologetic effort to unfold the true nature of Christianity, the writer insists on the glory inherent in Christ's vocation as Captain of Salvation. In doing so he is self-consistent. In his view of the glory of Christ there is the same duality we found in his view of the Christian era. The world to come is future and it is here. Even so the exaltation of Christ is in heaven, and yet also on earth.

CHAPTER V

THE CAPTAIN OF SALVATION

Chap. ii. 10

The statement contained in this verse is so weighty that a separate chapter must be devoted to its elucidation.

The writer here affirms that the career of suffering to which Christ was subjected was worthy of God. The affirmation is made to justify the assertion of the previous sentence that the appointment of Jesus to taste death for others was a manifestation of grace or favour on God's part towards His well-beloved Son. "By the grace of God I have said, and I said so deliberately; for it became Him who is the first and final cause of all to accomplish this great end, the salvation of men, in a way which involved suffering to the Saviour,"—such is the connection of thought. The author feels that this is a position which must be made good in order to reconcile his readers to the humiliation and sufferings which Christ underwent. This he virtually acknowledges by the periphrastic manner in which he names God. If God be the last end of all, and the first cause of all, He must be the final and first cause of Christ's sufferings among other things; and unless it can be maintained that the end for which Christ suffered was worthy of Him who is the great end of the universe, and that the means employed for the attainment of that end were worthy of Him who is the first cause of everything that happens, the defence of the Christian faith is a failure. Knowing perfectly well what is at stake, the writer, having full confidence in the goodness of his cause, fearlessly maintains that everything relating to the matter of salvation, means not less than end, is worthy of the Maker and Lord of all. "It became Him." The point of view is peculiar. In one respect it goes beyond the usual biblical manner of regarding Divine action, the Bible writers ordinarily being content to rest in God's good pleasure. In another it is defective, as compared, for example, with Paul's way of treating the death of Christ as necessitated by the righteousness of God. The apologetic aim explains both features. The writer is dealing with men to whom Christ's sufferings are a stumbling-block, to whom therefore it will not suffice to say, "It pleased the Lord to bruise Him." On the other hand, he is glad to be able to show them the fitness of Christ's sufferings from any point of view, even though his statement should come far short of presenting a complete theory. The statements of apologists are apt to appear defective from a dogmatic point of view, as they sometimes learn to their cost. At the same time it must be remarked that the statement of this inspired apologist is not so defective as has sometimes been represented, as when it is said that the reason for the death of Christ here given is related to the Pauline as the Scotist theory to the Anselmian, or the Socinian to the Lutheran.[1] It points to a congruity between the experience of Christ and the moral nature of God. It is in the same line with the Pauline doctrine, only it is less definite and more general.

The sentence in which the Godworthiness of the method of salvation is asserted is so constructed as to be in a manner self-evidencing. The writer, as he proceeds, uses words charged with persuasive virtue, so that by the time we arrive at the end of the verse we are disposed to give a cordial assent to the doctrine enunciated. Not that the whole evidence is either stated or even suggested in this single sentence; for all that remains of the second chapter may be regarded as an expression and elucidation of the thought contained therein. But the words are so fitly chosen, and the clauses so skilfully arranged, as to win our sympathy in behalf of the truth stated, and to dispose us to lend a favourable ear to what may be further advanced in its illustration and defence. This will appear as we consider in detail the separate members of the sentence.

First comes the clause in which God's end in the mission of Christ is set forth: "In bringing many sons unto glory" ($\pi o \lambda \lambda o \grave{v} \varsigma \ v i o \grave{v} \varsigma \ \epsilon i \varsigma \ \delta \acute{o} \xi a \nu \ \grave{a} \gamma a \gamma \acute{o} \nu \tau a$). The reference is to God, not to Christ, notwithstanding the change of case from the dative ($a \grave{v} \tau \hat{\omega}$) to the accusative ($\grave{a} \gamma a \gamma \acute{o} \nu \tau a$). The aim of the whole sentence makes this certain. The intention is to ascribe to God, in connection with the sufferings of Christ, an end indisputably worthy of Him who is the final end of all things. The Godworthiness of that end is not, indeed, expressly

[1] So Pfleiderer, *Paulinism*, vol. ii. p. 71, English edition.

declared, and that because the whole stress of the difficulty lies not on the end but on the means. But though not formally asserted it is plainly implied. The end is alluded to by way of suggesting that thought as an aid to the understanding of the more difficult one— the Godworthiness of the means. Skill in the art of persuasion is exhibited in placing it in the forefront. For no one could doubt the Godworthiness of the end— the salvation of men. It might be presumptuous to say that God was bound to become a Saviour, but it may confidently be asserted that to save becomes Him. The work He undertook was congruous to His position as Creator and to His relation to men as Father. It was worthy of God the Creator that He should not allow His workmanship in man to be frustrated by sin. The irretrievable ruin of man would have compromised the Creator's glory by making it possible to charge Him with failure. Speaking of this, Athanasius says: "It would have been unbecoming if those who had been once created rational had been allowed to perish through corruption. For that would have been unworthy of the goodness of God, if the beings He had Himself created had been allowed to perish through the fraud of the devil against man. Nay, it would have been unbecoming that the skill of God displayed in man should be destroyed, either through their carelessness or through the devil's craftiness." [1]

The Godworthiness of the end is still more apparent in view of man's filial relation to God. What more worthy of God than to lead His own sons, however degenerate, to the glory for which man was destined and

[1] From the treatise on the *Incarnation of the Word*.

fitted when he was made in God's image, and set at the head of creation? The title "sons" was possibly suggested by the creation story, but it arises immediately out of the nature of salvation as indicated in the quotation from the 8th Psalm,—lordship in the world to be. This high destiny places man alongside of *the* Son whom God "appointed heir of all things." "If sons, then heirs," reasoned Paul; "if heirs, then sons," argues inversely the author of our Epistle. Both reason legitimately, for sonship and heirship imply each other. Those who are appointed to lordship in the new world of redemption are sons of God, for what higher privilege or glory can God bestow on His sons? And on those who stand in a filial relation to God He may worthily bestow so great a boon. To lead His sons to their glorious inheritance is the appropriate thing for God to do.

We have next to notice the title given to Him who for men tasted death. He is designated "the Captain (or Leader) of salvation" (τὸν ἀρχηγὸν τῆς σωτηρίας). This rendering, that of the Authorised Version, is preferable to that of the Revised Version, which, with some recent interpreters,[1] for the suggestive title "Captain" substitutes the weak general term "Author." The only

---

[1] Opinion is divided on the point. Davidson cautiously remarks, "The idea that the Son goes before the saved in the same path ought perhaps to be retained." Professor W. R. Smith (*Expositor*, 2nd Series, vol. ii. p. 422), while acknowledging that the idea of leadership is suitable enough to the thought of the Epistle, remarks that the phrase "leader in their salvation" is "awkward." Vaughan says, "The meaning of ἀρχηγός varies (like that of ἀρχή) between the ideas of *beginning* and *rule*; of *principium* and *principatus*." He admits that the idea of leader or prince is the more common, and is the proper sense of ἀρχηγός in Acts iii. 15. On the other hand, he

objection to the rendering "Captain" is its predominantly military associations—an objection to which the equivalent title Leader is not liable. The idea of leadership serves admirably the apologetic purpose, and is therefore by all means to be retained. There is no good reason for excluding it. It is in harmony with the general thought of the Epistle. It sympathises with the idea of salvation embodied in the phrase: lordship in the world to come. The lordship is not yet actual, the world to come is a promised land into which the redeemed have to march. And as the Israelites had their leader under whose guidance they marched from Egypt to Canaan, so the subjects of the greater salvation have their Leader who conducts them to their inheritance. This parallelism, there can be little doubt, was present to the writer's thoughts. He speaks of Moses and Joshua, in different senses leaders of Israel, further on, and it is not a violent supposition that he has them in view even at this early stage. Then we have found reason for believing that the expression "crowned with glory and honour" might be thus paraphrased: "Crowned with the glory of a Moses and the honour of an Aaron." Therefore we expect to find him, in the immediate sequel, applying epithets to Christ descriptive of the respective offices of the two brothers, as both united in Him. And this is what we do find. Here he calls Christ the

thinks the sense "author" "slightly more appropriate" in Heb. ii. 10, and the use of the word in Heb. xii. 2 he allows to decide in favour of it. Rendall quite decidedly favours "captain," as being the invariable sense of the Greek word in the Sept. Reuss is equally decided. He gives as the French equivalent "*guide*," and says that the Greek word never means *l'auteur*.

archegos, answering to Moses; a little further on we find him calling Him the *archiereus*, answering to Aaron. Finally, it is to be noted that Christ as *archegos* is said to be perfected by *sufferings* (παθημάτων), not by the one suffering of death. The use of the plural is not accidental, it is intended to convey the idea of all sorts of suffering. But the experience of sufferings of all kinds fits into the idea of leader better than to that of priest, in which the suffering of death is the thing to be emphasised. The writer, indeed, knows how to adapt a wide experience of suffering to the priestly aspect of Christ's work, through the medium of a sympathy acquired by such experience, in virtue of which He becomes a trusty High Priest. But the connection between the experience and the office is not immediately obvious in the case of the priestly office; on the other hand, it is immediately obvious in the case of the office of leader.

Adopting, then, the rendering "Leader of salvation," let us consider the apologetic value of the title.

It implies a particular method of saving men, and readily suggests certain things likely to be involved in the adoption of that method.

As to the method of salvation, the title teaches that, while God is the supreme Saviour of men, He performs the office through a *Mediator*. He might conceivably have saved men by a direct act of sovereign power and mercy. But He chose to save by mediation. And this method, if not the only possible one, is at least fitting. It became Him for whom are all things, and by whom are all things, to bring His sons to glory in this way. It became Him, for this reason among others, that He was thereby following the analogy of providence, doing this work of deliverance in the manner in which we see Him performing all works of deliverance recorded in history, *e.g.* the deliverance of Israel out of Egypt, which was, as we have seen, most probably in the writer's thoughts as the great historical type of the work of redemption. How did God deliver Israel? The poetical account of the transaction is: "As an eagle stirreth up her nest, fluttereth over her young, spreadeth abroad her wings, taketh them, beareth them on her wings: so the Lord alone did lead him."[1] In a high, ideal sense it is a true as well as a beautiful representation. Nevertheless, the sole leadership, while excluding all strange gods, did not exclude the subordinate leadership of men. God led His ancient people from Egypt to Canaan, like a flock, "by the hand of Moses and Aaron."[2]

The method involves that salvation is a *gradual process*. It is a march under the guidance of a Leader to the promised land. With this view the aorist participle in the clause preceding, ἀγαγόντα, is not incompatible. This aorist has puzzled interpreters. Some render it "who had led," understanding it as referring to Old Testament saints whom God in His providence had led to glory, or to disciples whom Jesus had brought into the kingdom of heaven during His earthly ministry.[3] This rendering is in accordance with the grammatical rule that "the aorist participle generally represents an action as past with reference to the time of its leading

---

[1] Deut. xxxii. 11.   [2] Ps. lxxvii. 20.
[3] So the Vulgate, which translates "qui multos filios in gloriam adduxerat."

verb," [1] but it has no other recommendation. If we will insist on assigning to the participle its temporal force as required by this rule, it is better to lift the writer's thought out of the region of history into that of Divine intention, wherein the end ideally precedes the means. The resulting sense will be: it became God, having formed the purpose of leading sons to glory, to appoint for His chosen agent an experience of suffering. From this point of view the aorist becomes in effect a future, and signifies, not "having done," but "being about to do." [2] Such a reference to eternal purpose is in keeping with the phrases employed to describe God's relation to history ("for whom all things," "by whom all things"). It was natural that one who had used these phrases should look at the events of time *sub specie æternitatis*. The possible effects of this mode of contemplation are threefold. It may invert the temporal order, making that which is posterior in time prior in purpose; it may make events which are successive in history synchronous for thought; it may make events which are distinct in the historic order, virtually identical. In each of these cases the use of the aorist participle would be appropriate; [3] certainly so in the last mentioned, for one of the well-ascertained facts about the use of the participle is that it "may

---

[1] Goodwin, *Syntax of Greek Moods and Tenses*, p. 48.

[2] Bleek takes ἀγαγόντα in a future sense.

[3] Vaughan favours the first alternative: "The bringing of many sons to glory is (conceptionally) prior to the perfecting of Christ through suffering." Westcott adopts the second: "Though the objects of ἀγαγόντα and τελειῶσαι are different, the two acts which they describe are regarded as synchronous, or rather as absolute without regard to the succession of time."

express time coincident with that of the verb, when the actions of the verb and the participle are practically one."[1] *Sub specie æternitatis* the leading of sons to glory is the perfecting of Christ, and the perfecting of Christ is the leading of sons to glory, and both together are the act of a moment.

But the temporal order, nevertheless, has its rights, and in that order the leading to glory, not less than the perfecting of the Leader, is no mere momentary act, but a *process*. The sons of God are led to glory step by step. The new heavens and the new earth are not brought in *per saltum*, but by a gradual process of development, during which the teaching, example, and suffering of Jesus work noiselessly as a leaven. Redemption has a history alike in Leader and in led. Redemption after this fashion became Him for whom and by whom are all things better than an instantaneous deliverance. The latter might reveal Divine omnipotence in a signal way, but the former affords scope for the display of all Divine attributes: power, wisdom, patience, faithfulness, unwearied loving care.

The method of salvation by a Leader involves certain things for the Leader.

1. He must, of course, be a man visible to men whom He has to lead, so that they can look unto Him as Leader and Perfecter of faith, and, inspired by His example, follow Him in the path which conducts to glory.

---

[1] Goodwin, p. 52. A familiar example of this use of the aorist is supplied in the phrase often occurring in the Gospels, ἀποκριθεὶς εἶπεν. The speaker did not answer first, then say. He answered in saying.

2. Out of this primary requirement naturally springs another. He who in person is to lead the chosen people out of the house of bondage into the promised land must, in the discharge of his duty, *encounter hardship and suffering*. He must share the lot of those whom he has to deliver. He not only ought, he must; it arises inevitably out of the nature of the task. Whether we take the word ἀρχηγός as signifying a leader like Moses, or a military captain like Joshua, the truth of this statement is apparent. Neither Moses nor Joshua had an easy time of it. The leadership of Israel was for neither a dilettante business, but a sore, perilous, often thankless toil and warfare. And there never was any real leader or captain of men whose life was anything else than a yoke of care, and a burden of toil and sorrow. They have all had to suffer with those they led, and more than any of the led. What wonder, then, if the Captain or Leader of the great salvation was acquainted with suffering? Must He be the solitary exception to the rule which connects leadership with suffering? Ought we not rather to expect that He, being the ideally perfect Captain given by God to be a leader and commander to the people whom He purposes to conduct to glory, will likewise be more than any other experienced in suffering? If out of regard to His dignity as the Son He must be exempted from suffering, then for the same reason He must forfeit the position of leader. To exempt from suffering is to disable for leadership. Companionship in suffering is one of the links that connect a leader with those he leads and give him power over them. For the led, especially those who are

being led to "glory," have their troubles too, and no leader can win their hearts who does not share these. For one thing they have all to die, therefore their Leader also must "taste death" for their encouragement. Therefore it certainly became Him for whom are all things, and by whom are all things, in leading many sons to glory through tribulation, to make the Captain of salvation a participant in tribulation. He was thereby only fitting Him to be the better Captain.

3. This brings us to a third implicate of the method of salvation by a Captain for the Captain Himself. It is, that experience of suffering is not merely inseparable from His office, but useful to Him in connection therewith. It *perfects Him for Leadership.* Here at length we reach the climax of the apologetic argument, the final truth in which, when understood, the mind finds rest. If this be indeed true, then, beyond doubt, it became God to subject His Son to a varied experience of suffering. To proclaim its truth is the real aim of the writer. For while his direct affirmation is that it became God to perfect His Son by suffering, the really important thing is the indirect affirmation that the Son *was* perfected by suffering. It is one of the great thoughts of the Epistle, to be printed, so to speak, in large capitals.

How are we to understand the perfecting of Jesus? The term τελειῶσαι has been variously rendered. Some take it in a ceremonial sense, as meaning that Jesus by His death was consecrated to the priestly office which He exercises in heaven. Others take it as equivalent to "glorify," finding in the statement the truth Jesus Himself taught that it behoved Christ to enter into the glory and felicity of heaven through suffering. On this view the "perfecting" of verse 10 is synonymous with the "crowning" of verse 9, understood as referring to the state of exaltation. Others, again, favour an ethical interpretation, finding in the statement of the text the idea that through His curriculum of suffering Christ was made perfect in character by learning certain moral virtues, *e.g.* sympathy, patience, obedience, faith. Finally, some contend that the precise sense of the verb here is to *fit for office*. Briefly put, the four alternative meanings are: *consecration, beatification, perfected moral development, official equipment*.

The four senses in reality shade into each other. The author of our Epistle does not bind himself to one precise technical sense throughout, but uses the word in an elastic way. He employs it in reference to Christ in various connections of thought, now apparently in relation to office, now in relation to character, and now in relation to state. He uses it in reference to men in a quite different sense, as when he speaks of worshippers being perfected as pertaining to the conscience, where to "perfect" is equivalent to "justify" in Pauline phraseology. Through all the various special senses one radical sense runs, namely, to bring to the end. The special senses vary with the nature of the end. If the end be to become a leader, the special sense will be to make one a perfect leader, a thoroughly efficient captain. If it be to get into right relation with God as a pardoned sinner, the special sense will be to justify.[1]

Other opportunities will occur for considering more

[1] For an instructive statement on the meanings of τελειόω, *vide* Davidson, *The Epistle to the Hebrews*, pp. 65, 207.

fully the various uses of the word. Meantime we are concerned with the specific sense of τελειῶσαι in chapter ii. 10. Without hesitation I take it in the last of the four senses above distinguished. The writer means to say that Christ was perfected by suffering, in the sense that He was perfected for leadership. The perfecting of Christ was a process resulting in His becoming a consummate Captain of salvation. It was a process carried on *through* sufferings, taking place contemporaneously with these. It was a process begun on earth, carried on throughout Christ's whole earthly life, reaching its goal in heaven; just as the crowning with glory and honour began on earth and was completed in heaven. The crowning was the appointment of Jesus to the vocation of Saviour, the perfecting was the process through which He became skilled in the art of saving. The theatre or school of His training was His human history, and the training consisted in His acquiring, or having opportunity of exercising, the qualities and virtues which go to make a good leader of salvation. Foremost among these are sympathy, patience, obedience, faith, all of which are mentioned in the course of the Epistle. Whether we should say of Christ that He acquired these virtues and became more and more expert in them, or merely that He had an opportunity in His earthly life, with its experiences of temptation and suffering, of displaying them, is a question of dogmatic theology rather than of exegesis. Our author declares in another place that Christ *learned obedience*. We know what that would mean as applied to an ordinary man. It would imply growth, development in moral character. Whether that can be predicated of Christ without prejudice to His sinlessness is a question for dogmatic theology to settle. If it were, we should then be entitled to include in the official perfecting of Christ a personal ethical element, that it might be as real, full of contents, and significant as possible. The official perfecting of every ordinary man includes an ethical element. An apprentice during the course of his apprenticeship not only goes through all the departments of his craft and acquires gradually skill in each branch, but all along undergoes a discipline of character, which tends to make him a better man as well as a good tradesman. It is consonant to the general view taken by the writer of Christ's earthly state as one of humiliation, that he should conceive Jesus as subject to the law of moral growth; that was one of His humiliations.[1]

In any case, whatever view we take on the question as to Christ's personal growth in virtue, the point of importance is, that the process of His official perfecting took place *within the ethical sphere.* The supreme qualification for a leader of salvation is the possession and exercise of high heroic virtues, such as those already enumerated. He leads by inspiring admiration and trust; that is, by being a moral hero. But a moral hero means one whose life is hard, tragic. Heroes are produced by passing through a severe, protracted curriculum of trial. They are perfected by sufferings—sufferings of all sorts, the more numerous, varied, and severe the better; the more complete the training, the more perfect the result, when the discipline has been successfully passed through. Hence the fitness, nay the

[1] *Vide* on this the last chapter.

necessity, that one having Christ's vocation should live such a life as the Gospels depict and our Epistle hints at: full of temptations, privations, contradictions of unbelief, ending with death on the cross; calling into play to the uttermost the virtue of fortitude, affording ample scope for the display at all costs of fidelity to duty and obedience to God, and, in the most desperate situations, of implicit filial trust in a heavenly Father; and, through all these combined, furnishing most satisfactory guarantees for the possession of unlimited capacity to sympathise with all exposed to the temptations and tribulations of this world. How can any son of God who is being led through fire and flood to his inheritance doubt the value of a Leader so trained and equipped? I know not whether those commentators be right who say that $\delta\iota\grave{\alpha}$ $\pi\alpha\theta\eta\mu\acute{\alpha}\tau\omega\nu$, in the intention of the writer, applies to the "many sons" who are being led to glory, as well as to their Leader;[1] but I am quite sure that he regarded their experience of suffering as an aid to the understanding of the doctrine of Christ's perfecting, not less than as an occasion for administering the comfort of it.

From the foregoing exposition it will be evident what apologetic force resides in this skilfully worded and constructed sentence. Its didactic import may be summed up as follows:—

1. The end in view—the conducting of sons to glory —is manifestly Godworthy.

2. The carrying out of this end naturally demands a human Leader.

3. Leadership inevitably involves arduous experiences

[1] So Grotius, and likewise Pfleiderer; *vide* his *Paulinism*, ii. 72.

common to Leader and led, but falling more heavily on Him than on them.

4. These experiences fit the Leader for His work, establishing comradeship between Him and the led, inspiring in them admiration and confidence.

It is not less apparent that a firm grasp of the apologetic aim is the key to the true interpretation. Lose sight of it, or faintly recognise it as a bare possibility, then the idea of leadership sinks into a mere "perhaps," or is merged in the vague general idea of authorship, and it is no longer apparent how suffering should be an indispensable part of Christ's experience. A self-evidencing proposition becomes a comparatively obscure assertion.

It may be objected that what we gain apologetically by adopting the title "Leader" or "Captain" we lose dogmatically. Leader signifies little more than example. The death of Christ as Leader simply takes its place among His many earthly experiences of suffering, and possesses no exceptional significance. It is but the last and severest event in a tragic career. He died for men as their Leader, but only in the sense that He made death another thing—no longer terrible—for all who look to Him as their Captain—

"The Saviour hath passed through its portals *before* thee,
And the lamp of His love is thy guide through the gloom."

All this is true. The rationale of the suffering experience of Christ offered to us by the author of our Epistle, *so far as we have yet gone*, is, theologically, meagre. But the view given is true so far as it goes; it is one side of a many-sided doctrine, which embraces all the fragments of truth that form the basis of the various theories concerning the meaning of Christ's Passion. The writer was not a one-sided theorist, but a man of prophetic insight, looking at truth with spiritual versatility, from diverse points of view, and knowing how to use them all in turn. And he was thankful, to begin with, to be able to exhibit the fitness and necessity of Christ's sufferings from any point of view which had a chance of commending itself to the minds of his Hebrew readers. If it was true, important, useful, and above all obvious, it was enough. It was a point gained to have lodged in their minds the one thought: the sufferings of Christ a useful discipline for Him in sympathy with men and in obedience to God, and therefore a good training for being the Leader of salvation. It may seem incredible that at that time of day, after many years of Christian profession, they should need to be taught truths which are but the alphabet of the doctrine concerning Christ's death. But we have the writer's own word for it that such was the fact. And if we wish to understand the Epistle, we must keep the fact steadily in mind, and beware of falling into the error of supposing that the writer and his readers stood, in religious thought and belief, pretty much on a level. The error may be applied in either of two ways: by lifting the readers up to the writer's level, or by degrading him down to theirs. Both mistakes are alike fatal to successful exposition. In the one case we shall find in the book a collection of lifeless theological commonplaces; in the other we shall find in it a conception of Christianity which has not surmounted Judaism.

CHAPTER VI

THE WAY OF SALVATION

CHAP. II. 11–18

THIS section contains a further elucidation of the way or method of salvation in its bearing on the personal experiences of the Saviour. It may be analysed into three parts: First, the statement of a principle on which the argument proceeds (ver. 11); second, illustrations of the principle by citations from the Old Testament (vers. 12, 13); third, applications of the principle to particular facts in the history of Jesus (vers. 14–18).

The writer at this point seems at first sight to be making a new start, looking forward rather than backward, and with the priesthood of Christ, of which express mention is made in ver. 17, specially in his eye. Further reflection, however, satisfies us that, as the "for" at the commencement of ver. 11 suggests, he looks backward as well as forward, and that the new truth therein enunciated has its root in the statement contained in ver. 10. The assertion that the Sanctifier and the sanctified are all of one may be viewed as answering two questions naturally arising out of ver. 10, to which it furnishes no explicit answer. First, Christ is called the Captain or Leader of salvation: how does He contribute to salvation? Is He simply the first of a series who pass through suffering to glory? or does He influence all the sons whom God brings to glory so as to contribute very materially to the great end in view, their reaching the promised land? Second, what is the condition of His influence? what is the nexus between Him and them, the Leader and the led, that enables Him to exert over them this power? The answer to the former question is, Christ saves by *sanctifying*; the answer to the latter, that He and the sanctified are *one*. The answer in the first case is given indirectly by the substitution of one title for another, the "Leader of salvation" being replaced by the "Sanctifier"; the answer in the second case is given directly, and forms the doctrine of the text: the Sanctifier and the sanctified are all of one.

The new designation for Christ is presumably selected because it fits in both to that view of His function suggested by the title Leader, and to that implied in the title High Priest, introduced in the sequel. No good reason can be given for limiting the reference to the latter. The probability is that the writer meant to imply that Christ sanctifies both as a Captain and as a Priest, at once as the Moses and as the Aaron of the great salvation. It is probable that he introduces the title "the Sanctifier" to adjust the idea of salvation to the Saviour's priestly office, but it is reasonable to suppose that he does this without any breach in the continuity of thought.

These are simple observations, but they involve a very

important question, namely, In what sense are the terms "Sanctifier" and "sanctified" used in this place? and, generally, what conception of sanctification pervades the Epistle? In the ordinary theological dialect "sanctification" bears an ethical meaning, denoting the gradual renewal of his nature experienced by a believing man. The usage can be justified by New Testament texts in Paul's Epistles, and as I believe also in the Epistle to the Hebrews; but the notion of holiness thus reached is secondary and derivative. In the Old Testament holiness is a religious rather than an ethical idea, and belongs properly to the sphere of worship. The people of Israel were holy in the sense of being consecrated for the service of God, the consecration being effected by sacrifice, which purged the worshippers from the defilement of sin. It was to be expected that the ritual or theocratic idea of holiness should reappear in the New Testament, especially in an Epistle like that to the Hebrews, in which Christian truth is largely stated in terms suggested by Levitical analogies. Accordingly we do find the word "sanctify" employed in the Epistle in the Old Testament sense, in connection with the priestly office of Christ, as in chapter x. 10: "Sanctified through the offering of the body of Jesus Christ once for all." In such texts sanctification has more affinity with "justification" in the Pauline system of thought than with the sanctification of dogmatic theology. But it might also be anticipated that the conception of holiness would undergo transformation under Christian influences, passing from the ritual to the ethical sphere. The source of transforming power lay in the nature of the

Christian service. The sacrifices of the new era are spiritual: thankfulness, beneficent deeds, pure conduct. A good life is the Christian's service to God. Thus while formally considered sanctification might continue to mean consecration to God's service, materially it came to mean the process by which a man was enabled to live soberly, righteously, godly. Traces of this transformed meaning are to be found throughout the New Testament. The Epistle to the Hebrews is no exception to this statement. The term "holiness" (ἁγιασμός, ἁγιότης) is used in an ethical sense twice in the twelfth chapter. In ver. 10 it is stated that God's end in subjecting His children to paternal discipline is to make them partakers of His own holiness; in ver. 14, Christians are exhorted to follow peace with all men and holiness—holiness being prescribed as a moral task, and as an end to be reached gradually. In the one case, God is the Sanctifier through the discipline of life; in the other, Christians are summoned to sanctify themselves by a process of moral effort. In another class of texts Christ appears as a fountain of sanctifying influence. The word is not used, but the thing, help to godly living, is there. "Looking unto Jesus" the Leader in faith is commended as a source of moral strength and steadfastness (xii. 2). Even in His priestly character He is set forth as a source of moral inspiration. Through Him, the great High Priest, we receive "grace for seasonable succour" (iv. 16); from Him, the tempted one, emanates aid to the tempted (ii. 18). God's paternal discipline, our own self-effort, Christ's example, priestly influence, and sympathy, all contribute to the same end, persistency and progress in the Christian life. In connection with the first, we may say God sanctifies; in connection with the second, we may say we sanctify ourselves; why may we not, in connection with the third, call Christ the Sanctifier?

It thus appears that sanctification is spoken of in the Epistle both in a ritual and in an ethical sense, and that Christ is represented, in effect if not in express terms, as performing the part of a sanctifier, not merely by consecrating us once for all to God by the sacrifice of Himself, but likewise by being to us in various ways a source of gracious help. This double sense of the word "sanctify" is analogous to the double sense of the word "righteousness" in the Pauline literature. In stating his doctrine of salvation, Paul uses the word in an objective sense. The righteousness of God is an objective righteousness, given to us for Christ's sake. But in the Pauline apologetic, in which the apostle seeks to reconcile his doctrine with apparently conflicting interests, such as the claims of the law, the prerogatives of Israel, and the demands of morality, we find the word used in a subjective sense—to denote a righteousness within us.[1] Repelling the insinuation that we may continue in sin that grace may abound, he strives to show how every believer in Christ becomes a servant of righteousness. Even so in the Epistle to the Hebrews we find sanctification used in a double sense, a ritual and an ethical. But there is a failure in the parallelism between the two writers in this respect, that whereas in Paul what one might call the artificial or technical sense

---

[1] On the senses in which Paul uses the term δικαιοσύνη, vide my *St. Paul's Conception of Christianity*.

of righteousness appears in his doctrinal statement, and the ethical sense in his apologetic, in the author of our Epistle the ritual sense of sanctification appears in those parts of his writing which are dominated by his apologetic aim, and the ethical chiefly in the practical or hortatory passages, where he is set free from the trammels of his apologetic argument.[1]

If it be indeed true that Christ appears in the Epistle as a sanctifier in a twofold sense,—in a specific sense as a priest, in a general sense as a fountain of grace,—then it is natural to suppose that in introducing the title "the Sanctifier" for the first time the writer would employ it in a comprehensive sense, covering the whole extent of Christ's sanctifying influence. This comprehensive sense, as we have seen, suits the connection of thought, the text standing midway between two views of Christ's function as Saviour,—that suggested by the title Captain of salvation, on the one hand, and that suggested by the title High Priest, on the other—looking back to the one and forward to the other. I feel justified therefore in putting upon the designation "the Sanctifier" this pregnant construction, and shall now proceed to consider the affirmation in ver. 11, that the Sanctifier and the sanctified are all of one.[2]

---

[1] Another point will come up for comparison in due course. Paul discovers, in faith, in the very heart of his system a nexus between objective and subjective righteousness. Does the system of thought in this Epistle provide for the union of the two kinds of sanctification? or do they stand side by side, external to each other? Are religious and ethical interests reconciled by a principle inherent in the system? On this *vide* Chapter xvi. of this work.

[2] The present participle, οἱ ἁγιαζόμενοι, fits into the view that an ethical progressive sanctification is included, but it does not prove

This statement, as indicated at the outset, I regard as the enunciation of a *principle*; by which is meant that the unity asserted is involved in the relation of Sanctifier to sanctified. Whether there be only one or many exemplifications of the relation is immaterial. Though only one Sanctifier were in view or possible, the proposition would still continue to be of the nature of a principle. The point is, that Christ, *as* Sanctifier, must be one with those whom He sanctifies, could not otherwise perform for them that function. Some, as if bent on reducing the significance of the statement to a minimum, take it as the mere assertion of a fact: that this Sanctifier, Jesus Christ, and those whom He sanctifies are all of one God, that is, are all the children of God, the purpose of the statement being to justify the use of the title "sons" in the previous verse, or to repeat the truth implied in it. But that title, as we have seen, rests on its own foundation, the lordship of men, and needs neither justification nor repetition. Viewed as the mere statement of a fact, the first member of verse 11 becomes almost purposeless and superfluous. Viewed as the statement of a principle, on the other hand, it becomes a very necessary and fruitful proposition. The relative terms "Sanctifier" and "sanctified" imply one very obvious and wide difference between the parties. The Sanctifier is holy; the sanctified, when He takes them in hand, are unholy. That being so, it needs to be said that, notwithstanding the separation between the parties, there is a unity between them sur-

it, for the participles may be timeless designations of the parties. οἱ ἁγιαζόμενοι are those who need sanctification. That is their characteristic, as to be able to sanctify is that of the Sanctifier.

mounting the difference. And that can be said with truth, for otherwise the two parties could not stand in the relation of Sanctifier to sanctified; they could only stand permanently apart as holy and unholy. Unity is involved in the nature of the case. That is precisely what the writer means to say. He states the truth as an axiom, which he expects even his dull-minded readers to accept immediately as true; and he means to use it as a key to the cardinal facts of Christ's human experience.

Unity to some extent or in some sense is involved; that is clear. But in what sense; to what extent? This is indicated very laconically by the phrase "of or from one, all" (ἐξ ἑνὸς πάντες). The sentence has no verb, and is worn down to the fewest possible words, after the manner of a proverb. "For the Sanctifier and the sanctified—of one, all." Commentators have been much exercised over this elliptical utterance, and have made innumerable suggestions as to the noun to be supplied after "one." One seed, blood, mass, nature; or one Adam, Abraham, God. The consensus is in favour of the last. But if the writer had a particular noun in his mind why did he not insert it, and so make his meaning clear? It does look as if his purpose were to lay stress, not on descent from one God, one Divine Father, but rather on the result, the brotherhood or comradeship between the two parties. Is not his idea that Sanctifier and sanctified are all "of one piece, one whole,"[1] two parties welded into one, having *everything* in common except character? The phrase ἐξ ἑνός does

[1] The phrase is Professor Davidson's, who admits that ἐξ ἑνός might bear this meaning.

not necessarily imply that descent or origin is in his view. As in the text "every one that is of the truth heareth My voice" the phrase ἐκ τῆς ἀληθείας means *true*, in sympathy with the truth, so ἐξ ἑνός in our text may mean "one"; one as a family is one, having a common interest and a common lot. The connecting particle τε is in consonance with this view. It binds the two parties closely together as forming a single category: "Sanctifier and sanctified, all one."

We can now answer the question, To what extent one? Surely, *as far as possible*! The nature of the relation craves unity in everything but the one ineffaceable distinction of character. From whatever point of view we regard the Sanctifier's function, this becomes apparent on reflection. Conceive Christ first as Sanctifier in the ethical sense: in that capacity it behoved Him to be in all possible respects one with those to be sanctified. For in that case the sanctifying power lies in His example, His character, His human experience. He makes men believing in Him holy by reproducing in His own life the lost ideal of human character and bringing that ideal to bear on their minds; by living a true, godly life amid the same conditions of trial as those by which they are surrounded, and helping them by inspiration and sympathy to be faithful. His power to sanctify depends on likeness in nature, position, experience.

Conceive Christ next as Sanctifier in the ritual sense, as a priest, consecrating us for the service of God by the sacrifice of Himself, and the same need for a pervading, many-sided unity is apparent. The priest must be one with his clients in God's sight, their accepted representative, so that what He does is done in their name and avails for their benefit. He must be one with them in death, for it is by His death in sacrifice that He makes propitiation for their sins. He must be one with them in the possession of humanity, for unless He become partaker of human nature He cannot die. Finally, He must be one with them in experience of trial and temptation, for thereby is demonstrated the sympathy which wins trust, and unless the priest be trusted it is in vain that He transacts. All these unities except the first are unfolded in the sequel of the second chapter, and are common to the two aspects of Christ's function as the Sanctifier. The first unity, that before God, is peculiar to the priestly office, and is reserved for mention at a later stage, when the priesthood of Christ becomes the subject of formal consideration.[1]

Having enunciated this great principle of unity, the writer next proceeds to show that it has its root in Old Testament Scripture. The manner in which he does this is very lively and impressive. In abstract language the import is this: "The unity asserted implies a brotherly relation between Sanctifier and sanctified. But traces of such a brotherhood are discernible in the Old Testament, as in the following passages, where Messiah appears saying, 'I will declare Thy name unto My brethren'; 'I will put My trust in Him'; 'Behold, I and the children which God hath given Me.'" But the writer does not put the matter in this cold, colourless way. He introduces his quotations in an animated, rhetorical manner with the spirit-stirring sentiment, "for which cause He is

[1] *Vide* chap. v. 1.

not ashamed to call them brethren." Observing that the quoted passages are all of the nature of personal declarations or exclamations, observing also that they are all utterances of an impassioned character, he strives to reflect the spirit of the original texts in his own language. Therefore he says not, Messiah is represented as the brother of men, but He calls Himself their brother; and, not content with that, he introduces another word to bring out the fact that Messiah does not barely admit or reluctantly acknowledge the brotherhood, but proclaims it with ardour and enthusiasm, rejoicing, glorying therein. "He is not *ashamed* to call them brethren. On the contrary, He calls them brethren with all His heart, with the fervour of love, with the eloquence of earnest conviction." The reference to shame points significantly to the one cardinal difference, sin, which constitutes the temptation to the Holy One to be ashamed.

The quotations so spiritedly introduced are well selected for the purpose in hand. In all, brotherhood is expressed or clearly implied. In the first, the speaker, primarily the Psalmist,[1] represents himself as a member of a congregation of worshippers whom he calls his brethren; in the second, the speaker, primarily the prophet Isaiah,[2] declares his purpose to trust God, implying that he is in a situation of trial in which trust is necessary; in the third, taken from the same place,[3] he associates himself with the children God has given him, as of the same

---

[1] Ps. xxii. 22.

[2] Isa. viii. 17, as in Septuagint. The rendering in the English version is, "I will look for Him."

[3] Isa. viii. 18.

family and sharing the same prophetic vocation. The utterances put into the mouth of Messiah imply brotherhood in worship and in trying experience, and even the closer kind of brotherhood involved in family connections and a common calling.[1]

We now come to the applications of the principle enunciated in verse 11. They are three in number, together covering the whole earthly history of Christ, beginning with His birth and ending with His death, and all viewed as belonging to the category of humiliation. Incarnation, sorrowful experience, death, such are the three grand exemplifications of the brotherly unity of the Sanctifier with the sanctified; not arranged, however, in this order, the second changing places with the third, because the incarnation is exhibited in subordination to the death as a means to an end: Christ took flesh that He might die. The applications are as obvious as they are important. If the principle has validity and value, it must and will prove true in those particulars. What we have to do therefore is not to justify these deductions, but to study the terms in which they are expressed, which are in many respects curious and instructive.

First comes the incarnation (ver. 14). The sanctified are here referred to in terms borrowed from the last of the three quotations, "the children." The use of this designation is not only rhetorically graceful but logically apt, as suggesting the idea of an existence derived from

---

[1] The children of Isaiah prophesied by the very names they bore, e.g. Maher-shalal-hash-baz = "making speed to the spoil, he hasteneth the prey." On the reason for proving the solidarity of Jesus with sinners by prophetic texts rather than by reference to evangelic facts recorded in the Gospels, *vide* the last chapter of this work.

birth. Children is an appropriate name for men as born of blood, and therefore possessing blood and flesh. These terms, "blood and flesh," in their turn are employed to denote human nature as mortal, as it exists under the conditions of this earthly life: for flesh and blood have no place in the eternal life. Of man's mortal nature, as thus designated, Christ is said to have taken part "likewise" ($\pi\alpha\rho\alpha\pi\lambda\eta\sigma\iota\omega\varsigma$),[1] similarly. The scope of the whole passage requires that this word be emphasised, so that the similarity may be as great as possible. Therefore not merely is participation in man's mortal flesh implied, but entrance into human nature by the same door as other men—by birth. We may not, with Irving and the Adoptianists, include sinfulness in the likeness, for the application of the principle of unity is necessarily limited by the personal holiness of the Sanctifier. The rule is, Like in all things, sin excepted.

The second application of the principle is to the death of Christ, which, as already indicated, is next mentioned because it supplies the *rationale* of the incarnation (vers. 14b, 15). As a mere corollary to the principle it would have been enough to have said, Because the brethren die, He too died. But the objection might be raised, Why should the sinless One die, if, as we have been taught, death be the penalty of sin? Therefore the application of the principle to the death of Christ is so stated as to bring out at the same time the service He thereby rendered to His brethren. This is done, however, in a very peculiar way, which has

[1] "From the idea of *close alongside* comes that of *in precisely like manner*. The adverb occurs here only in Scripture."—Vaughan.

greatly perplexed commentators. The difficulty arises in part from our trying to put too much theology into the passage, and to bring its teaching into line with other more familiar modes of exhibiting the significance of Christ's death. It must be recognised once for all that the writer has various ways of showing that it behoved Christ to die, and that he gladly avails himself of any way that tends to throw light on a subject ill-understood by his readers. This is one of the ways; and although from its isolation in the Epistle it looks obscure and forbidding, the text yields a good, clear, intelligible sense, if we will be content not to find in it the whole mystery and theory of the atonement. For the materials of explanation we do not need to go outside the Bible: they are evidently to be found in the account of the Fall in the third chapter of Genesis. According to that account, death came into the world because Adam sinned, tempted by the serpent. The text before us is a free paraphrase of that account. The serpent is identified with the devil, death is represented as a source of slavish fear, embittering human life,[1] because it is the penalty of sin: the power of death is ascribed to the devil, because he is the tempter to sin which brought death into the world, and the accuser of those who sin, so that they, having sin brought to mind, fear to die. Christ destroys the devil by destroying his power, and He destroys his power by freeing mortal men from the cruel bondage of the fear of death.

[1] The universal fact is here described, though τούτους ὅσοι might seem to imply limitation. "There is no limitation intended."—Vaughan.

All this is plain enough. But the question now arises, How did Christ through death free from the fear of death? We, steeped in theology, would naturally reply, By offering Himself an atoning sacrifice for sin. But that is certainly not the writer's thought here. He reserves the great thought of Christ's priestly self-sacrifice for a more advanced stage in the development of his doctrine. What, then, is his thought? Simply this. Christ delivers from the fear of death by dying *as a sinless one*. Death and sin are connected very intimately in our minds; hence, fear. But lo, here is one who knows no sin dying. His point is not that the sinless One dies instead of the sinful, but that the sinless One, though sinless, dies. The bare fact breaks the association between sin and death. But more than that: He who dies is our brother, has entered into our mortal state in a fraternal spirit for the very purpose of lending us a helping hand. We may not fully know how His death avails to help us. But we know that the Sanctifier in a spirit of brotherhood became one with us, even in death: and the knowledge enables us to realise our unity with Him in death, and so emancipates us from fear. "Sinners may die, for the Sinless has died." The benefit thus derived from the death of the sinless One is but the other side of the great principle, Sanctifier and sanctified all one. For it has two sides; it applies both ways. The Sanctifier becomes one with the sanctified in brotherly love; the sanctified become one with the Sanctifier in privilege. They are mutually one in both directions in God's sight; they are mutually one in both directions for the spiritual instincts of the believer, even before he knows what the twofold validity for God means. In proportion as we realise the one aspect of the principle, the Sanctifier one with us, we are enabled to realise and get benefit from the other. While the Holy One stands apart from us in the isolation of His sinlessness, we, sinners, fear to die; when we see Him by our side, even in death, which we have been accustomed to regard as the penalty of sin, death ceases to appear as penalty, and becomes the gate of heaven.[1]

Thus with consummate tact does the writer turn the one thing that divides Christ from ordinary men, and seems to disable Him for helping them, into a source of consolation. Sanctifier, that presupposes sinlessness; sanctified, that presupposes sin; and being sinners we fear to die. Yes; but the sinless One *died*, and we feeling our unity with Him cease to fear. He cannot be one with us in sin, but He is one with us in that which comes nearest to sin, and derives all its terror from sin.

Before passing to the third application of the principle, the writer throws in a truism to relieve the argument and make it more intelligible to persons to whom the train of thought is new and strange (ver. 16). Simply rendered, what the verse states is this: "For, as

---

[1] So in effect Professor Davidson, p. 70. Rendall renders the last clause of ver. 14, "that through *His* death He might bring to nought him that had the power of *that* death," limiting the devil's power to the death of Christ. He takes the article τοῦ before θανάτου as referring to a particular instance of death. But it is rather a case of the article prefixed to abstracts. Ὁ θάνατος is simply death as a familiar human experience. The omission of the article in ver. 15 makes no difference; it is still the abstract idea of death. The use of the article with abstracts, though common, is not necessary.

you know,[1] it is not of angels that He taketh hold (to be their Helper), but He taketh hold of the seed of Abraham." The rendering of the Authorised Version (an inheritance from patristic times) is due apparently to inability to conceive of the writer penning so self-evident a truth as that Christ did not undertake to save angels. That inability, again, is due to failure to gauge the spiritual ignorance of his Hebrew readers. To the same cause it is due that some recent commentators have not been content to regard ver. 16 as the statement of a truism, but have laboured hard to assign to it an important place in the chain of argument. To me this text is one of the most significant indications of the dark condition of the Hebrew Christians in reference to the nature of Christianity. They were so little at home, it appears, in Christian truth, that nothing could be taken for granted, and they had to be coaxed like children to engage in the most elementary process of thought on the subject. Such coaxing I find here. The writer stops short in his argument, and says in effect: "Please to remember that Christ is not the Saviour of the angels of whom I have lately been speaking, but of men, and reflect on what that implies, and it will help you to go along with me in this train of thought."

But we observe that he does not say, Christ taketh

---

[1] This is one of the comparatively few instances of the use of the particle δή (δή που) in the New Testament. It is not well rendered either in the Authorised or in the Revised Version, here or anywhere. It always points to something familiar, matter of course, or specially noteworthy. Here "it implies that the statement made is a familiar truth. 'For He doth not, as we well know.'"—Westcott. The combination δή που occurs here only in the New Testament.

hold of *men*, but, "of the seed of Abraham." We must beware of attaching too much importance to this, as if the reference implied that the Christian salvation concerned only the people of Israel. Here, again, the apologetic exigencies and aim are our best guide. The writer is not enunciating a theological proposition, but having recourse to an oratorical device to bring home his teaching to the hearts of his readers. He means to say, "Christ took in hand to save, not angels, but yourselves, my Hebrew brethren." His argument up to this point has been stated in terms applicable to all mankind; to charge it with a warmer tone and an intenser interest he gives it now a homeward-bound turn. To infer from this that he considered the gospel the affair of the Jews exclusively, is to sink to the rabbinical level in exposition. At the same time it may be noted that the introduction of a reference to Israel just here is convenient, as from this point onwards things are to be spoken of, *e.g.* the office of the high priest,[1] in which persons belonging to the chosen people were specially interested.

The writer now resumes and completes his application of the principle enunciated in ver. 11, giving prominence in the final instance to Christ's experience of temptation (vers. 17, 18). In doing, so he takes occasion from the parenthetical remark about the subjects of Christ's saving work (ver. 16) to make a new start, and go over the

---

[1] Von Soden remarks: "The expression σπέρμα ’Αβραάμ is chosen here because it prepares for the introduction of the high-priest idea," so making the use of the phrase intelligible even on the hypothesis of Gentile first readers.

ground again with variations. The thoughts contained in these closing sentences are similar to those expressed in verses 14, 15. Here, as there, it is inferred from the fact that the subjects of Christ's work are men, that He must have a human nature and experience likewise. Here also, as there, the ends served by the assumption of human nature and endurance of a human experience are set forth. But neither in stating the fact of the incarnation nor in explaining its end does the writer repeat himself. He varies not only the forms of expression, but also the aspects under which he presents the truth, so as to give to his unfolding of the doctrine variety, richness, and fulness. While before he said that because the children were partakers of blood and flesh Christ also took part of the same, here he says that for the same reason it behoved Christ in all things to be made like unto His brethren. And whereas in the former place he set it forth as the end of the incarnation to deprive the devil of his power over man through death, and to rob death itself of its terrors, in this concluding passage he represents the human experience of Jesus as serving these two ends: first, the fitting of Him to transact as a priest for men towards God; and second, the qualifying of Him for being a sympathetic friend in need to all the tempted.

To be noted specially are the terms in which the unity between the Sanctifier and the sanctified is stated here. It behoved Him to be *in all respects* (κατὰ πάντα) made like unto His brethren. Likeness is asserted without qualification, and yet there are limits arising out of the nature of the case. One limit, of course, is that there can be no likeness in moral character. This limit is implied in the very titles applied to the two parties, Sanctifier and sanctified, and it is expressly stated in the place where Christ is represented as "tempted in all respects similarly, apart from sin" (iv. 15). Another limit, nowhere referred to in words, but tacitly assumed, is, that the likeness is in those respects chiefly in which our life on earth is affected by the curse pronounced on man for sin. Overlooking this principle, we might fail to be impressed with the likeness of Jesus to other men in His experience; we might even be impressed with a sense of unlikeness. There are respects in which Christ's life was unlike the common life of men. He was a celibate; He died young, and had no experience of the temptations of middle life, or the infirmities of old age; in outward lot He was the brother of the poor, and was well acquainted with their griefs, but of the joys and temptations of wealth He had no experience. But these features of difference do not fall under the category of the curse. Family ties date from before the Fall. The doom pronounced on man was death immediate, and prolonged life is a mitigation of the curse. Wealth too is a mitigating feature, another evidence that the curse has not been executed in rigour, but has remained to a considerable extent an unrealised ideal, because counteracted by an underlying redemptive economy. It will be found that Christ's likeness to His brethren is closest just where the traces of the curse are most apparent: in so far as this life is (1) afflicted with poverty, (2) exposed to temptations to ungodliness, (3) subject to death under its more manifestly penal forms, as when it comes as a blight in early life, or as the judicial penalty of crime. Jesus was like His brethren in proportion as they need His sympathy and succour—like the poor, the tempted, the criminal.[1]

This likeness had for its final cause that the Sanctifier might become an effective helper of those to whom He was thus made like.

"*That He might be a merciful and trusty High Priest in things pertaining to God, to make propitiation for the sins of the people.*" These weighty words form an important landmark in the Epistle, as containing the first express mention of a topic which the writer has had in view from the outset, and on which he will have much to say in the sequel, namely, the Priesthood of Christ. He has now arrived at a point in his argument at which he can introduce the great thought with some chance of being understood; though how well aware he is of the difficulty likely to be felt by his readers in taking it in appears from the fact that, immediately after announcing the new theme, he invites them to consider carefully the Apostle and High Priest of their confession (iii. 1). In effect he says, "Now this is a great and glorious topic, but for you it is a difficult one; give your minds to it; come, study it with me, it will well repay your pains." Here he does little more than introduce the subject. The priestly function of Christ he describes in general terms

---

[1] Westcott, always careful to report patristic opinion, gives the following from Chrysostom: ἐτέχθη, φησίν, ἐτράφη, ηὐξήθη, ἔπαθε πάντα ἅπερ ἐχρῆν, τέλος ἀπέθανεν = "He was born, nourished, grew, suffered what was needful, at last died."

as exercised towards God and as consisting in the expiation of sin.[1] No mention as yet of the means of propitiation, "gifts and sacrifices" (v. 1); still less of the fact that Christ accomplishes the result by the sacrifice of *Himself*. He will take care not to introduce that master-thought till he can do so with effect. Here on the threshold of the subject he gives prominence rather to the moral qualities of a well-equipped High Priest, mer<u>ciful</u>ness and trust<u>worth</u>iness; moved partly by a regard to the connection of thought, and partly by a desire to present Christ as Priest in a winsome light. The stress laid on these attributes is one of the originalities of the Epistle, whether we have regard to the legal requirements for the priestly office as specified in the Pentateuch, or to the view of Christ's atoning work presented by other New Testament writers. It is one of the writer's favourite themes.

Of the two attributes the former is the chief, for he who is merciful, compassionate, will be faithful. It is want of sympathy that makes officials perfunctory. Hence we might read, "a merciful and *therefore* a faithful, trustworthy High Priest." So reading, we see the close connection between the experiences of Christ and His fitness for the priestly office. For all can understand how an experience of trial and temptation might help to make Christ compassionate, while it is

---

[1] εἰς τὸ ἱλάσκεσθαι τὰς ἁμαρτίας τοῦ λαοῦ. Note that the object of the <u>verb is *sin*</u>, not *God*, as it would have been in a Pagan <u>writer</u>. The present tense points to a habitual exercise of the function of propitiation. "The real thought is to secure the forgiveness of sin from day to day and from hour to hour, by His presence with God as the Propitiation."—Vaughan.

not so easy to see why it behoved Him to suffer *all* He suffered in order to perform the essential duty of a Priest—that of atoning for sin. One might think that for the latter purpose it were enough to die; but to ensure that a High Priest should be heart and soul interested in His constituents, it behoved Him to be made in all respects like unto His brethren.

The other end served by Jesus being made in all things like His brethren is thus stated: "*For having Himself been tempted in that which He suffered, He is able to succour those who are being tempted.*" This rendering of verse 18 is one of several possible ones which it is not necessary to enumerate or discuss, as the general sense is plain, namely, that Christ having experienced temptation to be unfaithful to His vocation in connection with the sufferings arising out of it, previously alluded to as a source of perfecting, is able to succour those who, like the Hebrew Christians, were tempted in similar ways to be unfaithful to their Christian calling. The words show us, not so much a different part of Christ's ministry as Priest, as a different aspect of it. In the previous verse His work is looked at in relation to sinners for whose sins He makes propitiation. In this verse, on the other hand, that work is looked at in relation to believers needing daily succour amid the temptations to which they are exposed. Both aspects are combined when, further on, mercy and grace for seasonable succour are named as the things to be sought in our petitions at the throne of grace (iv. 16).

CHAPTER VII

CHRIST AND MOSES

CHAP. III

THE remarkable statement concerning the nature and way of salvation contained in the section which we have been considering in the three last chapters supplies ample material for a new exhortation. The writer has shown that the Christian salvation consists in nothing less than lordship in the world to come. He has set forth Christ as the Captain of this salvation, and the High Priest of the new people of God, the Moses and the Aaron of Christendom, and in both capacities as the Sanctifier of the sons of God whom He leads to glory, and, in order to the efficient discharge of that function, one with His brethren in nature and experience. The immense supply of motive power stored up in this densely packed group of thoughts he now brings to bear on the tempted Hebrew Christians as an inducement to steadfastness: " Wherefore, holy brethren, partakers of a heavenly calling, consider the Apostle and High Priest of our confession, Jesus."

Every word here is an echo of something going before, and is instinct with persuasive virtue. " Brethren," of

Him who in a fraternal spirit identified Himself with the unholy, and for their sakes took flesh and tasted death. "Holy," at least in standing, in virtue of the priestly action of the Sanctifier; and because holy in this sense, under obligation to make their consecration to God a reality by living a truly Christian life. "Partakers of a heavenly calling"—thus described, at once with truth and with rhetorical skill, with a backward glance at the greatness of the Christian's hope as the destined lord of the future world, and with a mental reference to the contrast between that glorious prospect and the present state of believers as partakers of flesh and blood, and subject to death and the fear thereof; reminding them at the same time of the blessed truth, that as Christ became partaker of their present lot, so they were destined to be partakers of His glorious inheritance, the unity and fellowship between Him and His people being on both sides perfect and complete. The epithet "heavenly" gracefully varies the point of view from which the inheritance is contemplated. The world to come becomes now a world above, a celestial country. The change in the mode of expression is an oratorical variation; but it is more, even a contribution to the parenetic force of the sentence, for the heavenly in the thought of the writer here and throughout the Epistle is the *real*, the *abiding*. Heaven is the place of realities, as this material world is the place of shadows. Such is our author's philosophic view-point, if we may ascribe such a thing to him—his way of contemplating the universe, supposed by some to be borrowed from Philo and the Alexandrine school of philosophy; certainly a marked peculiarity, whencesoever derived.[1] With the heavenly world Christianity is identified, and thereby its absolute and abiding nature is strongly asserted, as against Judaism, which as belonging to the visible world is necessarily doomed to pass away. This contrast indeed does not find open expression here, but that it is in the writer's mind the sequel abundantly shows. He uses his philosophy for his apologetic purpose, employing it as a vehicle for expressing and defending the thesis: Judaism transient, Christianity for aye.

The titles here ascribed to Jesus also arise out of the previous context, and are full of significance. Specially noteworthy is the former of the two, "Apostle," here only applied to Christ. The use of this epithet in reference to our Lord is one of several indications of the fresh creative genius of the writer, and of the unconventional nature of his style. When he calls Christ an apostle he is not thinking of the twelve apostles, or of Christ's prophetic office. Christ's claim to attention as one through whom God has spoken His last word to men he has sufficiently recognised and insisted on in the first exhortation (ii. 1-4). He is thinking rather of the apostleship of Moses. The basis for the title is such a text as Exodus iii. 10: "Come now therefore, and I will send thee (ἀποστείλω, Sept.) unto Pharaoh, that

[1] Among the thought-affinities between our Epistle and Philo are the distinction between the visible world (τὰ φαινόμενα, xi. 3 = Philo's ὁ ὁρατὸς κόσμος) and the invisible (μὴ ἐκ φαινομένων, xi. 3 = Philo's κόσμος νοητός); the conception of heaven as the country or home of the soul (πατρίς, xi. 14); the application to Christ of attributes ascribed by Philo to the Logos, e.g. πρωτότοκος, (= πρωτόγονος in Philo, or πρεσβύτερος υἱός) θεός, (i. 8) ἀρχιερεύς.

thou mayest bring forth My people the children of Israel out of Egypt." Moses was an apostle, as one sent by God on the important mission of leading the enslaved race of Israel out of Egypt into Canaan. Christ was our Apostle, as one sent by God to be the Leader in the greater salvation. The Apostle of our Christian confession and the " Captain of salvation " are synonymous designations. Something indeed might be said for taking it as a generic title, including all Christ's functions. In that case it might have stood alone, though even then special mention of the priestly office would have been appropriate, as having been previously named, and as a source of peculiar comfort and inspiration, and also because it is in the sequel the subject of a lengthened consideration. As applied to it, the exhortation to consider has a somewhat different meaning from that which it bears in reference to the title Apostle. " Consider the Apostle " means, consider for practical purposes a subject already sufficiently understood ; " consider the High Priest " means, consider the doctrine of Christ's priesthood, that ye may first understand it, and then prove its practical value.

Christ the Apostle is the immediate subject of contemplation. That aspect is in view throughout the third and fourth chapters, the priestly aspect being presented at the close of the latter, as an introduction to the long discussion which commences with the fifth chapter and extends to the tenth. " Consider the Apostle of our confession " is the rubric of this new section.

To guide consideration, a point of view is suggested

congruous to the practical aim. The aim being to promote steadfastness in the Christian faith and life, the selected point of view is the fidelity of Jesus our Apostle. "Who was faithful to Him that made Him." In other words, "faithful to His vocation." God made Jesus, as in 1 Samuel xii. 6 He is said to have made Moses and Aaron. The underlying idea is, that it is God in His providence who raises up all great actors in human affairs and prepares them for their position as public men. God "made" Jesus by giving Him His unique place in the world's history, as the chief agent in the work of redemption. And Jesus was faithful to God by discharging faithfully the high duties entrusted to Him. What the Hebrews are invited to do, therefore, is to consider Jesus as the faithful Captain of salvation, who never betrayed His trust, shirked His responsibilities, or neglected duty to escape personal suffering, and who at the last great crisis said, "Not My will, but Thine be done." For of course the theatre in which Christ's fidelity was displayed was His earthly life of trial and temptation. True, it is present fidelity that is asserted ($\pi\iota\sigma\tau\grave{o}\nu$ $\check{o}\nu\tau\alpha$), nevertheless the rendering "who was faithful" is practically correct. What is meant is, that Jesus is one who by His past career has earned the character of the Faithful One: that is the honourable title to which in virtue of a spotless record He is fully entitled. The field of observation is His public ministry on earth, assumed to be familiar to readers of the Epistle, either through our written Gospels, or through the unwritten evangelic tradition. What end could be served by pointing to a fidelity displayed in heaven? Fidelity there costs no effort; but fidelity maintained amid constant temptation to unfaithfulness is worth remarking on, and may fitly be commended to the admiring contemplation of the tempted. Then how inappropriate the comparison between Christ and Moses, if the fidelity ascribed to the former were that exercised in the heavenly state! The faithfulness of Moses, which drew forth the Divine commendation, was certainly exercised on earth, and could fitly be compared to that of Jesus only if the virtue were in both cases practised under similar conditions. This, then, is what the writer holds up to the view of his readers as an example and source of inspiration—the faithfulness of Jesus to God in the fulfilment of His vocation during His earthly life. He has already held up Jesus as Priest, as one who is faithful to the interests of those for whom He transacts before God, and therefore entitled to their confidence. The two views supplement each other, and complete the picture of the Faithful One. Faithful as Priest to men in virtue of sympathies learned on earth, faithful as Apostle to God in the execution of the arduous mission on which He was sent to the world; in the one aspect inspiring trust, in the other exciting admiration and inciting to imitation.

The following comparison between Christ and Moses at once serves the general end of the Epistle by contributing to the proof of the superiority of Christianity to Judaism, and the special end of the present exhortation by affording the opportunity of extracting wholesome lessons from the fate of the people whom Moses led out of Egypt. The task of exalting Christ above Moses was a delicate one, requiring careful handling; but the tact of the writer does not desert him here. With rhetorical skill he first places the lesser apostle beside the greater One, as one who like Him had been faithful to his commission. In doing this, he simply does justice to the familiar historical record of the Jewish hero's life, and to God's own testimony borne on a memorable occasion, the substance of which he repeats in the words, "as also Moses (was faithful) in his house." "My servant Moses, faithful in all My house, he,"[1] God had said emphatically, to silence murmuring against him on the part of his brother Aaron and his sister Miriam. In presence of such strong commendation proceeding from the Divine lips, our author, writing to Hebrews proud of their great legislator, might well have been afraid to say anything which even seemed to disparage him; and one wonders what words he will find wherewith to praise Christ and set Him above Moses, without appearing to set aside the testimony of Jehovah to the worth of His servant. But the gifted Christian doctor knows how to manage this part, as well as all other parts of his argument. He lays hold of the suggestive words "house" and "servant," and turns them to account for his purpose, saying in effect, "Moses was as faithful as any servant in a house can be: still he was only a servant, while He of whom I now speak was not a mere servant in the house, but a son; and that makes all the difference."

Verses 3 to 6a are substantially just the working out of this thought. So much in general is clear; but when we look closely into these sentences, we find them

[1] Num. xii. 7.

a little hard to interpret, owing to an apparent confusion of thought. There seem to be two builders of the house: Christ (ver. 3), it being natural to assume that he who hath builded the house is the same with him who is said to have more glory than Moses, and God (ver. 4), the builder of all things. Then the same man Moses figures in two characters: first, as the house (ver. 3), then as a servant in the house (ver. 5). The former of these puzzles is disposed of in various ways by the commentators. Some say there are two houses and two builders: the Old Testament house, whereof God was builder; and the New Testament house, whereof Christ was the builder. Others say there is one house and one builder; the one house being God's supremely, Christ's subordinately, and the builder God as the first great cause, using His Son as His agent in building the spiritual house as well as in making the worlds. A third class, agreeing that there is but one house and one builder, make the builder Christ, and render the last clause of ver. 4, "He that buildeth all things is Divine," taking $θεός$ without the article as a predicate, and finding in it an argument for Christ's divinity. The truth doubtless is, that the house is one, even God's, in which Moses was servant, in which Christ is the Son, that house being the Church, essentially one and the same though varying in form under the earlier and the later dispensations; whereof the builder and maker is He that made all things, building it through His Son. The other difficulty regarding the double character of Moses disappears when it is explained that the word $οἶκος$ is used in a comprehensive sense, as signifying not merely the stone and lime, so to speak, or even the furniture, but likewise the household, or establishment of servants. In this sense Moses, being a servant in the house of God, was a part of the house, and therefore inferior to the builder; for if he who builds a house hath more honour than the whole house, *à fortiori* he hath more honour than any part of it.

Jesus is a Son, Moses was a servant: such, apart from all minute questions of interpretation, is the ground on which the greater glory is claimed for the former. But it may be asked, the subject of comparison being the respective fidelities of the two apostles, is not a reference to their positions irrelevant? What does it matter whether Moses was son or servant, if he was faithful in all God's house, in all parts of his work as the leader of Israel? If one were comparing two commanders in respect of bravery and military genius, would it not be an irrelevance to say of one of them, he was the better man, for he was the king's son? The question is pertinent, but it admits of a satisfactory answer. Reference to the superior dignity of Christ is relevant, if His position as Son tended to enhance His fidelity. That it did the writer doubtless meant to suggest. Further on we find him saying, "Though He was a Son, yet learned He obedience." Similarly he says here in effect, "Christ, though a Son, was faithful to His vocation amid trial." It is a just thought. Beyond doubt, we have in Christ as Son a more sublime moral spectacle of fidelity than in any ordinary man called to play a great and responsible part in history. To the fidelities which He has in common with other men the Son adds this other: resolute resistance to the temptation to use His Sonship as an excuse for declining arduous heroic tasks. "If Thou be the Son of God, use Thy privilege for Thine own advantage," said the tempter in the wilderness, and all through life. "Get thee behind Me, Satan," was the Son's constant reply, giving to His faithfulness to God and duty a unique quality and value.

But there is more than this to be said. The reference to the dignity of Christ looks beyond the immediate parenetic purpose to the ultimate aim of the whole Epistle. It is designed to insinuate the great truth that Christianity is the absolute, eternal religion. For there is more in this statement concerning Christ and Moses than meets the ear, thoughts suggested though not plainly expressed. One great idea never absent from the writer's mind is here quietly insinuated by aptly chosen phrases and pregnant hints—the transient nature of the old dispensation in contrast to the abiding nature of the new. This idea casts its shadow on the page at three different points:

1. In the contrast between Moses and Jesus as respectively servant and Son.

2. In the representation of the ministry of Moses as being for a testimony of things to be spoken afterwards, ver. 5: εἰς μαρτύριον τῶν λαληθησομένων.

3. In the representation of Christians as pre-eminently though not exclusively God's, Christ's, house: οὗ οἶκός ἐσμεν ἡμεῖς, ver. 6.

In the first, because, as Christ Himself once said, "The servant abideth not in the house for ever: but the Son abideth ever." And with the servant the service also must pass away. In the second also, in spite of the difficulties which have been raised by Bleek and others, who hold that the things to be spoken of were the things spoken by Moses himself to the people of Israel, and the idea intended, that the fidelity he had hitherto exhibited ought to secure respect for all he might say in future, and protect him from such assaults as were made upon him by his brother and sister. Bleek thinks that, had a reference to Christ been meant, the writer would have written, "to be spoken in the end of the days," or "by the Son." But over against the verbal difficulty arising out of the use of λαληθησομένων, without qualifying phrase, is to be set the far greater difficulty of believing that the writer meant to utter in such a connection so paltry a thought as the one above indicated. How much more congenial to the whole style of the Epistle to find here a hint of the truth that Moses in his whole ministry was but a testimony to things to be spoken in the future by another greater Apostle!

The transient nature of the Mosaic ministry as subservient to the enduring ministry of the Son is a third time hinted at in the words, *whose house are we.* This is not a claim to monopoly of family privileges for Christians, but it is an assertion that the Christian community is in an emphatic sense the house of God. The assertion manifestly implies the transiency of the Mosaic system. It suggests the thought that the house as it stood in the times of Moses was but a rude, temporary model of the true, eternal house of God; good enough to furnish shelter from the elements, so to speak, but unfit to be the everlasting dwelling-place of the children of the Most

High, therefore destined to be superseded by a more glorious structure, having the Spirit of God for its architect, which should be to the old fabric as was the "magnifical" temple of Solomon to the puny tabernacle in the wilderness.

At ver. 6*b* transition is naturally made from Moses to the lessons of the wilderness life of Israel. The writer is haunted by the fear lest the tragic fate of the generation of the Exodus should be repeated in the experience of the Hebrew Christians. He hopes that the powerful motives arising out of the truths he has stated may bring about a better result. But he cannot hide from himself that another issue is possible. For the future fortunes of Christianity he has no anxiety; he is firmly persuaded that it will prosper, though the Hebrew Church, or even the whole Hebrew nation, should perish. That fatal catastrophe he dreads; therefore with great solemnity he proceeds to represent retention of their position in the house of God as conditional: *Whose house are we, if we hold fast the boldness and the boasting of the hope.* He does not express himself so strongly here as in ver. 14, where the thought is repeated by way of applying the lesson taught in the quotation from the Psalter concerning the conduct of Israel in the wilderness.[1] He is content for the present simply to indicate that there is room for doubt or fear. By the use of the qualifying words "boldness and boast-

---

[1] ἐάν strengthened by the particle περ, which intensifies the doubt, and the words "to the end" (μέχρι τέλους) added : "We are made partakers of Christ *if*, that is to say, we hold fast the beginning of our confidence firm *to the end*."

ing" (παρρησίαν, καύχημα) he teaches by implication that the Christian hope is worth holding fast. It must be a sure and glorious hope which inspires in those who cherish it confidence and exultation.

In the sequel the grounds both of the hope and of the fear are set forth. Of the fear first, the material for the demonstration being drawn from the wilderness history of Israel, as referred to in a quotation from the 95th Psalm. First comes the quotation itself, in vers. 7–11, connected with what goes before by διό, and introduced as an utterance of the Holy Spirit. The quotation keeps pretty close to the Septuagint, materially diverging only at ver. 9, where "forty years" is connected with the clause "they saw My works," instead of with "I was grieved with this generation," as in the Hebrew and the Septuagint. This change led to another, the insertion of διό at the commencement of ver. 10. This divergence is intentional, as we see from ver. 12, where the writer reverts to the original connection, which there suits his purpose, asking, "But with whom was He grieved for forty years?" He prefers here to represent the people of Israel as seeing God's works forty years, rather than to speak of God as grieved with them for the same space—both being equally true,—because he is anxious to make the case of the ancient Israel as closely parallel as possible to that of the Hebrew Christians, with a view to enhanced impressiveness. For both parties were very similarly situated in this very respect of seeing God's works for forty years. From the time when Jesus began His public ministry, to the destruction of Jerusalem, an event probably very nigh at hand when the Epistle was written, was, as near as can be calculated, forty years. What a significant, solemn hint to beware is contained for the Christian Hebrews in this statement concerning their forefathers, *And saw My works forty years!*[1] It says more powerfully than express words could: "You too have seen the works of the Lord, greater works than the ancient ones wrought by the hand of Moses, for the very same space of time. Take care that ye see them to better purpose, lest their doom, or a worse, overtake you."[2]

Next follows the application of the quotation to the case of the Hebrew Christians (vers. 12–14). *Take heed, brethren, lest haply there shall be in any one of you an evil heart of unbelief, in departing from the living God. But exhort each other every day, while the word "to-day" is named, lest any one of you be hardened by the deceit of sin. For we are become*

---

[1] The liberty taken with the words of the Psalm in altering the connection might be adduced as a fact helping to fix the date of the Epistle. The manipulation of the forty years may reasonably be regarded as evidence that such a period of time had elapsed since the beginning of the Christian Church.

[2] One other point in the quotation may be noticed. The Psalmist, in using the wilderness history for the instruction of his own generation, alludes to two instances in which God was tempted, namely, at Massah, at the beginning of the forty years, and at Meribah, towards their close. This point is obscure in the Septuagint, which takes the names as abstract nouns, in which it is followed by our author. The Psalmist selects the incidents at the beginning and the end of the wilderness history as examples of the conduct of Israel throughout the whole period of the wandering. "From these two learn all," he would say; the behaviour of Israel being such that God might justly complain, "Forty years was I grieved with this generation," the very similarity of the events serving to show how incorrigible a generation it was, given to repeating its offences, learning nothing from experience.

Companions of Christ, if we hold the beginning of our confidence firm to the end. The διό of ver. 7 is to be taken along with βλέπετε, all that lies between being regarded as a parenthesis. "Wherefore—beware," the beware being charged with solemn significance by the intervening quotation, conceived by the writer as spoken by the Holy Ghost directly to the Christian Church living in the era of the final revelation. The earnest exhortation follows closely the sense of the passage quoted from the Psalter. First, the brethren are warned against an unbelieving heart revealing its wickedness in apostasy from the living God, in allusion to the hardness of heart charged against Israel, and spoken of as the source of their unbelief and misbehaviour. Then homiletic use is made of the hortatory word: *To-day if ye will hear His voice.* "Exhort each other daily while to-day is named, while there is a to-day to speak of, while the day of grace lasts. Let each cry in the ear of a brother negligent or slothful, To-day, brother, to-day hear His voice, lest your heart become hardened by the deceit of sin, every to-morrow making repentance and faith more difficult." The solemn character of the admonition is excused by the remark, "for we are become Companions of Christ, if we hold the beginning of our confidence steadfast unto the end." This is the sentiment of ver. 6 expanded, with a new designation for Christians (μέτοχοι τοῦ Χριστοῦ) to be considered forthwith, and with marked emphasis on "beginning" and "end" (ἀρχή and τέλος). The writer wishes to impress on his readers that it is not enough to have begun, not enough to have once known the confidence and joy of the Christian hope, that all turns on persevering to the end. And he would have them further understand that perseverance is not a matter of course, that there is a real risk of an ill ending where there has been a fair beginning. For this purpose he again falls back on his quotation, to show that a disastrous ending after a fair beginning is not an imaginary evil (vers. 15–19).

In ver. 15 we have the formula by which the writer makes reference to the previously given quotation. It is loose and vague, and has given rise to much difference of opinion. Literally rendered it is, "In its being said, 'To-day if ye will hear His voice, harden not your hearts, as in the provocation'"; and the question is, What does the phrase "in its being said" mean? My own idea is, that its sole object is to recall attention to the quotation with a view to some further reflections on it intended to substantiate the statement made in ver. 14. The writer, as it were, says to his readers, "Look at that Scripture again, my brethren, and after you have carefully re-perused it let me ask you a series of questions on it." He means them to read or recall to mind the whole passage, though he quotes only the first verse; for the questions which follow go over the whole ground, and bring to bear the whole teaching of the extract for the purpose he has in view.

The first verse having been repeated with an etc. understood, the questions, six in all in three pairs, follow, the first pair, founded on the verse quoted, being put in ver. 16. For it is now universally admitted that this verse in both its members is to be rendered interrogatively, not as in the Authorised English Version, which makes sad havoc of the sense in rendering, "Some when they had heard did provoke: howbeit not all that came out of Egypt by Moses." In this version our translators were but following the all but unanimous exegetical tradition of previous ages,[1] and till the time of Bengel it hardly occurred to anyone that the τινες at the beginning of the verse was the interrogative τίνες, not the indefinite pronoun τινὲς. The fact that for ages men could be content with so unmeaning an interpretation as the latter yields is an extreme illustration of the sequacious habits of commentators. It requires courage to forsake fashion in exegesis no less than in other things.

"Who," asks the writer, "having heard, provoked? Was it not all they who came out of Egypt by Moses?" Thus rendered, the words manifestly bear very directly on the purpose in hand, which is to impress on the Hebrews that a warning against apostasy is not superfluous or impertinent as addressed to persons who have believed in Jesus. The questions asked remind them that the men who provoked God in the desert were all of them persons that had *started* on the journey from the land of bondage to the land of promise. The second of the two questions, which answers the first, reminds the Hebrews of the notorious fact that the persons who were guilty of the sin of provoking God were so numerous, and the exceptions so few, that they might be represented as coextensive with the whole generation that came out of Egypt.

The following verse (17) contains a second couple of questions based on the statement: "Wherefore I was

[1] Weiss (Meyer) mentions a few exceptions, including Chrysostom.

grieved with this generation." "And with whom was He grieved for forty years? Was it not with them that sinned, whose carcases fell in the wilderness?" In other words, the men who grieved God for forty years were men who for their sins were not permitted to enter Canaan, though they left Egypt in that hope and expectation, but were doomed to die in the desert, leaving their flesh to feed the vultures and their bones to bleach on the burning sands. A fact surely full of warning to those who had set out with high hopes on the way to the heavenly country to beware of coming short through unbelief and ungodliness.

Ver. 18 contains a third pair of questions based on the last sentence of the quotation: "So I sware in My wrath, They shall not enter into My rest." "And to whom sware He that they should not enter into His rest? Was it not to them that were disobedient?" The aim here is to point out the cause of failure in the case of ancient Israel, namely, disobedience, having its root in unbelief, to give weight to the warning addressed to the Hebrew Christians. To make the meaning if possible still more plain and emphatic, there is appended to the series of questions the final reflection: "So we see that they could not enter in because of unbelief."

Summing up the import of these questions: the first pair shows that it is not enough to begin the life of faith, that it is necessary to hold fast the beginning of our confidence firm unto the end. The second shows that a good beginning does not of itself ensure a good ending, that many begin well who end ill. The third points out the cause of such disastrous failures—unbelief in the heart, manifesting itself in disobedience and apostasy in the outward life. The drift of the whole is the same as that of 1 Corinthians x., in which, after reminding the Corinthians how many of the Israelites perished in the wilderness for their sins, though they had been baptized into Moses in the cloud and in the sea, and had eaten of the heavenly bread, and drank of the water that flowed out of the smitten rock, the apostle goes on to say, "Now all these things happened unto them for ensamples, and they are written for our admonition upon whom the ends of the world are come. Wherefore let him that thinketh he standeth take heed lest he fall."

Reverting now to the designation of Christians as $\mu\acute{\epsilon}\tau o\chi o\iota$ $\tau o\hat{v}$ $X\rho\iota\sigma\tau o\hat{v}$, rendered in our Authorised Version "partakers of Christ," let us consider its precise import. "Partaker of" is undoubtedly the meaning of $\mu\acute{\epsilon}\tau o\chi o\varsigma$ in several places in the Epistle where it is used with reference to things.[1] But here, as in i. 9, it is used in reference to a person, the Christ, and therefore here as there it may well bear the sense of companions, fellows, or partners. This is the uniform sense of the word in the Septuagint, and the presumption is therefore in favour of that sense here. It is indeed not difficult to assign a true and valuable meaning to the rendering in the Authorised Version, by viewing "Christ" as a compendium of salvation, just as "Moses" stands as a synonym for the redemption he achieved for Israel in

[1] It is so used in iii. 1, vi. 4, xii. 8. The corresponding verb is used in the same way in ii. 14, v. 13, vii. 13.

the passage above cited from Paul's Epistle to the Corinthians. But an equally valuable and much more vivid and impressive idea is conveyed by the other rendering. It is an idea which fits in to the connection of thought. How natural that in a passage which runs a parallel between Moses and Jesus Christians should be thought of as the companions or comrades of the New Testament Captain of Salvation, just as the sons of Israel were the companions of Moses in the march through the wilderness to the promised land?[1] Then one can easily imagine that the echo of the words, "the oil of gladness above thy fellows" (i. 9), still lingers in the writer's ear, and suggests the use of the phrase here in a cognate sense. The conception "fellows of Christ" is in full accord with the thought in ver. 6, that Christians are God's house. At the head of that house is God's Son, the Christ, and Christians are in the house as sons, not as servants, therefore as brethren of Christ, in intimate, familiar relations with Him, and sharing with Him all the privileges of the common home.

Fellowship, comradeship is pointed at, then, and that in the superlative degree. We have become and remain (γεγόναμεν) "fellows" of the Christ when the conditions specified are fulfilled—fellows in the full, final sense. All the Israelites in the wilderness were in a sense comrades of Moses, but it was the faithful men, like Caleb and Joshua, who were his comrades in the highest sense. Our author's thought is, that those who hold fast the beginning of their confidence steadfast unto the end

[1] So Hofmann, who favours the rendering "fellows" (Genossen). Vide *Die Heilige Schrift*, vol. v.

enter into a Caleb-like relation of intimate fellowship with the Leader of Salvation.[1]

Who the μέτοχοι of Messiah in i. 9 may be is uncertain. Perhaps they are the angels. Be that as it may, angels are not the true "fellows" of Christ. They are rather *men*, men who have passed bravely through the tribulations of life and been faithful even unto death. We have here a complementary truth to that stated in ii. 16. Christ took not hold of angels, it is said there; Christ's fellows are not angels but faithful men, it is in effect said here. It is a thought worthy of one who grasped the significance of the great principle: Sanctifier and sanctified all one. It is but the other side of that truth. The side first exhibited is Christ's unity with those He undertakes to sanctify, and His willing acceptance of all the conditions necessary to His complete identification with them. The other side is the unity of the sanctified with Christ, complete equality with Him in privilege. In crediting the writer with the sentiment, "faithful men the fellows of Christ," we merely assume that he understands his own system of thought; and I may add that he is familiar with the teaching of Christ, and with the conception of the relation between Christ and His people that pervades the entire New Testament. For the sentiment in question is no "fine modern idea," but one which we find again and again stated in bold, inspiring terms. "Ye are they which have continued

---

[1] Among those who adopt the rendering "fellows," *socii*, are, besides Hofmann, Delitzsch, Weiss (Meyer), von Soden, Rendall. Vaughan hesitates; Westcott adopts the traditional rendering without even referring to the one now coming into favour.

with Me in My temptations. And I appoint unto you a kingdom, as My Father hath appointed unto Me; that ye may eat and drink at My table in My kingdom." "Well done, good and faithful servant: enter thou into the joy of thy Lord." "If children, then heirs; heirs of God, and joint-heirs with Christ; if so be that we suffer with Him, that we may be also glorified together." "Blessed is the man that endureth temptation: for when he is tried, he shall receive the crown of life." "To him that overcometh will I grant to sit with Me in My throne, even as I also overcame, and am set down with My Father in His throne." Christ, Paul, James, John, all say the same thing. Is it strange to find a thought common to them, and familiar to the minds of all heroic men in the ages of fiery trial, getting recognition also in this Epistle?

On all these grounds I conclude that the true rendering of this text is: "We are become companions, partners, or fellows of Christ, if we hold the beginning of our confidence steadfast unto the end." Its aim is to proclaim the fulness of joy awaiting those who play the hero's part, not to assert the total forfeiture of salvation—of even a minimum share in the blessing of Christ, by those who sink below the heroic level. It presents the motives to steadfastness under the most attractive and stimulating form; for what can be conceived more desirable than comradeship with the Faithful One in the "land of the leal"?

CHAPTER VIII

THE GOSPEL OF REST

CHAP. IV

THE interest of an ordinary reader of our Epistle is apt to flag at this point, in consequence of the obscurity overhanging the train of thought and the aim of the whole passage relating to a "rest that remaineth." It helps to rescue the section from listless perusal to fix our attention on this one thought, that the Christian salvation is here presented under a third aspect as a rest, a sabbatism, a participation in the rest of God; the new view, like the two preceding, in which the great salvation was identified with lordship in the world to come and with deliverance from the power of the devil and the fear of death, being taken from the beginning of human history as narrated in the early chapters of Genesis.

One aim of the writer of the Epistle in this part of his work was doubtless to enunciate this thought, and so to identify the gospel of Christ with the Old Testament gospel of rest. But his aim is not purely didactic, but partly also, and even chiefly, parenetic. Doctrine rises out of and serves the purpose of exhortation. The obscurity of the passage springs from the interblending of the two aims—the theoretical and the practical; which makes it difficult to decide whether the object of the writer is to prove that a rest really remains over for Christians, or to exhort them to be careful not to lose a rest, whose availability for them is regarded as beyond dispute. In the latter case one is apt to think it might have been better to have omitted vers. 2–10 and to have passed at once to ver. 12, where comes in the solemn statement concerning the word of God. As in the previous chapter he had asserted without proof, "whose house are we," why could our author not here also have contented himself with asserting, "which rest is ours, if we lose it not by unbelief, as did Israel of old," and adding, "let us therefore, one and all of us, be on our guard against such a calamity"? Would his exhortation not have gained in strength by being put in this brief, authoritative form, instead of being made to rest on an intricate process of reasoning?

As proof offered naturally implies doubt of the thing proved, it is a ready inference that the Hebrew Christians required to be assured that they had not come too late for participation in the rest promised to their fathers. Evidence of this has been found in the word δοκῇ (ver. 1), rendered not "seem," as in the Authorised Version, but "think": "lest any of you imagine he hath failed of it by coming too late in the day."[1] The exhortation to

---

[1] So a number of the older commentators, and, among more recent writers, Rendall, who says the rendering "seem" conveys no meaning to his mind; also Weiss (Meyer), who refers to Luke xii. 51, xiii. 2, 4, 1 Cor. iii. 18, viii. 2, as parallel instances. Vaughan takes

fear, however, does not suit such a state of mind. It is more likely that the writer was led to argue the point, that the promised rest was still left over, simply because there were Old Testament materials available for the purpose. He chose to present the truth as mediated through Old Testament texts fitted to stimulate both hope and fear: hope of gaining the rest, fear of losing it.

In so far as the section, vers. 1–10, has a didactic drift, its object is to confirm the hope; in so far as it is hortatory, its leading purpose is to enforce the warning, "let us fear."

The hortatory interest predominates at the commencement, vers. 1, 2, which may be thus paraphrased: "Now with reference to this rest I have been speaking of (iii. 18, 19), let us fear lest we miss it. For it is in our power to gain it, seeing the promise still remains over unfulfilled or but partially fulfilled. Let us fear, I say; for if we have a share in the promise, we have also in the threat of forfeiture: it too stands over. We certainly have a share in the promise; we have been evangelised, not merely in general, but with the specific gospel of rest. But those who first heard this gospel of rest failed through unbelief. So may we: therefore let us fear." When we thus view the connection of thought in these two verses, we have no difficulty in understanding the omission of the pronoun ($\dot{\eta}\mu\epsilon\hat{\iota}\varsigma$) in the first

δοκῇ in a forensic sense, in which it would be the way of pronouncing a verdict. "Did ὁ δεῖνα commit such or such a crime? δοκεῖ (he seems to have done it; I am of opinion that he did it)." Von Soden also takes the word in this forensic sense = "be convicted." This is probably the true sense of the word here.

clause of ver. 2, which might surprise one. As in the previous chapter (ver. 6) the writer had said, "whose house are *we*," so we expect him here to say "*we* not less than they have received the good tidings of rest." But his point at this stage is not "*we* have been evangelised" —that is, "the ancient gospel of rest concerns us as well as our forefathers,"—but "we have been *evangelised*, and therefore are concerned in the threatening as well as in the promise."

To be noted is the freedom with which, as in the case of the word "apostle" (iii. 1), the writer uses the term εὐηγγελισμένοι, which might have been supposed to have borne in his time a stereotyped meaning. Any promise of God, any announcement of good tidings, is for him a gospel. Doubtless all God's promises are associated in his mind with the great final salvation, nevertheless they are formally distinct from the historical Christian gospel. The gospel he has in view is not that which "began to be spoken by the Lord," but that spoken by the Psalmist when he said, "To-day if ye will hear His voice, harden not your hearts." Only when this is lost sight of can it create surprise that the statement in the text runs, "We have had a gospel preached unto us as well as they," instead of, "They had a gospel preached unto them as well as we."

Not less noteworthy is the way in which the abortive result of the preaching of the gospel of rest to the fathers is accounted for. "The word preached did not profit them, not being mixed with faith in them that heard it." The remarkable point is the idea of *mixing*, instead of which one might have expected the introduction of some simple commonplace word such as "received": "The word did not profit, not being received in faith." Had this form of language been employed, we should probably have been spared the trouble of deciding between various readings. The penalty of originality in speaker or writer is misconception by reporters, copyists, and printers. Uncertain how the idea of mixing was to be taken, the copyists would try their hand at conjectural emendation, changing συγκεκερασμένος into συγκεκερασμένους, or *vice versâ*. In this way corruption may have crept in very early, and it is quite possible that none of the extant readings is the true one.[1] Of the two most important variants given above, the second, according to which the participle has the accusative plural ending, and is in agreement with ἐκείνους, is the best attested,[2] but it does not give the most probable sense: "The word did not profit them, because they were not mixed by faith with the (true) hearers." On this reading the word "mixed" receives the intelligible sense of "associated with," but it is open to the serious objection that the writer has assumed in the previous chapter that there were no true hearers, or

---

[1] Bleek conjectures that instead of ἀκούσασι may have stood originally ἀκούσμασι. Among the various readings are several varieties of spelling and form in the participle συγκεκερασμένος, of no importance to the sense, but showing an unusual amount of uncertainty as to the original text. In their critical notes on Select Readings, Westcott and Hort say: "After much hesitation we have marked this very difficult passage as probably containing a primitive corruption." In his Commentary on the Epistle Westcott gives a preference to συνκεκερασμένος.

[2] The other variant has only the Sinaitic, of the great MSS., on its side.

so few that they might be left out of account (iii. 16).[1] Assuming that the other reading is to be preferred, according to which the participle is in agreement with λόγος, it is difficult to decide how the mixing is to be conceived of. Is the word mixed with faith in the hearer, or by faith with the hearer? and what natural analogy is suggested in either case? Obviously, this reading points to a more intimate and vital union than that of association suggested by the other; such a union as takes place when food is assimilated by digestion and made part of the bodily organisation. But how the matter presented itself to the writer's mind we can only conjecture. The one thing certain is, that he deemed faith indispensable to profitable hearing: a truth, happily, taught with equal clearness in the text, whatever reading we adopt.

At ver. 3 the didactic interest comes to the front. The new thought grafted into ver. 1 by the parenthetical clause, "a promise being still left," now becomes the leading affirmation. The assertion of ver. 2, "we have been evangelised," is repeated, with the emphasis this time on the "we"; for though the pronoun is not used, οἱ πιστεύσαντες stands in its stead. "We do enter into rest, *we believers in Christ.*" More is meant than that the rest belongs only to such as believe. It is a statement of historical fact, similar to "whose house are we" —Christians. Only there is this difference between the

---

[1] Vaughan thinks that this rendering brings Caleb and Joshua into such prominence as to make it impossible the writer could have left them out of account in iii. 16. That is, it forces us to take τινες as meaning "some," not "who?"

two affirmations: that whereas in the earlier it is claimed for Christians that they are God's house principally, if not exclusively, here the more modest claim is advanced in their behalf that they share in, are not excluded from, the rest. The writer, indeed, believes that the promise in its high ideal sense concerns Christians chiefly, if not alone; that thought is the tacit assumption underlying his argument. But the position formally maintained is not, We Christians have a monopoly of the rest, but, We have a share in it, it belongs to us also. A rest is left over for the New Testament people of God.

The sequel, as far as ver. 10, contains the proof of this thesis. The salient points are these two: *First*, God spoke of a rest to Israel by Moses, though He Himself rested from His works when the creation of the world was finished; therefore the *creation*-rest does not exhaust the idea and promise of rest. *Second*, the rest of Israel in Canaan under Joshua did not realise the Divine idea of rest, any more than did the personal rest of God at the creation, for we find the rest spoken of again in the Psalter as still remaining to be entered upon, which implies that the *Canaan*-rest was an inadequate fulfilment: "For if Joshua had given them rest"—*i.e.* given rest adequately, perfectly—"then would He (God or the Holy Spirit) not afterward have spoken of another day." The former of these two points contains the substance of what is said in vers. 3–5, the latter gives the gist of vers. 7, 8; whereupon follows the inference in ver. 9: a rest is left over. A third step in the argument by which the inference is justified is passed over in silence. It is, that neither in the Psalmist's day nor at any subsequent period in Israel's history had the promise of rest been adequately fulfilled, any more than at the creation or in the days of Joshua. Had the writer chosen he might have shown this in detail, pointing out that even Solomon's reign did not bring complete rest; the Solomonic rest containing within its bosom the seeds of future disturbance, division, and warfare, and proving to be but a halcyon period, followed by wintry storms, bringing desolation and ruin on a once happy land. As for the rest after the return from Babylon, the only other point in Jewish history at which the promise could find a place whereon to set its foot, he would have no difficulty in showing what a poor, imperfect, disappointing fulfilment it brought. Who that reads the sad, chequered tale of Ezra and Nehemiah would say that it realises all the meaning of the twice-spoken oracle of Jeremiah: "Therefore fear thou not, O My servant Jacob; neither be dismayed, O Israel: for, lo, I will save thee from afar, and thy seed from the land of their captivity; and Jacob shall return, and shall be in rest, and none shall make him afraid." [1]

Our author takes the oracle in the Psalter as the final word of the Old Testament on the subject of rest, and therefore as a word which concerns the New Testament people of God. God spake of rest through "David," implying that up till that time the long promised rest had not come, at least in satisfying measure. Therefore a rest remains for Christians. Is the inference cogent? Because a certain promised good

---

[1] Jer. xxx. 10, xlvi. 27. The idea of rest is in these texts, but it is not rendered by καταπαύω in the Septuagint.

had not come up to a certain date, must it come now? Let us review the situation. The ancient Scriptures speak of a Divine rest which God enjoyed at the beginning of the world's history, and in which man seemed destined to share. But man's portion in this rest has never yet come in any satisfying degree. It came not at the creation, for after that came all too soon the Fall; it came not at the entrance into Canaan, for the people of Israel had to take possession sword in hand, and long after their settlement they continued exposed to annoyance from the Canaanitish tribes; it came not from Joshua till David, for even in his late time the Holy Spirit still spoke of another day. Extending our view, we observe that it came not under Solomon, for after him came Rehoboam and the revolt of the ten tribes; it came not with the return of the tribes from Babylon, for envious neighbours kept them in a continual state of anxiety and fear, and they rebuilt their temple and the city walls in troublous times. Is not the natural inference from all this that the rest will never come, all actual rests being but imperfect approximations to the ideal? So reasons unbelief, which treats the *summum bonum* in every form as a mere ideal, a beautiful dream, a pleasure of hope, like that of the maniac, to whom

> "Mercy gave, to charm the sense of woe,
> Ideal bliss that truth could never know."

Far otherwise thought the writer of our Epistle. He believed that all Divine promises, that the promise of rest in particular, shall be fulfilled with ideal completeness. "Some must enter in"; and as none have yet entered in perfectly, this bliss must be reserved for those on whom the ends of the world are come, even those who believe in Jesus. "There remaineth therefore a rest for the people of God."

A *sabbatism* our author calls the rest, so at the conclusion of his argument introducing a new name for it,[1] after using another all through. It is one of the significant thought-suggesting words which abound in the Epistle. It is not, we may be sure, employed merely for literary reasons, as if to vary the phraseology and avoid too frequent repetition of the word κατάπαυσις. Neither is it enough to say that the term was suggested by the fact that God rested on the seventh day. It embodies an idea. It felicitously connects the end of the world with the beginning, the consummation of all things with the primal state of the creation. It denotes the *ideal* rest, and so teaches by implication that Christians not only have an interest in the gospel of rest, but for the first time enter into a rest which is worthy of the name, a rest corresponding to and fully realising the Divine idea. This final name for the rest thus supplements the defect of the preceding argument, which understates the case for Christians. It further hints, though only hints, the nature of the ideal rest. It teaches that it is not merely a rest which God gives, but the rest which God Himself enjoys.[2] God rested on the *seventh day*, and by the choice of this name the writer happily hints

---

[1] It is not a coinage of our author's. It occurs in Plutarch. The verb σαββατίζω occurs in the Septuagint.

[2] The writer takes the pronoun "my" in the expression "my rest" in the latter sense.

that it is God's own rest into which Christians enter. It is God's own rest for God's own true people, an ideal rest for an ideal community, embracing all believers, all believing Israelites of all ages, and many more; for God's rest began long before there was an Israel, and the gospel in the early chapters of Genesis is a gospel for *man*, as the writer of our Epistle well knows, though he does not plainly say it. Into this sabbatic rest cessation from work enters as an essential element; for it is written that God "rested on the seventh day from all His work which He had made." That this is the thought which our author chiefly associates with the term σαββατισμός appears from ver. 10, which may be thus paraphrased: "One who enters into rest ceases, like God, from work, and therefore may be said to enjoy a sabbatism." But this yields only a negative idea of the rest, and the *summum bonum* can hardly be a pure negation. The rabbinical conception of the Sabbath was purely negative. The Rabbis made a fetich of abstinence from whatever bore the semblance of work, however insignificant in amount, and whatever its nature and intention. Christ discarded this rabbinised Sabbath, and put in its place a humanised Sabbath, making man's good the law of observance, declaring that it was always lawful to do well, and justifying beneficent activity by representing Divine activity as incessant, and Divine rest therefore as only relative, a change in the manifested form of an eternal energy. We do not know how far our author was acquainted with the sabbatic controversies of the Gospels, but we cannot doubt on which side his sympathies would be. It has been suggested that he coined a name for the rest that remains, containing an allusion to the seventh day rest, that he might wean the Hebrews from its external observance by pointing out its spiritual end.[1] This view rests on no positive evidence, but it is far more credible than that the bliss of the future world meant for him the eternal prolongation of a rabbinical Sabbath, as it meant for the Talmudist who wrote: "The Israelites said, Lord of all the world, show us a type of the world to come. God answered them, That type is the Sabbath." He took his ideas of the perfect rest, not from the degenerate traditions of the rabbis, but from the book of Origins. That being the fountain of his inspiration, it is probable that he conceived of the ideal rest, not as cessation from work absolutely, but only from the weariness and pain which often accompany it. There was work for man in paradise. God placed him in the garden of Eden to work it[2] and to keep it; and the whole description of the curse implies that it is the sorrow of labour, and not labour itself, that is the unblessed element. The ἔργα which pass away when the ideal rest comes are the κόποι—the irksome toil and worry—of which John speaks in the Book of Revelation: "They shall rest from their labours," and "pain shall be no more."[3]

We have seen that our author borrows three distinct conceptions of the great salvation from the primitive history of man. It is reasonable to suppose that they

---

[1] So Calvin.   [2] ἐργάζεσθαι in Septuagint.
[3] Rev. xiv. 13, xxi. 4. Very significant for the sense of κόπος are the texts Luke xi. 7, xviii. 5; Gal. vi. 17. Worry, annoyance, enter into its meaning in all three places.

were all connected together in his mind, and formed one picture of the highest good. They suggest the idea of paradise restored: the Divine ideal of man and the world and their mutual relations realised in perpetuity; man made veritably lord of creation, delivered from the fear of death, nay, death itself for ever left behind, and no longer subject to servile tasks, but occupied only with work worthy of a king and a son of God, and compatible with perfect repose and undisturbed enjoyment. It is an apocalyptic vision: fruition lies in the beyond. The dominion and deathlessness and sabbatism are reserved for the world to come, objects of hope for those who believe.

The perfect rest will come, and a people of God will enter into it,—of these things our author is well assured; but he fears lest the Hebrew Christians should forfeit their share in the felicity of that people: therefore he ends his discourse on the gospel of rest as he began, with solemn admonition. "Let us fear lest we enter not in," he said at the beginning; "Let us give diligence to enter in," he says now at the close. Then to enforce the exhortation he appends two words of a practical character—one fitted to inspire awe, the other to cheer Christians of desponding temper.

The former of these passages (vers. 12, 13) describes the attributes of the Divine word, the general import of the statement being that the word of God, like God Himself, is not to be trifled with; the word referred to being, in the first place, the word of threatening which doomed unbelieving, disobedient Israelites to perish in the wilderness, and, by implication, every word of God. The account given of the Divine word is impressive, almost appalling. It is endowed in succession with the qualities of the lightning, which moves with incredible swiftness like a living spirit, and hath force enough to shiver to atoms the forest trees; of a two-edged sword, whose keen, glancing blade cuts clean through everything—flesh, bone, sinew; of the sun in the firmament, from whose great piercing eye, as he circles round the globe, nothing on earth is hid. "Living is the word of God, and energetic, and more cutting than every two-edged sword, penetrating even to the dividing of soul and spirit, of joints and marrow, and discerning and judging the affections and thoughts of the heart. And there is not a creature invisible before it, but all things are bare and exposed to the eyes of Him with whom we have to reckon."

The description falls into four parts. First, "living and forceful is the word." I have suggested a comparison to the lightning as interpretative of the epithet "living." But possibly the allusion is to a seed, in which life and force lie dormant together, capable of development under fitting conditions. The blade of grain is the witness both of the life and of the power latent in the seed from which it springs. Or perhaps the thought intended is that the word of threatening, though spoken long ago, is not dead, but living still, instinct with the eternal life and energy of God who spake it, a word for to-day, as well as for bygone ages.

There is no difficulty in determining to what the Divine word is likened in the next member of the sentence, for it is expressly compared to a sword. The only difficulty lies in the construction and interpretation of the words descriptive of its achievements in this capacity. Does the word divide soul from spirit, or both soul and spirit, not only soul, but even spirit? And what are we to make of the mention of joints and marrow, after soul and spirit? Have we here a mingling of metaphor and literal truth, and an accumulation of phrase in order to heighten the impression? or is it meant that "joints and marrow" are the subject of a distinct action of the word? Believing that we have to do here with rhetoric and poetry rather than with dogmatic theology, I prefer a free, broad interpretation of the words to that which finds in them a contribution to biblical psychology and a support for the doctrine of the trichotomy of human nature, which, with all respect for its patrons, savours, in my opinion, of pedantry. The simple meaning of the passage is this: The word of God divides the soul, yea, the very spirit of man, even to its joints and marrow. It is a strong, poetical way of saying that the word penetrates into the inmost recesses of our spiritual being, to the thoughts, emotions, and hidden motives, whence outward actions flow, as easily and as surely as a sword of steel cuts through the joints and marrows of the physical frame. Thus understood, the second part of the description leads naturally up to the third, which speaks of the critical function of the word, in virtue of which it is "the candle of the Lord searching all the inward parts."

In the concluding part of the eloquent panegyric on the word, it is spoken of in a way which suggests the idea, not of a candle, but of the sun, which beholdeth all things; and in the final clause, it is said of God Himself that all things are naked and exposed to His eyes.

The word which I have rendered *exposed* is one of uncertain meaning, and untranslatable except by periphrasis. When a Greek writer used it he had a picture in his mind which charged it with a significance and force no English word can reproduce; but what the picture was it is not easy to determine. The most probable opinion is that τραχηλίζω, not found in classical Greek authors, was a coinage of the wrestling school, to express the act of a wrestler who overmastered his antagonist by seizing him by the neck. Hence the participle τετραχηλισμένος might come to mean one overpowered, as by calamity, or by passion. The verb and its compound ἐκτραχηλίζω occur frequently in Philo, in this tropical sense. In the Epistle to the Hebrews the meaning must be more specific, involving a reference to the effect of the grip of the wrestler on the head of his antagonist, which might be either to force it downwards, or to throw it backwards, according as he seized him behind or before. In the one case we should render "downcast,"[1] in the other "exposed"; the one epithet suggesting the desire of the guilty one to hide his face from the searching eye of God, the other implying that no one, however desirous, can so hide himself from the Divine gaze.[2]

---

[1] So Rendall, whose note on the passage is well worth consulting; as is also that of Vaughan, who remarks that there are two chief lines of explanation, one being to take it as a wrestler's word, the other as a sacrificial word = to bare the neck for the knife. Weiss adopts the latter view. Westcott quotes the Fathers to show that the word puzzled them.

[2] The reference to Philo reminds me that another word in this eulogy on the word of God recalls him to the thoughts of one

In the closing sentences of the chapter the writer winds up the long exhortation to steadfastness by an inspiring allusion to the sympathy of the great High Priest, who has passed out of this time-world, through the veil of the visible heavens, into the celestial world; taking care that his last word shall be of a cheering character, and also so managing that the conclusion of this hortatory section shall form a suitable introduction to the next part of his discourse. On this account vers.

familiar with his writings. I refer to the epithet τομώτερος, which sounds like an echo of Philo's doctrine concerning the cutting or dividing function of the Logos in the universe, set forth at length in the book *Quis div. rer. heres.* Indeed, one bent on establishing a close connection between our author and Philo might find a copious supply of plausible material in this part of the Epistle. Besides these two words, there are the epithet "great high priest," and the attribute of sinlessness, applied here to Christ, and to the Logos by Philo, and in the next chapter the unusual word μετριοπαθεῖν, also occurring in Philo. Then does not the expression ὁ λόγος τοῦ Θεοῦ seem like an allusion to the mystic personified Logos of whom one reads everywhere in Philo? and is not this fervent eulogy on the word almost like an extract from the praises of the Logos unweariedly sung by the philosophic Jew of Alexandria? The resemblance in style is certainly striking, yet I concur in the judgment of Principal Drummond, that "there is nothing to prove conscious borrowing, and it is probable that the resemblances are due to the general condition of religious culture among the Jews" (*Philo Judæus*, vol. i. Introduction, p. 12). In any case, whatever is to be said of the style, it is certain that our Epistle is independent of Philo in thought and spirit. The word of God here is not Philo's Logos, nor is his cutting function the same. Philo calls the Logos the "cutter" (ὁ τομεύς), as cutting chaos into distinct things, and so creating a kosmos. The cutting function of the word in our Epistle is wholly ethical. The originality of the Epistle in thought is all the more remarkable if the writer was acquainted with Philo's writings, so that there is no cause for jealous denial of such acquaintance. It is a mere question of fact.

14–16 might have been reserved for consideration in the next chapter, but I prefer to notice them here, in accordance with the traditional division of the Epistle. How truly they form a part of the exhortation which began at chapter iii. 1 appears from the repetition of phrases. "Consider the High Priest of our confession," the writer had said there; "having a High Priest, let us hold fast our confession," he says here. But it is to be noted that he does not simply repeat himself. The movement of his thought is like that of the flowing tide, which falls back upon itself, yet in each successive wave advances to a point beyond that reached by any previous one. Here for the third time Christ is designated a High Priest, and attributes are ascribed to Him as such which are to form the theme of the next great division of the Epistle, wherein the priestly office of Christ is elaborately discussed. The writer re-invites the attention of his readers to the High Priest of their confession, and in doing so uses words every one of which contains an assertion which he means to prove or illustrate, and which being proved will serve the great end of the whole Epistle, the instruction and confirmation of the ignorant and tempted.

The first important word is the epithet "great" prefixed to the title High Priest. It is introduced to make the priestly office of Christ assume due importance in the minds of the Hebrews. It serves the same purpose as if the title High Priest had been written in large capitals, and asserts by implication not merely the *reality* of Christ's priestly office, but the superiority of Christ as the High Priest of humanity over all the high priests of Israel, Aaron not excepted. As an author writing a treatise on an important theme writes the title of the theme in letters fitted to attract notice, so the writer of our Epistle places at the head of the ensuing portion this title, JESUS THE SON OF GOD THE GREAT HIGH PRIEST, insinuating thereby that He of whom he speaks is the greatest of all priests, the only real Priest, the very Ideal of priesthood realised.

The expression "passed through the heavens" is also very suggestive. It hints at the right construction to be put upon Christ's departure from the earth. There is an obvious allusion to the entering of the high priest of Israel within the veil on the great day of atonement; and the idea suggested is, that the ascension of Christ was the passing of the great High Priest through the veil into the celestial sanctuary, as our representative and in our interest.

The name given to the great High Priest, "Jesus the Son of God," contributes to the argument. Jesus is the historical person, the tempted Man; and this part of the name lays the foundation for what is to be said in the following sentence concerning His power to sympathise. The title "Son of God," on the other hand, justifies what has been already said of the High Priest of our confession. If our High Priest be the Son of God, He may well be called the *Great*, and moreover there can be no doubt whither He has gone. Whither but to His native abode, His Father's house?

Having thus by brief, pregnant phrase hinted the

thoughts he means to prove, our author proceeds to address to his readers an exhortation, which is repeated at the close of the long discussion on the priesthood of Christ to which these sentences are the prelude.[1] In doing so he gives prominence to that feature of Christ's priestly character of which alone he has as yet spoken explicitly: His power to sympathise, acquired and guaranteed by His experience of temptation.[2] He presents Christ to view as the Sympathetic One in golden words which may be regarded as an inscription on the breastplate of the High Priest of humanity: "We have not a High Priest who cannot be touched with the feeling of our infirmities; but one that hath been tempted in all points like ourselves, without sin."

It is noteworthy that the doctrine of Christ's sympathy is here stated in a defensive, apologetic manner, "We have not a High Priest who cannot be touched," as if there were someone maintaining the contrary. This defensive attitude may be conceived of as assumed over against two possible objections to the reality of Christ's sympathy—one drawn from His dignity as the Son of God, the other from His sinlessness. Both objections are dealt with in the only way open to one who addresses weak faith, namely, not by elaborate or philosophical argument, but by strong assertion. As the Psalmist said to the desponding, "Wait, I say, on the Lord," and as Jesus said to disciples doubting the utility of prayer, "I say unto you, Ask, and ye shall receive," so our author says to dispirited Christians, "We have *not* a High Priest who *cannot* be touched

[1] Chap. x. 19-23.   [2] Chap. ii. 17, 18.

with sympathy"—this part of his assertion disposing of doubt engendered by Christ's dignity—" but one who has been tempted in all respects as we are, apart from sin" —this part of the assertion meeting doubt based on Christ's sinlessness. How this can be is a question theologians may discuss, but which our author passes over in silence.[1]

To this strong assertion of Christ's power to sympathise is fitly appended the final exhortation: " Let us therefore draw near with boldness unto the throne of grace, that we may receive mercy and grace for seasonable succour." Specially noteworthy are the words, *Let us approach confidently* (προσερχώμεθα μετὰ παρρησίας). They have more than practical import—they are of theoretic significance; they strike the doctrinal keynote of the Epistle: Christianity the religion of free access. In the opening chapter I said that this great thought first finds distinct, clear utterance in chapter vi. 20, where Christ is called our *forerunner*. But it is hinted, though not so plainly, here, it being implied that the priesthood of Christ, in virtue of His sympathy, and of other properties remaining to be mentioned, for the first time makes free, fearless, close approach to God possible. There is a latent contrast between Christianity and Leviticalism, as in a corresponding passage in Paul's Epistles there is an expressed contrast between Christianity and Mosaism. "Having therefore," writes the apostle, " such a hope, we use great boldness (of speech,

[1] The sinlessness of Christ here asserted means, in the first place, that He never yielded to temptation, but that implies as its source absolute sinlessness.

παρρησίᾳ), and are not as Moses, who put a veil upon his face"; [1] the contrast being between the free, frank, unreserved speech of the minister of a religion of life, righteousness, and good hope, and the mystery observed by the minister of a religion of condemnation, death, and despair. The one cannot be too plain-spoken, because he has good news to tell; the other has to practise reserve, to keep up respect for a rude, imperfect *cultus* which cannot afford to have the whole truth told. Paul's contrast relates to a diversity in the attitude assumed by the ministers of the two religions towards *men*. That latent in the text before us, on the other hand, relates to diversity of attitude towards *God*: the Christian has courage to draw near to God, while the votary of the old religion lacks courage. But the reason of the contrast is the same in both cases, namely, because Christianity is the religion of good hope. "Having such hope (as is inspired by the nature of Christianity), we are outspoken," says Paul; "having the better hope based on the priesthood of Christ, we draw nigh to God confidently," says the author of our Epistle.

The contrast is none the less real that the expression "to draw near" was applied to acts of worship under the Levitical system. Every act of worship in any religion whatever may be called an approach to Deity. Nevertheless, religions may be wide apart as the poles in respect to the measure in which they draw near to God. In one religion the approach may be ceremonial only, while the spirit stands afar off in fear. In another the approach may be spiritual, with mind and heart,

[1] 2 Cor. iii. 12, 13.

in intelligence, trust, and love, and with the confidence which these inspire. Such an approach alone is real, and deserves to be called a drawing near to God. Such an approach was first made possible by Christ, and on this account it is that the religion which bears His name is the perfect, final, perennial religion.

CHAPTER IX

CHRIST NOT A SELF-ELECTED, BUT A GOD-APPOINTED PRIEST

CHAP. v. 1-10

AT length the priesthood of Christ, already three times alluded to, is taken up in earnest, and made the subject of an elaborate discussion extending from this point to chapter x. 18.

The writer begins at the beginning, setting forth first of all that Christ was a legitimate priest, not a usurper: one solemnly called to the office by God, not self-elected. For this is the leading thought in this introductory statement. It seems indeed to be only one of two. *Primâ facie* the writer's aim seems to be to specify, as of equal and co-ordinate importance, two fundamental qualifications for the office of a high priest, and then to show that these were both possessed in a signal manner by Jesus. Every properly qualified high priest, he seems to say, must both sympathise with men, and have a call from God; accordingly, Jesus had such a call, and He was also eminently sympathetic. And he evidently does regard sympathy as, not less than a Divine call, indispensable, the terms in which he speaks of it being remarkable for vividness and emphasis. But he does not put the two on the same footing. The chief thing in his mind is the call; the sympathy is referred to, in connection with its source personal infirmity, as explaining the need for a call, so as to suggest the question, Who, conscious of the infirmity which is the secret of sacerdotal mildness, would dream of undertaking such an office without a Divine call? Hence, in the application of the general principles stated regarding the high-priestly office (vers. 1–4) to the case of Christ (5–10), no reference is made to His sympathy, but only to His call, and to experiences in His earthly life which showed how far He was from arrogating to Himself the priestly office. These experiences were indeed a discipline in sympathy, but that aspect is not spoken of.

If sympathy is not co-ordinate with the call in the writer's mind, still less is it his main theme. This it would have been had the Hebrew Christians been familiar with the doctrine of Christ's priesthood and stood in no need of its being *proved* or elaborately expounded, but only of its being used for their encouragement under trial. To those who take this view of the situation, chapter v. 1–10 appears a mere pendant to the statement in chapter iv. 14–16, to this effect: "Compassion may be counted on in every high priest, for he is conscious of his own infirmity, and moreover he is called to office by God, who takes care to call only such as are humane in spirit. On both grounds you may rest assured of the sympathy of Jesus." The real drift of the passage is rather this: "Sympathy is congruous to the high-priestly office in general. It arises out of the sense of personal infirmity, whence also it comes that no right-minded man would undertake the office voluntarily, or without being called of God. Jesus assuredly undertook the office only as called of God. He was called to the priesthood before His incarnation. He came to the world under a Divine call. And during the days of His earthly life His behaviour was such as utterly to exclude the idea of His being a usurper of sacerdotal honours. All through His incarnate experiences, and especially in those of the closing scene, He was simply submitting to God's will that He should be a priest. And when He returned to heaven He was saluted High Priest in recognition of His loyalty. Thus from first to last He was emphatically One called of God." Thus viewed, the passage before us is obviously the proper logical commencement of a discourse on the priesthood of Christ, *intended to instruct readers who had next to no idea of the doctrine, and needed to be taught the very rudiments thereof.* Was this their position, or was it not? It is a question on which it is very necessary to make up our minds, as the view we take of it must seriously influence our interpretation of the lengthy section of the Epistle of which the passage now under consideration forms the introduction.[1]

What is said of the sympathy that becomes a high priest, though subordinate to the statement concerning

---

[1] Of all recent expositors, Mr. Rendall seems to have this question most distinctly before his mind, and to realise its importance for the interpretation of the Epistle. He decidedly advocates the view I have indicated above, holding that the Hebrew Christians "did not connect the idea of priesthood with Christ, though they knew Him as their Prophet and their King."—*The Expositor* for January 1889, p. 32.

his call, is important and interesting. First, a description is given of the office which in every clause suggests the reflection, How congruous sympathy to the sacerdotal character! The high priest is described as taken *from among* men, and the suggestion is that, being a man of like nature with those for whom he transacts, he may be expected to have fellow-feeling with them. Then he is further described as ordained *for* men in things pertaining to God, the implied thought being that he cannot acquit himself satisfactorily in that capacity unless he sympathise with those whom he represents before God. Lastly, it is declared to be his special duty to offer sacrifices of various sorts *for sin*, the latent idea being that it is impossible for anyone to perform that duty with any earnestness or efficiency who has not genuine compassion for the sinful.

What is implied in ver. 1 is plainly stated in ver. 2, though in participial form, in accordance with the subordinate position assigned to the requirement of sympathy in relation to the Divine call. "Being able to have compassion on the ignorant and erring."

Very remarkable is the word employed to describe priestly compassion, μετριοπαθεῖν. It does not, like συμπαθῆσαι in iv. 15, signify to feel with another, but rather to abstain from feeling *against* him; to be able to restrain antipathy. It was used by Philo to describe Abraham's sober grief on the loss of Sarah and Jacob's patience under affliction. Here it seems to be employed to denote a state of feeling towards the ignorant and erring balanced between severity and undue leniency. It is carefully selected to represent the spirit which becomes a high priest as a mean between two extremes. On the one hand, he should be able to control the passions provoked by error and ignorance: anger, impatience, disgust, contempt. On the other hand, he must not be so amiable as not even to be tempted to give way to these passions. Ignorance and misconduct he must not regard with unruffled equanimity. It is plainly implied that it is possible to be too sympathetic, and so to become the slave or tool of men's ignorance or prejudices, and even partaker of their sins; a possibility illustrated by the histories of Aaron and of Eli, two high priests of Israel. The model high priest is not like either. He hates ignorance and sin, but he pities the ignorant and sinful. He is free alike from the inhuman severity of the pharisee, who thinks he has done his duty towards all misconduct when he has expressed himself in terms of unmeasured condemnation regarding it, and from the selfish apathy of the world, which simply does not trouble itself about the failings of the weak. He feels resentment, but it is in moderation; disgust, but it is under control; impatience, but not such as finds vent in ebullitions of temper, but such rather as takes the form of determined effort to remove evils with which it cannot live on friendly terms. All this, of course, implies a loving, kind heart. The negative virtue of patience implies the positive virtue of sympathy. The model high priest is one in whose heart the law of charity reigns, and who regards the people for whom he acts in holy things as his children. The ignorant, for him, are persons to be taught; the erring, sheep to be brought back to the fold. He remembers that sin is not only an evil thing in God's sight, but also a bitter thing for the offender; realises the misery of an accusing conscience, the shame and fear which are the ghostly shadows of guilt. All this is hinted at in the word μετριοπαθεῖν, whereby, instantaneously, the writer *photographs* the character of the model high priest.

The character thus drawn is obviously congenial to the priestly office. The priest's duty is to offer gifts and sacrifices for sin. The performance of this duty habituates the priestly mind to a certain way of viewing sin: as an offence deserving punishment, yet pardonable on the presentation of the appropriate offering. The priest's relation to the offender is also such as demands a sympathetic spirit. He is not a legislator, enacting laws with rigid penalties attached. Neither is he a judge, but rather an advocate pleading for his client at the bar. Neither is he a prophet, giving utterance in vehement language to the Divine displeasure against transgression, but rather an intercessor imploring mercy, appeasing anger, striving to awaken Divine pity.

But the special source to which sacerdotal sympathy is traced is the consciousness of personal infirmity. " For that he himself also is compassed with infirmity." The explanation seems to labour under the defect of too great generality. A high priest is no more human in his nature and experience than other men: why, then, should he be exceptionally humane? Two reasons suggest themselves.

The high priest was *officially* a very holy person, begirt on all sides with the emblems of holiness:

copiously anointed with oil, whose exquisite aroma typified the odour of sanctity; arrayed in gorgeous robes, significant of the beauty of holiness; required to be so devoted to his sacred calling and so dead to the world that he might not mourn for the death of his nearest kin. How oppressive the burden of this official sanctity must have been to a thoughtful, humble man, conscious of personal infirmity, and knowing himself to be of like passions and sinful tendencies with his fellow-worshippers! How the very sanctity of his office would force on the attention of one who was not a mere puppet priest the contrast between his official and his personal character, as a subject of solemn reflection. And what would the result of such reflection be but a deepened self-knowledge, a sense of unworthiness for his sacred vocation, which would seek relief in cherishing a meek and humble spirit, and in manifesting a gracious sympathy towards his brethren, considering himself as one also tempted; and would gladly hail the return of that solemn season—the great day of atonement—when the high priest of Israel offered a propitiatory sacrifice *first* for his own sins, and then for the people's?

Another source of priestly benignity was, I imagine, habitual converse in the discharge of duty with the erring and the ignorant. The high priest had officially much to do with men, and that not with picked samples, but with men in the mass; the greater number probably being inferior specimens of humanity, and all presenting to his view their weak side. He learned in the discharge of his functions to take a kindly interest in all sorts of people, even the most erratic, and to bear with inconsistency even in the best. The poet or philosopher, conversant chiefly with ideal men, heroes invested with all imaginary excellences, is prone to feel disgust towards real common men, sadly unheroic and unromantic in character. The high priest had abundant opportunities for learning that the characters even of the good and devout are very defective, and he was thankful to find that their hearts were right with God, and that when they erred they were desirous to confess their error and make atonement. He looked not for sinless, perfect beings, but at most only for men broken-hearted for their sins, and bringing their trespass offering to the altar of the Lord.

The account given of priestly sympathy prepares us for appreciating the statement which follows concerning the need for a Divine call to the priestly office. "And no one taketh the honour to himself, but only when called by God, as indeed was Aaron" (ver. 4).

No one, duly impressed with his own infirmities, would ever think of taking unto himself so sacred an office. A need for a Divine call is felt by all devout men in connection with all sacred offices involving a ministry on men's behalf in things pertaining to God. The tendency is to shrink from such offices, rather than to covet and ambitiously appropriate them. The sentiment, *nolo episcopari*, which has ever been common in the best days of the Church, is not an affectation of modesty, but the expression of a deep reluctance to undertake the onerous responsibilities of a representative man in religion by all who know themselves, and who realise the momentous nature of religious interests.

The sentiment is deepened by the reflection that the office is honourable as well as sacred. For it is a maxim which calls forth a response from every healthy conscience, that men should not seek honours, but be sought for them, it being but an application of the proverb, " Let another man praise thee, and not thine own mouth."

Having stated the general principle that a Divine call is necessary as an inducement to the assumption of the priestly office, the writer passes to the case of Jesus Christ, whom he emphatically declares to have been utterly free from the spirit of ambition, and to have been made a high priest, not by self-election, but by Divine appointment. Of the two texts quoted in proof of the assertion, the second, taken from Psalm cx., naturally appears the more important, as containing an express reference to Messiah's priesthood. This oracle, the key to the whole doctrine of the Epistle on the subject in question, is introduced here for the first time, very quietly, as if by the way, and in subordination to the more familiar text already quoted from the 2nd Psalm bearing on Messiah's Sonship. Here once more we have occasion to admire the oratorical tact of the writer, who, having in mind to present to his readers a difficult thought, first puts it forth in a stealthy, tentative way, as if hoping that it may thus catch the attention better than if more obtrusively presented; just as one can see a star in the evening twilight more distinctly by looking a little to one side of it, than by gazing directly at it.

It is difficult to understand, at first, why the text from the 2nd Psalm, " My Son art Thou," is introduced here at all, the thing to be proved being, not that Messiah was made by God a Son, but that He was made a Priest. But on reflection we perceive that it is a preliminary hint as to what sort of priesthood is signified by the order of Melchisedec, a first attempt to insinuate into the minds of readers the idea of a priesthood belonging to Christ altogether distinct in character from the Levitical, yet the highest possible, that of one at once a Divine Son and a Divine King. On further consideration, it dawns on us that a still deeper truth is meant to be taught: that Christ's priesthood is coeval with His Sonship, and inherent in it. Only when we find this idea in it do we feel the relevancy of the first citation to be fully justified. So interpreted, it contains a reference to an eternal Divine call to the priesthood in consonance with the order of Melchisedec, which is described further on as "having neither beginning of days nor end of life"—eternal *a parte ante*, as well as *a parte post*. Thus viewed, Christ's priestly vocation ceases to be an accident in His history, and becomes an essential characteristic of His position as Son: Sonship, Christhood, priestliness, inseparably interwoven.

From the preincarnate state to which the quotations from the Psalter refer, the writer proceeds to speak of Christ's earthly history: "Who, in the days of His flesh" (ἐν ταῖς ἡμέραις τῆς σαρκὸς αὐτοῦ). For a Philo the Son and Logos of God could have no such days, contact with flesh being beneath the dignity of so exalted a spirit. If our author had ever been a disciple of Philo's, he had surmounted that difficulty. The solution of the problem in which his mind found rest was not speculative, but ethical. It lay in this that the life in the flesh, with all that went along with it, was seen to be invested with moral grandeur, not only in spite of, but in virtue of, its humiliations. Hence, as we see, these humiliations are not glozed over or understated in the following sentences, but allowed to appear in their naked grim reality. Not every Christian teacher in the apostolic age could have dared to speak of the experience of Jesus in Gethsemane as is done here; not Luke, *e.g.*, whose account of that experience in his Gospel, if one omit the critically doubtful passage concerning the bloody sweat, is very much toned down as compared with the parallel accounts in Matthew and Mark.[1]

"Who, in the days of His flesh." The writer here conceives, as further on he expressly represents,[2] the Christ as coming into the world under a Divine call to be a priest, and conscious of His vocation. In vers. 7, 8, his purpose is to exhibit the behaviour of Jesus during His life on earth in such a light that the idea of usurpation shall appear an absurdity. The general import is: "Jesus ever loyal, but never ambitious; so far from arrogating, rather shrinking from priestly office, at most simply submitting to God's will, and enabled to do that by special grace in answer to prayer." It is implied that this is a true account of Christ's whole behaviour on earth; but the special features of the picture are taken from the prelude to the Passion, the Agony, where the

---

[1] On this *vide* my book, *With Open Face*, chap. xii. In view of Luke's treatment of the Agony, it is clear that he could never have been the author of the Epistle to the Hebrews, as some have imagined.

[2] Chap. x. 5.

truth of the representation becomes startlingly conspicuous.

In the description of the tragic experiences of that crisis, we note the pains taken to lay bare the *infirmity* of Jesus, the object being to show the extreme improbability of one who so behaved assuming the priestly office without a Divine call. The familiar fact that Jesus prayed that the cup might pass from Him is stated in the strongest terms: " When He had offered prayers and supplications with strong crying "; and a particular is mentioned not otherwise known, that the prayers were accompanied with " tears." Jesus is thus made to appear manifesting, confessing, His weakness, frankly and unreservedly ; even as the high priest of Israel confessed his weakness when he offered a sacrifice for himself before he presented an offering for the people. Whether the writer had in his view a parallel between Christ's agony in the garden and the high priest's offering for himself it is impossible to decide, although several things give plausibility to the suggestion, such as the use of the sacrificial term προσενέγκας in reference to Christ's prayer in the garden.[1] What is certain is that he is careful to point out that Christ was compassed with infirmity not less real, though sinless, than that which in the case of the Jewish high priest made it necessary that he should offer a sacrifice for himself before offering for the people ; the moral being: How unlikely that one who so shrank

[1] Hofmann, *Schriftbeweis*, ii. 399, earnestly contends that such a parallel is intended. Vide *The Humiliation of Christ*, p. 277, where I have stated and adopted his view. I still feel its attraction, but I am not so sure that the alleged parallel was present to the writer's mind.

from the cup of death should be the usurper of an office which involved the drinking of that cup!

The hearing of Christ's prayer referred to in the last clause of ver. 7 belongs to the description of His sinless infirmity. Whether we render, "And being heard for His piety," or "and being heard (and delivered) from the fear" (of death, as distinct from death itself), is immaterial;[1] in any case the answer consisted in deliverance from that fear, in courage given to face death. Some have supposed that the reference is to the resurrection and ascension. But it is not permissible to read into the passage a hidden allusion to events of such importance. Moreover, the reference is excluded by the consideration that all that is spoken of in ver. 7 leads up to the main affirmation in ver. 8, and must be included under the category of learning obedience. The last clause of ver. 7 describes the attitude of one who shrank from death, and who was at length enabled to face death by special aid in answer to prayer delivering him from fear; that is to say, of one who in all that related to the passion was *only learning obedience.* The point to be emphasised is, not so much that the prayer of Jesus was heard, as that it *needed* to be heard: that He needed heavenly aid to drink the appointed cup.

To perform, or even to attempt, such a task without a conscious Divine call was impossible. Even with a clear

---

[1] Opinion is very much divided as between these two renderings of the words εἰσακουσθεὶς ἀπὸ τῆς εὐλαβείας, many weighty names being on either side. Bleek supports the first view, Bengel the second. On the whole, the weight of authority and of argument inclines to the rendering, "being heard for His piety, or His godly fear."

consciousness of such a call it was difficult. That is the truth stated in ver. 8, in these terms: "Though He was a Son, yet learned He obedience from the things which He suffered." Freely paraphrased these words mean: "In His earthly experience Christ was so far from playing the part of one who was taking to Himself the honour of the priesthood, that He was simply throughout submitting to God's purpose to make Him a Priest, and the circumstances were such as made obedience to the Divine will anything but easy, rather a painful process of learning." Reference is made to Christ's Sonship to enhance the impression of difficulty. Though He was a son full of love and devotion to His Father, intensely, enthusiastically loyal to the Divine interest, ever accounting it His meat and drink to do His Father's will, yet even for Him so minded it was a matter of arduous learning to comply with the Father's will *in connection with His priestly vocation*. For it must be understood that the obedience here spoken of has that specific reference. The aim is not to state didactically that in His earthly life Jesus was a learner in the virtue of obedience all round, but especially to predicate of Him learning obedience in connection with His priestly calling—obedience to God's will that He should be a Priest.

But why should obedience be so difficult in this connection? The full answer comes later on, but it is hinted at even here. It is because priesthood involves for the Priest death (ver. 7), mortal suffering (ver. 8); because the Priest is at the same time victim. And it is in the light of this fact that we clearly see how impossible it was that the spirit of ambition should come into play with reference to the priestly office in the case of Christ. Self-glorification was excluded by the nature of the service. One might be tempted to take unto himself the honour of the Aaronic priesthood, though even with reference to it one who fully realised its responsibilities would be disposed to exclaim, "Nolo pontifex fieri." A vain, thoughtless, or ambitious man might covet the office of Aaron, because of the honour and power which it conferred. In point of fact, there were many ambitious high priests in Israel's last, degenerate days, as there have been many ambitious ecclesiastics. But there was no risk of a self-seeker coveting the priestly office of Christ, because in that office the Priest had, not only to offer, but Himself to be the sacrifice. With reference to such a priesthood, a self-seeker would be sure to say, "I do not wish it; I have no taste for such an honour." Yea, even one who was no self-seeker might say, "If it be possible, let me escape the dread vocation"; and he would accept its responsibilities only after a sore struggle with the reluctance of sentient nature, such as martyrs have experienced before appearing with serene countenance at the stake. The holy, sinless Jesus did indeed say "no" for a moment in reference to this unique sort of priesthood. His agony in Gethsemane, so touchingly alluded to in our Epistle, was an emphatic "no," which proved that, far from proudly aspiring, He found it hard even to humbly submit to be made a priest.[1]

---

[1] Referring to the Agony, I have made this strong statement in *The Humiliation of Christ*: "That agony was an awfully earnest, utterly sincere, while perfectly sinless *Nolo pontifex fieri* on the part

The verses which follow (9, 10) show the other side of the picture: how He who glorified not Himself to be made a priest was glorified by God; became a priest indeed, efficient in the highest degree, acknowledged as such by His Father, whose will He had loyally obeyed. "And being perfected became to all who obey Him author of eternal salvation, saluted by God 'High Priest after the order of Melchisedec.'" A weighty, pregnant sentence, setting forth the result of Christ's earthly experience in terms suitable to the initial stage of the discussion concerning His priestly office, implying much that is not expressly stated, and suggesting questions that are not answered, and therefore liable to diverse interpretation.

"Being perfected" — how? In obedience, and by obedience even unto death; perfected for the office of priest, death being the final stage in His training through which He became a *Pontifex Consummatus*. Some think the reference is to the resurrection and ascension. It is a plausible and tempting suggestion, but one cannot help feeling that the writer has studiously avoided such specific references, and expressed himself in general terms fitted to convey the moral truths involved, independently of time and place. I therefore see no reason for assigning to τελειωθείς a different sense from that which seemed to be most appropriate in chapter ii. 10.

Being made perfect in and through death Jesus became

of one who realised the tremendous responsibilities of the post to which He was summoned, and who was unable for the moment to find any comfort in the thought of its honours and prospective joys" (p. 276).

ipso facto author of eternal salvation, the final experience of suffering by which His training for the priestly office was completed being at the same time His great priestly achievement. This interpretation of our author's meaning takes for granted that in his view the death of Christ was a priestly act, not merely a preparation for a priesthood to be exercised afterwards, in heaven. Nay, not merely a priestly act, but the great priestly act, the factbasis of the whole doctrine of Christ's priesthood. I have no doubt this is a correct impression. In this connection it is noteworthy that the first and last times the writer refers to the subject of our Lord's priestly work (chap. ii. 9 and chap. x. 10) it is to this death that he gives prominence: "that He should taste death for every man"; "we are sanctified through the offering of the body of Jesus Christ." That Christ's priestly ministry is placed in the heavenly sanctuary is not less certain, and the two views seem to be in flat contradiction to each other. Whether they can be reconciled, and how, are questions which will come up for discussion hereafter; meantime let us be content to leave the two views side by side, an unresolved antinomy, not seeking escape from difficulty by denying either.[1]

The statement that through death Jesus became *ipso facto* author of salvation is not falsified by the fact that the essential point in a sacrifice was its presentation before God in the sanctuary, which in the Levitical system took place subsequently to the slaughtering of the victim, when the priest took the blood within the

[1] For the solution *vide* Chapter xvi., also passage towards the close of Chapter xiv.

tabernacle and sprinkled it on the altar of incense or on the mercy-seat. The death of our High Priest is to be conceived of as including all the steps of the sacrificial process within itself. Lapse of time or change of place is not necessary to the accomplishment of the work. The death of the victim, the presentation of the sacrificial blood—all was performed when Christ cried Τετέλεσται.[1]

It is not the writer's object in this place to indicate the nature of "salvation,"—that is, the precise benefit procured for men by Christ as Priest,—but simply to indicate the fact that He attained to the high honour of being the source or author of salvation. Two facts, however, he notifies respecting the salvation of which Christ is the author: that it is *eternal*, and that it is available for those who *obey* Him. The epithet αἰώνιος, here used for the first time, frequently recurs in the sequel. It is one of the great, characteristic watchwords of the Epistle, intended to proclaim the absolute final nature of Christianity, in contrast to the transient nature of the Levitical religion. Possibly it is meant here to suggest a contrast between the *eternal* salvation procured by Christ and the *annual* salvation effected by the ceremonial of the great day of atonement. More probably its introduction at this place is due to the desire to make the salvation correspond in character to the Melchisedec type of priest-

---

[1] Some theologians, such as Professor Smeaton, contend for an entrance "within the veil" by Christ, with His blood, in His disembodied state, immediately after His death on the cross. The feeling which dictates this view is right, but the view itself takes too literally and prosaically the parallel between Christ and the Jewish high priest. For Professor Smeaton's view *vide The Apostles' Doctrine of the Atonement*, p. 48.

hood, whose leading feature is perpetuity: "Thou art a Priest for ever." To the same sense of congruity it is due that obedience to Christ is accentuated as the condition of salvation. Christ became a Saviour through obedience to the will of His Father, and it is meet that He in turn should be obeyed by those who are to receive the benefit of His arduous service. It is a thought kindred to that expressed by Christ Himself when He spake of the Son of Man laying down His life for the many as the way He took to become the greatest, and to be ministered unto by willing subjects.

The Divine acknowledgment of Christ's priestly dignity, referred to in ver. 10, is not to be prosaically interpreted as a formal appointment; whether a first appointment, as some think, to an official position now commencing in the state of exaltation, or a second confirming a first made long before, alluded to in the Messianic oracle quoted in ver. 6 from Psalm cx.[1] It is rather the animated recognition of an already existing fact. Christ, called from of old to be a priest in virtue of His Sonship, and made a priest indeed by His arduous training on earth, is cordially owned to be a priest when

---

[1] Mr. Rendall takes this view. He says: "The language of this verse and the context alike point to a new appointment quite distinct from that recorded in the Psalms, though both refer to the same Melchisedec priesthood. Psalm cx. has been cited as evidence of the earlier appointment of God's Anointed by prophetic anticipation to a priesthood. This verse declares the formal recognition of His *high* priesthood by a Divine salutation addressed personally to Jesus" (*The Epistle to the Hebrews*, p. 45). I agree with him so far as to recognise the distinction between the two appointments, only I cannot regard the expression "*formal* recognition" as true to the spirit of the passage commented on.

the death which completed His training, and constituted Him a priest, had been endured—whether immediately after the passion or after the ascension must be left undetermined. The style is dramatic, and the language emotional. God is moved by the spectacle of His Son's self-sacrifice, as of old He had been moved by the readiness of Abraham to sacrifice Isaac, and exclaims, "Thou art a Priest indeed!" That the writer is not thinking of a formal appointment, which creates a position previously non-existent, appears from the liberties he takes with the words of the oracle which contains the evidence that Christ was a God-called Priest: "high priest" substituted for "priest," and "for ever" omitted. The former of these changes is specially noteworthy. It is not accidental and trivial, but intended and significant. The alteration is made to suit the situation: Christ, already a High Priest in virtue of functions analogous to those of Aaron, and now and henceforth a priest after the order of Melchisedec. The oracle, as adjusted, combines the past with the future, the earthly with the heavenly, the temporal with the eternal.

Translated into abstract language, ver. 10 supplies the *rationale* of the fact stated in ver. 9. Its effect is to tell us that Christ became author of eternal salvation because He was a true High Priest after the order of Melchisedec: author of *salvation* in virtue of His being a priest, author of *eternal* salvation because His priesthood was of the Melchisedec type—never ending.

The words put into the mouth of God serve yet another purpose: to indicate the lines along which the writer intends to develop the subject of Christ's priesthood. His plan is to employ two types of priesthood to exhibit the nature of the perfect priesthood of the absolute final religion—the order of Aaron, and the order of Melchisedec. I say not that he means to teach that Christ occupied successively two priestly offices—one like that of Aaron, the other like that of Melchisedec, the former on earth, the latter in heaven. That is too crude a view of the matter. His plan rather is to utilise the Aaronic priesthood to set forth the nature of Christ's priestly functions, and the Melchisedec priesthood to set forth their ideal worth and eternal validity; and he here as it were lets us into the secret. The plan in both its parts is based on Scripture warrant, to be produced at the proper place. This view of the writer's method is not to be summarily set aside by the assertions that priest and high priest are synonymous terms, and that the functions of all orders of priesthood are the same. As to the one point, it is enough to say that the writer uses the two words with discrimination: "priest" when likening Christ to Melchisedec, "high priest" when comparing Him with Aaron. As to the other, it is to be remarked that no mention is made of sacrificial functions in connection with Melchisedec's history as given in Genesis, and that the writer evidently does not choose to ascribe to him functions not spoken of in the record. Arguing from his way of drawing inferences from the silences of history, one might rather conclude that because he found no sacrificial functions mentioned in the story, he therefore assumed that such duties as were performed by Aaron about the tabernacle did not enter into the idea of the Melchisedec priesthood.

The words, "high priest after the order of Melchisedec," containing the programme of the discussion about to be entered on, we expect to find the two topics suggested taken up in this order: first, Christ as High Priest; next, Christ as Priest after the order of Melchisedec. In point of fact, they are taken up in the inverse order. Why, we may be able to discover in another chapter.

CHAPTER X

THE TEACHER'S COMPLAINT

CHAPS. V. 11-14; VI. 1-8

"OF whom," *i.e.* Melchisedec, continues the writer, taking up the second part of his programme first, "we have many things to say." Yet he does not forthwith say these things; he refrains from entering on ample discourse ($\pi o \lambda \grave{v}\varsigma$ $\lambda \acute{o} \gamma o \varsigma$) on the Melchisedec priesthood, because his spirit is disturbed by the recollection that he writes to persons dull of apprehension, at once ignorant, indolent, and prejudiced, unable and unwilling to take in new ideas, and, like horses with blinders on, capable of seeing only straight before them in the direction of use and wont, and therefore certain to find the thoughts he is about to express hard to understand. The haunting consciousness of this painful fact obscures the subject of discourse as a cloud hides the glory of the sun on an April day; and even as our Lord was not able to proceed with His farewell address to His disciples till He had rid Himself of the presence of the traitor, so this man of philosophic mind and eloquent pen cannot proceed with his argument till he has given expression to the vexation and disappointment caused by the inaptitude of his scholars. This he does with very great plainness of speech, for which all Christian teachers have reason to thank him; for what he has written may be regarded as an assertion of the right of the Church to be something more than an infant school, and as a defence of the liberty of prophesying on all themes pertaining to Christ as their centre against the intolerance always manifested by ignorance, stupidity, indolence, and prejudice towards everything that is not old, familiar, and perfectly elementary.

The teacher's complaint is severe—too severe, if the things to be said concerned some curious point in theology on which the complainer had some pet notions. A man may be a good Christian, and yet be ignorant or indifferent in reference to the mysteries of predestination and free will and their reconciliation. Might not the Hebrews be sufficiently good Christians, and yet remain ignorant of, or incapable of understanding, the transcendental doctrine of the Melchisedec priesthood? No; because the question at issue is not a mere curious point in theology. It is rather the fundamental question whether Christ was really a priest. The priesthood of Christ in its reality and ideal worth is not understood, unless it is seen to be of the Melchisedec type. Therefore the incapacity complained of, if not fatal, is at least serious.

The account given of the spiritual state of the Hebrew Christians is not flattering. In effect, they are represented as in their dotage. They have *become* dull of hearing, have *become* children having need of milk, and not able to receive the solid food of full-grown men. They are not merely children, but in their second childhood; in which respect it is interesting to compare the

Hebrew Church with the Corinthian as described in Paul's First Epistle. The members of the Corinthian Church were in their first childhood spiritually; hence they were unruly, quarrelsome, and had an indiscriminate appetite for all sorts of food, without possessing the capacity to discern between what was wholesome and what unwholesome, or the self-control to choose the good and reject the evil. The members of the Hebrew Church, on the other hand, were in that state of dotage so affectingly described by Barzillai with reference to the physical powers: "I am this day fourscore years old; and can I discern between good and evil? can thy servant taste what I eat or what I drink? can I hear any more the voice of singing men and singing women? wherefore then should thy servant be yet a burden unto my lord the king?"[1] The Hebrew Christians had once had a certain capacity of discernment, but they had lost it. Their senses had become blunted by the hebetude of old age: they had, so to speak, no teeth to eat solid food, no taste to discern the excellency of new, strong meat, but simply enough taste to detect that the meat was new; no ear to appreciate the new songs of the Christian era, but just enough hearing left to tell them that the sounds they heard dimly were strange, not the familiar melodies of the synagogue; no eyes to see the glory of Christ's self-sacrifice, but simply vision enough to perceive as through a haze the gorgeous robes of the high priest as he moved about the temple precincts performing his sacerdotal duties. All the symptoms of senility were upon them as described by the preacher; decay was present and death near. Melancholy end of a

---
[1] 2 Sam. xix. 35.

Christian profession that had lasted some forty years! Dotage at an advanced age, in the physical sphere, is natural and blameless, exciting only tender pity; in the spiritual sphere it is unnatural and blameworthy. What ought to be is steady progress towards moral and religious maturity (τελειότητα), characterised by practised skill to discern between good and evil, and settled preference for the good: a wise, enlightened mind, and a sanctified will.[1] That so few reach the goal, that healthy growth in the spiritual life is so rare, is for all earnest souls a wonder and a deep disappointment.

Having uttered these sharp words of reproof, the writer proceeds (vi. 1) to exhort his readers to aspire to that state of Christian maturity which is capable of digesting solid food, and not to remain always at the beginnings of the Christian life. Perhaps we should rather say that the writer intimates his own purpose to go on in his discourse from the milk of elementary truth that suits babes to the solid food of advanced doctrine that suits men. The commentators are divided in opinion as to which of these two interpretations is the more correct; but it is scarcely worth while to discuss the question, as the one view implies the other. The writer

---

[1] The words τέλειος and τελειότης (v. 14, vi. 1) are used here in a sense distinct from that in which Christ is said to have been perfected by suffering, and from that in which men are said to have been perfected by His one offering of Himself. To be perfect is always to be in the position of having reached the end; but the end in the present instance is not training for an office, or purgation of the conscience from the guilt of sin, but the attainment of manhood, with the characteristics named above. Of the two characteristics only the wise mind, or experienced judgment, is referred to, because defective spiritual intelligence is the thing complained of.

does not wish merely to express his own thoughts concerning Christ's priestly office, but to communicate them to others. He desires to *teach*; but he can teach only in so far as there is receptivity in his scholars. Teaching and learning are correlative, and teacher and scholar must keep pace with each other. No man can teach unless his pupils let him. Therefore this Christian doctor, minded to discourse not of the *principia* of Christianity—"the beginning of Christ"—but of its higher truths, appropriately says, "Let us go on," expressing at once a purpose and an exhortation.

In declining to make the Christian elements his exclusive theme, the writer takes occasion to indicate what these are. We scan with eager interest the list of fundamentals setting forth what, in the view of our author, and we may assume also of the Church in his time, a man was required to do and believe when he became a Christian. What first strikes one in this primitive "sum of saving knowledge" is how little that is specifically Christian it contains.[1] There is no express reference to Christ, not even in connection with faith, where it might have been expected. In his address to the elders at Miletus, Paul claimed to have testified to Jews and Greeks "repentance towards God, and faith towards our Lord Jesus Christ." Here, on the other hand, mention is made of "repentance from dead works, and faith towards God," as if it were a question of theism as against polytheism, rather than of Christian belief.[2]

---

[1] A similar remark may be made in reference to "The Teaching of the Twelve Apostles."

[2] M'Giffert too confidently remarks: "Nearly all the principles

It is superfluous to remark that the priesthood of Christ
finds no place in the list; that topic evidently is regarded
as belonging to the advanced doctrine. To us, who have
been accustomed to regard faith in the atoning death of
Christ, and even in a particular theory of the atonement,
as essential to salvation, all this must appear surprising.
Yet the meagre account here given of the catechumen's
creed is no isolated phenomenon in the New Testament.
It is in entire accord with what we learn from Paul's
First Epistle to the Thessalonians, which may be said
to show the style of his instructions to young converts
during the period of missionary activity antecedent to
the rise of the great controversy concerning the law.
Paul's purpose in that Epistle seems to be to remind the
Thessalonian Christians, for their encouragement and
strengthening, of the things he had taught them at the
time of their conversion, such phrases as "ye remember,"
"ye know," being of frequent occurrence. Yet throughout
the Epistle we can find no trace of the doctrine of justification
in the specifically Pauline sense, or of the doctrine
of Christ's atoning death. Christ's death is indeed referred
to, but in such a way as to suggest that the fact
of vital importance to faith was not that He died, but
that He rose again. "If we believe that Jesus died and
rose again, even so them also which sleep in Jesus will
God bring with Him."[1]

enumerated in this passage were common to Jews and Christians;
and a Christian, therefore, in writing to Jewish disciples could not
refer to them in such a way. Only a heathen would need to lay
such a foundation in accepting Christ" (p. 468).

[1] 1 Thess. iv. 14. *Vide* my work, *St. Paul's Conception of Christianity*, chap. i.

The apparently non-Christian character of the Christian *principia* is not the only perplexing feature in the list of fundamentals. It is not easy to determine how the various matters mentioned are related to each other. Judging from the rhythmical structure of the sentence, one's first thought is that the list contains six co-ordinate articles, grouped in pairs: first, repentance and faith; second, the doctrines of baptism and laying on of hands; third, the doctrines of resurrection and eternal judgment; the members of each pair being of kindred nature, and the whole six forming together the foundation of the Christian religion. But doubt arises when it is observed that in this view things are mixed together which belong to different categories; repentance and faith, which are spiritual states, with *doctrines* about other matters of greater or less importance. If there are six articles in the list of fundamentals, why not say, "Not laying again a foundation in doctrine concerning repentance, faith, baptisms," etc.? And so we are tempted to adopt another hypothesis, namely, that the last four are to be regarded as the foundation of the first two, conceived not as belonging to the foundation, but rather as the superstructure. On this view we should have to render, "Not laying again a foundation for repentance and faith, consisting in instruction concerning baptisms, laying on of hands, resurrection, and judgment." In favour of this construction is the reading διδαχήν (ver. 2, clause 1) found in B, and adopted by Westcott and Hort, which being in apposition with θεμέλιον (ver. 1) suggests that the four things following form the foundation of repentance and faith.

It is possible that the mixing up of states and doctrines in the list is due to the double attitude of the writer, as partly exhorting his readers, partly expressing his own purpose. "Not laying again a foundation, you by renewed repentance and faith, I by repetition of elementary instructions." But I cannot help thinking that there is discernible in this passage, notwithstanding its graceful rhythmical structure, on which Bengel and others have remarked, a slight touch of that rhetorical carelessness which recurs in much more pronounced form in chapter ix. 10, where the writer, referring to the ineffectual ordinances of Levitical worship, characterises them, in language difficult to construe, as "only, with their meats and drinks and diverse washings, ordinances of the flesh imposed until a time of reformation." In that place the loose construction of the sentence is an oratorical device to express a feeling of impatience with the bare idea that Levitical rites could possibly cleanse the consciences of worshippers. Of course the writer has no thought of putting the elementary truths of Christianity on a level with these rites. But the feeling of impatience with never getting beyond the elements seems to influence his manner of referring to them, giving rise to an elliptical abruptness of style which leaves room for questions as to the construction that cannot with certainty be answered.

On the whole, our first thought as to the connection is probably the correct one, according to which the passage is to be paraphrased thus: "Leaving discourse on the beginning of Christ, let us go on unto maturity, and unto the doctrine that suits it, not laying again a foundation in reiterated exhortations to repentance and faith, and in instructions about such matters as baptisms, laying on of hands, resurrection of the dead, and eternal judgment."

The only points needing explanation in this summary of elements are those included in the middle pair. Repentance and faith, the resurrection and the judgment, are obviously suitable subjects of instruction for persons beginning the Christian life. In the teaching of Jesus repentance and faith are the cardinal conditions of entrance into the kingdom of God. "The time is fulfilled, and the kingdom of God is at hand: repent ye, and believe the gospel" (Mark i. 15). There is room for dispute as to the import of the phrase employed to indicate the things to be repented of—"dead works." The phrase recurs in chapter ix. 14, where it will be made the subject of discussion. I will merely say here that it is by no means so clear as most commentators assume it to be, that "dead works" are synonymous with sinful works in general, and that there is no reference to the religious works of an artificial and servile legalism which first our Lord and then Paul declared to be worthless and pernicious. But be that as it may, there can be no doubt that repentance in some form, with faith, has a very appropriate place in the list of fundamentals. So have resurrection and judgment; for though, as events, they come at the end of the Christian's career, the doctrine concerning them comes fitly at the beginning, as tending to inspire an awe and a hope that are strong motives to holiness.

But what is the doctrine of baptisms? If instruction as to Christian baptism be mainly referred to, its appropriateness at the commencement is beyond question. But why baptisms and not baptism? Commentators generally concur in replying: because the writer has in view not merely Christian baptism, but all the symbolic uses of water with which Jewish converts might be familiar. Where various forms of such use were known comparison would be natural, and might be helpful as a means of conveying instruction as to the distinctive significance of Christian baptism. Against the reference to baptism in the specifically Christian sense it has been urged that it is never called βαπτισμός, the word used here, but always βάπτισμα. To this it seems a sufficient answer that the former term is employed because Christian baptism is included in a more comprehensive category along with Levitical purifications.

The "laying on of hands" is to be understood in the light of the apostolic practice of imposing hands on the heads of baptized persons, as a sign of the communication of the Holy Ghost. According to the accounts in the Book of Acts, this symbolic action was often followed by the communication of the Holy Ghost in the sense of a power to perform marvellous acts, such, *e.g.*, as speaking with tongues. This gift, in the view of the primitive Church, appears to have been regarded as the chief effect of the Divine Spirit's influence. Our present way of thinking is entirely different. We conceive of the Holy Spirit, not as a transcendent power descending occasionally on men, enabling them to exercise miraculous charisms, but as an indwelling influence enabling Christians to be good men. This happy change in our conceptions is due to the Apostle Paul, who, in his Epistles, while not denying the reality of the so-called "spiritual gifts" or their utility, yet placed the ethical above the charismatic, and represented love as of more value than all the charisms put together. His treatment of the subject in his Epistle to the Corinthians probably led to the decline of the "gifts."[1] But while they lasted there had to be something said about them, a doctrine of charisms—tongues, prophesyings, and the like. The miraculous charisms having passed away, a doctrine of the laying on of hands is no longer needed. With the doctrine the symbolic action has also ceased, save in the case of ordination of ministers. It might be for the advantage of the Church if it also passed away, as in connection with it the tendency of religious symbols to become causes of superstition has received baleful illustration.

Such are the fundamentals. What is meant by leaving them? Not, of course, ceasing to believe in them, or to think and speak of them, or to attach importance to them; for, though elementary, they *are* the foundation ($\theta\epsilon\mu\epsilon\lambda\iota o\nu$). They are to be left in the sense in which a builder leaves the foundation of a house—by erecting an edifice thereon. They are not to be treated as if they were everything, building as well as foundation. There has always been a Christianity of this sort, stationary, unprogressive; always concerned about the initial stage, and never getting beyond it. With reference to Christian teachers, the lesson is not to confine themselves to elementary truths, but to teach wisdom also to the "perfect," not forgetting their needs, though the number of them in the Church be small. Even for the sake of the immature, it is well not

[1] Vide *St. Paul's Conception of Christianity*, chap. xiii.

to tarry too long by the elements, lest they imagine they have nothing more to learn, when in truth they are in the state of the disciples to whom Jesus said, " I have yet many things to say to you, but ye cannot bear them now."

What he has just declared to be desirable the writer intimates his own purpose to do, cherishing the wish, if not the hope, that he may carry his readers along with him. "And this will we do," you and I, "if, that is,[1] God permit." This "if God permit" is an ominous hint at the more than possibility of the Hebrews having become so spiritually hidebound that they will prove totally incapable of receiving new truth. And so it forms a suitable introduction to the solemn passage which follows. And yet, though when a grave, earnest man makes reference to God's sovereign will, we feel that he must have some serious thought in his mind, we are hardly prepared for the very sombre picture of the apostate which this passage contains. Nor is it quite easy to see how it is connected with what goes before. Does the writer mean, "It is useless to keep insisting on foundation truths relating to repentance, faith, and the like topics; for if any one have fallen away you cannot bring him to repentance by any amount of preaching on the old trite themes"? or is his meaning rather, "I do trust you and I will go on together to manhood and its proper food, though I have my fears concerning you, fears lest you be in the position of men who have lapsed from a bright initial experience, whose outlook for the future is necessarily very gloomy"? Possibly both of these thoughts were passing through his mind when he wrote.

[1] ἐάνπερ, the περ intensifying the force of the ἐάν.

In these verses (4–6) there is a vivid description of a happy past, a supposition made regarding those whose past experience is portrayed, and a strong assertion hazarded regarding any in whom that supposition is realised.

The description of initial Christian *experience* is a companion picture to the preceding account of initial Christian *instruction*. It points to an intense religious life, full of enthusiasm, joy, and spiritual elevation, not, however, to be regarded as the exceptional privilege of the few, but rather as the common inheritance of the Church in the apostolic age. The picture is painted in high colours, but the outlines are not very distinct; and the spectator, while powerfully impressed, fails to carry away a clear idea of the scene. The writer's purpose is not to give information to *us*, but to awaken in the breasts of his first readers sacred memories, and breed godly sorrow over a dead past. Hence he expresses himself in emotional terms such as might be used by recent converts rather than in the colder but more exact style of the historian. "The heavenly gift"—precious doubtless, but what is it? "The good word of God"—ineffably sweet, but what precise word gave such rare enjoyment? Five distinct elements in the initial Christian experience of converts seem to be specified, yet on further analysis they appear to be reducible to three: the *illumination* conveyed by elementary Christian instruction (φωτισθέντας), the *enjoyment* connected with that illumination (γευσαμένους, ver. 4, repeated in ver. 5);[1] and the spiritual *power* communicated by

[1] The repetition of γευσαμένους suggests that the clause in which the participle occurs for the second time may be explanatory of that

the Holy Ghost, and manifesting itself in the miraculous charisms whereof we read in Acts and in Paul's First Epistle to the Corinthians (δυνάμεις μέλλοντος αἰῶνος, ver. 5). The cardinal fact is the illumination. The light of heaven breaking in on the soul awakens strong emotions, which find vent in speaking with tongues and prophesying—the powers and signs of the Messianic age. That illumination is the epoch-making event of the Christian life. It takes place once for all (ἅπαξ); there ought to be no need for its repetition, nay, it cannot be repeated. It comes like a revelation, and produces mighty effects; and woe to the man who lets the light go out!

"If they fall away" (καὶ παραπεσόντας): such is the supposition made with reference to persons who have gone through experiences so remarkable. The case put is that of persons who once knew, believed, and loved Christian truth, did wonderful works in Christ's name and by the power of His Spirit, lapsing into ignorance, unbelief, indifference, or even dislike of what they once found sweet to their taste—God's word and the gift of

in which it occurs for the first time. In that case the "heavenly gift" would be practically identical with the "word of God," which the convert finds good to his taste = the gospel of grace; and the "Holy Spirit" in which the convert participates would be synonymous with the "powers of the world to come." That is to say, the Holy Spirit would be referred to, not as the indwelling source of Christian sanctity, but as the source of spiritual gifts or miraculous charisms. The change in the construction (the genitive after the participle in the first case, the accusative in the second) may suggest slightly differing shades of meaning: sharing, having part in the heavenly gift; appreciating the quality of the Divine word, receiving the truth, feeling its value.

grace to which it bears witness. The very putting of such a case seems a rude contradiction of the dogma of perseverance, and hence this passage has been a famous battlefield between Arminians and Calvinists. The expositor who is more concerned about the correct interpretation of Scripture than about the defence of any system of theology will not find himself able to go altogether with either side in the controversy. The Bible is an excellent book for the purposes of practical religion, but rather a tantalising book for the systematic theologian. Its writers know nothing of the caution and reserve of the system-maker, but express themselves in strong, unqualified terms which are the torment of the dogmatist and the despair of the controversialist. The author of this Epistle in particular writes, not as a theorist, but as an observer of facts. Cases of the kind described have actually come under his eye. He has seen many bearing all the marks of true believers fall away, and he has observed that such men do not usually return to the faith from which they have lapsed. He speaks as his experience prompts. He does not call in question the reality of the faith and gracious affections of *quondam* Christians, but describes these after their fall, as he would have described them before it, admitting them to have been blossoms, though they were blighted by frost; or leaf-bearing branches, though they afterwards became dead and withered.

As little, on the other hand, does he hesitate to affirm that recovery in such cases is impossible, reasoning again from past observation, and also doubtless in part from the nature of the case, apostates appearing to him like a fire whose fuel has been completely consumed so that nothing remains but *ashes*. This brings us to the third point in the passage before us—the strong assertion made regarding those who lapse: "It is impossible to renew them again unto repentance." Two questions suggest themselves. Is the assertion to be taken strictly? and, so taken, is it true? That the writer uses the word "impossible" strictly may be inferred from the reason he gives for his assertion. When men have got the length of crucifying Christ to themselves, and putting Him to an open shame before others, their case is hopeless.[1] But possibly he puts too severe a construction on the facts. There may be a lapse from the bright life of a former time, serious and perilous, but not amounting to a crucifying of Christ, or so hardening the heart as to make repentance impossible.

Now two things may be admitted here. First, there are phases of the spiritual life liable to be mistaken for symptoms of apostasy, which are truly interpreted only when looked at in the light of the great law of gradual

[1] Dr. Edwards takes the participles ἀνασταυροῦντας and παραδειγματίζοντας, not as explanatory of παραπεσόντας, but as putting a hypothetical case, and renders, "they cannot be renewed after falling away if they persist in crucifying." The change from the aorist to the present may be in favour of this view, yet one cannot help feeling that the writer means to say something more serious than that falling away is fatal *when* it amounts to crucifying Christ. Mr. Rendall has another way of softening the severity of the dictum, namely, to take ἀνακαινίζειν as expressing continuous action, and render "it is impossible to keep renewing" = the process of falling and renewing cannot go on indefinitely: the power of impression grows weaker, and at length becomes exhausted by repetition. This view is certainly in keeping with the spirit of the whole passage (v. 11-14, vi. 1-8).

growth enunciated by our Lord in the parable of the blade, the green ear, and the full corn in the ear.[1] The difficult problem of Christian experience cannot be mastered unless we grasp the truth taught in that parable, and know the characteristics of each stage, and especially of the second, which are most liable to be misunderstood. For lack of such knowledge many a Christian, destined to reach a splendid spiritual manhood, has seemed to himself and others to have fallen away utterly from grace, faith, and goodness, while he was simply passing through the stage of the green fruit, with all its unwelcome yet wholesome experiences. In this crude stage of his religious history Bunyan thought he had committed the sin against the Holy Ghost, and "an ancient Christian," supposed to be wise in counsel, whom he consulted, told him he thought so too. Yet he was on the way to Beulah through the valley of the shadow of death; and few reach that blessed land without passing along the same dark, dreary road. How far the writer of our Epistle, or indeed any of the New Testament writers, understood the law of growth by broadly discriminated stages, enunciated by Christ, does not appear. It is certain that nowhere else in the New Testament can there be found a statement approaching in scientific clearness and distinctness to that contained in the parable referred to.[2] In absence of a

[1] Mark iv. 26-29. On this parable see *The Parabolic Teaching of Christ*.

[2] It has been disputed whether there be any distinct doctrine of growth or gradual sanctification in Paul's Epistles. Pfleiderer maintains the affirmative. Reuss, a more orthodox theologian, denies, maintaining that Paul conceives the new life as perfect

theory of sanctification to guide them, however, their spiritual sagacity might be trusted to keep them from confounding a case like Bunyan's with that of an apostate.

Second. Bible writers often state in unqualified terms as an absolute truth what is in reality only an affair of tendency. Translated into a statement of tendency, the doctrine taught is this. Every fall involves a risk of apostasy, and the higher the experience fallen from the greater the risk. The deeper religion has gone into a man at the commencement of his Christian course, the less hopeful his condition if he lapse. The nearer the initial stage to a thorough conversion the less likely is a second change, if the first turn out abortive; and so on, in ever-increasing degrees of improbability as lapses increase in number. The brighter the light in the soul, the deeper the darkness when the light is put out. The sweeter the manna of God's word to the taste, the more loathsome it becomes when it has lost its relish. The fiercer the fire in the hearth while the fuel lasts, the more certain it is that when the fire goes out there will remain nothing but ashes. The livelier the hope of glory, the greater the aversion to all thoughts of the world to come when once a Christian has, like Atheist in the *Pilgrim's Progress*, turned his back on the heavenly

---

from the first. There is a noticeable difference between Paul and our Lord in their respective manner of dealing with the defects of young Christians. Paul blames, as if they were full-grown men; Christ corrects, as one who knows that nothing else is to be looked for in children, and that the future will bring wisdom: "I have many things to say unto you, but ye cannot bear them now." Vide *St. Paul's Conception of Christianity*, chap. xix.

Jerusalem. Action and reaction are equal. The more forcibly you throw an elastic ball against a wall the greater the rebound; in like manner the more powerfully the human spirit is brought under celestial influences, the greater the recoil from all good, if there be a recoil at all. The gushing enthusiasts of to-day are the cynical sceptics of to-morrow. Have promoters of "revivals" laid these things duly to heart?

But the wise teacher whose complaint of his dull scholars we are considering has something more serious in view, when he speaks of falling away, than the coldness and languor, or even the moral lapses, which are apt to overtake converts after a period of great excitement. It is not a question of loss of feeling, or of unstable, inconsistent conduct, or of falls through infirmity, but of deep alienation of heart. He thinks of such as are capable of cherishing towards Christ the feelings of hatred which animated the men who crucified Him, and of openly renouncing the Christian faith. This was the crime the Hebrew Christians were tempted to commit. A fatal step it must be when taken; for men who left the Christian Church and went back to the synagogue became companions of persons who thought they did God service in cursing the name of Jesus.

The writer proceeds (vers. 7, 8), by a comparison drawn from agriculture, to illustrate the danger to which those are exposed who, having had a pronounced spiritual experience, afterwards fall away from the faith and life of the gospel. The parable does not really afford us much help to the understanding of the matter; as it is rendered in the Authorised Version it affords no help at all. As the case is put there, a contrast seems to be drawn between two kinds of soil, one of which is well watered, and therefore fertile, while the other is unwatered, and therefore sterile or productive only of thorns and thistles. Such a contrast would bring out the difference between those who have and those who have not enjoyed gospel privileges, not the difference between two classes of Christians who have both equally enjoyed such privileges, or the two possible alternatives in the case of every professing Christian. It is a contrast fitted to serve the latter purpose that really is made. Exactly rendered it runs thus: "For land which, after drinking in the rain that cometh oft upon it, bringeth forth herbage meet for those for whose benefit it is tilled, receiveth blessing from God; but if *it* (the same land well watered) bear thorns and thistles, it is worthless, and nigh unto a curse, whose end is unto burning."

When we compare this parable with any of our Lord's, there is a great falling off in point of felicity and instructiveness. One purpose it doubtless serves, to make clear the matter of fact, that the same Christian privileges and experiences may issue in widely different ultimate results. The soil is supposed in either case to be well watered, not only rained upon, but often saturated with water, having drunk up the blessing of the clouds, and moreover to be carefully tilled; for though that point is left in the background, it is alluded to in the words "for whose benefit it is tilled" ($\delta i'$ οὓς καὶ γεωργεῖται). Yet in one case it yields a useful crop, in the other only a useless crop of thorns and thistles. But why? On this important question the parable throws no light. The land which bears the useless crop is not a barren rock; for it drinks in the rain, and it is considered worth ploughing. Nay, it is doubtful if the case supposed in the second alternative can occur in the natural world. Was there ever a land well tilled and watered that produced nothing but thorns and thistles? It seems as if the natural and the spiritual were mixed up here, and that were said of the one which is strictly true only with reference to the other. The writer describes a case in the natural world which can hardly happen to represent a case which may happen in the spiritual world, that, namely, of men whose hearts have been sown with the seed of truth and watered with the rain of grace becoming so utterly degenerate and reprobate as in the end to produce nothing but the thorns and thistles of unbelief and ungodliness.[1] Mixture of metaphor and literal sense is indeed manifest throughout, the phrases " receiveth blessing," " reprobate " ($ἀδόκιμος$), " nigh to a curse," " whose end is unto burning," expressing moral ideas rather than physical facts. This is particularly evident in the case of the last phrase. It plainly points to a judicial visitation of the severest kind, the appointed penalty of spiritual unfruitfulness. But in the natural

---

[1] Natural improbability occurs in some of our Lord's parables; *e.g.* in the Parable of the Great Supper. Such a thing as all the guests invited to a feast with one consent refusing to come does not happen in society. The truth is, it is impossible to describe the essentially unreasonable behaviour of men in regard to the kingdom of God in parabolic language, without violating natural probability. On the other hand, the parables which describe Christ's own conduct, much assailed by His contemporaries, are all thoroughly true to nature; *e.g.* those in the fifteenth chapter of Luke. I have remarked on this contrast in *The Parabolic Teaching of Christ*.

sphere burning is remedial rather than punitive, to burn land which has become foul being a good method of restoring it to fertility.

In yet another respect the comparison fails us. Supposing there were such a thing as burning unprofitable land by way of judicial visitation, as the land of Sodom was destroyed by fire and brimstone,—an event which may have been present to the writer's thoughts,—the fact might serve to symbolise the Divine judgment on apostasy. But the matter on which we most of all need light is the asserted impossibility of renewal. That the finally impenitent should be punished we understand, but what we want to know is, how men get into that state: what is the psychological history of irrecoverable apostasy? To refer to Divine agency in hardening human hearts does not help us, for God hardens by means naturally fitted and intended to soften and win. Neither can we take refuge in the supposition of insufficient initial grace, at least from the point of view of the writer of our Epistle; for he assumes that the fruitful and the unfruitful have been equally favoured. The rain falls not less liberally on the land that bears thorns and thistles than on the land that brings forth an abundant crop of grass or grain; and the rain represents the enlightenment, enjoyment, and power previously mentioned.

In the Parable of the Sower the diversity in the results is traced to the nature of the soil. In each case the issue is exactly such as we should expect from the character of the soil. In the parable before us opposite results are supposed to be possible in the same soil. The effect, that is to say, is conceived to depend on the will of the individual, on the use he makes of his privileges. The Hebrew Christians might have been teachers instead of childish learners, had they chosen to take the necessary pains. They might have been full-grown men, had they only properly exercised their spiritual senses in the art of discerning between good and evil.

CHAPTER XI

THE TEACHER'S CHARITY

CHAP. VI. 9-20

AT this point the teacher of the Hebrew Church suddenly and decidedly changes his tone. He will not let his last word be one of complaint and despondency. He refuses to believe that the apostate's doom is in store for any of those to whom he writes. Therefore he hastens to assure them that he cherishes hopeful thoughts of their present and future state, calling them, in this solitary instance, "beloved," as if to make amends for the severity of his rebuke, and declaring that he fully expects to see realised in their experience the better alternative of the foregoing contrast—fruitfulness connected with, leading up to, salvation—instead of the cursing and perdition appointed for the land that bears only thorns and thistles.

So the teacher's complaining gives place to the charity that believeth all things and hopeth all things. It is the way of all New Testament writers, eminently of Paul. How he labours to persuade himself of the better things in regard to unbelieving Israel in that section of his Epistle to the Romans in which he deals with the hard problem, how to reconcile Israel's position as God's elect people with her attitude towards the gospel! Having faced first the dark alternative, that the facts meant the cancelling of the election, and shown that in that case no one was to blame but Israel herself, he declares his belief that the state of matters is not so serious. "I say then, Hath God cast away His people? God forbid." The recurrent phrases, "I say then" and "God forbid," show how hard he finds it to make good this position. But the ingenuity of love discovers a ground of hope even in the very terms in which rejection was threatened: "I will provoke you to jealousy by a no-people"; whence the apostle extracts the theory, that God has temporarily cast away Israel, and called the Gentiles to make the former jealous, and so lead her to value privileges hitherto despised. It is only a new, roundabout method of working for Israel's good (Rom. xi.).

Such was Paul's ground of hope for Hebrew unbelievers. And what is the ground of the hope the writer of our Epistle cherishes for Hebrew Christians? It is their Christian work, and more especially the love they have shown to the name of God, and of His Son Jesus, by past and present ministries to the necessities of saints. Verily a good, solid foundation for a judgment of charity and hope! And in adducing it for that purpose, the writer shows himself to be a man thoroughly imbued with the spirit of Christ's teaching. He evidently knows what value the great Master set upon even a cup of cold water given to a disciple in the name of a disciple, and how in the representation of the last judgment He made charity the great decisive test of character. He hopes that it is well with these poor Hebrew Christians, in spite of their vacillations in opinion and their hankering after old religious customs, because they have manifested, and are still manifesting, love to the name of Christ by deeds of kindness to Christians afflicted with the common ills of life, or exposed to persecution for the gospel's sake. In cherishing such a hope on such a ground he acted on a sound instinct. Men were still a long way from crucifying Christ afresh who continued to show kind feelings towards His followers. Their hearts were right, though their heads might be confused, and their minds in a state of painful oscillation between the old and the new religions, between the traditions of the synagogue and the simple, spiritual, free, revolutionary principles of the gospel, as preached first by the Lord Jesus and then by His apostles. Had these Hebrews really been apostates, or on the point of becoming such, they would have hated, not loved, their former brethren; they would have addicted themselves to the bad work of persecuting believers in Jesus, rather than to the blessed work of ministering to the necessities of the saints. Renegades are ever the most ruthless persecutors: witness James Sharp, Archbishop of St. Andrews in the reign of Charles II., formerly a Covenanting Presbyterian minister, whose cold-blooded cruelty towards his old fellow-religionists horrified even his unscrupulous associates in the bad work of persecution, and brought at length its own penalty in the murder of the apostate by a band of daring men whom his iniquity had driven mad.

Recalling the kindly deeds of his slow-minded pupils,

the teacher almost repents of the alarming tone in which he has addressed them, and becomes apologetic, saying in effect: "I do not think so badly of you as to believe that the fearful doom I have depicted will befall you, but I have thought it right to put the dark picture before your eyes, that you might look at it; for I wish to rouse you out of your torpor, and stir you up to diligence to make your calling and election sure, that your salvation may be a matter of certainty, and not merely of charitable hope" (vers. 11, 12).

Noteworthy in these verses is the individualising character of the pious solicitude of this man of God for the spiritual wellbeing of the Hebrews. *Every one of you.* The good shepherd goeth after even one straying sheep. The expression may signify that while there was no reason to take a despairing view of the Hebrew Church as a whole, there were some of its members in imminent danger of apostasy. It may also be legitimately taken as an index of personal relations—a proof that the writing we are studying was really an epistle addressed to a particular community well known to the writer.

The teacher desires to see faith and hope in as lively exercise as charity, in the characters of these Hebrews. With their love it appears he had no fault to find, but their faith was weak and their hope was dim. Even at the worst, even if they should suffer shipwreck of faith, he trusts that men so kindly affectioned towards Christ's people would get safe to heaven's shore, "some on boards, some on broken pieces of the ship"; but he is not content that they should be saved in this precarious manner. He would have them go into the haven with ship intact, with the rudder of faith in good working condition, and with sails filled with the favouring breeze of the hope of glory.

He further expresses his desire that the Hebrews should become imitators of those who through faith and patience inherit the promises. He has in view, doubtless, the roll of heroes who have made their lives sublime, and who receive honourable mention in the eleventh chapter. The reference is not merely to the patriarchs, though the mention of Abraham in the next verse might lead us to suppose that they are specially intended, but to all in all ages, living or dead, present or past, who by steadfast faith and firm endurance do make sure the inheritance, and do in a sense possess it even before life's close. What is wished for the Hebrews therefore is, that they may have a faith so clear that it shall be the substance of things hoped for, the future inheritance in present possession; and that by a great-souled, indomitable patience, proof against all temptation, they may persevere in the faith even to the end, and so obtain the promise, not merely by way of earnest, but in full fruition.

This expression of his *pium desiderium* the writer follows up by a reference to Abraham, as the most signal example of patient, magnanimous faith, and as one whose history served to show how reliable are the promises of God (vers. 13–17). All New Testament writers, Paul, James, our author, utilise the story of the great patriarch of the Jewish race for the purpose of establishing a doctrine or enforcing a moral lesson. Nothing was more likely to touch the Hebrew heart. The part of Abraham's history alluded to is that in which the pathos of his life reaches its climax, the words quoted being those spoken to him by God after his sublime manifestation of implicit obedience and trust in offering up for sacrifice his only son. What God said is not quoted in full, only the kernel of the promise being given, and the Divine eulogy on Abraham's magnanimity being passed over in silence. The point on which stress is laid is the oath accompanying the promise; for the writer's purpose is to make prominent the trustworthiness of the promises, as amply justifying the desiderated "full assurance of hope," not to pass an encomium on Abraham. He does not indeed lose sight of the latter object entirely. The patriarch's patient faith gets honourable mention in ver. 15, where it is said in effect that, having received the *word* of promise, confirmed by an oath, Abraham persevered in faith, and, persevering, at length obtained the fulfilment of the promise. Even here, it is to be observed, the leading thought is not Abraham's patience, but the certainty of the promise. The patriarch's patience is referred to only in a participial clause (οὕτως μακροθυμήσας); that he obtained the promise is the main affirmation. And the purpose of that affirmation again is not to assert that Abraham personally entered into full possession of the thing promised. This was that his seed should be multiplied as the stars of heaven, and as the sand of the seashore, and that in his seed all the nations of the earth should eventually be blessed. It was in truth *the* promise of the great Messianic salvation, the object of hope for humanity at large, and for the Hebrew Christians in particular. That promise, of course, was not fulfilled exhaustively and comprehensively in Abraham's lifetime. Of Abraham, as of all the patriarchs, it was true that he died in faith, not having received the promises, but having only seen them afar off. This is our author's own reflection (xi. 13), and he does not mean to say anything inconsistent therewith here. His aim in the two places is not the same. In the eleventh chapter his object is to extol the faith of the patriarchs; here it is chiefly to extol the reliableness of God's promises, that it may appear that a fully assured hope is justifiable and attainable. Viewed in the light of this purpose, what he says is in effect this: the promise made to Abraham, extravagant as its terms may seem, and however unlikely to be fulfilled, regarded before the event, shall be fulfilled to the letter. Important instalments of fulfilment lie behind us in the history of Israel; there was even an initial fulfilment in Abraham's own lifetime, in the giving back to him of his son Isaac from the dead, in the marriage of Isaac to Rebekah, and in the birth of grandchildren through their marriage.[1]

[1] In what sense the statement that Abraham received the promise is to be understood, is a point on which interpreters are not agreed. Bleek understands it as meaning that he obtained the promise itself, but not the thing promised; or the latter, only *de jure* (Grotius), not *de facto*. In support of this view he adverts to the fact that the word used to express the idea of obtaining in chapter vi. 15 (ἐπέτυχεν) is not the same as in chapter xi. 13, 39 (προσδεξάμενοι, ἐκομίσαντο). Similarly, among recent interpreters, Kendall. The great majority of commentators have found in the words a reference to fulfilment; and it does seem as if the scope of the argument

The writer's purpose being to insist on the trustworthiness of God's promises for the strengthening of hope in dejected hearts, he naturally makes the oath accompanying the promise to Abraham the subject of some reflections designed to bring out its significance, proceeding on the assumption that the oath, like the promise, concerned not Abraham only, but all his spiritual seed. That oath is indeed remarkable in many ways, and in a high degree provocative of thought. It is the first instance in Scripture in which God is represented as binding Himself by an oath to the keeping of His word. It is further remarkable as an expression of admiration awakened in the Divine bosom by the spectacle of self-sacrifice presented by the patriarch in offering up his only son Isaac. Looking down thereon God exclaims: "As I live, this is a great, heroic deed; it shall not go unrewarded; out of the son with whom this man is willing to part at the call of duty shall spring a seed multitudinous as the stars or the sand of the seashore, and destined to be a channel of grace and mercy to all the peoples that dwell on the face of the earth."

But it is not in either of these senses that our author wishes to fix the attention of his readers on the oath, but in a third respect, namely, as a reliable guarantee of the

required this. There would not be much encouragement to hope in the mere fact of believing men getting promises, if there were not at least partial fulfilments to point to. Westcott's view is similar to that stated in the text. Weiss thinks the birth of Isaac and of his sons was not the fulfilment referred to, but the growth of a great people out of them. Vaughan thinks the fulfilment was that of the promise of the heavenly rest realised, though not exhaustively, by Abraham.

absolute certainty of the promise to which the oath was attached. To commend it in this view, he enlarges on the oath, exhibiting it particularly on two sides: (1) as a manifestation of *Divine condescension*, in gracious solicitude for man's good, therefore a *moral* argument for the truth of the promise; and (2) as pledging the Divine *nature*, and therefore a *metaphysical* argument for the truth of the promise. The former aspect is suggested by the words, "because He could swear by no greater, He sware by Himself" (ver. 13). That is as much as to say, that if it had been possible for God to find any being greater than Himself of whom He stood in awe, as men stand in awe of Him, He would have been glad to swear by that being, to show to the heirs of the promise the immutability of His counsel, for their encouragement and confirmation. But the Divine condescension is still more strikingly exhibited in the words ἐμεσίτευσεν ὅρκῳ (ver. 17), weakly rendered in the Authorised Version "confirmed it by an oath," but which literally signify, "interposed Himself as a middle party or mediator by an oath." The idea is a very bold but also a very grand one: that God, in taking an oath, made Himself a third party intermediate between God and Abraham. Men, as is remarked in ver. 16, swear by the greater, and so in a sense did God. God swearing became inferior in His condescension to God sworn by: "descended as it were" (to quote Delitzsch) "from His own absolute exaltation, in order, so to speak, to look up to Himself after the manner of men, and take Himself to witness; and so by a gracious condescension confirm the promise for the sake of its inheritors." Thus God, in taking an oath, does a thing analogous to God becoming man. The acts are kindred, being both acts of condescension and love. In these two acts and in covenant-making God stoops down from His majesty to the weakness and want and low estate of man. In taking an oath, He submits to indignity, imposed by man's distrust, and, instead of standing on His character for truthfulness, puts Himself under oath, that there may be an end of gainsaying (ἀντιλογίας, ver. 16). In becoming man, God condescends to man's sin, submits to the lot of a sinner, that man may be delivered from the power of evil. In making a covenant, He makes Himself a debtor to His creatures, and gives them a right to claim what is in reality a matter of grace, and not of debt.

The other aspect of the oath is presented in ver. 18. The point here is the utter impossibility of God perjuring Himself. Apart altogether from God's *love*, it is simply impossible for the Divine Being to make a promise on oath which He does not mean to keep. But it may be asked, What are the two unchangeable (ἀμεταθέτων) things? God's oath is one of the things, of course, but what is the other? It is the bare *word* of promise without the oath. It is right to count the *word* separately among the immutabilities. By so doing our author does not weaken the argument drawn from the oath, but rather strengthens it. The very stress he lays on the oath requires him to attach not less value to the bare word of God. For if God's word were not immutable, His oath would not be immutable either. Unless His word were as good as an oath, His oath would be worthless. For He has nothing to fear as the penalty of perjury. Men have something to fear, but not God; the only influence that can affect Him is reverence for Himself, and that will influence Him not less when He simply pledges His word than when He seals His word with the solemnity of an oath.

The fitness of God's word, backed by His oath, to encourage even the weakest faith, is strongly asserted by implication in the description of those for whose benefit the whole argument is intended, as persons who have fled as for refuge to lay hold upon the forelying hope. The words suggest the idea of a person fleeing to a sanctuary, and laying hold of the horns of the altar. Or perhaps, as the image of an anchor occurs in the next verse, the writer had in his mind the case of a sailor running his vessel into the most convenient harbour of refuge, to escape the fury of the storm and the danger of shipwreck.

In addition to all that has been said on the oath, it may be remarked that, without doubt, the writer made it the subject of the foregoing reflections, because they well served the purpose of preparing his readers for attaching importance to another oath of God—that sworn in announcing the introduction of a new order of priesthood. He wished to suggest the thought, that it is always an important occasion when God swears an oath. An oath reveals a great tide of emotion in the Divine heart, which nothing short of an epoch-making event in the history of the world can give rise to. Note well the crises when God plays the part of mediator between Himself and men by oath-taking, and mark their profound significance. In the case of Abraham, the oath expressed the Divine delight in self-sacrifice, and the certainty of ultimate renown and bliss for all who rise to the heroic pitch in faith and patience. They shall be the founders of enduring races, the originators of great beneficent movements for the good of mankind, and their memory shall live while the world lasts. In the case of the Melchisedec priesthood, the oath meant the Divine weariness of a rude Levitical ritual, and the inbringing of a new order that should perfectly realise the ideal, and therefore be eternal. The two events, the giving of the promise to Abraham, and the institution of the Melchisedec priesthood, had, it thus appears, this much in common, that they were both occasions sufficiently important to be worthy of a Divine oath. Had they no other connection? Was it a mere accident that God took an oath in these two cases, and so tied together by a slight string events otherwise unrelated? This is not the view of the writer of our Epistle. The promise to Abraham and his seed—the object of the Christian hope—and the Melchisedec priesthood are in his mind closely related. In referring to the oath sworn to Abraham, he gives a premonitory hint of the intimate connection between the two things, which is plainly declared in the closing verses of the chapter (19, 20).

These beautiful words form the happy, cheering conclusion of a passage, which as a whole, and especially at its commencement, is of a very stern and sombre character. Here the frown passes away from the teacher's face, and is replaced by a benignant smile, and his style of writing relaxes from prophetic severity to evangelic geniality and tenderness. While in the early part of this section we were conducted to the edge of a precipice, and bid look down and behold the appalling fate of apostates, or carried away back to the plain of Sodom, and shown there a land rendered sterile for ever by fire and brimstone for the sins of its inhabitants, we are here privileged to witness the pleasing sight of a ship riding safely at anchor, an emblem of the security of a Christian who cherishes the hope of eternal life, and is thereby enabled to hold fast his profession of faith in spite of all the stormy tribulations of time. Then how fitted to reassure the Christian pilgrim on his heavenward way, that view of Jesus gone within the veil as our Forerunner, reminding us of His own words to His disciples on the eve of His passion: "In My Father's house are many mansions; . . . I go to prepare a place for you. And . . . I shall come again, and receive you unto Myself; that where I am, there ye may be also" (John xiv. 2, 3).

Which (hope) we have as an anchor of the soul, secure and firm, and entering into the place within the veil.

The two epithets (ἀσφαλῆ τε καὶ βεβαίαν) describe the qualities of a good anchor. Being connected by τε καί they may be regarded as expressing only a single idea. But we may refer the first epithet to the anchoring ground, as good for anchorage, and the second to the anchor, as one which will keep its hold.

The comparison of hope to an anchor is apt in respect both to its use and to the way in which it is used. The use of an anchor is to keep a ship fixed to one spot, and prevent it from drifting before wind and tide; and it is made available for this purpose by being thrown out of the ship into the sea, that it may sink to the bottom and lay hold of the unseen ground. Even so the function of hope is to keep the soul in peace and safety amid trouble, and it does this by entering into the unseen future, and laying hold of good not now enjoyed. This is true of hope in general. The peculiarity of Christian hope is, that it finds its anchorage, not in the nearer future lying between the present moment and death, but in the remote future beyond the tomb. Its anchoring ground lies deep beneath the dark waters of time, invisible to sense, existing only for faith.

Assuming that the former of the two epithets by which the anchor is described refers to the anchoring ground, it amounts to a testimony that the Christian hope is objectively true. If it be asked, What is the evidence for such an assertion? to find the answer of the writer we must fall back on the "two immutable things." God's promises and His oaths, and His covenant with men, and the whole history of His dealings with men in the execution of a redemptive purpose, as recorded in the Scriptures,—these are the guarantees that we strike the anchor of our eternal hope into a firm, unyielding bottom. If we are to doubt the reality of the thing hoped for, then we must give up the idea of a revelation and all that it implies; for it is not credible that God would act towards men as the Bible represents, if human existence was limited to threescore years and ten. If man's destiny be to "be blown about in desert dust, or sealed within the iron hills," not only is man "a monster then, a dream, a discord," but the faith which revelation inspires, that "God was love indeed, and love creation's final law," is a delusion.

The image of the anchor is in itself very appropriate and pathetic, but the conception of it as entering into the place within the veil, *i.e.* the Holy of Holies, strikes one at first as artificial and frigid. It seems incongruous to speak of an anchor in connection with the inner shrine of the tabernacle. Some seek escape from the incongruity by taking the "entering" (εἰσερχομένην) as referring, not to the anchor, but to the hope, the figure being dropped at this point. The truth appears to be, that we have here a combination of two metaphors, with the connecting link suppressed. The full thought is this: Hope is an anchor entering into the eternal, invisible world, like the anchor of a ship entering into the waters, and laying hold of the bottom of the sea; and that eternal world whereof hope lays hold may in turn be likened unto the place within the veil, because it is hid from view, as by a veil suspended before our eyes, to be drawn aside at the hour of our decease.

The allusion to the Holy of Holies as an emblem of the eternal world is made, it seems to me, with the purpose of bringing the train of thought back to the old theme. In the long digression into which he has been drawn, the writer has, to use a familiar phrase, gone off the rails, and he employs this expression as a switch to bring the train back to the main line. It is another example of the rhetorical tact by which the whole Epistle is so notably distinguished. But the expression is more than a switch: it contributes to the argument, and serves to justify the representation of the anchor of Christian hope as one sure and steadfast. This appears when we reflect what is "the place within the veil." It is the place where are the ark of the covenant, and the mercy-seat, and the cherubim with outstretched wings—which were just Israel's grounds of hope that God would fulfil His promise, and keep His covenant with His people, maintaining them in peace and prosperity in the Promised Land. This the Hebrews well knew, and their friend would have them understand that the new covenant of grace, and the gospel of mercy, and the outstretched wings of redeeming love, in the New Testament holy of holies, are not less reliable grounds of hope for believers in Christ with respect to the "world to come" than was the furniture of the inner shrine of the tabernacle for the people of Israel with respect to the temporal blessings God had promised them.

And now we come to the crowning thought: *Where, as Forerunner for us, entered Jesus, become, after the order of Melchisedec, our High Priest for ever* (ver. 20). The word πρόδρομος is, as Bengel remarks, *verbum valde significans*, though in common with nearly all commentators he fails to perceive, or at least to express in any adequate manner, its significance. It lies really in this, that it expresses an idea entirely new, lying altogether outside the Levitical system. The high priest of Israel did not go into the most holy place as forerunner, but only as the representative of the people. He went into a place whither none might follow him, entering once a year, in the people's stead, not as their pioneer. The glory and privilege of the new Christian era, the peculiar excellence of the perfect religion, is, that Christ, as the High Priest of humanity, goes nowhere where His people cannot follow Him. He is our pioneer, clearing our way. There is no longer any envious veil screening off some specially holy place, and shutting it against us. The veil was the sure sign that the Levitical religion was not the absolute religion, not the *summum bonum*, but only a shadow of good things to come. The absolute religion demands an unrestricted fellowship of the human spirit with a Divine Father, who is not merely in a place technically holy, but wherever there is a contrite, humble, devout worshipper; a Father who dwells in heaven, doubtless, but not in a heaven which He keeps to Himself, but rather in a heaven into which He means to gather together all His children. Not till such unrestricted fellowship has been established has the perfect, perennial religion come. That it has been established, is what the writer of our Epistle means to suggest by the use of the term πρόδρομος in reference to Jesus as our great High Priest entering into the place within the veil. He means to point out a contrast between the two religions, saying in effect: That which was lacking in the old religion is at length come. Where the High Priest goeth we may also go, instead of, as of old, standing without, waiting anxiously for the exit of the high priest from that inaccessible, dark, awful, perilous, most holy place beyond the veil. The great thought forms a worthy close to a discourse designed to revive hope in drooping hearts.

To what extent it served this purpose we know not; possibly the Hebrew Christians failed to perceive the point, and so lost the intended benefit. This certainly has been the case with most commentators; why, I find it hard to understand. How completely the authors of the old English version missed the sense appears from their rendering "whither *the* Forerunner is for us entered, even Jesus," as if the idea of a high priest being a forerunner were a perfectly familiar one, instead of being a startling, beneficent originality. Familiar to us of course it is, but we must consider what it was to the first readers of the Epistle. Some of the more recent commentators fail not less completely, by connecting the idea of forerunner, not with Christ's high-priestly office, but with His function as the Captain of salvation, leading God's people into the Promised Land. Jesus is our Forerunner, not as the Aaron, but as the Joshua of the new era,[1] though He is represented as entering for us and before us, not the heavenly Canaan, but the heavenly holy of holies —the place beyond the veil. Thus what the author, as I believe, intended to be a striking contrast becomes a parallel between the two dispensations. Without doubt, the main cause of all this miscarriage is failure to grasp

---

[1] So Dr. Edwards and Mr. Rendall, and apparently also Dr. Weiss; for he refers back to chapter ii. 10, and the title ἀρχηγὸς there. Vaughan's note on πρόδρομος is purely verbal, except that he weakens the religious value of the truth it expresses by the remark, "We might have expected the simple genitive (ἡμῶν) after πρόδρομος. But the insertion of ὑπὲρ is reverential, and marks the disparity of the πρόδρομος and the followers." Westcott sees the point dimly, but he does not put the contrast with adequate sharpness. "Thus to the fulfilment of the type of the high priest's work another work is added. The high priest entered the Holy of Holies on behalf of the people, but they never followed him. Christ enters heaven as Forerunner of believers."

firmly the apologetic character of the Epistle, as intended to show the superiority of the Christian religion over the Levitical, and never losing an opportunity of promoting that end. Here surely was an excellent opportunity, a glaring contrast between the two religions offering itself for remark, a contrast in which the advantage was altogether and manifestly on the side of Christianity: the high priest of Israel going within the veil as a substitute, the High Priest of humanity going within the veil as a Forerunner. A competent writer of an apologetic work, such as I take the Epistle to the Hebrews to be, could not omit this thought; and if it is to be found anywhere in the Epistle, it is here.

Probably a subsidiary misleading influence, preventing expositors from finding the thought referred to in this text, has been the notion that Christ's priestly office did not begin till He entered the heavenly sanctuary. If Jesus became our High Priest only after He had reached the place within the veil, then His function as Forerunner must not be connected with that office, but is to be accounted for in some other way. But are we really required to date the commencement of His priesthood so rigidly from His arrival in heaven? Not certainly by the closing words of the text now under consideration: *having become*, or *becoming, after the order of Melchisedec, a High Priest for ever*. We may think of Jesus as becoming a High Priest in the very act of entering, becoming Priest by doing a priestly act. On this principle of becoming by doing, we must go back further still for the commencement of His priesthood, and include His death among His priestly functions. He dies as Priest, He enters the heavenly sanctuary as Priest, He takes His seat on the throne as Priest. He does not become a High Priest after His entrance. He only becomes a High Priest *for ever* then. His likeness to Melchisedec lies, not in His being a High Priest, but in the eternal endurance of His priestly office, the imperishable value of His priestly work, whereof His session on the throne is the symbol and evidence.

While the idea of Jesus as Forerunner serves to bring into strong relief the superiority of the Christian religion over the Levitical, yet it does not give adequate expression to the worth of the religion of free access. It makes salvation a thing of the future, an object of hope, the point of view from which it is regarded in this whole section. This conception of salvation as future is not the exclusive, though it is the predominant viewpoint of the Epistle. In some places the *summum bonum* appears as a present good. The way into the most holy place is already consecrated, and we may boldly come even now into the very presence of God (x. 19–22). We are come unto Mount Zion (xii. 22). The same truth is implied in the exhortation in chapter iv. 16 to come with boldness unto the throne of grace. The Christian faith not only has a promise of lordship in the world to come, but possesses that world now. Christianity, in fact, is the future world. This paradox, as Pfleiderer has remarked,[1] expresses in the most pregnant form the peculiar point of view of the Epistle, and gives

[1] *Paulinism*, vol. ii. pp. 57, 58.

to its teaching a place intermediate between the Jewish-Christian conception, according to which salvation was purely future, and the Johannine, according to which it is, as an ideally perfect thing, present: eternal life, not merely in prospect, but now enjoyed to the full by believers.

CHAPTER XII

THE ORDER OF MELCHISEDEC

CHAP. vii. 1-10

HAVING unburdened his heart by these words of complaint and charitable hope, our author proceeds to determine the nature of the Melchisedec order of priesthood, and to demonstrate its superior and supreme value. Before considering his method of fixing the type, and showing its ideal worth, it may be helpful to offer here some introductory observations on the writer's aim in introducing into his treatise this remarkable speculation, if I may so designate it, or the function which the latter performs in his argument.

The section concerning the Melchisedec type of priesthood serves, I think, a double purpose. First, and in some respects foremost in importance, there is the apologetic purpose. The writer eagerly lays hold of the Melchisedec priesthood, as a means of showing that Christ might be a priest, though not possessing the legal qualifications for the Levitical priesthood. Here is a priesthood, represented in the oracle of Psalm cx. as of a different order, to which Jesus, as the Messiah, may lay claim. This new type of priesthood, other than

Levitical, further serves well the apologetic aim by its priority in point of time. The new type is older than the Levitical, supposed alone to possess legitimacy; nay, is the oldest type known to sacred history. In comparison with this ancient order, the Levitical priesthood is an upstart. But what if this order were only a rude, imperfect, irregular sort of priesthood, good enough for those old-world times, and graciously accepted by God in absence of a better, but destined to pass away when a regularly established priesthood came in, not worthy to continue side by side therewith, and not fit to be referred to as establishing a new sort of priesthood, claiming to supersede the Levitical? In that case it would be a mere impertinence to refer to that rude, primitive priesthood to justify the antiquation of the divinely instituted, not merely graciously tolerated, priesthood of the sons of Levi. This would be a very natural view of the matter for Jewish minds to take; and the apologist of Christianity could not be sure that it would not suggest itself to the Hebrew Christians whom he sought to establish in the faith. The possibility was present to his mind, and he amply provides for it in his argument by unfolding the full significance of the oracle in Psalm cx., pointing out that the priesthood of Melchisedec is there referred to, not as a rude, irregular, inferior sort of priesthood, the continuance of which, in times of established order, were absurd or impious, but as the highest sort of priesthood, the very ideal of priesthood, a priesthood fit for kings, as opposed to sacerdotal drudges. "'Thou art a priest for ever, after the order of Melchisedec.' Here," says our apologist in effect, "here is

Melchisedec's priesthood erected into the dignity of an eternal priesthood, a priesthood worthy to be established by an oath, a priesthood which would not dishonour a king, nay, a priesthood fit even for Messiah; for you, my readers, believe this to be a Messianic psalm. See how possible it is for Jesus to be not only *a* priest, but *the* Priest *par excellence*, though not of the house of Aaron."

The Melchisedec priesthood a distinct type, the most ancient, and, though ancient, yet not rude, but rather the better, and the best possible: such are the moments in the apologetic argument, which has for its aim to prove that the priesthood of Christ is at once real, and of ideal worth. One cannot help comparing this use of the Melchisedec priesthood in our Epistle with that made by Paul of the *promise* in the Epistle to the Galatians.[1] The promise, argued Paul, was *before* the law, and therefore above it: the law came in afterwards, not to supersede the promise, but to serve a purpose in subordination to it; and when that purpose is fulfilled, the law must pass away, that the promise may come into full effect, and the reign of grace begin.[2] Both lines of thought

---

[1] For some interesting observations on this parallel between Paul and the writer of the Epistle to the Hebrews, *vide* Pfleiderer's *Paulinism*, vol. ii. p. 94. The idea of Christ as a Priest after the order of Melchisedec, he represents as strictly a pendant to the Pauline philosophy of religion. The apologetic value of the Melchisedec priesthood is not destroyed by the fact of his not belonging to the Jewish people. No Jew could say, "What is Melchisedec or his priesthood to us? He was a mere heathen." The priest of Salem was drawn into, and, as it were, naturalised in the history of Israel by Abraham receiving the benefit of his priestly benediction, and recognising him as the priest of the most high God.

[2] Gal. iii. 17.

tend in the same general direction, that of establishing the independence and absolute worth of Christianity over against Judaism. Paul, by his line of thought concerning the promise, establishes the absolute worth of Christianity as against *legalism*; the author of our Epistle, by his line of thought concerning the Melchisedec priesthood, establishes the same truth as against *Leviticalism*, thereby exhibiting himself as in full sympathy with the Pauline system, if not as a direct disciple of the great Gentile apostle.

Besides the apologetic purpose of the Melchisedec section, we may distinguish a dogmatic one. In saying this, I do not mean that the writer himself makes any such formal distinction, or deals with the relative material successively from the apologetic and the dogmatic points of view; but merely that we may regard what he has written on the subject from the latter point of view as well as from the former. Dogmatically considered, the section exhibits the Melchisedec priesthood as a symbol of the eternal validity of Christ's priestly functions. In this connection, the expression "for ever" in the oracle from the Psalter is the point emphasised. In his scheme of thought, our author employs the Aaronic type of priesthood to convey an idea of the nature of Christ's priestly functions, and the Melchisedec type to symbolise the everlasting duration of His priestly office. Hence, in determining the characteristics of the latter type, it is to the attribute of eternity that he gives prominence (ver. 3). But it would be a mistake to suppose that he attaches no importance to any other attribute, or means to suggest that none but the one emphasised enters into the idea of the type. The contrary is evident, from the way in which he deals with the history of Melchisedec, in order to determine the nature of his priesthood. It is further evident from the nature of the case. Eternity is the main fact, but the question inevitably arises, Why is the Melchisedec type of priesthood eternal? The answer must be, Because it is perfect, because it possesses ideal value. Eternity and ethical worth go together. We see this, and that the writer saw it will forthwith appear. The "order of Melchisedec," as he conceived it, did not mean merely an eternal priesthood, but a priesthood of such a nature that its eternity follows of course.

To the above-mentioned uses the Melchisedec priesthood could be put, and for the sake of pointing them out the discourse concerning it was well worth while. It remains to state that that peculiar priesthood was not an adequate medium for conveying all the writer had to say on the subject of Christ's priesthood. It indeed failed to teach precisely the supreme, vital lessons that Christ's sacrifice was Himself, and that self-sacrifice is the highest kind of sacrifice—indeed the only real sacrifice.[1]

It is not surprising that the ancient priest of Salem took so strong a hold of an imaginative, philosophic mind like that of our author. Melchisedec is a striking figure in the early history of mankind. The reference to him in the Hebrew Psalter shows that from of old he had attracted the attention of men of prophetic gifts in Israel, and that in the few facts narrated concerning

[1] *Vide* on this the last chapter of this work; also some observations towards the close of the following chapter.

him such men had been able to discern an ideal significance. That Philo would have something to say about him might have been anticipated. But what he says is not important or stimulating. One searching the writings of the Alexandrian philosopher, in quest of thoughts concerning Melchisedec similar to those in our Epistle, and fitted to support the hypothesis that the writer drew his inspiration from him, is doomed to disappointment. Philo does not, so far as I have observed, quote or refer to the text in Psalm cx., and there is nothing in all his writings to show that he followed the Psalmist in ascribing to Melchisedec an ideal significance. What Bleek says is strictly true, that in Philo the significance of Melchisedec is always treated of in an incidental manner.[1] On the whole, he speaks of the priest of Salem with respect, though one phrase might almost suggest that he conceived of his priesthood as of the rude character above indicated. I refer to that passage in which he describes it as a "self-learned, self-taught priesthood."[2] There is certainly nothing in his writings to justify the representation that on the subject

---

[1] *Hebräerbrief*, ii. p. 323, note.
[2] ὁ τὴν αὐτομαθῆ καὶ αὐτοδίδακτον λαχὼν ἱερωσύνην, in the tract *De Congr. Erud. Gr.* cap. xviii. In another place Philo speaks of God having made Melchisedec a priest by an act of grace, without regard to any meritorious work of his: ἱερέα ἑαυτοῦ πεποίηκεν ὁ Θεὸς, οὐδὲν ἔργον αὐτοῦ προδιατυπώσας (*Leg. Allegor.* iii. 25). In the same place Melchisedec is compared to reason, the point of the comparison being, that reason is able to discourse worthily of God, the highest of all themes, and Melchisedec was the priest of the most high God: ἱερεὺς γάρ ἐστι λόγος (not ὁ λόγος), κλῆρον ἔχων τὸν ὄντα, καὶ ὑψηλῶς περὶ αὐτοῦ λογιζόμενος. "For Reason is a priest, having Him who is for his inheritance, and reasoning loftily concerning Him."

of Melchisedec the writer of our Epistle borrowed from him. We can fairly claim for our author originality, so far, at least, as Philo is concerned. He got his inspiration, not from the Jewish philosopher, but from the Hebrew prophet who wrote Psalm cx. And what he got from the poet's brief pregnant word was but an impulse, a starting-point, a slight hint, which only a mind of an equally high order could appreciate, and which for generations of Bible-readers had remained dead, unproductive, almost unobserved. All honour to the man through whose philosophic genius, illuminated by the Spirit of Christ, the grain of precious wheat, after abiding alone for ages, at length attained to abundant fruitfulness, in the form of a theory concerning the Melchisedec priesthood of Jesus Christ, preserved for our instruction in the seventh chapter of this Epistle, whose contents we now proceed to consider![1]

The first part of the chapter (vers. 1–10) has for its object *to determine the type*, or to fix the meaning of the expression, "after the order of Melchisedec." In the opening paragraph (vers. 1–3), the writer condenses into one closely packed sentence every particular of typical significance in reference to the mysterious personage whose

---

[1] Dr. Edwards regards the passage relating to Melchisedec as an allegory borrowed from Philo, which "cannot be intended by the apostle to have direct inferential force." I can hardly think that, on reflection, this excellent commentator, who has made a real contribution to the elucidation of the Epistle, would abide by this view. It appears to me fatal to the whole doctrine of Christ's priesthood set forth in the Epistle. If Christ's priesthood is not proved at this point, it is not proved at all. The writer certainly thinks he is proving it. The whole stress of his argument lies on the apologetic value of the Melchisedec priesthood.

priesthood is represented in Psalm cx. as the model of Messiah's. Of the things here said, some are plain enough, being simply a repetition of the historical facts as stated in the Book of Genesis; others are indeed hard to be understood, and have given rise to great variety of interpretation. Yet it is possible to exaggerate the difficulty of these enigmatical statements, and so to make the whole discourse about Melchisedec a cloud of mist, obscuring the great truth of Christ's priestly office, rather than a light shining in a dark place, through which a subject ill understood becomes clearer to the mental eye. The meaning of this remarkable passage can be ascertained, in proof whereof it is enough to adduce the fact that the leading expositors of ancient and modern times are in the main agreed as to the sense.

Let us note first the structure of this long sentence. The main proposition, stripped of all adjuncts (and these are so numerous that the fact might escape notice), is, "For this Melchisedec abideth a priest for ever, or continually." Hence the word γάρ (for), with which the chapter begins. At the close of chapter vi. it is said of Jesus that He entered heaven, to be there a High Priest for ever, after the order of Melchisedec; the idea implied being, that eternal endurance is an essential characteristic of the Melchisedec priesthood. Here this thought is justified by the assertion that the typical Melchisedec had a priesthood, whose nature it is to abide for ever.

Of the participial or relative clauses lying between the beginning and the end of the sentence, the first five, down to the words ἐμέρισεν Ἀβραάμ (ver. 2, clause 1), recapitulate the historical facts concerning Melchisedec; the remaining eight are a comment on the history, intended mainly to justify the statement that Melchisedec abideth a priest continually, and incidentally to suggest other characteristics of the priesthood that abideth. This analysis yields three categories under which the contents may be ranged: first, the *facts*; second, the *commentary*; third, the main proposition or *doctrine*.

1. The facts are simple, and need little explanatory comment. Melchisedec is called "king of *Salem*," which most commentators regard as the name of a *place* to be identified with Jerusalem. He is next called "priest of the most high God," the title being exactly reproduced from the Septuagint. The third fact referred to is the meeting between Melchisedec and Abraham, on the return of the latter from his victorious battle with the kings. That the writer has his eye on the page of the Septuagint appears from the use of the Hellenistic word κοπή, employed by the Seventy to express the idea of defeat or slaughter.[1] The fourth fact mentioned is that Melchisedec blessed Abraham. The words of blessing are not quoted, the aim being simply to emphasise the fact that Abraham was blessed by Melchisedec. Last in the list of facts comes the gift of a tenth of the spoil to Melchisedec by Abraham, an act of worship on the patriarch's part, whereby he recognised God as the universal proprietor and Melchisedec as His priestly vice-regent.

2. For the better understanding of the writer's *commentary* on these facts, we must recall to mind the

[1] Gen. xiv. 17.

practical design of this whole excursus concerning Melchisedec. It is to determine the notes of the ideal perfect priesthood of the Christ, as typified by the priest of Salem. For this purpose he finds it necessary to attach importance, not merely to what is said of Melchisedec in the history, but to what is *not* said. He gets at the ideal by laying stress on the *silences* as well as on the *utterances* of the narrative in Genesis. To Western minds the method of reasoning may appear strange, but there can be no doubt of the fact that the writer does so reason, and the fact must be frankly recognised if we are to get at his real thought. He finds, *e.g.*, that no mention is made of the parentage or genealogy of Melchisedec, and he regards that as significant. And on reflection one sees that he has some reason for doing so, and that his method of fixing the notes of the Melchisedec order is not so arbitrary or fanciful as at the first blush we are apt to imagine. This inspired commentator is by no means a blind disciple of the Rabbis in his method of exegesis. The lack of a genealogy in the case of Melchisedec is undoubtedly a significant circumstance, at once suggesting the thought that here we have a priesthood of a different sort from that of the tribe of Levi. For in connection with the Levitical priesthood, parentage, genealogy, was of fundamental importance. To be a priest in Israel it was necessary to belong to the tribe of Levi, and no man might exercise sacerdotal functions who could not trace his lineage to the house of Aaron. If therefore, so far as the history is concerned, Melchisedec was fatherless, motherless, without genealogy, it must signify, for the typical interpretation, that his was a sort of priesthood that had no connection with parentage or descent, depending on personal, not on technical, external qualifications.[1]

That this is the true explanation of those mysterious epithets, ἀπάτωρ, ἀμήτωρ, ἀγενεαλόγητος, there is no room for doubt. Equally certain is it that the two following phrases, "having neither beginning of days, nor end of life," are to be explained on a similar principle. Here also significance is attached to the silences of history. The narrative in Genesis makes no allusion to the birth or the death of Melchisedec; so far as the record is concerned, he is without beginning of days and end of life. He makes a mysterious, momentary appearance out of eternity on the stage of time, then disappears for ever from view, to be mentioned only once again in Old Testament Scripture in a psalm which represents his priesthood as the ideal priesthood, and, on the principle that whatever is ideal is Messianic, as the type of Messiah's priesthood. Our author assumes that, in fixing on the Melchisedec priesthood as the ideal, the Psalmist laid stress on the absence of all reference to birth or

[1] In Philo, Sarah is called ἀμήτωρ because the name of her mother is not mentioned. But, as Bleek has pointed out, by the epithet Philo does not mean merely that Sarah was motherless so far as the record is concerned, but that she had no mother. There can be no doubt, however, that the method of reasoning from silences was practised by Philo. Instances are given in Siegfried's *Philo von Alexandria*, p. 179. That the writer of our Epistle uses the method is admitted by so cautious commentators as Vaughan and Westcott. "For all that the narrative in Genesis tells of him, Melchisedec might have been all these."—Vaughan. "The silence of Scripture, the characteristic form, that is, in which the narrative is presented, is treated as having prophetic force."—Westcott, who then proceeds to mention Philo's use of the same method.

death in the historical account, and so obtained eternal duration as one of the marks, as the outstanding mark, of the kind or order. He, for his own part, sees no other way whereby the attribute of eternity can be shown to be a mark of the Melchisedec order; and that it is a mark is a point settled for him by the fact that it is so represented in the prophetic oracle.

The last clause in the commentary need not now cause us much trouble. "Made like unto the Son of God." The words simply put in different form the thought contained in the previous clause. The intention is to suggest a parallel between Melchisedec and the Son of God in their respective relations to time. The Son of God as Son of man, like Melchisedec, had both a birth and a death; yet as Son of God He had neither beginning of days nor end of life. And Melchisedec is likened unto Him in this, that his life, so far as the record is concerned, is "shrouded in the mystery of eternity."[1]

Having thus explained the more difficult part of the commentary, let me revert now to the easier portion, hitherto overlooked. "Being first by interpretation (of the name Melchisedec) king of righteousness, and then also king of Salem, which is king of peace." A mystic significance is assigned to the priest's name, and to the name of the city over which he ruled. It is assumed that these names, mystically interpreted, are to be taken into

[1] For a strenuous, almost fierce attack on this method of interpreting the passage Heb. vii. 1-3, vide *The Authorship of the Epistle to the Hebrews*, by the Rev. A. Welch, 1898. Mr. Welch holds that the Melchisedec of Genesis and Ps. cx. *is* Christ, *i.e.* that Christ *is* Melchisedec, not merely *after the order of Melchisedec*.

account in determining the marks of the "order of Melchisedec." No other reason can be given why the writer thinks it necessary to explain their meaning. He did not need to tell his Hebrew readers the literal meaning of the words *Melchi, Zedec, Salem.* He interprets them because he wishes to suggest ideas entering into the "order" of which these words are the symbols, the ideas of *royalty, righteousness,* and a royal priesthood resulting in *peace,* or exercised in a region of peace remote from the passion, temptation, and strife of this world. And this is just what was to be expected. For it is not enough to know that the new (yet most ancient) order of priesthood is eternal. We want, further, to know the intrinsic nature of a priesthood to which it belongs to be eternal. That the new order is eternal is a fact—if you please, it is the main fact; but the fact has its *rationale,* and our demand is to know the *rationale.* Our author recognises the demand as reasonable, and does his utmost to meet it; and we accept these interpretations of names as a welcome contribution to the solution of the problem. The above-mentioned attributes, royalty, righteousness, etc., are therefore by no means to be regarded as "only accessories," which "might conceivably be absent without derogating from His Melchisedec priesthood."[1] They are no more accessory than is perfection accessory to the Christian religion, which throughout the Epistle is declared to be eternal. Christianity is the final, perennial religion, because it is the perfect religion, the religion which for the first time established a real, unrestricted fellowship between man

[1] So Davidson.

and God. In like manner the priesthood after the order of Melchisedec is eternal, because in it for the first time the ideal of priesthood is realised, and all the conditions of an absolutely efficient exercise of priestly functions are fully satisfied.

Not one merely, but five notes are specified as belonging to the Melchisedec type of priesthood. Taking them in the order in which they are referred to in the text, it is, first, a *royal* priesthood (*king* of righteousness); second, a *righteous* priesthood (king of *righteousness*); third, a priesthood promotive of *peace*, or exercised in the country of peace (king of *peace*); fourth, it is a *personal*, not an inherited dignity (without father, without mother); fifth, it is an *eternal* priesthood (without beginning of days or end of life). The first four are related to the last as cause to effect. Because the priesthood after the order of Melchisedec possesses these characteristics, it is eternal.

3. A word now on the main affirmation, that Melchisedec "abideth a priest continually." The variation in expression ($εἰς\ τὸ\ διηνεκές$ instead of $εἰς\ τὸν\ αἰῶνα$, vi. 20) is probably made out of regard to style, rather than to convey a different shade of meaning. The point to be noted is, that it is affirmed of the historical Melchisedec that he is a priest for ever. In what sense is this true? The statement is to be understood in the same way as all the others of similar startling character. Melchisedec had neither predecessor nor successor in office. We know of one priest of Salem, and but one. He lives in Scripture and in our imagination the priest of the city of peace. If he had had in the history, as

doubtless he had in fact, a successor in office, we should have said of him that he *was* the priest of Salem in the days of Abraham. As the case stands, he *is* the priest of Salem. He is known and lives in sacred history by that name, and in that respect, as well as in others, is an apt type of the one, true, eternal Priest of humanity. More than this may be said. Not only does Melchisedec abide in name the priest of Salem, but his priestly acts have an abiding value. His blessing on Abraham had a lasting effect. Levi was blessed (as well as tithed) in Abraham; all the generations of Israel got the benefit of that blessing. It is a great thing for a people to have a Melchisedec at the fountain-head of its history, a man fitted by genuine holiness and righteousness to transact on behalf of his fellow-men with God. The prayer of a righteous man availeth much, and the life of a saintly man availeth much. Such prayers and such lives are the bread and wine of life to men, from generation to generation.

Such, then, is the "order of Melchisedec," and such are the notes of that august order. The question might now be raised, Does the order thus determined absolutely coincide with the ideal order? in other words, Is the order of Melchisedec, possessing the above-mentioned characteristics, the highest order of priesthood conceivable? It is a question in speculative or philosophical theology. To answer it, it would be necessary to form a conception of an ideally perfect priesthood, and then to ascertain how far the marks of the Melchisedec order covered the ground. Thus we might say, The ideal priest must be really, not merely ritually, holy; he must not be a mere sacerdotal drudge, offering daily *ex officio* the statutory tale of sacrifices, but one whose whole priestly ministry is a course of gracious condescension—a royal priest, whose sacrifice is the outcome and highest manifestation of free, sovereign love—is, in fact, the sacrifice of himself; he must be one who by his personal worth and official acts is able to establish a reign of righteousness, peace, and perfect fellowship between man and God; finally, he must be one who never dies, ever lives, hath a priesthood that does not pass from him to another, as a guarantee for the maintenance of peace and fellowship. If this be the ideal, then the Melchisedec order comes at least near to its realisation, though failing apparently at one vital point—self-sacrifice; its notes all point that way, though they are so rapidly indicated that their full import cannot be certainly determined, but can only be guessed at. The words *king, righteousness, peace* are very suggestive, but the writer has not attempted to appreciate their precise value in relation to the order, preferring to leave them vague, provocative of thought, rather than satisfying the intellectual craving for knowledge, as is the way of Scripture writers in general.[1]

While not attempting the philosophical task of showing that the order of Melchisedec satisfied the requirements of the ideal, our author takes pains to show that that order is, at least, vastly superior to the order of Levi.

[1] Mr. Rendall suggests that the kingly aspect of Christ's Melchisedec priesthood, while evidently regarded by the writer as of essential importance, is not made prominent, from prudential reasons. "The title in the mouth of Hebrews was readily susceptible of a treasonable construction at the time of the national Jewish rebellion."

This is the burden of what follows of chapter vii. (vers. 4–28). No less than five arguments are adduced in support of the thesis: one based on the personal dignity of Melchisedec, three on the oracle in Psalm cx., and the fifth based on the contrast between *many* and *one*: many priests under the order of Levi, one priest under the order of Melchisedec. The first, as a pendant to the statement concerning the nature of the order, may be considered here; the rest will form the subject of the next chapter.

"How great was this man, Melchisedec! He was greater even than Abraham, the great, august patriarch of our race; therefore greater than his descendants, including the tribe of Levi." Such is the drift of vers. 4–10.

Two facts are adduced as showing that Melchisedec was greater than Abraham. He received tithes from the patriarch, and he gave him his blessing. To bring out the significance of the former fact, a comparison is made between the tithe-taking of Melchisedec and the similar privilege of the Levitical priesthood (vers. 5, 6). "It is true, indeed, that those of the sons of Levi who receive the office of the priesthood have a commandment, are entitled by statute, under the Mosaic law, to tithe the people, though they be their brethren descended from the same ancestor. But Melchisedec, who hath no part in their genealogy (and therefore no legal right), nevertheless tithed [1] Abraham." Such is the drift of these

---

[1] Literally "hath tithed" (δεδεκάτωκεν). The perfect is what Vaughan calls a *Scripture* perfect, the fact having a permanent place in the written record. As Vaughan puts it: "The γέγραπται (so to say) *quickens the dead*, and gives to the *præterite* of the history the permanence of a perfect." There are many such perfects in the

verses, and the point specially emphasised is, that the right of the Levitical priest is only a legal right. He is not intrinsically superior to his fellow-Israelites; they are all his brethren. Only a positive statute gives him the right of tithing his brethren as the means of his support, so that the fact of his receiving tithes is no evidence of personal superiority. But in Melchisedec's case it is different. He had no legal right. There was no law entitling him to receive, or compelling Abraham to give, tithes. The gift on the patriarch's part was entirely spontaneous. And just because it was so, it was, in the view of our author, unmistakable evidence of Melchisedec's personal greatness. He was so great a man in every sense, that the high-souled patriarch, who scorned to play the part of sycophant towards the king of Sodom, of his own motion, no law or custom compelling, out of pure reverence for worth, offered to the priest of Salem a tenth of the spoil taken in battle. Surely the priesthood of this man, who inspires reverence in the noblest, is of a very high order, superior to that based on a statute, a mere hereditary trade or profession.

In giving tithes to Melchisedec, then, Abraham voluntarily acknowledged his superiority. And Melchisedec in turn accepted the position accorded to him by bestowing on the donor his blessing: "And blessed him who had the promises. And without all contradiction, the less is blessed by the better" (vers. 6, 7). The fact is held to be conclusive evidence as to the relative position of the

Epistle, *e.g.* εὐλόγηκεν in this same verse and κεχρημάτισται in chapter viii. 5. For a long list of perfects in the Epistle, *vide* Westcott on vii. 6. These perfects are in effect presents.

parties, in accordance with the axiom that it belongs to the superior person to bless. The axiom is certainly true, though it is subject to limitations, holding chiefly with reference to *solemn* benedictions, and with regard even to these only when the parties understand and accept their proper relative positions. The inferior in age, status, worth, influence may assume the position of blessing-giver if he be conceited, forward, impudent. But in all cases it is true that it belongs to the better to bless the less. It is the place of the father to bless his son, of age to bless youth, as when Jacob blessed his son Joseph and his two grandsons, or Simeon blessed Mary the mother of Jesus. It is no exception to the rule that Jacob blesses Pharaoh; for such is the dignity of age, that the humblest peasant whose head is hoary, and whose feet have walked through life in the paths of righteousness, may with perfect propriety give his blessing to a king.

To enhance the greatness of Melchisedec as the bestower of blessing, it is carefully noted that the receiver of blessing was he who had the promises. It was no small matter to bless the man who had the promises! How great must he have been, who, without presumption, might give his blessing to the man whom the Maker of heaven and earth had called to be the father of a great nation, and to be a fountain of blessing for all the nations!

But it is Melchisedec's superiority over the Levitical priests that our author is really concerned to establish. For this purpose he states or suggests no less than four arguments. First, greater than the ancestor, therefore a *fortiori* greater than all or any of his descendants. This argument is suggested by the epithet "patriarch" (ὁ πατριάρχης) attached to the name of Abraham in ver. 4, and placed at the end of the sentence for emphasis. Second, greater than the sons of Levi, even in the respect in which they were superior to their brethren of the other tribes; they receiving tithes in virtue of a legal right, he receiving tithes in virtue of a higher moral right freely and cordially acknowledged by the giver. Third, greater in this, that in receiving tithes from Abraham, he virtually received tithes from his descendants, including the tribe of Levi (vers. 9, 10). Fourth, he received tithes as one who continues to live, the Levitical priests receive tithes as men that die (ver. 8).

The third argument is curious. The reasoning may appear to us more subtle and ingenious than convincing; and the writer himself seems to hint that it must be taken *cum grano* by introducing it with an apologetic phrase: "And *so to say* (καὶ ὡς ἔπος εἰπεῖν) through Abraham Levi also, the receiver of tithes, was tithed; for he was yet in the loins of his father, when Melchisedec met him." Yet the statement will bear examination. It simply proclaims in a concrete form the principle that Abraham, in all the leading transactions of his life, was a representative man. To many this idea of solidarity appears a mere theological fiction. But it is not so, indeed: it is a great law whose operation is discernible in the whole course of human history. There are individuals in whose personal life the history of whole races is, as it were, summed up. Abraham was one of these. God's call to him was a call to Israel. God's blessing to him was a blessing to the human family. In like manner we may say that Melchisedec's blessing on Abraham was a blessing on all his descendants, and that Abraham's offering of tithes was an act of homage from the people of Israel to the priest of Salem. Therefore, in addressing Hebrews, who recognised the federal principle, and gloried in some of its applications, *e.g.* in being the people to whom belonged the covenants and the promises and the fathers, the writer of our Epistle was justified in pressing this thought into the service of his argument, and so inviting his readers to open their minds to the truth that, while within the race there were men bearing the title of priest, there was a higher priesthood, with reference to which these priests were simple laymen, paying tithes, doing homage thereto, receiving blessing therefrom, just like ordinary men.

The fourth argument seems the least cogent of all. Even the fact-basis of it may appear questionable. Melchisedec is described as a person testified to as living. Where is the testimony borne? Not in Psalm cx., for the statement there is made concerning Messiah, not concerning the historical Melchisedec. If it be supposed that the testimony is implicitly contained in the expression, "the order of Melchisedec," that order having eternity for one of its attributes, we are still thrown back on the narrative in Genesis as the basis of that attribute, and therefore as the original source of the witness. But the witness of the history is not positive, but negative. The story does not say that Melchisedec continued to live; it simply omits to say that he died. We have here therefore another inference from the *silence* of Scripture. The meaning is: though the historical Melchisedec doubtless died, the Melchisedec of the sacred narrative does nothing but live. Stress is laid on the omission of all reference to the death of the priest of Salem to hint that the receiving of tithes from Abraham has significance for all time. The type is regarded as continuing to receive tithes from Abraham's descendants, because the antitype is entitled to receive tribute from all men of all generations. Under the Levitical system dying men received tithes, and when they died their claim died with them or was transmitted to their successors. The true Priest never dies, and therefore is ever able to save, and therefore ever also entitled to receive a Saviour's homage, the tithes of grateful love and faithful service.

I must not close this chapter without remarking on one feature in the "order of Melchisedec" which is conspicuous by its absence—its universalism. Melchisedec, though priest of the most high God, did not belong to the Jewish race. The order of priesthood named after him ought, therefore, to exist for the benefit not of Jews only, but of humanity. The Priest after that order ought to be the great High Priest of mankind. Here, as throughout the Epistle, the writer is silent as to the universal reference, but doubtless he has it in his mind. It is the latent unexpressed postulate of his whole system of thought.

CHAPTER XIII

THE PRIEST AFTER THE ORDER OF MELCHISEDEC

Chap. vii. 11-28

THE didactic significance of this section is, that in Jesus Christ, as the Priest after the order or type of Melchisedec, the ideal of priesthood is realised. The truth is established by the method of comparison. That Jesus is the best possible Priest is proved by showing that He is better than the familiar Levitical priest. The emphasis lies now on the inferior, unsatisfactory nature of the Levitical priesthood, now on the supreme, absolute worth of the Messianic Priest.

Having demonstrated the superiority of the Melchisedec priesthood over the Levitical, by setting forth the personal dignity of the priest of Salem as attested by the history, the writer proceeds next to make use of the text from the 110th Psalm for the same purpose. From this famous prophetic oracle he draws no less than three arguments in support of his position. The first infers the inferiority of the Levitical priesthood from the mere fact of another priesthood being promised (vers. 11–14); the second infers its transient nature from the eternal duration ascribed to the new order (vers. 15–19); the third emphasises the fact that the new order of priesthood, in contrast to the old, is introduced with an oath, implying the transcendent importance of the one as compared with the other (vers. 20–22).

The first of these arguments, stripped of all adjuncts, is expressed in these terms: "*If then perfection were by the Levitical priesthood, what further need was there that a different priest should arise after the order of Melchisedec?*" The remaining matter of vers. 11–14 is of the nature of explanatory comment. On two points the writer deemed it necessary to offer explanations: on the term *perfection* (τελείωσις); and on the expression, *the order of Melchisedec*, as implying the origination of a new, different (ἕτερον) type of priesthood, not to be called after the order of Aaron (οὐ κατὰ τὴν τάξιν Ἀαρὼν λέγεσθαι). The parenthetical clause, "for under (rather, upon) it the people received the law" (ver. 11), is his comment on the word τελείωσις. The purpose is to justify the demand of perfection from a priesthood laying claim to finality. It is assumed that a priesthood worthy of and destined to perpetuity must make men "perfect," in the sense of bringing them really near to God, establishing between them and God a true, unimpeded fellowship by the removal of sin. It is further assumed that if perfection in this sense was possible at all under the Mosaic law, it was so in virtue of the Levitical priesthood, seeing that thereon, undeniably, as a foundation, the people was legally constituted as a people in covenant with God. On both grounds, because it is the function of all priesthoods to perfect the worshipper as to conscience, and because of the central position occupied by the Levitical priesthood in the Mosaic law, it is held to be reasonable to demand of that priesthood, conceived of as laying claim to finality and refusing to be superseded, nothing less than "perfection." To the advocates of Levitical finality is offered the alternative: either perfection or supersession. To the plea, "Our time-honoured priesthood may be permanently useful in its own place, as part of a greater whole, though it come short of what you call perfection, and aspire not to a virtue which can rightfully be ascribed only to the whole legal system," the stern reply is, "No; it must be all or nothing." And from the oracle in the Psalter it is inferred that it is not capable of being all. By that oracle it is, as matter of fact, superseded; therefore it cannot have been able to provide "perfection." Such is the inexorable logic of the Christian apologist.

Here again we have occasion to note the affinity between our author and the Apostle Paul. Paul said, The law must be everything in salvation, or nothing. To the Judaistic compromise, law *and* grace, he replied by an "either—or." Either the law *or* grace, choose your alternative. The same "either—or" reappears here in an altered form. Either perfection must come by the Levitical priesthood, the soul or kernel of the law, or that priesthood must pass away as unprofitable, and give place to a different order of priesthood, which can perform the task for which it has been found incompetent.

We come now to the writer's comment on the expression, "the order of Melchisedec." He regards it as involving a *legal revolution*. It means the origination of a different type of priesthood, to be called after Melchisedec, not after Aaron; and it involves therefore change in the law in at least one point: a priest for the Israel of God who does not belong to the Levitical tribe—a mark of the Messianic priest inferable from prophecy, and verified as a matter of fact in the history of Jesus (vers. 13, 14); this one apparently minute change implying many more. But why insist on the revolutionary effect of the introduction of the new order of priesthood? Would it not have been more prudent in the apologist of Christianity to have concealed or minimised the legal change that was to accompany the advent of the Messianic priest? Such timid, time-serving apologetic did not suit the temper of New Testament writers. Jesus boldly claimed to have brought to the world "new wine," and all New Testament writers accentuate the innovating effect of Christianity, the writer of our Epistle not least. He has the courage to look the revolutionary character of the new religion straight in the face. And his courage is true wisdom. For, in the first place, there is the undeniable fact to be reckoned with, that Jesus Christ sprang out of Judah, "as to which tribe Moses spake nothing about priests." The only way to deal with such a fact is to find a broad principle that covers and justifies it: such as, that the priesthood is the foundation of the legal system, so that a change in the priesthood prepares us to expect manifold change in the law. Then the bold proclamation of this principle, while accounting for the evident fact, at the same time serves admirably the main purpose of the argument, which is to show the radical defectiveness of the Levitical priesthood. Men think twice before they make any change in an existing state of things which involves a political revolution. They bear with innumerable abuses loudly calling for reform, because they fear that if one stone of the building (not to speak of the foundation) be removed, the whole edifice may come tumbling down. What then may be inferred from the fact, that God, by the mouth of a prophet, declared His intention to inaugurate a new priesthood that should supersede the old, and by consequence abrogate the whole legal system whereof it was the foundation? Surely this, that in His view, and in very truth, the Levitical priesthood was hopelessly insufficient, incapable of fulfilling the ends for which a priesthood exists, fit only to foreshadow the true priesthood by which perfection might come, and by its defectiveness to prepare men for thankfully embracing the "better hope," no matter with how much innovation on existing usage it might be ushered in.

It is probable that the "evident fact," that our Lord did not belong to the tribe of Levi, appeared to Hebrew Christians an insuperable objection to His claim to be a priest.[1] We cannot therefore but admire the tact with which our author virtually turns it into an argument in support of that claim. It is not difficult to construct such an argument out of his rapid hints. It is to this effect. In the 110th Psalm, the rise of a new order of priesthood is predicted. This change is revolutionary: it involves the upsetting of the whole Mosaic

[1] That our Lord's connection with the tribe of Judah is spoken of as "evident," implies acquaintance on the part both of writer and first readers with a current tradition to that effect. The writer knew that Jesus was popularly called "The Son of David," and he may even have seen a genealogy justifying the title.

law, whereof the Levitical priesthood was the foundation. Any amount of innovation may be looked for under the new order of priesthood. We need not be surprised if we find that the Messianic Priest when He comes does not belong to the tribe of Levi: on the contrary, we ought to regard that circumstance as a matter of course, for a descendant of Aaron would not be a suitable person to inaugurate an entirely new order of priesthood.

This is one use to which our Lord's descent from Judah might be put, that, namely, of showing that in so far as He did not trace His descent to Levi His history corresponded to what the oracle in the Psalter would lead one to expect. There is another service which it could be made to render, and which possibly it did render to some of the Hebrew Christians as they reflected thereon. It might help to cure inordinate fondness for the religious ordinances of the old dispensation by suggesting a process of reasoning backwards thus: Jesus is the Christ, we all believe that; but Jesus is descended from David, not from Aaron. Yet is He a priest, according to the oracle. But a priest not connected with the tribe of Levi—what an innovation, what a revolutionary transgression of the law that is! It is no light thing to set aside, virtually to disannul, a law given thousands of years ago to our fathers. If such a momentous step was necessary, what an unsatisfactory affair must the Levitical system of priests and sacrifices, after all, have been! Why then cling to such poor, beggarly elements when that which is perfect is come?

The second argument drawn from Psalm cx. to prove the inferiority of the Levitical priesthood is stated in these terms: *And it is yet more abundantly evident, if, according to the similitude of Melchisedec, there ariseth a different priest, who hath become priest, not according to the law of a fleshly commandment, but according to the power of an indissoluble life. For He is witnessed to that " Thou art a priest* FOR EVER, *after the order of Melchisedec."*

The thing that is said to be evident here is, not that which is declared to be evident in ver. 14, but the general thesis which the writer is engaged in establishing, namely, the unsatisfactory character of the Levitical priesthood, making change of the priesthood, and consequently of the whole law, necessary. The use of a different word (κατάδηλον [1] instead of πρόδηλον) puts us on our guard against supposing that the reference is still to the fact that our Lord sprang out of Judah: it possibly points to a different kind of evidence, that which comes through logical inference, as distinct from that supplied by facts. The writer means to say, that the argument he now proceeds to state makes it even more evident than the one previously advanced, that by the Levitical priesthood perfection could not and never was intended to come.[2] And the justice of the affirmation becomes apparent when we consider the drift of this new argument. The emphasis lies on the expression *for ever* (εἰς τὸν αἰῶνα).

[1] The use of this word is all the more noticeable that it is found here only in the New Testament or the Septuagint. It means literally "downright evident" (Vaughan).

[2] Many commentators think that what is declared evident in ver. 14 is the change in the law. But it is not the mere fact of change, but the *need* for it, created by the defect of the Levitical priesthood, that the writer has in view. So Bengel: "*Patet*, scilicet illud quod versu 11 asseritur (*nullam consummationem factam esse per sacerdotium leviticum*").

The writer views the phrase as at once signalising the peculiar excellence of the new order, and dooming to decay and death the old order for its weakness and unprofitableness. From the mere fact that a new order is instituted he has already inferred that the old order was inadequate; and now from the *eternal* character of the new order he infers with, if possible, even more cogency the transient nature of the old.

The terms in which, under this new point of view, the two priesthoods are contrasted are very forcible. They transcend the limits of the argument, and suggest thoughts which an expositor must refrain from expatiating on, lest the connected chain of reasoning be lost sight of. There is a double contrast hinted at in ver. 16: first, one between *law* and *power*; and next, one between a *fleshly* commandment and an *endless* life. The former distinguishes the Levitical priesthood, as resting on positive law, from the Messianic, as resting on spiritual fitness and energy. The Levitical priest was law-made, without reference to spiritual qualifications; the Messianic Priest becomes a priest because He hath inherent spiritual fitness for, and therefore inherent right to, the office. The latter contrast distinguishes the Levitical priest as liable to death from the Messianic Priest as one over whom death has no power. For the epithet fleshly ($\sigma\alpha\rho\kappa\acute{\iota}\nu\eta\varsigma$),[1] applied to the commandments regulating appointments to the

---

[1] This is the true reading, not $\sigma\alpha\rho\kappa\iota\kappa\hat{\eta}\varsigma$ as in T.R. Adjectives in $\nu o\varsigma$ denote the material of which anything is made. Thus we have, in 2 Cor. iii. 3, οὐκ ἐν πλαξὶν λιθίναις ἀλλ' ἐν πλαξὶν καρδίαις σαρκίναις: "not on stone tablets, but on tablets consisting in fleshen hearts." The adjective σαρκικός expresses a moral idea, for which the word "carnal" should be reserved.

priestly office, points to the fact that all the conditions had reference to the corruptible body. A man's fitness for office was determined by physical considerations. He must be the son of this or that father, without blemish in his body, and so forth. It was altogether an affair of physical descent and fleshly qualities. And just on that account it was transient, not merely in the individual, but in the kind. A priestly order whose existence was based on the properties of corruptible flesh must share the fate of its unstable foundation. Of it, as of the flesh with which it is so closely associated, it was written, " Dust thou art, and to dust shalt thou return." All flesh is grass, and a priesthood based on fleshly requirements must of necessity fall before the scythe of Time, while the priesthood of spirit and righteousness, like the word of God, and all things Divine, liveth and abideth for ever.

Just such a thought is it that our author finds in the 110th Psalm. The oracle uttered there sounds to his ear as an echo of the voice from the wilderness. He hears in it the death-knell of the priesthood of Levi and of the whole law with which it was connected, and at the same time the Divine fiat which calls into being a new dispensation. Hence the sentences which follow (vers. 18, 19), wherein the writer states what he takes to be the practical effect of the solemn announcement in the Psalm. The rendering of these verses in the Authorised Version totally misses the sense; it is perhaps the greatest and most serious of numerous failures occurring in the Epistle. What is really said is this: " There takes place (through the oracle in the Psalm), on the one hand ($\mu\acute{\epsilon}\nu$), a disannulling of the commandment going before, on account of its weakness and unprofitableness (for the law perfected nothing); and (there takes place through the same oracle), on the other hand (δέ), the introduction thereupon of a better hope, through which we draw nigh to God." In short, the text from the Psalm is to our author a bell, which with solemn tones rings out the old order of things, and at the same moment rings in the new; rings out the priesthood of Levi and the Levitical sacrifices, and rings in the Christ that is to be and that sublime sacrifice of Himself which once offered shall possess eternal worth and undying virtue. As he listens with devout attention to the solemn peal, he feels as if it said to him: "The priesthood of physical descent is weak and unprofitable. It must pass away, so must the whole ritual law; for it is all alike weak and useless; it makes nothing perfect, it fails of its professed end throughout. But be of good cheer; Christ is coming; another and a very different Priest shall arise, one who is really and perfectly holy, and of regal dignity, and whose priesthood rests on personal merit, not on fleshly descent. He will make all things perfect. What the old law could not do, because of its weakness, He will do effectually. Place your hope in Him; for He will meet all your need, sanctify you, bring you nigh and keep you nigh to God."

"A BETTER HOPE, THROUGH WHICH WE DRAW NIGH UNTO GOD." If one were to attempt by typography to indicate the great, salient thoughts of this Epistle, these words would certainly have to be printed in capitals. They contain the dogmatic centre of the Epistle, setting forth Christianity as the religion of the better hope by comparison with the earlier religion; absolutely as the religion of good hope, because the religion through which men for the first time enter into intimate fellowship with God. This, as has been indicated in the introductory chapter, is the distinctive conception of the Christian religion, or of the good which came by Jesus Christ, contained in our Epistle. In the Synoptical Gospels the *summum bonum* appears as the kingdom of God; in the Fourth Gospel, as eternal life; in Paul's Epistles, as the righteousness of God; in the Epistle to the Hebrews, as free access to, unrestricted fellowship with, God. The thing is one, though the names and the view-points are diverse: and under any of the four aspects Christianity is well entitled to be called the religion of good hope, the religion that absolutely satisfies the highest hopes and aspirations of mankind. Corresponding to the four phases of the good He brings are the functions of the Saviour. He introduces into the kingdom of God as the Son of God and Son of man; He communicates eternal life as the Logos; He makes men partakers of the Divine righteousness as their federal Head; He brings them nigh to God as their great High Priest, the aspect under which He is appropriately presented in this Epistle.[1]

[1] One is so accustomed to find in commentaries blunt, commonplace generalities where one expects, or at least desires, to find distinct recognition of great broad truths, that it has given me sincere pleasure to discover in Vaughan a sharp precise statement of the radical contrast between Leviticalism and Christianity. "The *uselessness* (*unhelpfulness*) of the priesthood was proved by its inability to aid men in that ἐγγίζειν τῷ θεῷ which is their one want." "In the Old Testament we have the *limitation* and *prohibition* of this drawing nigh." At this testing-place of the Epistle Westcott is disappointing.

The third argument taken from the text in Psalm cx. to prove the inferiority of the Levitical and the incomparable superiority of the Messianic priesthood rests on the fact that the new order is introduced with an oath (vers. 20-22). By a lengthy parenthesis (ver. 21) pointing out the difference between the two priesthoods in the matter of the oath, the statement of the argument is rendered elliptical but not obscure, for the meaning obviously is: "Inasmuch as not without an oath He was made priest, by so much more must the constitution in connection with which He exercises His sacerdotal functions be superior to the old."

The principle of the argument is, that God doth not swear oaths lightly. When He says, "I have sworn, and will not repent," the matter on hand must be supremely important, and of an enduring nature. The new priesthood must be one of whose institution He will never have any cause to repent. It is implied that the old priesthood was one of which God had cause to repent. The oracle insinuates that God had found the Levitical institute after trial unsatisfactory; and as if weary of its law-made officials, and of their daily task of butchery and bloodshed, He swears a solemn oath saying: "As I live, I will bring this fleshly system to an end. I will ordain a new Priest not of Aaron's line, who shall perform His work in a very different way, whose character and service shall be to Me an everlasting delight, and whose merit shall benefit sinners time without end."

But it is noteworthy that in connection with this final argument from the Psalm, based on the oath, it is not so much the inferiority of the Levitical priest that is insisted upon, as the inferiority of the dispensation under which he served. What is said is not, Because He is made a Priest with an oath, therefore He exercises a superior kind of priesthood; but, Because He is made a Priest with an oath, therefore He is become surety of a *better covenant*. It is now not the men of the olden time, but the whole system of things with which they are associated, that is found wanting, the very fundamental constitution of the Israelitish commonwealth, by which it was made a people of God. The writer waxes ever bolder as he advances. First the priesthood is condemned; then the law creating and regulating it; then the covenant, which gave birth, not merely to the priesthood, but to the very people for which it transacted in holy things. The introduction of this reference to the covenant at first surprises us. We partly understand it when we observe that, in the next section of the Epistle, the covenants old and new become a leading subject of discourse. It is another instance of the skilful interweaving of a new theme into the one about to be dismissed. But we understand the new turn of thought fully only when we perceive that it fitly belongs to what goes before. When we attach due importance to the great idea expressed by the words, "*Through which we draw nigh to God*," this becomes clear. By the covenant at Sinai Israel became a people related to God, theoretically near to Him. But only theoretically. Israel was nigh, yet not nigh, not merely because of her sin, but through the very ordinances that were designed to express and maintain the intimacy; witness the Levitical priesthood, the veil, and the inaccessible holy place.

Thinking of this, our author feels that the Sinaitic covenant, which brought Israel nominally near to God, was a poor, disappointing thing, a failure, like all else belonging to the old religion. It might have cost him an effort to say so, had not Jeremiah with prophetic liberty said it before him. But, encouraged by Jeremiah's famous oracle of the new covenant, he does say so, by implication, by speaking of Jesus as the surety or guarantor of a *better* covenant. It is for him a better covenant, because it does really what the old covenant did only in name, *i.e.* brings men nigh to God. And he calls Jesus "surety" (ἔγγυος) of the better covenant, because it is He who prevents it also from being a failure like the old. There is literary felicity in the use of the word, as playfully alluding to the foregoing word ἐγγίζομεν. There is more than literary felicity, for the two words probably have the same root, so that we might render ἔγγυος: *the one who insures permanently near relations with God*.[1]

[1] On the word ἐγγύς, Passow remarks: "Probably of the same origin with ἔγγυος, ἐγγύη, from γυῖον = lying to the hand." Referring to the view that ἔγγυος forms a *paronomasia* with ἐγγίζομεν, Bleek expresses doubt, on account of the distance between the two words, and thinks it more probable that ἔγγυος is used out of regard to the similarity of sound between it and γέγονεν going before. The question has been much discussed among commentators, whether Jesus is surety for men to God (so the old theologians of the Lutheran and Reformed Churches), or for God to men (so Schlichting, Grotius, and others), or both (so Limborch, Baumgarten, etc.). The question really cannot be decided. The word occurs here only in the New Testament (it is not found in the Septuagint), and all that can be certainly taken out of it is the general idea that Jesus insures the stability of the new covenant and of the close relations between God and men which it establishes.

We have now to notice the last of the five arguments adduced to prove the inferiority of the Levitical priesthood, as compared with that of the Priest after the order of Melchisedec, which turns on the contrast between *many* and *one*. It is to this effect. The old priesthood was imperfect in this, that it was exercised by many priests in succession; the new is perfect in this, that the office is held in perpetuity by one Person, who continueth for ever, and therefore hath a priesthood that is inviolable, or that doth not pass from Him to another (ἀπαράβατον:[1] vers. 23, 24). To appreciate the full force of the argument, it is well to remember that even under the Levitical system the importance of having a continuous priesthood was felt. To such a feeling may be ascribed the fact that Aaron and his sons were consecrated simultaneously. Some think that this simultaneous consecration is alluded to in the text, when it is said that "they indeed have been made many priests." There can be no doubt, at all events,

---

All beyond has to be read into it. ἔγγυος expresses more than μεσίτης (connected with διαθήκη in viii. 6, ix. 15, xii. 24), adding to the general idea of mediation the more specific idea of "one who *makes himself responsible* for the validity and effectuation of the διαθήκη" (Vaughan).

[1] This is a ἅπ. λεγ.; a word of late Greek and disapproved by Phrynichus (p. 313). It may be taken passively when it will bear the meaning "not to be invaded," inviolable; or actively, when it will mean "not passing over from one person to another." Commentators are divided as to the rendering to be preferred. Vaughan and Westcott adopt the first, Weiss and von Soden the second. Weiss refers to Exodus xxxii. 18, and Sirach xxiii. 18, where παραβαίνω is used in the sense of passing from (ἄνθρωπος παραβαίνων ἀπὸ τῆς κλίνης αὐτοῦ—a man passing from his bed. Sir. xxiii. 18). The latter meaning seems the more appropriate.

that one end served by simultaneous ordination was to provide for the office being continuously occupied. From the nature of the case this was desirable. If there was need for a priest at all, there was need for one at all times; the office must abide without intermission, though the official might change. It is interesting to notice in this connection, that Eleazar was invested with the office of high priest before Aaron his father died. Moses took both father and son up to Mount Hor, and stripping the sacerdotal garments from the father put them on the son, whereupon the first occupant of the office breathed out his life.[1] Such precautions might serve after a fashion to secure for Israel an unchangeable priesthood. But if it were possible to have one priest never dying, and performing efficiently his duties perennially, that were obviously a more excellent way. If not only the priesthood, but the pri_est_ were continuous, that were the ideally perfect state of things. Our author here informs his readers that such is the actual state of things under the priesthood of Jesus. He, because He abideth for ever, hath the priesthood unchangeably.

The New Testament Priest was not exempt from death. He too, like Aaron, ascended a hill to die. But that fact is not in contradiction to the doctrine enunciated. He did not require to hand over His office to another, for death was not to have power over Him. He died as one possessing the power of an indissoluble life, taking death up as an element into His life, through which its power, instead of being destroyed or impaired,

[1] Num. xx. 28.

was rather enhanced. He rose again, and after forty days ascended another hill, not to die, but to be translated to the celestial sanctuary, there to abide a Priest for ever.

So we come back, at the close of the argument, to the point from which we started: the Priest after the order of Melchisedec, superior to the Levitical priests in all respects, but especially in this, that He is a Priest for ever. And by an easy transition we pass on to the natural consequence of Christ's unchangeable priesthood. "Whence also He is able to save perfectly those that draw near unto God through Him, seeing He ever liveth to intercede for them" (ver. 25).

Noteworthy here are the terms in which Christ's power to help men is described. He is able *to save perfectly* all those who seek to attain the end of all religion, close fellowship with God. In making this statement, the writer has in view what he has said of the Levitical priesthood, namely, that perfection came not by it. He here says in effect, Perfection does come by Jesus. But he does not say this in so many words. He prefers to vary the phrase, aiming at the greatest possible breadth and strength of statement. "Perfection," τελείωσις, narrows the range of benefit, pointing chiefly if not exclusively to the pardon of sin. Therefore for this word is substituted the more general and comprehensive σώζειν, suggesting the idea of salvation in all its aspects. Then the root idea of τελείωσις, reaching the end, is thrown into the adverbial phrase εἰς τὸ παντελές, which may be rendered "perfectly," "completely," "to all intents and purposes."[1] Thereby is ascribed to Christ the power of conferring a salvation uniting in itself all possible "perfections," accomplishing all manner of devoutly to be wished beneficent ends: pardon of sin, spiritual renewal, defence against temptation to apostasy, maintenance of Christian fidelity even unto death. It has been discussed whether παντελές contains a reference to time. Such a reference is very natural in connection with the asserted unchangeableness of Christ's priesthood; and for us who live so far down in the Christian centuries, it is a legitimate homiletic use of the text. But as the writer expected the consummation soon, the temporal reference must, to say the least, have had a very subordinate place in his mind.[2] His aim was to ascribe the highest degree of saving power to Jesus, in contrast to the impotence with which he had previously charged the Levitical priesthood. The law, he would say, the Levitical priesthood, completed nothing, not even the cancelling of guilt; Christ completes everything that enters into the idea of salvation, as most comprehensively conceived. Thus understood, this text favours the broad construction I put upon the title "the Sanctifier," given to Jesus in chap. ii. 11, as including sanctification in the ethical Pauline sense, as well as the narrower sense of "justification," in which it is sometimes used in this Epistle.

Noticeable further in the remarkable sentence now

[1] The phrase occurs again in Luke xiii. 11, there bearing the meaning "completely."

[2] On the temporal sense Westcott remarks: "The old commentators strangely explain it as if it were εἰς τὸ διηνεκές (so Latt. in perpetuum)."

under consideration are the means or method by which Christ is represented as perfectly saving those who through Him approach God. He saves by *intercession*, for such doubtless is the meaning of the word ἐντυγχάνειν. In classic usage it signifies to meet with. In Acts xxv. 24 it is construed with a dative, and a genitive governed by περί, and signifies to deal with one concerning a matter. Here, as in Romans viii. 26, where it is compounded with ὑπέρ, it means to intercede, or more generally to transact on behalf of. That the notion of intercession, speaking for, is mainly intended appears from what follows, the object of which is to point out that Christ, in consequence of His perfection, does not need to offer sacrifice, or to do anything more than intercede, in contrast to the Levitical priests, who, by reason of their infirmity, had to offer up sacrifices daily. The writer would say: "A word from Him is enough. As by His word of power He created and upholds all things, so by a word He can bring to bear all the resources of the Almighty for the complete and final salvation of His brethren." What power can be greater than this?

A word of intercession—nothing more is required; one who by a mere word can save is the sort of High Priest that meets our need—such is the import of what remains of this chapter (vers. 26–28). The Priest that suits us, that can perfect us as to our relations with God, that can bring us nigh and keep us nigh to God, is one perfectly righteous in all relations, "holy" towards God, benevolent towards men, free from any fault that might disqualify Him for His priestly office, separated locally from sinners by translation to the blessed region of peace, where He is exempt from temptation and eternally secure against moral evil; exalted to a position of supercelestial glory and power in full and equal fellowship with His Father, needing not to offer repeated sacrifices, or to do anything whatever in our interest beyond interceding for us. Here at last is the writer's ideal of priesthood. In determining the marks of the Melchisedec type, he omitted to say how far they satisfied the ideal, or to indicate what the ideal was. Here, at the close of the discussion on the new type, he supplies the lack by sketching in a few rapid strokes an ideal priest. Does the ideal answer to the type? is it drawn with the type in view, and in order to assign more definite values to certain terms left vague—king, righteousness, peace? It is not improbable that the beginning and the end thus meet in the author's thought, and that the terms ὅσιος, ἄκακος, ἀμίαντος define "righteousness," that the phrase κεχωρισμένος ἀπὸ τῶν ἁμαρτωλῶν interprets "peace," and that ὑψηλότερος τῶν οὐρανῶν γενόμενος indicates the significance of "king."

Thus far all seems clear; but what shall we say of the last trait in the picture of the ideal Priest, which represents Him as one who needs not to repeat sacrifice? Is this an element in the ideal to which there is no counterpart in the type? In determining the marks of the Melchisedec type, our author said nothing about sacrifice. He may, however, have thought of Melchisedec as offering no sacrifices, and have regarded this fact also as possessing typical significance. In so doing he would simply have been applying his method of determining the type by laying stress on the silences as well as the utterances of Scripture. If this suggestion be correct, then we must regard the statement concerning the non-repetition of sacrifice as a supplement to the doctrine of the type reserved for the close of the discussion, as the place where it could most fitly and impressively be introduced.

In the writer's mind this last feature is connected with those going before, and especially with those relating to the moral character of the ideal Priest, as effect with cause. Because He is "holy, harmless, undefiled," *therefore* He needs not to repeat sacrifice; and this is His crowning merit. To the Hebrew Christians it would probably appear a grave defect, rather than a merit, in the Priest after the order of Melchisedec, that He was not constantly occupied in offering sacrifices like the priests after the order of Aaron. The morning and evening sacrifices, and the great day of atonement annually recurring, what a comfort! And what a blank would be created were these swept away, and nothing similar took their place! Their teacher gives them to understand that they are mistaken, and that the repetition of sacrifice in the Levitical system was due to the moral imperfection of the offerers. He does not mean to say that it was wholly due to this cause, for he elsewhere traces it to the nature of the sacrifices (chap. x. 1–11). But he does mean to say that it was due in part to this cause, and that is the point which he deems it needful to insist on here. The infirmity of the priest made it necessary that he should offer repeated sacrifices for himself, and because for himself, therefore for the people; for the priestly offices of sinful officials could not avail to remove the people's sins for ever, if indeed at all. On the other hand, the High Priest of the new, better order has no need to offer repeated sacrifices, either for Himself or for His people. Not for Himself, because He has been perfected both in character and in state for evermore.[1] Free from sin, even in His earthly state, when subject to temptation, though not free from sinless infirmity, and worthy even then to be described by the august attributes, "holy, harmless, undefiled," He is now in a position in which sin is out of the question. Not for others, because He offered for sinners a perfect sacrifice once for all.

That sacrifice was *Himself*. The great thought comes in here for the first time. Once struck, as Delitzsch says, the note sounds on ever louder and louder.[2] It comes in very relevantly here in connection with an argument designed to prove that repetition of sacrifice was a mark of inferiority and weakness adhering to the Levitical system, and that the non-repetition of sacrifice

---

[1] The term τετελειωμένος, ver. 28, here, as in ii. 10 and v. 9, means to fit for office. The fitness in this case embraces two elements: a character rendered temptation-proof, and a position inaccessible to temptation. That both elements are included appears from the description of the ideal priest in ver. 26. The idea of "consecration" is foreign to the connection of thought. The same remark applies to ver. 11. The rendering of Mr. Rendall, "seeing again that there was a consecration under the Levitical priesthood," seems to me to involve the argument in confusion.

[2] Delitzsch is honourably distinguished by his sense of the grave significance of the thought that Christ's sacrifice was Himself, in the development of the writer's argument. Many commentators treat it as if it were a matter of course. Such is the deadening effect of familiarity.

was an equally sure mark of the superiority of the Christian dispensation. For the nature of the sacrifice in either case had an important bearing on the question of repetition or non-repetition. The ancient priest of Israel, himself morally stained, had to offer a brute beast physically faultless, a mere shadowy emblem of holiness; and such offerings being intrinsically worthless, he had to present them again and again by way of renewing an impressive spectacle. The High Priest of humanity offered *Himself*, and by the very act demonstrated Himself to be perfectly holy, presenting in his death an embodiment of exact, loving obedience to the Divine will and of self-effacing devotion to the well-being of man; and just because the offering was the very ideal of sacrifice realised, it needed not to be repeated. The offering was presented once for all, and stands there before the universe a thing perfectly well done, recognisable as an eternally valid and valuable act by all men of purged vision, whose minds are not blinded, as were those of the Hebrews, by long familiarity with and doting attachment to the beggarly elements of a rude ritual.

But how does this sacrifice " of nobler name " stand related to the " order of Melchisedec " ? Does it lie within or without the type ? On first thoughts it seems as if the answer must be " without." Not only does it take place on earth, while the Melchisedec priesthood belongs to heaven, where no sacrifice is offered *de novo*, but there appears to be nothing in the history of Melchisedec which would lead us to look for such a sacrifice. Neither by the utterances nor by the silences of Scripture does it seem possible to arrive at *self-sacrifice* as one of the notes of the Melchisedec type. By the silences we might rather arrive at the conclusion that there was, not merely no repetition of sacrifice, but no sacrifice at all, in the new order, and that its functions were limited to prayer and benediction. There is only one way of escape out of the difficulty, though it may be doubted if it was in the writer's thoughts.[1] We have seen that the non-repetition of sacrifice results from the moral attributes of the ideal Priest. Because He is "holy, harmless, undefiled," therefore He needs not to be continually performing new sacrificial acts. What if the one sacrifice be also the result of the same moral attributes? What if the whole truth be, "holy, harmless, undefiled"—in one word, perfectly righteous, therefore *one* sacrifice and *only* one, and that sacrifice *Himself*? This would lead us to regard Christ's death as the natural effect of His fidelity to the interests of God and man in this evil world. And this is the actual historic fact. Whatever theological significance may attach to that death, this is the fundamental fact on which our theological construction must rest. The first lesson Jesus taught His disciples on the meaning of His passion was, that His cross came to Him through loyalty to duty, that He suffered for righteousness' sake.[2] In the light of this doctrine we comprehend why there was one sacrifice, and only one, and that one "Himself." There was one sacrifice, because the Holy One lived in an evil world, to which His holiness, even, yea above

---

[1] *Vide* on this the concluding chapter of this work.
[2] Matt. xvi. 24.

all, His love, His brotherly sympathy with man, was an offence; and they cried in fierce intolerance, "Crucify Him." There was only one sacrifice, because after His death He was raised to the region of peace, "where the wicked cease from troubling, and the weary are at rest."

By this train of thought an attempt might be made to show that self-sacrifice enters as an element into the Melchisedec type. But it is better to confess frankly that the thought, however true in itself, was not present to the writer's mind, and to content ourselves with saying that self-sacrifice is certainly an essential feature of the *ideal* Priesthood. The highest possible priesthood is that in which priest and victim are one, and the only true sacrifice is that which results from character, and reveals, is offered through, the indwelling spirit. The proof of this is the Spirit of Christ witnessing in our hearts. There is no other proof for us; there was no other proof for the writer of our Epistle. If a man does not see this for himself, typological arguments, whether from Melchisedec or from Aaron, will not help him. We see only what we bring. Another thing the man of open spiritual vision understands: that the real nature of Christ's sacrifice is to be learned from His life on earth. The perplexities arising out of the typological form into which the truth concerning Christ's priesthood is cast in our Epistle have driven some to find His true sacrifice in a perpetual service of love and praise rendered by Him to God in heaven.[1] It is rather

---

[1] For this view *vide* the late Professor Milligan's *The Ascension of our Lord*, and the work of his son, the Rev. George Milligan, B.D., on the *Theology of the Epistle to the Hebrews*, recently published.

to be found in His earthly career of heroic fidelity to God amid incessant temptation, culminating in the crucifixion. There lies the pathos, the moral power, and the inspiration which helps us to live well. Thence we know anything we do know of the spirit of Christ's life in heaven. His spirit is "eternal"; the mind that is in Him now is the same mind that animated Him while He lived in this world. But it is the mind that *was* in Him that interprets to us the mind that *is* in Him. And it is the spirit of His earthly life that gives value to His heavenly life for God and for men. The temporal at once illuminates and enshrines the eternal. Without those sacred years lived under Syrian skies the eternal life of the High Priest of humanity would be for us an infinite void, whence issued no light to our minds and no comfort to our hearts.

The view here contended for seems to be that of the author of our Epistle in this place. He speaks, not of a perpetual sacrifice in heaven, but of the sacrifice which Christ presented once for all "when He offered up Himself."[1] If he speak elsewhere of Christ offering sacrifice in heaven, that is an apparent antinomy to be solved, but it must not be solved by denying that His death on earth was a priestly act.

[1] The question has been discussed whether τοῦτο (ver. 27, last clause) includes both the previous clauses: "First for His own sins, then for those of the people." Verbal interpretation answers in the affirmative, but the nature of the case requires a negative. The doctrine of the Epistle being that Christ was ever sinless, the writer cannot have meant to represent Christ as offering a sacrifice for His own sins. Those who make τοῦτο include both have to take ἁμαρτιῶν in the sense of infirmities. So Schlichting and Hofmann.

CHAPTER XIV

CHRIST AND AARON

CHAP. VIII

THE discourse on Melchisedec is finished, and now Aaron comes to the front. Having used the priest of Salem to set forth the dignity and value of Christ's priesthood, the writer proceeds to use the high priest of Israel to convey an idea of His priestly functions. The aim of the next division of the Epistle, comprising the eighth and ninth chapters, is to show that the priestly ministry of Christ is as much superior to that of the Levitical priests as He Himself is personally superior to them. The rubric of the whole passage is "the more excellent ministry." But as comparison can be made only between things that have something in common, this comparison between Christ and the Levitical priest implies a certain resemblance which the writer intends to exhibit. By the one train of thought he accomplishes a twofold object, establishing superiority on a basis of similitude.

Thus he puts the crown [1] or copestone on the discourse

---

[1] The opening words of the next discourse—κεφάλαιον δὲ ἐπὶ τοῖς λεγομένοις—are happily rendered by Dr. Field in *Otium Norricense*: "Now to crown our present discourse," and by Rendall: "Now to crown what we are saying." κεφάλαιον may mean either "sum"

concerning the priestly Minister after the order of Melchisedec by a discourse on His priestly ministry, in terms drawn from the order of Aaron. That discourse runs on to the end of the theoretic part of the Epistle (chap. x. 18), and might have for its general heading "Christ and Aaron," though I have assigned to its divisions special headings, reserving the general title for the contents of chapter viii., which forms the introduction to the discourse.

For the new line of thought Scripture warrant is produced, as had been done in the case of the discourse on the Melchisedec type. The warrant for describing Christ's priestly functions in terms of those performed by the priests of the house of Aaron is found in the words: "See that thou make all things according to the pattern showed to thee in the mount,"[1] understood to mean that the Levitical system of worship was a copy or shadow of a higher heavenly reality. This principle was carried to absurd lengths by the Rabbis, whose notion was that there were in heaven original models of the tabernacle and its furniture, and that these were shown to Moses, somewhat as original pictures by famous artists, of which copies are made by obscurer men, are shown to travellers in the picture-galleries of European cities. Like most rabbinical notions, this was a prosaic caricature of the truth implied in the word of God to Moses.

or "principal matter." Most recent interpreters take it in the latter of these senses, as I have done above. As to the grammatical construction: κεφάλαιον is an accusative in apposition with the following sentence. A similar construction in Rom. viii. 3 (τὸ γὰρ ἀδύνατον τοῦ νόμου).

[1] Ex. xxv. 9, and again in ver. 40.

Our author was too much of a poet and philosopher to be capable of such pedantry as to imagine that of every article of furniture in the Jewish tabernacle—snuffers, candlesticks, tables, altars—there was an eternal material pattern in heaven. But he did believe, and he here teaches, that the material tabernacle with all its appurtenances was an emblem of a spiritual, Divine, eternal sanctuary, shown to Moses in vision on the mount. Hence he describes the Levitical priests as those who serve "that which is the pattern and shadow of the heavenlies," namely, the material, man-made tabernacle (ver. 5), and represents heaven itself as a sanctuary, the holy place *par excellence*, the true tabernacle which the Lord pitched, not man (ver. 2). In the same way he assumes that as there was a priesthood and a system of sacrifices in the religious establishment set up by Moses, so there must be a priest in the real heavenly sanctuary (ver. 1), and the Man who fills that office there must have something to offer (ver. 3). A celestial Sanctuary, High Priest, and Sacrifice: such are the transcendent realities whereof the material tabernacle, and the Levitical priests and sacrifices were the rude, shadowy copies.

It is worthy of note with what a firm, confident tone the writer asserts the superiority of the heavenly patterns over the earthly copies. The heavenly sanctuary is the true, genuine tabernacle, that which answers to the ideal ($ἀληθινῆς$ [1]); the material man-made tabernacle, on the

---

[1] The word is used in the same sense in the Fourth Gospel, *e.g.*, "I am the true vine" ($ἡ\ ἄμπελος\ ἡ\ ἀληθινή$). In this sense $ἀληθινός$ is opposed to the vulgar reality which comes short of the ideal, while $ἀληθής$ is opposed to the false or unreal in the common sense.

other hand, is but a rude sketch, or barely that, only such a dim, scarcely recognisable likeness as a shadow (σκιᾷ) supplies, of the fair spiritual sanctuary which, like Plato's republic, is to be found nowhere in this world, but only in the heavens. With this way of describing the things contrasted, the Hebrew Christians of course would not sympathise. They would feel disposed to invert the terms, and apply the epithet "true" to the material structure, and the epithet "shadowy" to the spiritual one. Yet what, after all, are the essential constituents of a holy place? Not the boards and the veil, not stone and lime; but a God present in His grace, and a priest competent to transact for man with God, and a people drawing nigh to God through his mediation. Given these, your religious establishment is complete in all essential points. And these essentials are found in connection with the celestial sanctuary more perfectly than they were in connection with the old tabernacle in the wilderness.

Corresponding to the transcendent excellence of the heavenly sanctuary is the incomparable dignity of its priestly Minister. He is "such an High Priest as sat down on the right hand of the throne of the Majesty in the heavens." He is a royal Priest, who does not stand ministering like the sacerdotal drudges of the tribe of Levi (chap. x. 11), but while He ministers, interceding for men, sits in regal state.

On the principle that all the great religious realities are to be found in heaven, there also must be the true offering, or sacrifice. What is it? That is the question on which the writer specially desires his readers to exercise their thoughts. For them it is the hardest question. They might recognise that heaven could, by a certain latitude of speech, be called a sanctuary, and that the glorified Christ could be conceived of as in some vague sense a priest; but sacrifice in heaven! What has He to offer? Their teacher does his best to help them to master this abstruse point. First, he remarks that if Christ were on earth He would not even be a priest at all, there being those who offer gifts according to the law (ver. 4). This statement does not mean that Christ while on earth was not a priest in any sense. The remark is meant for Hebrew ears, and is intended to provoke reflection on the question, What gift did the Priest of the new order offer? in the hope that readers slow to learn would at length get hold of the great idea (unfamiliar to them, though commonplace to us) first hinted in the close of the seventh chapter, and developed in the sequel, that Christ's offering was *Himself*. In catechetical form our author's meaning may be put thus: "Christ is a Priest, the true, high, highest, ideal Priest. He must therefore have something to offer; for the very duty of a priest is to offer gifts and sacrifices for sin. But what is it which He offers? It is not any such sacrifice as the Levitical priest offers, insomuch that were He on earth He could not be recognised as a priest at all. What then can it be? It cannot certainly be the blood of bulls and goats. The daily scenes of slaughter that took place before the door of the tabernacle would be utterly out of place in the celestial sanctuary. You cannot imagine such sanguinary work going on up yonder. The sacrifice that is to make even heaven pure must be of a very different character. No shadows, no dim emblems, no rude, barbaric rites will do there. All must be real, spiritual, and of the highest kind, and in the highest measure of perfection. The priest that gets entry yonder must be more than officially holy, and his offering must be as holy as himself. Can you not guess what it is? It is *Himself*, offered without spot or stain of sin unto God, through the eternal Spirit of filial obedience and lowly love. That will do even for heaven." This, or something like it, is what the writer has in his mind; but he does not utter all his thought just yet. He is content for the present to throw out the remark: "This Man must have something to offer," and to leave his readers for a while to puzzle over the question, What can it be?

At no point in the Epistle is it more needful to bear in mind its apologetic character, and to realise the ignorance of its first readers as to the nature of Christianity, which made an elaborate apology necessary, than at the place which now engages our attention. If we assume that the Hebrew Christians were familiar with the doctrine that Christ was a Priest, and that by His death He made atonement for sin, it is difficult to understand what the writer could mean by the statement that He must have something to offer. It degenerates into a mere truism. Why, of course He had His own blood shed on the cross to present to God in heaven. Or are we to suppose that the writer means something additional to that: such as intercessions for sinners, and presentation to God of the prayers and praises of His people? Assume, on the other hand, that the Hebrew Christians were ignorant of the great truth that in His death Christ offered Himself a sacrifice to God, and all becomes clear. The observation that Christ must have somewhat to offer gains point, and the added remark that if He were on earth He would not be a priest serves an important purpose. The former is no longer a theological commonplace, or dogmatic truism, but an apologetic device to force slow-witted men to think; and the latter is a friendly hint as to the direction in which the solution of the problem is to be found.

This Man must have somewhat to offer—what can it be? such was the puzzling question for the first readers of our Epistle. The puzzle for modern readers and interpreters is different. The priestly ministry is in heaven; and yet the sacrifice the Priest presents there appears to be none other than that offering of Himself which He made once for all; an event, so far at least as the initial stage of it, the blood-shedding, is concerned, happening on earth, and within this visible world. This is the antinomy to which reference has already been made.[1] For the final solution we must wait till we have come in the course of exposition to the writer's fullest expression of his conception of Christ's sacrifice. Meantime it will suffice to hint that in his view "true" and "heavenly" are synonyms; whatever is "true" is heavenly, belongs to the upper world of realities, and whatever belongs to that upper world is true and real. If Christ's sacrifice of Himself be a true sacrifice, it belongs to the heavenly world, no matter where or when it takes place. Then, secondly, Christ's sacrifice is for

[1] *Vide* Chapter ix. p. 190; for the solution, *vide* Chapter xvi.

him a true sacrifice, because it is an affair of *spirit*. Flesh and blood, whether of man or of beast, are of the earth, earthy, and belong to the realm of shadows. Even the blood of Christ, literally considered, can find no place in heaven; so that it is vain to distinguish between the first stage of the sacrifice, the death or blood-shedding, and the second, the sprinkling of the shed blood on the mercy-seat within the sanctuary, and to relegate the former to earth as something lying outside the sphere of Christ's proper priestly activity, and to locate the latter in heaven, regarding it as the point at which Christ's priestly ministry begins. Christ's sacrifice of Himself finds entrance into heaven only when blood is transmuted into spirit. In other words: the shedding of Christ's blood is a true sacrifice, as distinct from the shedding of the blood of bulls and goats, which was only a shadow of sacrifice, because it is the manifestation of a mind or spirit. And because it is that, it belongs to heaven, though it take place on earth. As in the Gospel of John, the Son of man living on the earth is represented as claiming to be in heaven,[1] so we may claim for the death of Christ, in virtue of the spirit it revealed, that it belongs to the heavenlies, though it took place on Mount Calvary. The magic phrase, "through an eternal spirit," lifts us above distinctions of time and place, and makes it possible for us to regard

[1] John iii. 13. I am aware that ὁ ὢν ἐν τῷ οὐρανῷ is a doubtful reading omitted by W. and H. (given in the margin). But it is retained by Tischendorf, and the thought is entirely in the manner of the Fourth Gospel, which contemplates history *sub specie æternitatis*, whereby distinctions of here and there, now and then, are abolished.

Christ's offering of Himself, in all its stages, as a transaction within the celestial sanctuary.

Leaving his readers for a while to their own meditations on the question, What is it Christ had to offer? our author proceeds to show that the ministry of the "true tabernacle," whatever its precise nature, must needs be one of surpassing excellence. For this purpose he reverts to the idea of the "better covenant" introduced in the previous chapter (ver. 22), of which he declares Christ to be the "Mediator," that is, the agent by whom it is established, as he has already declared Him to be its "surety," that is, the agent by whom its stability is guaranteed. "But now," he argues, "hath He obtained a more excellent ministry, by how much He is also Mediator of a better covenant, one which has been legally constituted upon better promises." From one occupying this position what may not be expected? Of the priestly service connected with the better covenant, based on better promises, too lofty ideas cannot be formed. Thus would the wise teacher entice backward pupils onward in the untrodden path that conducts to Christian enlightenment. Whether he was successful we know not. Not improbably he failed with his first readers because of the novelty of his thoughts, as he is apt to fail with us through their being too familiar. The "new covenant" is now a trite theme, and it requires an effort of historical imagination to conceive that at one time it was a great, spiritual, poetic thought: first for Jeremiah, whose prophetic soul gave birth to it; and then, ages after, for the author of our Epistle, who utilised it in his grand apology for the Christian religion. In so doing he certainly showed his wonted skill. For Jeremiah's oracle of the new covenant, here quoted at length, serves excellently the purpose of the whole Epistle, while it facilitates the exposition of the peculiar nature of Christ's priestly ministry. The oracle speaks of a *new* covenant, and is thus another Scripture text showing that a new order of things was contemplated even in long past ages, and that the old order was felt to be unsatisfactory. The oracle further represents the new, desiderated order as a *covenant*, implying an analogy as well as a difference between the new and the old, and preparing us to expect, in connection with the new not less than the old, a priestly ministry and sacrifice, serving a purpose analogous to that served by the Levitical system of worship, only serving it far more effectually.

After justifying the application of the epithet "better" to the new covenant by the remark that, if the first covenant had been faultless, no place would have been sought for a second (ver. 7), and by pointing out that the oracle of the new covenant is introduced with disparaging reflections on the old (vers. 8,[1] 9), the writer quotes the oracle (with its preface) at length (vers. 8–12), and leaves it to speak for itself as to the quality of its promises which he had declared to be "better" than those of the old covenant. Read the oracle, he says in effect, and judge for yourselves. It would certainly have been satisfactory if he had treated his readers of all ages

[1] μεμφόμενος γὰρ αὐτοῖς. B. has αὐτοῖς, which might be neuter, and refer to the details of the Sinaitic legislation, a reference to which seems to be required by the ἄμεμπτος in ver. 7. So Vaughan. Weiss thinks that even with αὐτοῖς, which he adopts, the reference is to the people.

as children so far as to think it necessary to give a succinct enumeration of the promises, that they might know on what he chiefly laid stress. Fortunately he returns to the subject farther on, and by a partial requotation lets us see what bulks most largely in his view (chap. x. 16–18). Two promises are covered by the second quotation: the writing of the law on the heart, and the everlasting oblivion of sin. One might have been quite sure, apart from any express indication, that our author had the last-mentioned promise very specially in mind when he characterised the promises of the new covenant as "better"; for the very aim of his whole work is to show that Christ for the first time deals effectually with the defilement of sin, so that we can indeed draw near to God. But it is important to observe that remission of sin, while of great moment in his view, is not everything. He includes the writing of the law on the heart within the scope of Christ's work. He thinks of that as one of the ends to be effected by Christ as the founder and guarantor of the new covenant. In other words, he conceives of Christ as the Sanctifier in the ethical or Pauline sense, as well as in the ritual or theocratic sense of putting men, through forgiveness, in right relations with God.

The new covenant might well be left to speak for itself as to the superior quality of its promises. Under the Sinaitic covenant God gave the people of Israel, through Moses as mediator, the Ten Commandments written on tables of stone, and promised to bless them if they kept these commandments, to be their God if they would be His people and do all the words of His law.

He gave them, further, detailed instructions with reference to their religious duties, and provided a priestly caste to keep them right in point of ritual, a thing very necessary under so complicated a system. Finally, God promised to His people temporary forgiveness of sins of ignorance and infirmity, on condition of their offering certain specified sacrifices, at certain stated times, and in accordance with certain prescribed forms; cancelling, *e.g.*, the "ignorances" of a year in consideration of the sacrifices offered by the high priest on the great day of atonement. Benefits these not to be despised, but how poor compared with those of the new covenant! Instead of a law written on tables of stone, and deposited in the ark, was to be a law written on the *heart*, and deposited in the safe custody of a renewed mind. And there is no "if" in the promise of the covenanting God. It is absolute, and runs: "I will be their God, and they shall be My people." Then, instead of instruction in the details of a cumbrous ceremonial system by the priest, or by any neighbour who happened to be better informed, there is to be intuitive, first-hand knowledge of God, of His will, and of His heart, possessed by all, accessible to laymen as well as to priests, to the poor as well as to the rich, to the least as well as to the greatest, to the illiterate as well as to the learned—the knowledge being of a kind not dependent on talent, status, or profession, but simply on moral disposition, the common possession of all the pure in heart. Finally, there is promised under the new covenant, not a temporary—say, annual—forgiveness of sins of a minor and artificial character, but forgiveness free, full, everlasting, of all sins, however heinous. "I will be merciful to their unrighteousness, and their sins and their iniquities I will remember no more"; words which in the mouth of a prophet meant something more serious than the pardoning of petty offences against a religious ritual.

The new, reformed covenant is evidently constructed on the principle of avoiding the defects of the old one. The oracle announcing it is in one aspect just a criticism of the Sinaitic covenant. When prophets thus boldly criticise the constitution of their nation, change more or less revolutionary may be looked for. The first item in the reform programme, the law written on the heart, may indeed appear a poet's dream, to be relegated to the realm of Utopia. No fault is found at this point with the old law in itself. The law referred to is the Decalogue, as we gather from the implied contrast between writing on the heart and writing on stone tablets. It was this law above all that the people of Israel broke when they provoked God to disregard His covenant, and send them into exile. They were banished to Babylon, not for neglecting religious ritual, but for neglecting the great duties of righteousness, which it was the glory of the prophets to preach. This law in itself was good, and accordingly in this case the old covenant is blamed merely for not providing that the law should be kept. The complaint may seem unreasonable, but there can be no doubt that a law which not only told men what to do, but insured compliance with its own precepts, would be a great boon.

The second item in the programme points not merely to a new method of enforcing old laws, but to abrogation.

The dependence of each man upon his neighbour for the knowledge of God's will arose out of the fact that under the ancient covenant the people of Israel were subject to a vast body of *positive* precepts, which had no reason except that God was pleased to enjoin them. Even under that covenant the moral law was to a certain extent written on the heart. But the heart, or the conscience, could give no guidance in reference to religious ritual or ceremonial purity. In such matters men had to seek the law at the priest's mouth. Yet ignorance might have serious consequences. Exact knowledge of God was at once necessary and difficult. It was so difficult, that the rise of a class like the scribes, whose business it was to interpret the law, became inevitable; it was so necessary, that a man could not be legally righteous without a minute acquaintance with the contents of the statute book, there being innumerable offences which were not sins against the Decalogue, but only against ceremonial precepts, having penalties attaching to them. This it was which made the legal yoke grievous. It was not enough to be a good man; you must likewise, as touching the positive precepts of the law, be blameless. And it was so difficult to be ritually blameless, that one might know God essentially very well, even as a prophet knew Him, and yet be in Divine things an *ignoramus*, from the point of view of the priestly code. For this incongruous state of matters abrogation was the only remedy. Sweep away the cumbrous and vexatious system of positive precepts, and let the things needful to be known in order to acceptable acquaintance with God be reduced to a few great moral and spiritual truths, comprehensible by all, without aid of priest, scribe, rabbi, or village schoolmaster, the all-sufficient organ of knowledge being a pure heart. This was one of the boons to be brought in by the days that were coming, the "time of reformation," the era of the "new covenant."

Another was the abolition of the Levitical priesthood, and the system of worship with which it was connected. For this is what is pointed at in the third complaint virtually brought against the old covenant, that it did not deal effectually with the problem of sin. This is the most serious charge, as it is the one which the author of our Epistle is most concerned to emphasise. It was well founded. The Levitical system might, without any breach of charity, be characterised as trifling with the great question, How can human sin be pardoned, and the sinner brought near to God? It really dealt only, or at least for the most part, with artificial sins, arising out of ignorance of the ritual law, and its tendency was to divorce religion from morality. A man might be ritually right who was morally wrong, and morally right who was ritually wrong. Perhaps it was not of this that Jeremiah was thinking when he wrote, "I will forgive their iniquity, and their sin will I remember no more." But an implied censure on the old religion is what our author finds in the words. For him they contain the promise of a boon which it was not in the power of that religion to confer; therefore by inference an intimation that it must and shall pass away, and give place to a better religion that shall effectually provide for the pardon of sin and the establishment of peace between man and God. He does not interpret the prophecy as pointing to the total abolition of priests and sacrifices; he finds in it rather the promise of a *better* priest and a *better* sacrifice. That is for him *the* promise of the new covenant, the fulfilment of which brings along with it the fulfilment of the other two. Give us only the true Priest and the true Sacrifice, then ritual worship becomes useless, and a simple worship of the living God takes its place, and obedience is made easy by law being transmuted into love.

How fully the revolutionary character of Jeremiah's oracle of the new covenant was present to our author's mind appears from the remark which he appends to the quotation from the prophet: "In that He saith 'new' He hath made old the first" (ver. 13). He regards the mere use of the fateful word "new" as implying that even in the prophet's time the Sinaitic covenant was in the Divine view moribund. It was therefore virtually a notice to the old order generally, and to the Levitical priesthood in particular, to be ready to quit. The obvious moral is pointed still more plainly for the benefit of Hebrew readers by the added reflection: "that which is becoming antiquated [1] and growing age-worn is nigh unto vanishing away." It is implied that the sentence of antiquation pronounced seven centuries ago through the mouth of Jeremiah has at length become ready for execution through the long process of decay to which legal institutions had been subject. It was necessary to point this out, because the Hebrew Christians

---

[1] παλαιούμενον, present participle, contrasting with πεπαλαίωκεν in the previous clause.

might think that a prophetic verdict of condemnation that had lain dormant so long, and been treated as *brutum fulmen* by triumphant Rabbinism, would remain for ever a dead letter. "Not so," says their teacher. "No word of God returns unto Him void of effect, least of all shall this word of censure on the old covenant fall to the ground. The time of fulfilment has arrived. Leviticalism is decrepit, and death must ensue. Think of this, ye Hebrews, who cling to Levitical ordinances! See: the high priest's head is white with age; his limbs totter from feebleness; the boards of the tabernacle are rotten; the veil of the sanctuary is moth-eaten. Everything portends approaching dissolution. Let it die then, the hoary system, and receive from devout men decent burial. Shut not your eyes to the white hairs and tottering steps, fanatically striving to endow the venerable with immortality, embalming that which is already dead. Accept the inevitable, however painful, and find comfort in the thought that though the body dies the spirit lives on, that when the old passes away something new and better takes its place. It is sad to lose such a one as Simeon the just and devout; but why mourn for him when a *Christ* is born?"

Wise counsel, accepted by all in reference to revolutions lying behind them in long past history. Good counsel, we say, for Hebrew Christians of the apostolic age, and for the men of the sixteenth century when Luther introduced his reforms. The difficulty is to accept and act on the counsel in connection with changes impending or now going on. Then the voice of wisdom seems to many a word of blasphemy. "Abolish the

Sinaitic covenant, and the God-given law, and the divinely instituted priesthood—what an impious proposal!" It is this that makes the prophet ever a heavy-hearted man. He sees so clearly to be a duty what to other men appears a crime. Well if they do not stone him to death, like Stephen!

CHAPTER XV

THE ANCIENT TABERNACLE

Chap. ix. 1-10

THE writer now proceeds to compare the old and the new covenants with reference to their respective provisions for religious communion between man and God, his purpose being to show the superiority of the priestly ministry of Christ over that of the Levitical priesthood. In the first five verses of the section now to be considered he gives an inventory of the furniture of the tabernacle pitched in the wilderness; in the next five he describes the religious services there carried on. Thereafter he proceeds to describe in contrast the ministry of Christ, the new covenant High Priest, as performed in the greater and more perfect tabernacle, not made with hands.

The first paragraph simply continues the train of thought, and hence the subject of the affirmation in ver. 1 is left to be understood: "Now (οὖν leading back to viii. 6) the first (covenant) had ordinances of Divine service and its mundane sanctuary."[1] The epithet κοσ-

---

[1] The δικαιώματα λατρείας and the ἅγιον κοσμικόν are joined together as one composite institution by τε. Service and sanctuary corresponded to each other, the sanctuary being adapted in its construction to the services therein carried on.

μικόν here applied to the tabernacle evidently signifies "belonging to this material world," in opposition to the heavenly sanctuary (ver. 11) not made with hands out of things visible and tangible. Some have rendered "ornate," or well ordered, for which, however, the usual Greek word is κόσμιος. The purpose of the writer is to point out that the tabernacle belonged to this earth, and therefore possessed the attributes of all things earthly, materiality and perishableness. The materials might be fine and costly; still they were *material*, and as such were liable to wax old and vanish away.

In vers. 2–5 is given a detailed description of the arrangements and furniture of this cosmic[1] sanctuary. It is represented as divided into two parts, each of which is called a tabernacle, distinguished as first and second; and the articles contained in, or belonging to, each compartment are carefully specified. "For there was prepared a tabernacle; the first, wherein were the candlestick, and the table, and the shewbread; which is called the Holy place. But behind the second veil, the tabernacle which is called the Holy of Holies; having a golden altar of incense, and the ark of the covenant covered on all sides with gold, wherein (was) a golden pot containing manna, and Aaron's rod that budded, and the tables of the covenant; and above it cherubim of

---

[1] I use this word simply as a synonym for "mundane," not as hinting sympathy with the idea that the sanctuary was cosmic in significance, representing the universe, or even as implying that κοσμικόν points to the universality of the worship, the temple being open to Gentiles. Neither of these ideas was present to the mind of the writer, though some interpreters, ancient and modern, have found them in the epithet he applies to the sanctuary.

glory overshadowing the mercy-seat; of which I cannot now speak severally." The tabernacle called in ver. 3 "the Holy of Holies" is in ver. 7 called "the second." The veil between the Holy place and the most Holy place is called the second veil, to distinguish it from the curtain at the door of the tent, which is regarded as the first.

The *inventory* of the tabernacle furniture here given offers several points for consideration. Looking at it as a whole, what strikes one is the great care taken to give a full list of the articles, and also to describe them, specially those of costly material. Several things are named which have no bearing on the comparison between the old and new covenants, no counterparts in the Christian sanctuary, apparently for no other reason than just that the list might be complete. No valuator could be more careful to make an inventory of household furniture perfectly accurate than our author is to give an exhaustive list of the articles to be found in the Jewish tabernacle, whether in the Holy place or in the most Holy. Indeed, so careful is he to make the list complete, not only in his own judgment, but in the judgment of his readers, that he includes things which had no connection with religious worship, but were merely put into the tabernacle for safe custody, as valuable mementoes of incidents in Israel's history; *e.g.*, the golden pot of manna, and Aaron's rod that budded. It is further to be noted, in regard to these articles, that they are represented as being within the ark of the covenant, though it is nowhere in the Old Testament said that they were, the direction given being merely that they should be placed before the

Testimony,[1] and it being expressly stated in regard to the ark in Solomon's temple that there was nothing in it save the two tables on which the Ten Commandments were inscribed.[2] Whether these things ever had been in the ark we do not know. The fact that they are here represented to have been does not settle the point. The writer speaks not by inspiration, or from his own knowledge, but simply in accordance with traditional belief. The Rabbis held that the golden pot and Aaron's rod were placed not only before, but inside the ark; and the Jews generally accepted this opinion. And our author is content to state the case as his readers might have stated it. He has no interest or wish to deny the truth of the opinion; on the contrary, his whole purpose in making the enumeration gives him rather an interest in acquiescing in current opinion on the point. For he desires to convince his readers of the superior excellence of the priestly ministry of Christ, and it is a part of his art as an orator to go as far as he honestly can in pleasing those whom he would persuade. If they think that it makes the golden pot and the budding rod more precious to have them inside the ark, why then, let it be so. He acts like a valuator describing certain articles greatly valued by surviving relatives as heirlooms that had belonged to a deceased friend. The valuator sees well enough that the articles in question are of little intrinsic worth, and knows that they would bring little money if sold. But he knows also the superstitious veneration with which the old relics are regarded by the kinsfolk of the

[1] Ex. xvi. 32-34; Num. xvii. 10.   [2] 1 Kings viii. 9.

departed; so he takes care how he speaks about them, that he may not shock natural feeling by assigning to them their real as distinct from their imaginary sentimental value.

To the same motive is due the careful manner in which notice is taken of the fact that certain articles of furniture—all pertaining to the inner shrine—had *gold* about them. The writer wishes to avoid the slightest suspicion of ungenerous disparagement. He is required by truth to disparage the old covenant as a whole, in comparison with the new; but he desires to speak of its ordinances and properties with becoming respect, as things regarded with peculiar reverence by his readers, and even held in high esteem by himself. While his doctrine is that the ancient tabernacle was at best but a poor, shadowy affair, he takes pains to show that in his judgment *it was as good as it was possible for a cosmic sanctuary to be*.[1] Its articles of furniture were of the best material; the ark of fine wood covered all over with gold, the altar of incense of similar materials, the pot with manna of pure gold. He feels he can afford to describe in generous terms the furniture of the tabernacle, because, after all, he will have no difficulty in showing the immeasurable superiority of the "true" tabernacle wherein Christ ministers. One single phrase settles the point—οι χειροποίητος (ver. 11). The old tabernacle and all its furniture were made by the hands of men out of

---

[1] Intention to praise the sanctuary as far as possible is revealed by the μέν in ver. 1, which finds its answering δέ in ver. 6, where the description of the worship begins. On the one hand, the highly ornamented sanctuary; on the other hand, the disappointing service!

perishable materials. The curtains might be fine in texture and ornamentation, and the wood employed in constructing the tables the most beautiful and durable that could be procured. Still all was material, all was fashioned by human handicraft, all was doomed to wax old and vanish away. The "gold, and silver, and brass, and the blue, purple, and scarlet cloths, and the fine linen, and goats' hair, and rams' skins dyed red, and badgers' skins, and shittim wood," were all liable to destruction by the devouring tooth of time, that spares nothing visible and tangible.

This eulogistic style of describing the furniture of the cosmic tabernacle was not only generous, but *politic*. The more the furniture was praised, the more the religious service carried on in the tent so furnished was in effect depreciated by the contrast inevitably suggested. In this point of view there is a latent irony in the reference to the precious materials of which the articles were made. The emphasis laid on the excellent quality of these really signifies the inferiority of the whole Levitical system. It says to the ear of the thoughtful: "The furniture of the tabernacle was golden, but its worship was poor; the outward aspect of things was fine, but the spiritual element was weak and defective; the apparatus was costly, but the practical religious result was of small account. The whole system was barbaric and beggarly, placing value in the outside, rather than in the inside, in matter rather than in mind, in the costliness of the furniture rather than in the high intelligence and refined purity of the cultus there carried on."

Looking now at the inventory distributively, let us note what articles are placed in either compartment of the tabernacle respectively. In the first are located the candlestick, the table, and the shewbread, which was arranged in two rows on the table; to the second are assigned what is called the θυμιατήριον, and the ark of the covenant, containing, as is said, the manna pot, Aaron's rod, and the tables of the covenant, and surmounted by the cherubim of glory shadowing the mercy-seat, or lid of the ark.

After finishing his enumeration, the writer adds that he cannot speak of the things enumerated in detail. Neither can I. The only article of which there is any need to speak "particularly" is the θυμιατήριον, concerning which there are two questions to be considered: What is it? and with what propriety is it assigned to the most Holy place? As to the former, the word θυμιατήριον may mean either "the altar of incense," as I have rendered it, or "the golden censer," as translated in the Authorised and Revised Versions. It is, as Alford remarks, "a neuter adjective, importing anything having regard to, or employed in, the burning of incense," and "may therefore mean either an altar upon which, or a censer in which, incense was burned." The word occurs in Greek authors in both senses, and great division of opinion has arisen among commentators as to which of the two senses is to be preferred here. In favour of the rendering "censer" is a passage in the Mischna, in which stress is laid on the censer to be used on the great day of atonement as distinguished from that used on any other day, on the fact of its being of gold, and not only so, but of a particular and precious kind of gold. No mention of such a golden censer occurs in the Pentateuch. In Leviticus xvi. 12, where directions are given to Aaron concerning the incense-offering, we read: "He shall take a censer full of burning coals of fire from off the altar before the Lord, and his hands full of sweet incense beaten small, and bring it within the veil: and he shall put the incense upon the fire before the Lord, that the cloud of the incense may cover the mercy-seat that is upon the testimony, that he die not." In this passage the Greek name for the censer in the Septuagint is τὸ πυρεῖον; the censer is not called golden; and, lastly, it could not from the nature of the case be kept in the most Holy place, for the high priest would then have had to go in for it in order to use it, a very unlikely procedure, considering that the very purpose of its use was to make it safe for the officiating priest to go within the veil. Still there may have been a censer, distinguished as the golden one, employed in after ages in the solemnities of the great day of atonement; and it is conceivable that, following Jewish tradition in this as in other particulars already referred to, the writer might include it in his enumeration.

Conceivable, but that is all: the supposition is highly improbable. For observe what would follow. One very important article of furniture, the golden altar of incense, would in that case find no place in the enumeration. Is it at all likely that so prominent a piece of furniture would be overlooked in an inventory designed to give a full list of the articles that were the glory and boast of the ancient sanctuary? It is by no means a strong argument against its being the article intended that it is not named as in the Septuagint, where it is designated τὸ θυσιαστήριον τοῦ θυμιάματος. In calling the altar of incense θυμιατήριον the writer followed the usage of his time, as illustrated in the writings of Philo and Josephus. The true cause of the hesitation to adopt this interpretation is not verbal, but theological—the consideration, namely, that by deciding that the altar of incense is intended, we seem to make the writer guilty of an inaccuracy in assigning it to the inner shrine of the tabernacle. I have little doubt that this consideration had its own weight with our Revisers in leading them to retain the old rendering, "the golden censer"; and the fact detracts from the value of their judgment, as based, not on the merits of the question, but on the ground of theological prudence. A clearer insight into the mind of the writer would have shown them that this well-meant solicitude for his infallibility was uncalled for.

This brings us to the question as to the propriety of placing the altar of incense among the things belonging to the most Holy place. On this point even such a considerate interpreter as Bleek has not hesitated to say that the writer has fallen into a mistake, not without its bearing on the question of authorship, as showing that the Epistle could not have been written by an inhabitant of Palestine, who would have known better, but may with more probability be ascribed to an Alexandrian, who might excusably be imperfectly informed. But it is not credible that so able and well instructed a writer as the author of our Epistle, whoever he was, shows himself on every page to be, could commit such a blunder as is imputed to him, that, namely, of locating the altar of incense within rather than without the second veil.[1]

But why then, it may be asked, does he not mention this altar among the articles to be found in the first division of the tabernacle? The answer is of vital importance in its bearing on the main doctrine of the Epistle, the utter insufficiency of the Levitical system. The fact is, that the altar of incense was a puzzle to one who was called on to state to which part of the tabernacle it belonged. Hence the peculiar manner in which the writer expresses himself in reference to the things assigned to the most Holy place. He does not say, as in connection with the first division, "in which were" (ἐν ᾗ), but represents it as "having" (ἔχουσα) certain things.

---

[1] In his latest work, *Das Urchristenthum*, Pfleiderer repeats the assertion that the writer makes a mistake as to the altar of incense, and presses it, along with other supposed mistakes (*e.g.* the daily offering of sacrifice by the high priest, chap. x. 11) into the service of his argument as to the destination and authorship of the Epistle. As the note on page 317 will show, he might have found in the writings of Philo, from which he supposes our author to have drawn freely, a hint of a solution that would have kept him from bringing so hasty a charge. Weiss and von Soden think that the expression ἔχουσα leaves it doubtful whether the writer conceived the altar of incense as within the Holy of Holies. Von Soden is of opinion that he would have some excuse for so thinking in some Old Testament texts, *e.g.* Ex. xxvi. 35, where only the candlestick and the table of shewbread are mentioned as being in the Holy place. Weiss says that it does not matter what the writer thought as to that. He has in his mind the high priest's service on the day of atonement in the most Holy place, when incense was there offered, so that the altar of incense appeared naturally as a piece of furniture belonging to it.

The phrase is chosen with special reference to the altar of incense. Of all the other articles it might have been said "in which were," but not of it. Nothing more could be said than that it *belonged* to the second division. The question is, whether even so much could be said, and why the writer preferred to say this rather than to say that the altar of incense stood outside the veil in the first division. Now as to the former part of the question, in so putting the matter our author was only following an Old Testament precedent, the altar of incense being in 1 Kings vi. 22 called the altar "that was by the oracle," or, more correctly, as in the Revised Version, the altar "that belonged to the oracle." Then the directions given for fixing its position, as recorded in Exodus xxx. 6, are very significant. The rubric runs: "Thou shalt put it before the veil that is by the ark of the Testimony, before the mercy-seat that is over the Testimony, where I will meet with thee." The purport of this directory seems to be: outside the veil for daily use (for within it could not be used save once a year), but tending inwards, indicating by its very situation a wish to get in, standing there, so to speak, at the door of the most Holy place, petitioning for admission. So the eloquent eulogist of the better ministry of the new covenant appears to have understood it. He thinks of the altar of incense as praying for admission into the inner shrine, and waiting for the removal of the envious veil which forbade entrance. And he so far sympathises with its silent prayer as to admit it within the veil before the time, or at least to acknowledge that, while materially without, it belonged in spirit and function to the most Holy place. It really did so at all times, and very specially in reference to the service on the great day of atonement, when incense was carried within the veil.

In stating the case as he does, our author was not only following usage, but utilising the double relations of the altar of incense for the purposes of his apologetic. He wanted to make it felt that the position of that altar was difficult to define, that it was both without and within the veil, that you could not place it exclusively in either position without leaving out something that should be added to make the account complete. And he wished to press home the question, What was the cause of the difficulty? The radical evil, he would suggest, was the *existence* of the veil. It was the symbol of an imperfect religion, which denied men free access to God, and so was the parent of this anomaly, that the altar of incense had to be in two places at the same time: within the veil, as there were the mercy-seat and the Hearer of prayer; without the veil, because the incense of prayer must be offered daily, and yet no one might go within save the high priest, and he only once a year. How thankful, then, should we be that the veil is done away, so that the distinction of without and within no longer exists, and we may come daily to offer the incense of our prayers in the very presence of God, without fear of evil, with perfect "assurance to be heard"![1]

[1] A thought similar to the one above stated occurs in Philo in reference, not to the altar of incense, but to the tree of the knowledge of good and evil. Observing that it is not expressly said in

After the inventory of its furniture comes an account of the ministry carried on in the Jewish sanctuary (vers. 6–10); the description of which, coming after the former, has all the effect of an anticlimax. One can hardly fail to say to himself, What a fall is here! The furniture was precious, but the worship how poor! I read first of golden arks, altars, and pots, and then of sacrifices, ceremonies, meats, drinks, divers washings— mere fleshly ordinances, utterly unfit to put away sin Without any commentary, the two lists placed side by side tell their own tale. Every one capable of reflection feels that a religious system in which the vessels of the sanctuary are so much superior to the *service* cannot be the final and permanent form of man's communion with God, but only a type or parable for the time of better things to come, that could last only till the era of reformation arrived.

This truth, however, the writer does not leave to be inferred, but expressly points out and proves. On two things he insists, as tending to show the insufficiency

Scripture where it was placed, he asks, "What shall we say?" and decides that it was both within and without paradise—within as to essence, without as to power: οὐσίᾳ μὲν ἐν αὐτῷ, δυνάμει δὲ ἐκτός; just the converse of what I have said of the altar of incense, which was within the Holy of Holies as to power, without as to essence. Vide *Alleg.* i. chap. xviii. I have not noticed any reference to this passage from Philo in any of the recent commentaries, nor indeed any such conception of the state of the case as to the location of the altar of incense, as would call for such a reference. Vaughan and Westcott both pronounce in favour of the view that θυμιατήριον means the altar of incense, but neither perceives the point above stated. Vaughan is very conscious of the difficulties for the *interpreter*, but has not thought of the difficulty for the *writer* in locating the θυμιατήριον, or of the lesson he means to teach thereby.

and therefore the transitiveness of the Levitical system, and all that pertained to it. First, he asserts that the mere division of the tabernacle into an accessible Holy place and an inaccessible most Holy place proved the imperfection of the worship there carried on; and, secondly, he points out the disproportion between the great end of religion and the means employed for reaching it under the Levitical system. The former of these positions is dealt with in vers. 6–8, the latter in vers. 9, 10.

The method in which religious worship was carried on in the tabernacle is stated in these terms: "These things being thus prepared, the priests go in continually into the first tabernacle, accomplishing their services; but into the second, once in the year, alone, the high priest, not without blood, which he offers for himself, and for the ignorances of the people."[1] The purpose of this statement is to convey a vivid impression of inaccessibility in reference to the most Holy place, which is done by emphasising three particulars: (1) that no ordinary priest, not to speak of lay persons, ever entered there, only the high priest; (2) that even the high priest entered only once a year;[2] (3) that he dared not enter without the blood of a victim, to make atonement for his own sins and for the sins of the whole people. The

---

[1] The present tenses (εἰσίασιν, προσφέρει) are held by some to prove that when the Epistle was written the temple service was still going on. But the argument is not conclusive. The present may be that of the Scripture record, the writer describing ideally as if the service were now going on.

[2] That is, on one day in the year; how often on that one day is of no consequence to the purpose on hand.

inaccessibility was not absolute, but the solitary exception made the sense of inaccessibility more intense than if there had been no exception. Had entrance been absolutely forbidden, men would have regarded the inner sanctuary as a place with which they had no concern, and would have ceased to think of it at all. But the admission of their highest representative in holy things on one solitary day in the year taught them that the most Holy place was a place with which they had to do, and at the same time showed it to be a place very difficult of access. The ceremonial of the great day of atonement said in effect : " You need to get in here, but it is barely possible to get in. You can be admitted only by deputy, as represented by your officially holy man ; and even he may enter only at rare intervals, and with fear and trembling, with blood in his hands to atone for his and your sins. The door of the second tabernacle is all but shut against you ; open just enough to keep alive in your hearts at once a sense of your need to get in, and the painful consciousness that your desire for admission is rather whetted than satisfied."

Our author proceeds to intimate that just this was the import of the arrangement. "The Holy Ghost this (or by this arrangement) indicating that the way of (into) the Holy place has not yet been manifested, while the first tabernacle has a standing" (ver. 8). The idea is, that the exclusion from the inner part of the Jewish tabernacle, and the all but entire restriction of religious service to the outer part, signified " perfect intercourse with God not yet granted, the highest and therefore abiding form of religion a thing yet to come." The writer would have his readers see, in the mere fact of such a division of the tabernacle into a first and second chamber, a Divine intimation that there was a higher boon, a nearer approach to, a more intimate fellowship with God in store for men, which for the present was denied. "The first part of the tabernacle," he would say, "is yours; the second in its spiritual significance belongs to the future, to the time of Messiah, when all things are to undergo renovation. To cling to legal worship, then, as something that must last for ever is to shut your ear to the voice of the sanctuary itself, by its very structure bearing witness to its own insufficiency, and saying to all who have ears to hear: 'I am not for aye. I have a first and a second chamber, a Near and a Nearer to God. The first and the Near is yours, O people of Israel, for daily use; the second and the Nearer is as good as shut against you. When that which is perfect is come, the Nearer will be accessible to all, and the veil and the place outside and all the services that now go on there will cease to exist.'"

In some such sense as this are to be understood the words in the first clause of ver. 9: "Which (the existence, *i.e.*, or standing of the tabernacle as a first chamber)[1] is a parable for the time being." The sense is, that the outer part of the tabernacle, by its position as a first chamber, was a parable, not in word but in a fabric, teaching the temporary, shadowy, imperfect nature of the dispensation. Some think the time re-

---

[1] The ἥτις refers to στάσιν, "a standing or position such as." So Mr. Rendall, who remarks: "It is not the chamber itself (as in A V.), but its position, which is a figure."

ferred to is the time of the gospel, and that the idea is, that the services carried on in the Holy place were a figure, and nothing more, of the spiritual services offered by Christians. But I think the Authorised Version is correct in making the time referred to, be the time present to the Old Testament worshippers. The tabernacle was a parable even to them, bidding them look forward to the future, to the reality whereof it was but a rude sketch or adumbration.

It will be evident from the foregoing exposition how central to the author's system of thought is the conception of Christianity as the religion of free access, and with what truth that conception may be represented as the dogmatic kernel of the Epistle.

We come now to the description of the service carried on in the Jewish sanctuary (vers. 9, 10). The aim and effect is to make the reader feel that the ritual was in keeping with the parabolic character of the sanctuary itself, the services not less than the structure of the tabernacle proclaiming it to be but a shadow of good things to come. "A parable in keeping with which are offered both gifts and sacrifices having no power to perfect as to conscience him that serveth" (τὸν λατρεύοντα, either the officiating priest, or the people worshipping through him). That the legal sacrifices could not perfect the worshipper, whether priest or layman, as to conscience, appears to the writer self-evident, and he states the truth as an axiom, hoping that his readers will say Amen to it. Of what limited avail those sacrifices were to put away sin is significantly hinted by the term ἀγνοήματα in ver. 7; which points to the fact that the sacrificial system dealt chiefly with mistakes in matters of ritual.[1]

The following sentence, which gives some details regarding the system, is very loosely connected with the foregoing context. "Only, with meats and drinks, and divers washings, ordinances of the flesh, imposed till a time of reformation" (ver. 10). Two questions may be asked in reference to this loosely constructed sentence: (1) What is it that is called "ordinances of the flesh"? (2) In what relation do the meats and drinks and washings stand to the gifts and sacrifices?— are they the same things under different names, or something additional? The "ordinances" are doubtless the gifts and sacrifices of the preceding verse. The connection of thought is: "gifts and sacrifices not having the power to perfect as to conscience; on the contrary, being mere ordinances of the flesh putting away ceremonial uncleanness." As to the meats, drinks, etc., I think they are neither altogether the same with the gifts and sacrifices, nor altogether different from them, but things that were very prominent in connection with sacrifices,—there being meat offerings and drink offerings

---

[1] Besides such ignorances there were other more real and serious offences for which sacrifices were prescribed=sins against the seventh, eighth, and ninth commandments. These were of the nature of exceptions proving the rule; they were included in the category of expiable offences for special reasons: *e.g.* in a case of keeping back something stolen, entrusted, lent, or found, when the sin was voluntarily confessed and could not otherwise have been proved. Similarly, in the case of suppressing truth as a witness, and of the least aggravated offence against chastity, when the offenders were allowed to offer a trespass-offering after the sin had been punished by scourging. (*Vide* Lev. vi. 1-6, xix. 20, 21.)

prescribed by the law, and many washings connected with sacrifices and their occasions. They are referred to in a loose way to illustrate the grossly material nature of the whole religious services, and to justify the application of the depreciatory term "ordinances of flesh." We may paraphrase the whole passage thus: "A parable in keeping with which are offered gifts and sacrifices not fit to perfect the worshipper as to conscience, but only, with their meats and drinks, and divers washings, and so forth, mere ordinances of flesh." Thus understood, the careless construction is studied, being an oratorical device to express impatience with the notion that such ceremonies could possibly cleanse the conscience. The writer speaks as Luther was wont to speak of penances, etc. The great reformer never came in the way of such things without getting into a holy rage at them, and relieving his feelings by a contemptuous enumeration, as if holding them up to scorn, and "making a show of them openly." A similar passage may be found in Paul's Epistle to the Colossians, just where the words now quoted occur: "If ye be dead with Christ, why, as though living in the world, are ye subject to ordinances, (or perhaps, why do ye dogmatise, saying,) Touch not, taste not, handle not?" The careless, offhand way in which the apostle gives examples of the habit he condemns, "Touch not this, taste not that, handle not a third thing," is expressive of the contempt he feels for the whole system which attached importance to such trivialities (Col. ii. 20, 21).

The expression, "time of reformation" ($\kappa\alpha\iota\rho\grave{o}\varsigma$ $\delta\iota o\rho\theta\acute{\omega}\sigma\epsilon\omega\varsigma$), is one of several names given to the new Christian era from an Old Testament point of view. For those who lived under the moonlight of Jewish ordinances, and, conscious of its insufficiency, waited eagerly for the dawn of day, that era, the object of their hope, was the age to come, the time of a better hope, the time of refreshing, the day of redemption, or, as here, the time of rectification. This last designation, if not the most poetical, is very appropriate. For when Christ, the High Priest of the good things to come, arrived, all defects inherent in the ancient system were remedied. The veil was removed; the multitude of ineffectual sacrificial rites was replaced by one all-availing sacrifice; the problem of the pacification of conscience was thoroughly dealt with; and religion became, not an affair of mechanical routine, but a rational spiritual service.

CHAPTER XVI

THE MORE EXCELLENT MINISTRY

Chap. ix. 11-14

In these remarkable sentences the priestly ministry of Christ is described in contrast to that of the Jewish high priest, the aim being to show that the former ministry is, as stated in chap. viii. 6, a more excellent one both in its nature and in its result.

Between things contrasted there must be some resemblance. Hence, to facilitate comparison, the essential facts which form the basis of the doctrine of Christ's priesthood, His death as a sacrificial victim, and His ascension into heaven as one whose blood had been shed, are here stated in terms suggested by the transactions on the great day of atonement, involving a parallelism between Christ and Aaron which at each point is at the same time a contrast in Christ's favour. This mode of stating the truth is dictated by the apologetic aim, and serves well the purpose of conveying rudimentary ideas on the subject to ill-instructed minds. But of course it has its drawbacks. It involves obscurity at points where the parallelism is faint, and provides in a very inadequate measure for the expression of the highest truth. In this respect teaching by types is like teaching by parables. It is good to begin with, but ill fitted to be the last word.

These remarks find illustration in the passage now to be considered, which bristles with difficulties of all sorts: uncertainty in the text, doubtful connections of clauses, expressions to which it is not easy to assign an intelligible meaning, and phrases suggestive of lofty thoughts, where the mind of the writer seems to break away from the trammels of typology and soar into the serene region of spiritual truth. In the circumstances I deem it best to state as plainly as possible the views which commend themselves to my own mind, without discussing at length others with which I am unable to agree. At one point only shall I depart from this attitude, namely, in connection with the expression "through the eternal spirit," which I deem the most important in the whole Epistle, and as at once needing and justifying the most careful exposition, both positive and defensive.

Vers. 11 and 12 I render as follows: "But Christ, appearing [1] as High Priest of the good things to come,[2] *did*, through the greater and more perfect tabernacle not made with hands, that is to say not of this creation (or,

---

[1] παραγενόμενος. This participle expresses the idea of appearing on the stage of history (*vide* παραγίνεται, Matt. iii. 1, in reference to the Baptist). We need not, however, confine its application to the advent of Christ, or to His life on earth, though it includes these; but take it as referring "to the whole accomplished course of Christ summed up in one" (Alford), from the birth to the entrance into heaven as a Priest after the order of Melchisedec.

[2] For μελλόντων Codex B. has γενομένων, adopted by W. and H. This reading may be an ancient error of the eye caused by παραγενόμενος going before.

not of common structure), and not through blood of goats and calves, but through His own blood, *enter in*, once for all, into the holy place, so obtaining eternal redemption."[1]

The ministry of Christ is set forth as the more excellent compared with Aaron's in four respects: (1) because He entered into the true sanctuary through a more perfect tabernacle; (2) because He entered "through His own blood," not through blood of goats and calves; (3) because He thereby obtained, not an annual but an "eternal redemption"; (4) because on that account He needed to enter only once (ἐφάπαξ).

The very first of these four particulars makes us aware of the difficulties created by the typological parallelism. The suggestion seems to be that, as Aaron on the day of atonement entered into the Holy of Holies through the first division of the tabernacle, so Christ entered into the celestial most Holy place through something corresponding thereto. We may indeed very excusably doubt whether that can be intended, seeing it is part of the author's doctrine that by Christ the distinction between holy place and most holy is abolished. But the veil might exist for Christ entering, and be abolished by His entering. Assuming then that Christ is conceived of as entering in through something correspond-

---

[1] I render εἰσῆλθεν periphrastically "did enter in," separating the auxiliary from the main verb by the intervening clauses, to make clear the dependence of these clauses on εἰσῆλθεν. This dependence is acknowledged by most recent interpreters. Rendall takes another view of the construction, and arranges thus: "Christ appearing, not through blood of goats and calves, but through His own blood, as High Priest of good things which came (γενομένων) through the greater and more perfect tabernacle," etc.

ing to the first division of the tabernacle, the question arises, What is the something? I am inclined to agree with those who think that we have nothing here but a form of thought dictated by the parallelism between Christ and Aaron. You may fill it in, if you please, by the lower or first heavens, or by the place of God's visible presence, where He is manifested as an object of worship to angels and spirits of just men made perfect, as distinguished from the proper abode of God, whom no eye hath seen or can see, the celestial holy of holies. I for my part prefer to leave it vague. Were I to yield to the temptation to become definite, I should take up with the antiquated view of the worthy Fathers who saw in Christ's body or human nature the greater and more perfect tabernacle through which our High Priest passed into the celestial sanctuary. Whatever one may think of its truth, it has at least the merits of intelligibility and moral interest. It is much easier to think of Christ's human nature as a tabernacle through which He entered into glory, than to form a definite conception of the heavens as divided into a holy and a most holy place. Then there is something fine in the idea that our Lord's human nature and earthly history were to Him what the transit through the first division of the tabernacle was to the Jewish high priest, namely, the condition of His gaining an entrance into the most holy place, the heavenly sanctuary, as the great High Priest of mankind. On this view, the space between the two veils becomes an emblem of the life of Jesus on earth between His mysterious advent as the holy Child and His no less mysterious exit when He ascended into heaven; and His career between these two points answers to the solemn passage of Aaron through the first tabernacle to the second on the day of annual atonement. I feel the beauty of this thought, while not prepared to affirm that it is the one intended; though in view of the representation of Christ's flesh as a veil in chapter x. 20, it cannot be said to be foreign to the writer's typological system. Acceptance of it is of course not facilitated by the description of the better tabernacle as not of this creation (οὐ ταύτης τῆς κτίσεως).[1] The body of Christ was of this creation, just like the bodies of other men. From this difficulty some take refuge in the glorified, spiritualised body of Christ, only to encounter trouble in another direction from the question, In what sense can it be said that Christ passed through His glorified body? The only possible solution is to say that *through* means *with*, not implying local transition, but a condition under which a particular action is performed.

At the next point in the comparison the typological parallelism brings us in front of a new difficulty. Aaron

[1] Though I have adopted here the rendering of the Revised Version, I am by no means sure that the words above quoted should not be rendered "not of common structure." Dr. Field, in *Otium Norvicense*, remarks on this passage, "By ταύτης I understand *vulgaris, quæ vulgo dicitur*." After giving several examples of this usage, which he thinks has been overlooked by lexicographers, he adds : "This being understood, there is no occasion to take κτίσις in any other sense than that in which κτίζειν is commonly applied to a city (3 Esd. iv. 53 : κτίσαι τὴν πόλιν) or to the tabernacle itself (Lev. xvi. 16 : οὕτω ποιήσεις τῇ σκηνῇ τῇ ἐκτισμένῃ αὐτοῖς)." Most recent commentators adopt the rendering "not of this visible creation," Weiss and von Soden referring to Sap. Sol. xix. 6 for this use of κτίσις.

entered into the inner shrine of the tabernacle with the blood of sacrificial victims in his hands. Is it suggested that Christ took His blood with Him into heaven? No such crude idea ever entered the writer's mind. Does the parallelism then fail at this point? In some respects it certainly does. In the Levitical system, blood-sprinkling within the sanctuary was an essential feature in sacrifice. In connection with the better ministry there is no blood-sprinkling, except in a figure which has no value save as the symbol of a spiritual truth. Blood belongs to this world, and can find no place in heaven. But an analogy can be established between Christ and Aaron by conceiving of blood as the means of gaining admission into the sanctuary. The blood in either case may be regarded as a key opening the door of the holiest. It is in the light of this idea that the phrases, "not through blood of goats and calves, but through His own blood," are to be understood. The writer seizes hold of the one point at which parallelism in the matter of blood is possible, and skilfully adapts his mode of expression (διά) to the state of the case.

Thus far of the parallelism, but now of the contrast: "not by blood of *goats and calves*, but by *His own* blood." To feel the force of this distinction we must understand that the comparison lies not between the *bloods*, but between the *victims*. Blood, whether of man or of beast, is a material, corruptible thing. Chemically considered, I suppose, there is not much difference between the blood of man and that of beast. But what a difference between the victims! In the one case a bullock or a goat, in the other Jesus Christ Himself. There is really no comparison here. "His own blood" takes us into a region of thought where typological conceptions serve no purpose, save to make a crude religious system a foil to show off the grandeur of spiritual truth. We pass *per saltum* from the ritual to the ethical; from a brute beast slain involuntarily, without foreknowledge, and without capacity to consent to, or appreciate the reason of, its dying, to a holy, loving Man, who laid down His own life deliberately, freely, devotedly, animated by an eternal spirit of goodness. Without knowing much of theology one can understand that the two kinds of sacrifice must have very different values in the judgment of God. How the Levitical sacrifice could have any value or any effect it is not easy to see; but that a self-sacrifice like that of Jesus has immeasurable value, however it is to be theologically formulated, for God and for man, one instinctively feels. The difficulty experienced by theologians in their attempts to express its worth in terms of theory is due to the vastness of its significance. Therein is revealed a "many-coloured wisdom of God."[1]

What virtue our author ascribed to Christ's sacrifice appears from the words which set forth the third and chief point of contrast between His ministry and that of Aaron: "obtaining *eternal* redemption" (αἰωνίαν λύτρωσιν εὑράμενος). This is what results from the entrance of Christ into the sanctuary through His own blood, *i.e.* as one who had Himself been the victim. When we come to consider the two following verses, we shall see more clearly why that fact should have so momentous a consequence. For the present we may

[1] Eph. iii. 10: ἡ πολυποίκιλος σοφία τοῦ Θεοῦ.

confine our attention to the exact force of the contrast between the two ministries at this point. It is this: By his sacrifice of bullocks and goats the high priest of Israel procured for himself and for the people an *annual* redemption; by His sacrifice of Himself Christ procured an *everlasting, perennial* redemption. The blood of bulls and goats taken within the veil and sprinkled on the mercy-seat procured, not by its intrinsic virtue, but by positive Divine appointment, remission of certain offences against the Levitical religious system, with the effect of restoring offenders to right theocratic relations for the time being, so giving the people a fair start, as it were, for another year. The blood of Christ shed freely and lovingly on Calvary, and conceived as taken up by Him into heaven, procured by its transcendent essential merit perpetual remission of all sin, took away the whole sin of the world, and so gave mankind a new start, not for a new year, but for a new, unending era of grace. Such is the contrast: on one side, an annual, partial, putative redemption; on the other, an eternal, complete, real redemption. There is no room to doubt where the superiority lies.

The final point of comparison is the number of entries into the most Holy place. The high priest of Israel went in once a year, our great High Priest went in once for all. To the legal, ceremony-loving mind the advantage in this respect might seem to be with the Levitical priesthood. What a fine, imposing service was that annual solemnity of expiation! With what pious delight the devout worshipper anticipated its return, with all its hallowed associations! How pleasant and comforting to have the year divided by sacred seasons! and what a blank would be created by their discontinuance! Tell him not of the insufficiency of those annual atonements; all he knows is that he finds much pleasure in them, and real satisfaction to his conscience in their periodic cancelling of the sins of each past year. Very natural feelings these. It is natural to men in all ages (yes, even in this Christian era, when we ought to have outgrown such childish practices) to observe "days and months and times and years." But such attachments to sacred times in no case settle the question as to the worth or unworth of religious institutions. In particular, it by no means followed that, because the day of atonement was an institution to which the pious Israelite fondly clung, therefore it was fitted to perfect the worshipper as to conscience, or to deal thoroughly with the problem of sin. On the contrary, the annual repetition of the solemnity was a standing testimony to its insufficiency. It needed to be repeated, because at no time did it fulfil the end of its existence. Repetition is not indeed in all cases evidence of insufficiency. The repetition of the passover did not show that it came short of its purpose. It was a commemorative festival, and its repetition served to keep alive the memory of the Exodus. The same remark applies to the feast of tabernacles, which commemorated the wilderness life of Israel. But the annual atonement was not commemorative of redemption achieved once for all. There was in it a remembrance of sin, not of redemption from sin, every year. It was a fresh act of expiation. Therefore in this case repetition implied insufficiency.

The atonement for sin was not, like the deliverance out of Egypt, a thing done thoroughly once for all; therefore it had to be done over and over again.

We pass now to vers. 13, 14. The purpose of these sentences is to justify the ascription to the one sacrifice of Christ virtue sufficient to procure for sinful men a real and eternal redemption. They contain the writer's fullest statement as to the nature of Christ's sacrifice, his final answer to the question, What has this Man to offer?

"For if the blood of goats and bulls, and ashes of a heifer sprinkling those who have been defiled, sanctifieth unto the cleanness of the flesh: how much more shall the blood of Christ, who through an eternal spirit offered Himself without spot unto God, purge our conscience from dead works to serve the living God?"

The point chiefly to be noted in ver. 13 is, that, while in the previous part of the argument mention is made only of the victims slain on the day of atonement, here, besides these, a reference is made to the legal provision for removing uncleanness contracted by accidental contact with a dead body. The reason readily suggests itself. Both things, the blood of victims on the day of atonement, and the ashes of the red heifer, are named together, because the two combined formed the complete legal provision for removing uncleanness, however contracted, *from the whole people of Israel*. The one dealt with the defilement of *sin*, the other with the defilement caused by contact with *death*. By thus uniting the two, our author protects himself from a possible charge of dealing partially with the subject under consideration. And while doing full justice to the law he has an eye to the glory of the gospel. He is preparing the way for the presentation of Christ's sacrifice as dealing effectually with the whole question of moral defilement in all its aspects. He mentions both the blood of sacrificial victims and the ashes of the heifer, because he means to exhibit Christ's blood as serving both the purposes for which these two kinds of legal purification were respectively provided, so proving itself to be a perfect cure for moral evil. On this view the mention of the two Levitical remedies for defilement over against the one remedy under the gospel suggests a subsidiary argument for the superiority of the priestly ministry of the new covenant.

Another point in ver. 13 is worthy of notice. Both the Levitical remedies for uncleanness are spoken of as availing merely for the purity of the flesh. The statement is strictly applicable to the ashes of the heifer, for the sole design of that peculiar institution was to make a man technically clean whose person had come into contact with a corpse. But it may seem rather depreciatory to say of the blood shed on the day of atonement that it availed only to the purifying of the flesh, seeing the express purpose of the sacrifices offered on that day was to make atonement for the sins of Israel. Yet practically, and in effect, the representation is correct. These sacrifices did not purge the conscience, but only the persons of the worshippers. Grave moral offences they did not even profess to deal with, but only with technical offences against religious ritual. And their effect was just that which followed application of the ashes of the heifer, the removal of technical disability to serve God. A man who touched a dead body was not allowed to approach the tabernacle till he had been sprinkled with holy water mixed with a portion of the ashes. In like manner the whole people of Israel were regarded as formally disqualified for the service of God by the accumulated "ignorances" of the past year, till the blood of victims had been duly applied for the purpose of purgation.

In ver. 14 Christ's sacrifice in its infinite worth and eternal validity is set over against these legal provisions for the purification of Israel. We have to note (1) on what the virtue of Christ's sacrifice is made to depend; and (2) what its effect is represented to be.

1. The reason why the sacrifice of Christ possesses transcendent virtue is given in these words, "Who through an eternal spirit offered Himself spotless to God" (ὃς διὰ πνεύματος αἰωνίου ἑαυτὸν προσήνεγκεν ἄμωμον τῷ Θεῷ); where stress must be laid on each of three particulars: Christ offered *Himself*; in offering Himself He presented a *spotless* offering; He offered Himself *through an eternal spirit*. I arrange them thus, because through the explanation of the first two particulars I hope to feel my way to the sense of the third and most difficult one.

First, then, Christ's sacrifice possesses incomparable worth and virtue because the victim was HIMSELF. The ἑαυτόν before the verb is emphatic, and is one of the words to be written here and throughout the Epistle in large letters. In this one fact is involved that Christ's sacrifice possessed certain moral attributes altogether lacking in the Levitical sacrifices: voluntariness and beneficent intention, the freedom of a rational being with a mind of his own and capable of self-determination, the love of a gracious personality in whom the soul of goodness dwells. Christ's sacrifice was an affair of mind and heart—in one word, of *spirit*.

Christ's sacrifice possesses incomparable worth and virtue, secondly, because in Himself He presented to God a *spotless* sacrifice—spotless in the moral sense. He was a perfectly holy, righteous Man, and He showed His moral purity precisely by being loyal and obedient even to the point of enduring death for righteousness' sake. The victims under the law were spotless also, but merely in a physical sense. Christ's spotlessness, on the contrary, was ethical, a quality belonging not to His body, but to His spirit.

We are now prepared in some measure to understand the third ground of the value attaching to Christ's sacrifice, namely, that He offered Himself *through an eternal spirit*. Putting aside for a moment the epithet "eternal," we see that Christ's sacrifice was one in which *spirit* was concerned, as opposed to the legal sacrifices in which flesh and blood only were concerned. The important thing in connection with the latter was the simple fact that the blood was shed and sprinkled according to the rubric. The important thing in Christ's sacrifice was, not the fact that His blood was shed, but the spirit in which it was shed. Then, further, we have no difficulty in determining the ethical character of the spirit in which Christ offered Himself. It was a *free, loving, holy* spirit. But the writer, it is observable, omits mention of these moral qualities, and employs instead another epithet, which in the connection of thought it was more important to specify, and which there was little chance of his readers supplying for themselves. That epithet is *eternal*. The apparent purpose it is meant to serve is, to explain how it comes that the sacrifice of Christ has perpetual validity, how it obtained *eternal* redemption. It meets a state of mind that might express itself thus: "I see the difference between a brute beast slain by the priest and a sacrifice in which the priest is himself the victim, a difference arising out of the introduction of the elements of will and intention; but how that one sacrifice of Himself offered by Christ, though presented through a free, loving, holy spirit, avails to procure an eternal redemption, so that no more sacrifices are needed, I do not see." The epithet "eternal" suggests the thought: the act performed by Jesus in offering Himself may, as an historical event, become old with the lapse of ages; but the spirit in which the act was done can never become a thing of the past. The blood shed was corruptible; but the spirit which found expression in Christ's self-sacrifice is the same yesterday, to-day, and for ever, and in its eternal self-identity lends to the priestly deed imperishable merit and significance.

This fitly chosen phrase thus makes the one sacrifice of Christ cover with its efficacy all prospective sin. But it does more than that. It is retrospective as well as prospective, and makes the sacrifice valid for the ages going before. For an eternal spirit is independent of time, and gives to acts done through its inspiration validity for all time. In this respect it might be said of Christ, that though He offered Himself in historical fact after the world had been in existence for some thousands of years, He offered Himself in spirit "before the foundation of the world." It does not follow from this that the value of His sacrifice was the same in all respects before and after its historical presentation. It was the same for God, but not for man. The sacrifice that was to be, influenced God's attitude towards the world from the first. But the mystery hid *in* God was hid *from* man for ages, and during that long period the beneficent influence of the Christ's eternal spirit could reach men only through the reflected moonlight of Levitical sacrifices, serving as aids to faith in Divine redeeming grace till the era of reformation arrived.

One virtue more must be ascribed to this magic phrase, "through an eternal spirit." It helps us over the difficulty created by the fact that Christ's real self-sacrifice took place on earth, and yet ideally belongs to the heavenly sanctuary. The contradiction, it will be observed, is similar to that I had occasion to note in reference to the altar of incense. Like it, this apparently hopeless antinomy is, when rightly viewed, easily soluble. When we think of Christ's sacrifice as offered through an eternal *spirit*, we see that we may place it where we please, in earth or in heaven, on Calvary or on high, as suits our purpose. For, to repeat what has been already stated,[1] a sacrifice offered through the spirit is a *reality* not a mere shadowy symbol, and the spiritually real belongs to the heavenlies even though it have its place

[1] *Vide* Chapter xiv. p. 294.

also as an historic event among the earthlies. Do you insist that Christ's proper offering of Himself took place in the celestial sanctuary after the ascension, even as Aaron's proper offering was the blood-sprinkling within the most holy place? I reply, Be it so: but it took place there through an eternal spirit which gave to it its value; and if we want to know what that spirit was, we must look to the earthly life of obedience and love culminating in the crucifixion, wherein it found its perfect manifestation. Through this *eternal* spirit Christ offered Himself before He came into the world, when He was in the world, after He left the world. All this the author of our Epistle understands full well, and here in effect teaches; though the apologetic method of his writing requires him to relegate the priestly work of Christ, for the most part, to heaven.

In the foregoing train of reflection we have been, as it were, feeling our way to the sense of this remarkable phrase, and not, I trust, without gaining some light on the place it occupies in our author's system of thought. In proceeding to make some further observations upon it, I begin by remarking, that it may be assumed that the phrase διὰ πνεύματος αἰωνίου serves an important purpose in the argument—really tends to throw light on the transcendent worth of Christ's sacrifice by explaining its unique nature. No interpretation can be accepted which reduces it to a mere expletive that might be omitted without being missed. On first thoughts, indeed, it may seem as if it only produced difficulty, and as if the sense would have been clearer had the sentence run, "Who offered Himself without spot to God." It is surprising indeed that among the variants found in ancient texts and versions there is not one consisting of just such an omission, and that the readings are limited to the omission of *αἰωνίου* and the substitution for it of *ἁγίου*, yielding the mutilated idea "through a spirit," and the commonplace idea "through the Holy Spirit." But whatever difficulty the added phrase may create, so long as we remain in ignorance as to the function it performs, we may be quite sure that the philosophic author of our Epistle uses it with a weighty meaning, which forms an important contribution to the argument, and "crowns" his doctrine as to the nature and worth of Christ's sacrifice. In absence of other instances of its use, our best guide is to try and discover for ourselves what links of thought are still wanting; what questions regarding Christ's sacrifice remain as yet unanswered.

Now one question at least arises naturally out of the foregoing argument, and urgently demands an answer. Why should the sacrifice of Christ possess a value out of all proportion to that of legal victims? To the blood of *goats and bulls* is assigned an extremely limited virtue; why should unlimited virtue be ascribed to the blood of *Christ*? The kernel of the reply given by the writer to this momentous question is contained in the word *spirit*. It stands in antithesis, not merely to the blood of bulls and goats, but to blood in general (the blood of Christ included). The expression "the blood of Christ" refers to His sacrifice in terms of *parallelism* with Levitical sacrifices; the expression "spirit" belongs to the category of *contrast*. It lifts the sacrifice Christ offered in Himself into a higher region, altogether different from that of blood,—the region of mind, will, conscious purpose. The sense in which it is used here may be partly illustrated by a passage in the writings of our author's contemporary Philo. Philo in one place speaks of man as having two souls: the blood, the soul of the man as a whole; the Divine spirit, the soul of his higher nature:[1] in the former part of his doctrine following the teaching of the Hebrew Scriptures, that "the life or soul of all flesh is the blood."[2] We may conceive our author as consciously or unconsciously re-echoing the sentiment, and saying: "Yes, the blood, according to the Scriptures, is the soul of a living animal, and in the blood of the slain victim its soul or life was presented as an offering to God by the officiating priest. But in connection with the sacrifice of Christ, we must think of the higher human soul, the Divine spirit. It was as a spirit He offered Himself, as a self-conscious, free, moral personality; and His offering was a spirit revealed through a never-to-be-forgotten act of self-surrender, not the literal blood shed on Calvary, which in itself possessed no more intrinsic value than the blood of Levitical victims."

Thus interpreted, the term "spirit" unfolds the implicit

[1] "Ἐπειδὰν γὰρ ψυχὴ διχῶς λέγεται, ἥ τε ὅλη καὶ ἡγεμονικὸν αὐτῆς μέρος, ὃ κυρίως εἰπεῖν ψυχὴ ψυχῆς ἐστι, καθάπερ ὀφθαλμὸς ὅ τε κύκλος σύμπας, καὶ τὸ κυριώτατον μέρος τὸ ᾧ βλέπομεν, ἔδοξε τῷ νομοθέτῃ διπλῆν εἶναι καὶ τὴν οὐσίαν τῆς ψυχῆς· αἷμα μὲν τὸ τῆς ὅλης, τοῦ δὲ ἡγεμονικωτάτου πνεῦμα θεῖον: "Since soul is spoken of in two senses, the whole soul and the ruling part of it, which, to speak truly, is the soul of the soul, as the eye is both the whole ball and the principal part by which we see, it seemed to the legislator (Moses) that the essence of the soul is double: blood of the whole, and the Divine spirit of the ruling part" (*Quis Rer. Div.* xi.).

[2] Lev. xvii. 11.

significance of "Himself," and gives us the *rationale* of all real value in sacrifice. It can have no value, we learn therefrom, unless mind, spirit be revealed in it. Death, blood, in its own place, may have theological significance, but not apart from spirit. This is the new truth which by a wide gulf separates Levitical from Christian sacrifice. It has been doubted whether the writer had any such truth in view: whether, that is, he meant to teach anything in advance of Leviticalism on the question, What determines the value of sacrifice? It has been argued that with the Levitical sacrifices before him he did not feel any need for seeking after a new principle, his idea being just that blood atoned, and that the higher efficacy of Christ's blood lay in its being the blood of *Christ*.[1] Had the Epistle to the Hebrews been a purely practical homiletic writing, I could have imagined this to be the writer's state of mind. In such a writing it would not be necessary to raise the question of the *rationale* of value, and the expression, "the blood of Christ cleanseth from all sin," could and would have been used without explanatory comment. But the author of an apologetic writing, if he really understands the Christian religion which he undertakes to defend as against those who fail to see its superiority to Levitical institutions, will have something more to say. It is not enough for him to say, "Blood atones." We understand what that means in reference to Levitical sacrifices: blood was sprinkled on the altar and the mercy-seat, and so made places and persons ritually holy. Was Christ's blood literally sprinkled on the holy things in the "true" tabernacle?

[1] So Davidson.

is it sprinkled literally on human consciences? If not, we are forced to ask what "blood" in New Testament dialect means, and wherein the cleansing virtue really lies. In the phrase, "through an eternal spirit," I see the evidence that the writer of our Epistle felt the pressure of the question, and knew how to answer it.

It goes without saying that the idea of spirit is essentially *ethical* in its import. Voluntariness and beneficent intention enter into the very substance of Christ's sacrifice. Only a frigid exegesis could suggest that the voluntariness of that sacrifice lies outside Christ's priestly action. It is in virtue of its moral contents that Christ is the ideal Priest, and that His sacrifice is the ideal sacrifice. But for the holy, beneficent will revealed therein, Christ's offering of Himself, instead of being a sacrifice "of nobler name" than those offered by Levitical priests, would be a reversion to the lowest type exhibited in human sacrifices. It passes at a bound from the lowest to the highest type by the introduction of the moral elements of free will and holy, gracious purpose. Sacrifice and priesthood are perfected when priest and victim are one, and when the sacrifice is the revelation of spirit. This is the doctrine of our Epistle taught in this famous text, for which we are indebted to the writer's clear, spiritual insight; for it came to him thence, not from reflection on either the Melchisedec or the Aaronic type of priesthood. These he used as the vehicle of his thoughts for apologetic purposes, but they were not the fountain of his own inspiration.

Another remark still may be added. In the light of

the foregoing discussion we can see the vital significance of the *death* of Christ in connection with His priestly work. The tendency of recent commentators, following in the wake of Bähr, has been to throw the death into the shade, and make the stress lie on the subsequent transaction, the entrance of Christ into heaven "through His own blood." In connection with this view much is made of the fact that in the case of most sacrifices under the Levitical system the victim was not slain by the priest, but apparently by the offerer,[1] the chief exception being the sacrifices offered on the day of annual atonement. Such was the fact, so far as we know; but in connection with the highest ideal sacrifice the case is otherwise. The least priestly act of the Levitical system becomes here the most important, the humble, non-

---

[1] Philo in the *Life of Moses* speaks of the victims as slain by the priests. The Septuagint leaves the point vague, using the expression, "they shall slay" (σφάξουσι), *vide* Lev. i. 5, iv. 29. Assuming that the victims, in cases of private or individual sacrifices, were slain by the offerers, we get a threefold gradation in the discharge of priestly functions. All that belonged to a sacrifice: presentation, laying on of hands, slaying, blood manipulation, burning on the altar, was priestly, but in different degrees. Some acts (the first three) were competent to lay offerers, who shared in the general priesthood of Israel, the "kingdom of priests." Other acts connected with ordinary sacrifices, without the tabernacle and within the first division, were competent to the general body of priests in the professional sense. The offices connected with the annual atonement were reserved for the high priest alone, *the priest par excellence*, as in the solemn service in which he exclusively officiated the whole Levitical system culminated. This gradation was a mark of imperfection and helped to increase the sense of distance from God. The people's part, though rudimentary, was very important. The pathos of the Levitical system came out in the acts which they might perform.

sacerdotal first step the essence of the whole matter. Through the death of the Victim His spirit finds its culminating expression, and it is that spirit which constitutes the acceptableness of His sacrifice in the sight of God; as Paul also understood when he said, "Walk in love, as Christ also hath loved us, and hath given Himself for us, an offering and a sacrifice to God for a sweet-smelling savour."[1] The death of Christ is indeed the cardinal fact, whatever theory we adopt as to the nature of the atonement: whether, *e.g.*, we regard the victim in a sacrifice as a substitute for the offerer, bearing the penalty of his sin, or, with Bähr and others, as the symbol of his own self-devotion, the blood presented to God representing a pure life and pledging the offerer to a life of self-consecration. On either view applied to Christ His death was of vital significance; obviously so if He bore the penalty of our sin, not less obviously if His death was but the consummation of a life of self-sacrifice, wherein He is the pattern to all His followers.

On the epithet "eternal" attached to "spirit" it is not necessary further to enlarge. As the term "spirit" guarantees the *real* worth of Christ's offering as opposed to the putative value of Levitical sacrifices, so the term "eternal" vindicates for it *absolute* worth. It lifts that offering above all limiting conditions of space and time, so that viewed *sub specie æternitatis* it may, as to its efficacy, be located at will at any point of time, and either in earth or in heaven. "Eternal" expresses the

---

[1] Eph. v. 2. Pfleiderer, regarding this Epistle as non-Pauline, finds in the text cited a different view of the atonement from that of Paul. Vide *Urchristenthum*.

speculative element in the writer's system of thought, as "spirit" expresses the ethical.[1]

At the close of this discussion I must once more point out how much the interpretation of this Epistle is biassed by the assumption that the priesthood of Christ was a theological commonplace for the writer and his readers. Had it been so, it would have been quite superfluous to insist on so elementary a truth as that, in virtue of being an affair of mind and spirit, Christ's sacrifice possessed incomparably greater value than Levitical sacrifices. One would have expected rather a statement as to the precise

---

[1] Among other interpretations of the expression, διὰ πνεύματος αἰωνίου, the most favoured by recent writers is that which makes it substantially identical in import with πάντοτε ζῶν in chap. vii. 25. So Bleek, and more recently Davidson, Edwards, Weiss, etc. On this view, the purpose of the expression is to explain how Christ could offer Himself in death, and yet *survive the operation*, so as to be able to offer Himself again to God in heaven. "Spirit" is taken, *i.e.*, not in an ethical, but in an ontological or metaphysical sense. On this interpretation I remark, *first*, that the eternal duration of Christ's person is sufficiently recognised in chap. vii. 16, 25, so that I cannot think it likely that, as Reuss puts it, the writer here says, "by a new turn of thought, what he has already twice said in other terms"; and, *second*, that what the connection of thought in chap. ix. requires to be emphasised and accounted for is, not the "eternal personality" of Christ, but the real and absolute worth of His sacrifice, or what it is that makes His priestly performance the "more excellent," perfectly efficacious, ministry. Rendall takes spirit in the ethical sense : "In the eternal spirit of redeeming love the Son had from the beginning planned this offering of Himself for man's redemption." The ethical interpretation finds at least partial recognition in Strack and Zöckler's *Commentar*; also in Vaughan, who offers alternative interpretations: the ontological, in case προσήνεγκεν refers to the self-presentation of Christ in heaven; the ethical, in case it refers to the death on earth. In the latter case the thought is that the Holy Spirit enabled Jesus to present Himself to God in life and death a *spotless* offering.

significance of Christ's death, a theory of the atonement. Such a theory modern readers are chiefly interested in, and expect an expositor to bring out of the Epistle. I am sorry that I am unable to gratify the natural wish, and can only offer as the result of inquiry what may appear a moral truism. My excuse must be the entirely different situation of the first readers, for whom the truism was the thing of vital importance, by no means self-evident, but needing to be insisted on. They were children who required instruction in the merest elements of the Christian doctrine of atonement, and nothing more is to be looked for in the Epistle. That the only true priesthood is that in which priest and victim are one, and that the only real sacrifice is that which reveals and is offered through the spirit, is its contribution—of inestimable, *not yet sufficiently estimated*, worth, however elementary. In what relations such a sacrifice stands to the moral order of the world, and to what extent and under what conditions it exerts its virtue, are questions left comparatively unanswered.

2. The *effect* of Christ's self-sacrifice is made to consist in purging the conscience from dead works. That "the blood of Christ" has, or must have, this effect is not proved. The writer is content to assert, and for the rest invites his readers to reflect, and appeals to their personal experience. The more the subject is thought on, the clearer it becomes; and the appeal to experience is most legitimate, seeing it is within the region of conscience or consciousness that the effect takes place. That this is the case is implied rather than asserted; but the implied truth, that the real source of disability to serve God is to be

found, not in bodily defilement, but in "an evil conscience,' is of cardinal importance, as forming one of the leading points of contrast between Christianity and Leviticalism.

Conscience being the sphere within which the blood of Christ exerts its cleansing power, its mode of action is correspondingly modified. The blood of Levitical victims and the ashes of the heifer were literally sprinkled, and the effect was immediate, *ex opere operato*. Christ's blood acts on the conscience through the mind interpreting its significance, and in proportion as it is thought on. It speaks to our reason and our heart, and the better we understand its language the more we feel its virtue. It has a minimum of virtue for those who, in their way of contemplating Christ's death, scarce rise above the Levitical point of view. "The blood of Jesus shed as a sin-offering, God's ordinance for salvation; I look to it, and believe, on God's word, that my sin is forgiven." This way of regarding Christ's death as a positive institution for procuring pardon, for which no account can be given save God's sovereign will, limits the range of benefit and lowers the quality of service. God's mind is not known. He may be thought of perhaps as one who demands the blood of a victim in satisfaction to His justice, and that goes so far in the way of insight. But there is no thought of satisfaction to His *love*, of His delight in His Son's love: no perception of the truth that the value of Christ's sacrifice is immensely greater for God and for man *propter magnitudinem charitatis*, as Aquinas expressed it—"on account of the greatness of His love." It is difficult to serve such a God in the spirit of filial trust and devotion. When the spirit in which Christ offered

Himself is taken into consideration, assurance of forgiveness is greatly strengthened. We then not merely believe that the sacrifice satisfies God, but understand in some measure why. We learn from the feelings it awakens in our own breasts that such an act of self-devotion must be well-pleasing to God, and we cannot doubt that our trusty Brother and High Priest is the beloved of His Father, and that we are accepted in Him.

Thus conscience is purged in the sense that we are assured of pardon, and are no more troubled by the sense of guilt. But the sense of guilt is not the only disability under which we labour. We are hindered from serving God at all, or effectively, by moral evil present in us even after we have believed in pardon, tempting us to doubt our standing and God's power to save, and to enter into the bypaths of legalism and self-salvation. Is there any reference to these serious disabilities in this text? If we think of the writer as a slave to Levitical forms of thought, and as dominated by the parallelism between the ancient sacrificial system and the Christian priesthood, we shall answer in the negative. In that case, we restrict the effect of Christ's sacrifice to the pardon of sin, and not of all sin, but only of sins within the covenant; the benefit being confined to those already in covenant relations, and consisting in being cleansed from sins of infirmity such as even God's people commit. I have consistently protested against this narrow interpretation of the Epistle, which puts the writer practically on a level with his ill-instructed readers, and not much, if at all, in advance of the position held by the Judaistic party in the Church, and have contended for an interpretation which makes the contrast everywhere prominent, and the parallelism subservient to apologetic purposes. In accordance with this view, I am inclined to take the term "purge," as I have already taken the term "sanctify," in a large sense, and to understand by the purifying of the conscience the removal of all disabilities whereby men are prevented from rendering an efficient, acceptable service unto God. I believe the writer of our Epistle means to claim for Christ's sacrifice, viewed in the light of the spirit in which it was offered, the power to deliver us from all manner of disabilities, to bestow on us "a plenteous redemption," to unloose all bonds which keep us from being in the highest, noblest sense God's servants.

Holding this view, I naturally sympathise with the interpretation of the expression "dead works" advocated by Bleek, according to which it signifies, not merely sinful works in general, but more specifically religious works done by men who serve God in a legal spirit, not in the filial spirit of trust and love. The epithet "dead" is appropriate under either interpretation, as describing the defiling influence of the works done, so that from the mere words the question cannot be decided. We must be guided in our decision by a regard to the connection of thought and the religious condition of the first readers. Looked at from the former of these two points of view, we may assume that the phrase is employed to express the completeness and thoroughness with which Christ's blood cleanses the conscience. It is very well fitted to do that if it refer to works of religious legalism, because deliverance from the bondage of a legal spirit is the most difficult part and last instalment of redemption.

The severest test of Christ's power to redeem is His ability to loose the bonds springing out of a legal religion, by which many are bound that have escaped the dominion of gross sinful habits. Nor is it a matter of small moment whether men be set free from these bonds or not; for though they do not prevent their victims from serving God after a fashion, they prevent them from rendering to the living God a service acceptable in spirit and intelligent in aim. Men under the dominion of a legal temper often think they do God service, when they are simply obstructing His work in their time and thwarting His chosen instruments. In view of this fact, abundantly exemplified in the history of the Church, it becomes very apparent what cardinal importance attaches to *redemption from legalism*. A man of prophetic spirit, in sympathy with Christ and Paul and reformers in every age, in their judgment on religion of a legal type, could not fail to refer to Christ's power to deliver from its influence in a eulogium on His redeeming work. And such a reference was equally apposite, in view of the religious state of the Hebrew Christians. For that they had not escaped the fetters of legalism is manifest from the simple fact that such an elaborate apologetic for Christianity *versus* Leviticalism was called for.

Complete redemption involves deliverance from the sense of guilt, from the power of moral evil, and from religious legalism. These combined cover at once all ethical and all religious interests, both "justification" and "sanctification" in the Pauline sense. All these benefits flow from Christ's sacrifice, *viewed in the light of the spirit through which it was offered*. We are now in a position to answer a question hinted at in an early chapter, namely, "Does the system of thought in this Epistle provide for the union of the two kinds of sanctification? or do they stand side by side, external to each other? Are religious and ethical interests reconciled by a principle inherent in the system?"[1] I answer confidently in the affirmative, and I point to the great utterance, "through the eternal spirit," as the key to the solution of the problem. That word not only demonstrates the immeasurable superiority of Christ's sacrifice to those offered by Levitical priests, but brings unity and harmony into Christian experience. Intelligent appreciation of the spirit by which Christ offered Himself inspires that full, joyful trust in God that gives peace to the guilty conscience. But its effect does not stop there. The same appreciation inevitably becomes a power of moral impulse. The mind of Christ flows into us through the various channels of admiration, sympathy, gratitude, and becomes our mind, the law of God written on the heart. And the law within emancipates from the law without, purges the conscience from the baleful influence of "dead works," that we may serve the Father in heaven in the free yet devoted spirit of faith and love. To say that the author of our Epistle understood all this, and here has it in view, is only to say that he was an enlightened Christian; that he walked in the broad daylight of the Christian faith, not in the dim morning twilight of Judæo-Christian compromise; that if not a Paulinist, he was at least not less sensible than Paul to what extent the world was indebted to Jesus Christ.

[1] *Vide* p. 111, note 1.

CHAPTER XVII

THE NEW COVENANT

CHAP. IX. 15–28

ONE is inclined to wonder that after making the consummate statement as to the significance of Christ's death in ix. 14 the writer of our Epistle did not at once pass on to the exhortation to Christian confidence and steadfastness which begins at x. 19. The terms of the exhortation (x. 19–23) fit exactly to those of the doctrinal statement: the free access in the blood of Jesus answers to the deliverance by the same blood from all that disables for the service of the living God, and the heart sprinkled from an evil conscience answers to the purging of the conscience from dead works. Indeed, so close is the correspondence between the two passages, that one is tempted to indulge the conjecture that in the first draft of the Epistle they stood in immediate contact, and that all lying between is an interpolation subsequently inserted by the writer in the final revision.

The introduction of this intervening train of thought, which contains some obscurities, and in which the interest seems to sink below the high-water mark reached in chapter ix. 14, like so much more in the

Epistle, is best understood in the light of apologetic aims and exigencies. In the section commencing with chapter viii. the writer has been putting two great thoughts before his readers: a better covenant than the Sinaitic, a better ministry than the Levitical, brought in by the Christian religion. Both these thoughts are new and unfamiliar to them, and to their conservative temper unacceptable, as involving religious innovation or revolution. Had either been familiar and accepted, it could have been used for the establishment of the other, which being done, there would be nothing more to be said. But both being unfamiliar, each must be used in turn to justify the other. From the better covenant prophesied of by Jeremiah, and assumed to be legitimised by his authority, it is inferred that there must be a better ministry, which, whatever its precise nature, shall be supremely effective. What that better ministry is chapter ix. 14 declares. On the strength of that statement the infinitely valuable self-sacrifice of Christ is next assumed to be the truth conceded, and from it in turn is deduced as a corollary the inauguration of a new covenant (ver. 15). The idea of the new covenant again is employed to throw light on the death of the Inaugurator, the writer being well aware how slow his readers are to take in the thought that the thing which this Man has to offer is *Himself*. Hence in this interpolated train of thought, if we may so call it, the emphasis with which is iterated and reiterated, in reference to Christ's death, the sentiment, "*Once*, but once *only*." This alternate use of two unaccepted truths to prove each other is reasoning in a circle, but there is no help for it; and the fact that the writer is obliged to have recourse to it shows conclusively how true is the assumption on which I have been proceeding in my exposition of the Epistle, that the whole system of ideas embodied in it was strange to its first readers.

"*For this cause He is mediator of a new covenant*" (ver. 15). "From the better covenant I inferred a better ministry, and I have just told you what the better ministry is. Judge for yourselves of its excellence. If what I said of it be true, the priestly Minister of the Christian faith is well entitled to inaugurate a new covenant involving the supersession of the old; nay, the direct effect of His ministry is to establish such a covenant, for the purification of the conscience from dead works to serve the living God is just the improved state of things to which Jeremiah's oracle pointed. It imports all sin forgiven, the law written on the heart, God truly known in His grace, and close relations subsisting between Him and His people." Such is the connection of thought. To make the new covenant welcome, its novelty notwithstanding, the writer hastens to specify two important benefits it brings: full redemption of the transgressions under the first covenant, and the consequent actual, effective attainment of the inheritance. To understand the former we must keep in mind the writer's doctrine as to the valuelessness of legal sacrifices. He conceives of the uncancelled iniquities of the covenanted people as going on accumulating, these sacrifices notwithstanding. In spite of annual expiations designed to clear the "ignorances" of the past year, in spite of the blood of goats and bulls profusely shed, in spite of countless sin-offerings presented by individual offenders, the mass of unpardoned sins went on increasing, till it had become a great mountain rising up between Israel and God, loudly calling for some Mighty One who could lift it and cast it into the sea. Christ is the Mighty One. Or, to use a figure more in keeping with the language of the text, the first benefit He confers is, that He pays off the immense mass of debts with which the promised inheritance is so burdened that it is hardly worth possessing, being an inheritance of pecuniary obligation rather than of a real, substantial estate.

This accomplished, there follows of course the second benefit: the heir enters on a not merely nominal but real possession of his inheritance. "*They that have been called receive the promise of the eternal inheritance.*" They get not only the promise, but the thing promised, real fellowship with God now, with the certain hope of completed fruition in the great hereafter, when, following the Captain of salvation, they shall have passed through death to the promised land.

Having thus used Christ's death to justify the establishment of a new covenant, the writer proceeds to use the idea of a covenant to justify or explain Christ's death. It was fitting and needful that the Inaugurator of the new covenant should die once, but once only: such is the drift of what remains of the ninth chapter. In entering on this line of thought the writer makes a statement which it is difficult to understand unless we assume that he uses διαθήκη in vers. 16, 17 in the specific sense of a testamentary disposition: in one simple word, a will, or deed of gift by which a man disposes of his property to his heir. The Greek word bears this specific sense, as well as the more general one of an agreement between two parties.[1] The two meanings are not exclusive of each other, for the same thing may be at once a covenant and a testament. The new constitution on which our Christian fellowship with God is based is both. It is a covenant; a rather one-sided one indeed, a covenant of promises or of grace, still a covenant thus far, that the promises of God are given to faith. It is also a testament or will; for the peace of the new dispensation was bequeathed by Christ to His disciples on the eve of His death, and it was in the same solemn circumstances that He said to them, " I appoint[2] unto you a kingdom." It is easy to see why at this point the " new covenant " becomes a testament, and the Mediator a Testator. It is because under that aspect it becomes apparent why the death of the Inaugurator should precede the actual obtainment of the inheritance. For in the case of wills, though not in the case of covenants, it is true that a death must occur,[3] the death, namely, of the testator. Of this fact the

---

[1] Vaughan (ad vii. 22) says: "διαθήκη has the comprehensive sense of an arrangement whether of relations (covenant) or of possessions (testament)." He finds the latter use in Heb. ix. 16, in common with most recent commentators, including Weiss and von Soden.

[2] Luke xxii. 29: διατίθεμαι, the verb corresponding to the noun διαθήκη. (Cf. "dispone" in Scotch law.)

[3] The Greek word here is φέρεσθαι, which is used probably to express, along with the idea of happening, that of becoming known. "It contains besides the idea of γενέσθαι that of evidence that it has taken place."—Von Soden.

writer takes advantage as a means of showing the congruity of death to Christ's position as Mediator of the new covenant. The view here presented of Christ's death is by no means so important as that given in the previous context; for the death of a testator is not sacrificial: it is enough that he die in any way, in order that the heir may enter into possession. But it was something gained if it could be made to appear that in some way or other, on one ground or another, Jesus as the Christ behoved to die. One wonders at the introduction of so elementary and inferior a view close upon the grand conception of ver. 14. But remember to whom the writer is addressing himself. He is not at all sure that his grand thought will strike his readers as it strikes him, and so he falls back on this cruder view as more level to childish apprehension. In patient condescension he steps down from the sublime to the commonplace. For lack of attention to his aim it may readily happen that what he meant to simplify, his argument may create for us confusion and perplexity. We have difficulty in understanding how a man could at this stage in his discourse say anything so elementary.[1]

The two views of Christ's death, though quite distinct, and of very different degrees of importance, are yet closely connected. It is because Christ's death is sacrificial, and in that capacity of infinite virtue, that it

[1] Even Westcott remarks: "The death of Christ was a chief difficulty of the Hebrews, and therefore the writer presents it under different aspects, in order to show its full significance in the Christian dispensation"; on ix. 16, 17. On this view the atonement cannot have been, as some think, a commonplace for the first readers.

is also the death of a testator. In other words, because Christ through the spirit offered Himself a spotless and most acceptable sacrifice to God, therefore He hath an inheritance to bequeath, and might say, "I appoint unto you a kingdom, as My Father hath appointed unto Me."

The writer goes on to mention the fact that the Sinaitic covenant was inaugurated by sacrifice, still by way of showing the close connection between death and covenanting, and the congruity between Christ's death and His position as the Inaugurator of the new covenant (ver. 18). In doing so he seems to drop the specific idea of a testament that had been suggested to his mind by the word "inheritance" (ver. 15), and to return to the more general meaning of the term $\delta\iota\alpha\theta\eta\kappa\eta$. Such a sudden transition, without warning, from one sense to another of the same word is, from a logical point of view, unsatisfactory, and one is tempted to try whether the old sense cannot be made to fit into the new connection of thought. In that case the covenant at Sinai would have to be regarded as a testamentary one, by which God bestowed on Israel a valuable inheritance. The victim slain in sacrifice would represent the testator shedding his own blood as the condition of the heir obtaining possession of the inheritance. In support of this view stress might be laid on the deviation from the original Hebrew and from the Septuagint in the report of the words spoken by Moses to Israel when he sprinkled the blood. "*Behold* the blood of the covenant," he said. In our Epistle the words are altered to, "*This* is the blood of the covenant," which sounds like an echo of the words spoken by Jesus in instituting the Holy Supper: "This is

My blood of the new testament." But this interpretation, besides putting on the first covenant a sense foreign to Hebrew customs, would involve us in a very complicated typology. Christ would have to play many parts, being at once testator, mediator, priest, and victim: God, Moses, young men, and sacrifices, all in one.

In stating the facts connected with the ratification of the covenant at Sinai, the writer is not careful to keep close to the narrative in Exodus. He says nothing of the burnt-offerings and peace-offerings made by the young men (firstborn sons?), acting *pro tempore* as priests, but mentions only the sacrificial acts of Moses. On the other hand, he adds particulars from tradition or conjecture to make the description as vivid as possible; the added particulars being the water, scarlet wool, and hyssop. Further, in the original narrative there is no mention of the sprinkling of the book, nor are goats alluded to as being among the victims slain. These discrepancies are of trifling moment. The phrase "calves and goats" is a convenient expression for all bloody sacrifices. The water, wool, and hyssop were doubtless used on the occasion: the water to dilute the blood, a hyssop wand whereon to tie the wool, the wool to lick up the blood and be the instrument for sprinkling. That the book was sprinkled is probable when we consider the fact stated in ver. 22, that almost all things were by the law purged with blood, and the reason of the fact, that all things with which sinful men had to do contracted defilement, no matter how holy the things in themselves might be, the very Holy of Holies standing in need of purification.

This copious use of blood in connection with the inauguration of the covenant naturally leads the writer to mention other instances of blood-sprinkling, and to make the general observation that under the law almost everything was purged with blood,[1] and especially that the important matter of remission of sin never took place except in connection with blood-shedding[2] (vers. 21, 22). The reference in ver. 21 appears to be to the ceremonies connected with the consecration of Aaron and his sons, and also to those connected with the consecration of the tabernacle, events which probably took place at the same time, though they are described in different places.[3] Here again we have an addition to the rites. There is no mention in the history of the sprinkling of the tabernacle and its vessels with blood, but only of an anointing with oil. It is to be noted, however, that both blood and oil were used in the consecration of holy persons,[4] which makes it probable that both were used in the consecration of holy *things*. The emblematic significance of the elements justifies such an inference. Blood-sprinkling signified sanctification in the negative sense of

---

[1] Literally "one may almost say (σχεδόν) that, according to the law, all things are cleansed in blood." "The σχεδόν qualifies the sweeping statement which it prefaces, and especially the πάντα." Vaughan.

[2] αἱματεκχυσίας, blood-shedding, or blood-outpouring. Mr. Rendall contends for the latter; but, as Professor Davidson remarks, "so far as the author's purpose here is concerned, which is to show the necessity of a death for remission of transgressions (ver. 15), it is immaterial to decide which is meant." Westcott renders "outpouring of blood," and remarks that the Greek word is found elsewhere only in patristic writings. It is found here only in the New Testament, and not in the Septuagint.

[3] Lev. viii. and Ex. xl. [4] *Vide* Lev. viii. 30.

purging away the uncleanness of sin; the anointing with oil signified sanctification in the positive sense of infusing grace, or the spirit of holiness. Now sacred things admitted of the former sort of sanctification more obviously than of the latter, which seems appropriate only to persons. The inference that the blood was sprinkled on the tabernacle and its furniture is justified by Josephus, who states that Moses, when he had rewarded the artificers who had made and adorned these things, slew a bullock and a ram and a kid in the court of the tabernacle as God had commanded, and thus with the blood of the victims sprinkled Aaron and his sons with their vestments, purifying them with spring water and oil, that they might be the priests of God. In this way he sanctified them for seven days in succession. The tabernacle likewise and all its vessels he sanctified, anointing them with fragrant oil, and sprinkling them with the blood of bulls and rams and goats.[1]

From this extensive use of blood under the law an inference is drawn as to the probability of its use under the new covenant (ver. 23). If, it is argued, the cosmic tabernacle, with all that belonged to it, required to be purified by the blood of victims slain for that end, it stands to reason that the heavenly things of which these were the rude emblems should have their sacrifices also, only *better* than the legal ones. Why better is thus explained: "For not into a holy place made with hands, a copy (ἀντίτυπα,[2] literally 'antitype') of the true, is Christ entered, but into heaven itself, now to appear before the face of God for us" (ver. 24). The

[1] *Antiquities*, iii. 18, 6.   [2] *Vide* note at end of this chapter.

point insisted on is: the tabernacle into which Christ hath entered being not the material, man-made one, but the spiritual, heavenly one, His sacrifice must be in keeping with the dignity of the sanctuary wherein He officiates, must, in fact, possess attributes to be found only in *Himself*; for the aim is still to press home the truth that that is what this Man has to offer.

With regard to this line of argument three observations may be made. First, seeing that blood-shedding and blood-sprinkling were so prominent features under the law, it was to be expected that there would be a sacrifice of some kind under the new dispensation. Wherever there is a shadow there must be a body that casts it. The sacrifices of the law were shadows of something better of the same kind, of a rare, perfect sacrifice offered for the same purpose, the purification of sin. Second, for the new dispensation better sacrifices (or one better sacrifice) were required. The blood of bulls and goats might do for the cosmic sanctuary, but not for "the true tabernacle which the Lord pitched, not man." One cannot read the directions for sacrifice in the law without feeling, "This is a system of beggarly elements, of rude, barbaric ritualism, in which flesh and blood are very prominent, and spiritual import very hidden and obscure. There must surely be something better than this to come, a sacrifice of moral and not merely ritual value." Third, that the new covenant sacrifice (for though the plural is used in ver. 23 to suit the parallelism of thought, there is and can be only one sacrifice), Christ *Himself*, is better than any sacrifice under the law, better than all of them put together, the best conceivable, it being absolutely impossible to imagine any quality of excellence not found in the sacrifice Christ made of Himself through an eternal spirit. There is only one point in the inference contained in ver. 23 that we may reasonably have difficulty in understanding, namely, the implied assertion that the heavenly things needed to be purified by sacrifice. Various modes of meeting the difficulty have been suggested. We are told, *e.g.*, that the heavenly things do not mean heaven proper, but only the things of the new covenant, the new testament Church, or something of that sort, the sphere and the means of men's relations to God; that purifying is predicated of heaven, only to make the second half of the sentence correspond to the first; that even heaven itself does need or admit of purification in the sense that it needs to be made by Christ's entry there, with or through His own blood, approachable to sinful man, by the removal of the shadow cast on God's face by human guilt. For my own part, I prefer to make no attempt to assign a theological meaning to the words. I would rather make them intelligible to my mind by thinking of the glory and honour accruing even to heaven by the entrance there of "the Lamb of God." I believe there is more of poetry than of theology in the words. For the writer is a poet as well as a theologian, and on this account theological pedants, however learned, can never succeed in interpreting satisfactorily this Epistle.

Thus far the leading thought has been, It behoved Christ to die once. Of what remains, the burden is, *once only*. It is not a new thought, but the repetition of a thought more than once already enunciated (vii. 27,

ix. 12), iteration being forced on the teacher by the dulness of his pupils. But while not new in itself, the truth is enforced by a new argument, drawn not from the same source as the argument for the necessity of Christ's dying once, the analogy between the old and the new covenants, but from an analogy between the course of Christ's experience and that of men in general. It behoved Christ as a Mediator to die once, for even the first covenant was inaugurated by death; but it behoved Him to die once only, because it is appointed unto all men to die once only. The writer could find nothing in the Levitical system, or in the history of the old covenant analogous to the "once-for-all" attribute of Christ's death; and it was this fact that made it hard for the Hebrews to be reconciled to the solitary sacrifice of the Christian dispensation. He makes here a last effort to enlighten them, skilfully seeking in the history of the human race what he could not find in the history of the Sinaitic covenant, an analogy fitted to popularise the truth he is bent on inculcating.

These verses (25–28) may be paraphrased thus: Christ has entered into the heavenly sanctuary to appear in the presence of God for us, and *to abide there*, herein differing from the Levitical high priest, who went into the most holy place, and came out, and went in again, repeating the process year by year, and making many appearances before God, with the blood of fresh sacrifices. Christ presents Himself before God once for all, remaining in the celestial sanctuary, and not going out and coming in again and again. It must be so; any other state of things would involve an absurdity. If Christ were to go in and come out, go in and come out, again and again, that would imply His dying over and over again ; for the object of the repeated self-presentations in the presence of God on the part of the Jewish high priest was to offer the blood of new victims : but as Christ's sacrifice was Himself, each new self-presentation would in His case imply a previous repetition of His passion. He must often on that supposition have suffered death since the foundation of the world. But such an idea is absurd. It is contrary to all human experience, for it is appointed to men to die once only. After death comes no new return to life, to be followed by a second death, and so on times without number. After death once endured comes only the judgment. In like manner it is absurd to think of Christ as coming to the earth to live and die over and over again. He will indeed come once again, a second time ; not, however, as a Saviour to die for sin, but as a Judge. As for us men, after death comes at the end of the world the judgment, so for Him after His passion comes at the end of the world the work of judging : that is to say, in the case of those who believe in Him and look for Him, the work of assigning to them, by a judicial award, the end of their faith, even eternal salvation.

To minds enlightened in Christian truth this train of thought is by no means so important as that contained in vers. 13, 14, where the sufficiency of Christ's one sacrifice of Himself to accomplish the end of all sacrifice is proved from the infinite moral worth of that one sacrifice. But though of little value intrinsically, because giving no insight into the *rationale* of non-repetition of sacrifice, this final argument is of a more popular character, and fitted to tell on minds unable to appreciate arguments of a higher order. Their need is its justification.

Three points here call for a few sentences of additional explanation:

1. In the statement that repeated self-presentation on Christ's part before God, after the manner of the Levitical high priest, would imply frequent experience of death, the date from which these hypothetical experiences are made to begin is remarkable. "Since in that case it would have been necessary that He should suffer often *from the foundation of the world*." Why go back so far? why not rather say, "Then must He suffer again and again hereafter"? The answer to the latter part of the question will appear when we come to the second point I mean to notice; but as for the former part of the question, it admits of a satisfactory answer offhand. When we consider the purpose for which Christ died, it becomes clear that if one dying was not enough, then the commencement of the series of His self-sacrifices would require to be contemporaneous with the origin of sin. If by a single offering of Himself He could take away the sin of the world, then it did not matter when it was made. It might be presented at any time which seemed best to the wisdom of God. For its efficacy in that case would be spread over all time; it would avail for the ages before Christ's advent as well as for the ages that might come after, in virtue of the eternal spirit by which it was offered. But if by one offering Christ could not take away absolutely the world's sin; if the efficacy of His blood, like that of legal victims, was only temporary, limited, say, to a generation, as that of the victims slain

on the day of atonement was to a single year,—then He must either die for each successive generation, or the sins of the world, those of one favoured generation excepted, must go unatoned for.

It is thus clear that if one offering had not sufficed, Christ would have had to begin His series of incarnations and atonements from the date of Adam's fall, and to carry them on as long as the world lasted. This is what the writer intended to say in the statement above quoted. But the same idea might have been expressed thus: "Then must He continue to offer Himself from time to time till the end of the world." The difference between the two ways of putting the matter is, that in the one it is virtually stated that the experience which Christ underwent eighteen centuries ago could not (in the case supposed) have been the first; while in the other it would be virtually stated that that same experience could not be the last, the whole truth being that it could neither be the first nor the last.

2. But why then not say, "Then must He often suffer hereafter"? The answer to this question is, that as the writer conceived the history of the world there was no room left for future Incarnations and Passions. The world's history was near its end. This view comes out in these words: "But now once for all, at the end of the ages, hath He been manifested for the cancelling of sin by the sacrifice of Himself" (ver. 26); and it is the second point calling for remark. Now as to the belief held by the writer in common with all who lived in the apostolic age, that the end of the world was at hand, there is nothing to be said about it, save that he

and his contemporaries knew no better. They had no revelation on the subject, but were left to their own impressions, which have turned out to be mistaken. The one true element in them was, that the Christian dispensation is the final one, so that we look for no new era, but only for the συντέλεια τῶν αἰώνων. But it is worthy of remark, that the conception of Christ's death, resulting from this belief, as taking place at the end of the world, is in its own way very impressive. The history of redemption implied therein is something like this: The sins of the world go on accumulating as the successive generations of mankind appear and disappear. In spite of all that legal sacrifices can effect, the mass grows ever bigger. At the end of the ages Christ makes His appearance on the earth to annihilate this immense accumulation of sins, to lift the load on His strong shoulders, and cast it into the depths of the sea, and so to bring in the new heavens and the new earth wherein dwelleth righteousness. Surely a sublime mode of conceiving Christ's work; not less so than that which is more natural to us living far down in the Christian centuries, according to which Christ, in His earthly life, bisects the course of time into two parts, appearing as the central figure in the world's history, spreading His healing wings over the whole race of Adam, one wing over the ages before He came, the other over the ages after.

3. The third point calling for mention is the representation of Christ as appearing in His second advent *without sin* (χωρὶς ἁμαρτίας, ver. 28).

The expression, "without sin," used in reference to the second coming, implies that in some sense Christ came with sin at His first advent. And, however hard the idea may be, the writer certainly does mean to represent Christ as appearing the first time with sin. His own words in the immediately preceding context explain the sense in which he understands the statement, "Christ, once offered to bear the sins of many." Christ came the first time with sin, but not His own: with the sins of the many, of the world, of all generations of mankind; with sin on Him, not in Him; came to be laden in spirit, destiny, and lot with the world's guilt, so that He might truly be called "the Lamb of God who taketh away the sin of the world." To say that Christ appeared the first time with sin is equivalent to saying that He came to be a Redeemer from sin. The difference between the two comings therefore is this: in the first, Christ came as a Sin-bearer; in the second, He will come as a Judge. After the first coming no more sacrifice for sin is needed; all that remains to be done is to gather up the results of the one great sacrifice.

Note on ἀντίτυπα referred to on p. 364.

I append here the remarks of Westcott and Vaughan on this word occurring in Heb. ix. 24. Westcott says: "In the two passages in which the word ἀντίτυπον is used in the N.T. the sense corresponds with the two fundamentally different ideas of τύπος. The τύπος may be the archetype (cf. Acts vii. 44), of which the ἀντίτυπον is the provisional copy, as here; or the τύπος may be the provisional adumbration (cf. Acts vii. 43) of that which the ἀντίτυπον more completely expresses. So the water of baptism answered as ἀντίτυπον to the water of the flood, which bore in safety the tenants of the ark (1 Pet. iii. 21)." Vaughan: "*Corresponding to.* The same word ἀντίτυπον may be either (1) *answering in type to* or (2) *answering to the type of.* Thus type and antitype may change places in its use. The χειροποίητα here (the Levitical Holy of Holies) are called ἀντίτυπα to the heavenly. *Corresponding typically* to the ἀληθινά. In 1 Pet. iii. 21 the water of baptism is said to *correspond antitypically* to the water of the deluge."

CHAPTER XVIII

SHADOW AND SUBSTANCE

Chap. x. 1–18

What might seem the last word is not quite the last. The writer makes a fresh start, not as having any absolutely new truths to utter, but with intent to reassert old truths with a power and impressiveness befitting the peroration of a weighty discourse. The " for " with which the chapter begins does not imply close connection with what goes immediately before, as if what follows were a continuation of the argument written at the same moment; it expresses merely a general connection with the drift of the preceding discussion, the value of Christ's one sacrifice as compared with the valuelessness of oft-repeated Levitical sacrifices. We may conceive the writer making a pause to collect himself, that he may deliver his final verdict on Leviticalism in a solemn, deliberate, authoritative manner. This verdict we have here: rapid in utterance, lofty in tone, rising from the didactic style of the theological doctor to the oracular speech of the Hebrew prophet, as in that peremptory sentence: "It is not possible that the blood of bulls and of goats should take away sins." The notable thing in it is, not any new line of argument, though that element is not wanting, but the series of spiritual intuitions it contains, stated or hinted, in brief, pithy phrases: the law a shadow; Levitical sacrifices constantly repeated inept; the removal of sin by the blood of brute beasts impossible: the only sacrifice that can have any real virtue that by which God's will is fulfilled. The passage reminds one of the postscript to Paul's Epistle to the Galatians, written in large letters by the apostle's own hand, in which, in the same abrupt, impassioned, prophetic style, he enumerates some of his deepest convictions: the legal zealots hollow hypocrites; the cross of Christ alone to be gloried in; circumcision nothing, the new creation everything; the men who take this for their motto, the true Israel of God.[1]

The first important aphorism in this prophetic postscript, if we may so call it, expressed in a participial clause, is that the Levitical law had but a shadow of the good things to come (σκιά), and not the substance of them (εἰκών). The terms σκιά and εἰκών are fitly chosen to convey an idea of the comparative merits of Leviticalism and Christianity. A σκιά is a *rude* outline, such as a body casts on a wall in sunshine; an εἰκών is an *exact* life-like image. But a shadow is, further, a likeness separate from the body which casts it: whereas the image denoted by εἰκών is inseparable from the substance, is the form of the substance, and here, without doubt, stands for it.[2] The difference in the one case

---

[1] Gal. vi. 11–18.

[2] The Greek patristic commentators understood by σκιά the first sketch of a picture before the colours were put in, and by εἰκών the

is one of degree, and points to the superiority of the Christian religion over the Levitical; in the other it is a difference in kind, and points to the absolute worth of Christianity.

The idea that the law had only a shadow, hinted for the first time in chapter viii. 5, there, in reference to the cosmic tabernacle as a shadow of the true, heavenly tabernacle, is here repeated to account for the insufficiency of the legal sacrifices. How can a shadow serve the purposes of the substance? The statement is made with special reference to the ceremonies connected with the annual atonement, as is evident from the second clause of ver. 1, and its truth in that view might be illustrated by going into details. In its comprehensive reference as an atonement for the whole people; in the sin-offering presented by the high priest for himself, before offering for the people; in the dress worn by the high priest on that occasion; in the proximity of the solemn season to the feast of tabernacles, which followed four days after, and to the jubilee, which began on the evening of the same day—the religious ceremonial of the tenth day of the seventh month bore a shadowy resemblance to the transaction by which the sin of the world was really atoned for. It foreshadowed an atonement for

picture when it was finished. Westcott remarks: "The word contains one of the very few illustrations which are taken from art in the N. T. The 'shadow' is the dark, outlined figure cast by the object—as in the legend of the origin of the bas-relief—contrasted with the complete representation (εἰκών) produced by the help of colour and solid mass." In harmony with the statement made in the text von Soden defines εἰκών as "the appearance-form bearing in itself the reality which casts the shadow that in itself includes no reality."

all, by a perfectly holy Person, humbling Himself unto death, and procuring for men true liberty, peace, and joy. But how rude and barely recognisable the resemblance! The atonement, annual, partial, putative; the holiness of the priest, not real but ritual; his humiliation an affair of dress, not an experience of temptation, sorrow, and pain; the feast of tabernacles, a halcyon period *of seven days*; the year of jubilee, a twelvemonth of freedom, preceded and followed by fifty years of servitude, not an unending era of freedom and gladness. Looking at a shadow on a wall, you can tell that it is the shadow of a man, not of a horse or a tree; but, of what particular man, even if it were your own brother, you know not. Who, reading the sixteenth chapter of Leviticus, could guess what the ideal redemption would be like?

The law, having only a shadow, is not able[1] through its sacrifices to perfect worshippers, by communicating to them the sense of forgiveness: such, in brief, is the next aphorism. Admirers of Leviticalism might reply, "Perhaps not by a single sacrifice, or by the ceremonial of one sacred season; but repetition might help, the system as a whole might bring satisfaction." "No," rejoins our author, "repetition does not mend matters:

---

[1] The reading δύνανται (ver. 1) has more diplomatic evidence in its favour than the singular δύναται; but it is intrinsically so improbable as to lead Bleek to remark, "Even if it had been found in the autograph of the author, I should have regarded it as an accidental mistake on his part." Westcott and Hort have δύνανται, but Westcott in his Commentary has δύναται, with an additional note on the reading of chap. x. 1, p. 339, in which he states that δύνανται was suggested by προσφέρουσιν. Weiss regards it as a case of mechanical conformation of the one verb to the other. Whatever reading we adopt, the sense remains the same.

on the contrary, it is part of the shadowiness, it but serves to proclaim the ineffectual character of the sacrifices repeated. 'Since otherwise would they not have ceased to be offered, on account of the worshippers having no longer any consciousness of sin, being once for all purified?'[1] But (so far is that from being the case, that, on the contrary) in them is a remembrance of sins year by year' (vers. 2, 3). A remembrance, mark, not an atonement; an acknowledgment that there is sin there to be atoned for, but not an effectual dealing with it such as can satisfy the conscience: not at least the enlightened conscience, for the unenlightened might be well enough content." "The annual atonement," the unenlightened conscience might say, " cancelled the ritual errors of the year past—that was what it was intended to do; what more is needed?" "Ritual errors," replies the enlightened conscience—" mere artificial offences against a code of arbitrary rules! What I want to be rid of is sin, real sin, offences against the moral law, which alone give me serious trouble." The conscience that takes up this attitude has broken with Leviticalism, lives in a wholly different world, and accepts as an axiom needing no proof, and admitting of no dispute, the blunt, downright assertion which follows: "For it is

[1] Most commentators read ver. 2 as a question. In some texts the negative is omitted, so that the sentence reads, "The sacrifices would then have ceased to be offered, on account of the worshippers having been cleansed once for all, and having no more conscience of sins." Mr. Rendall thinks both transcribers and translators have missed the meaning, and renders : " For these sacrifices would not have ceased to be offered by reason of those who serve having been cleansed once for all, and having no more conscience of sins"; that is, so good a reason for cessation of sacrifice would not have existed.

impossible that the blood of bulls and of goats should take away sin" (ver. 4).

Here, at last, is the whole truth, declared without periphrasis or qualifying clauses, by one to whose illuminated Christian consciousness it is as clear as noonday that the very notion that sin can be removed by the shedding or sprinkling of a beast's blood is monstrous and absurd. How refreshing to him, weary of elaborate argumentation, to have an opportunity of uttering in this direct way his spiritual intuition on the subject under consideration! And who does not feel that there is more force in this plain statement of conviction than in the lengthened argument foregoing, skilful and persuasive though it be? To every spiritually intelligent mind it is self-evident that sin cannot be removed by the blood of beasts, or even by blood at all, viewed simply as blood, whether of man or of beast, but only by a holy will revealing itself through an act of self-devotion, and sanctifying, not through the mere blood shed in death, but by the holy, loving mind revealed in dying. Such is the thought the writer has in view when he makes the round assertion above quoted, for he has not forgotten his great word, "through an eternal spirit"; and accordingly he goes on to unfold this very thought, employing as the vehicle yet another Old Testament oracle, taken from the 40th Psalm.

"Wherefore, coming into the world, He saith: Sacrifice and offering Thou didst not wish, but a body didst Thou prepare for Me. In whole burnt-offerings and sacrifices for sin Thou hadst no pleasure. Then said I,

Lo, I am come (in the roll of the book it is written of Me) to do Thy will, O God."

This oracle, as it stands in the Hebrew text, is an echo of the great prophetic maxim, "to obey is better than sacrifice." Instead of "a body didst Thou prepare for Me," taken by our author from the Septuagint Version, the original has, "Mine ears hast Thou bored or opened"; the meaning being, "Thou hast no pleasure in sacrifices, but Thou hast made Me obedient, and Thou hast pleasure in that." Thus read, the oracle might seem to point to the total abolition of sacrifice. As read by our author, it points to the supersession of one kind of sacrifice by another of a higher type. "He taketh away the first, that He may establish the second" (ver. 9). So he points the lesson, after requoting the passage. He finds in it a reference to the sacrificial death of Christ on the cross. He assumes it to be Messianic, and conceives of Messiah as uttering the words, put into His mouth on entering the world, an eternal spirit incarnate. The Christ, having assumed flesh, says: "Lo, I come, that in this body which Thou hast prepared for Me I may do Thy will, O God, by offering Myself as a sacrifice." From a critical point of view, the use made of the oracle may seem questionable; but on the spiritual side it is unquestionably grand, provided we interpret the writer's meaning sympathetically. We must understand him as teaching, not merely that it pleased God by a sovereign act of His will to supersede one kind of sacrifice by another, the blood of beasts by the blood of the Man Christ Jesus, but that Christ's self-sacrifice stood in an inner, intimate, essential relation to God's will, conceived of, not as sovereign only, but as an embodiment of the moral ideal, and that its virtue lay in its being a perfect fulfilment of that will. Some interpreters, bent on emptying all the great words of this Epistle of ethical contents, as if jealous lest its author should appear more than a common, contracted Jewish Christian, do their best to reduce the significance of this last great word to a minimum, by conceiving of Christ's sacrifice as standing, in the writer's view, in a purely external relation to the Divine will. According to them, all he means to teach is, that Christ's offering of Himself is the true and final offering for sin, because it is the sacrifice which, according to the prophecy in the Book of Psalms, God desired to be presented. In this way he is made to appear inferior in spiritual insight to the Psalmist, who, it is admitted, set obedience to the general moral will of God above sacrifice. I have no sympathy with such starved exegesis. I think that when the writer conceives of Christ, come into the world, as saying, " Lo, I am come to do Thy will, O God," he means something more than, " I am come to suffer in this body, since that is the way by which it pleaseth Thee to redeem man"; and that when he remarks, "In which will we have been sanctified, through the offering of the body of Jesus Christ once for all" (ver. 10), he means that it is God's will that sanctifies through the offering, and not merely that it is God's will that we should be sanctified in this particular way. His doctrine is, that Christ's self-sacrifice was a perfect embodiment of Divine righteousness, and on this account possesses sanctifying virtue. God is well pleased with it, and out of regard to it pardons sin. In short, the will of God in this text serves the same general purpose as the eternal spirit in chapter ix. 14, that, namely, of accounting for the value of Christ's sacrifice. I attach great importance to my interpretation of the two texts, because I believe that the author of the Epistle to the Hebrews had really surmounted Judaism, did really understand Christianity, had valuable light to throw on the momentous question, Why Leviticalism should be superseded by a new religion, a satisfactory explanation to offer why the blood of Christ should have more virtue than the blood of beasts.

In the following three verses (11–13) we have a pictorial representation addressed to the spiritual imagination, graphically depicting the contrast between the Levitical priest and the great High Priest of humanity. The picture might be named "The Sacerdotal Drudge and the Priest upon the Throne." The contrast is carefully worked out, that it may be as vivid and impressive as possible. The portrait of the Jewish priest in particular is minutely drawn, every word contributing to the pictorial effect. "And *every* priest [1] *stands day by day* ministering, and offering *often* the *same* sacrifices, such as can *never* take away [2] sins." First, "every"

---

[1] In the best texts is found ἀρχιερεύς (high priest), the objection to which is, that what is said of the Levitical priest applies to the ordinary priests rather than to the high priest, for it was not the high priest that offered the daily sacrifices. But in a rhetorical statement strict accuracy is not aimed at. The main point is, that there was periodic repetition of sacrifice under the Levitical system, in the high priest's department as well as in the ordinary priest's.

[2] περιελεῖν, literally "to strip off all round," implying thorough work.

($πᾶς$) suggests the idea of a multitude, and that is one note of imperfection, already remarked on in an earlier part of the Epistle.[1] Every priest *standeth* ($ἔστηκεν$): the attitude is servile, and as such is in contrast to the regal attitude of sitting on a throne ascribed to the exalted Christ. "Day by day" ($καθ'\ ἡμέραν$), a third mark of inferiority. The work never gets done, the wearisome round of duty is daily gone through by the sacerdotal drudge, without any result, and the poor official, as you look at him with the eye of the spirit, becomes an object of compassion to you, as if he were some criminal doomed to fruitless labour in the treadmill. "Offering the same sacrifices" ($τὰς\ αὐτὰς\ θυσίας$): yes, ever the same, no change from day to day, from year to year; evermore the same tale of lambs, and rams, and bullocks, and goats, slain and offered in the same stereotyped fashion as prescribed by rigid rule. "Often" ($πολλάκις$) are these same sacrifices offered. Had the service been confined to a few occasions, coming round at distant intervals, the sameness of the ritual would have been less felt. But as each day summoned the priest to his sacerdotal duties, his office would become in course of time unspeakably wearisome to him, and the only comfort available to the hapless official would be a beneficent stupidity, rendering him gradually insensible, as human ears grow insensible by custom to the unmelodious sounds emanating from a factory. "Sacrifices such as can *never* take away sin" ($οὐδέποτε$). Here was the most fatal defect of all. These Levitical sacrifices, daily repeated in the same invariable manner,

[1] vii. 23.

were of no real value. They were utterly unfit to do the very thing for which sacrifice exists. They could not divest the sinner of his sins, although the priest should live to the age of Methuselah, and offer the same sacrifices every day of his almost interminable life. This combination of *ever* and *never* is very pathetic to the reflecting mind. Ever, ever, ever at work; never, never, never doing any real good. What a dismal existence! How welcome death, coming as a kind friend to take the melancholy official from the treadmill to the grave, making his place vacant for his son and successor!

Turn your eye now from the sacerdotal drudge, and fix it on the Priest on the throne. This Man has a different career and destiny. "This one, having offered *one* sacrifice for sins, for ever sat down on the right hand of God, thenceforth waiting till His enemies be made the footstool of His feet." This Priest too had His experience of drudgery; but it had a glorious end and a magnificent result. He was a priest, but He is a king; a priest for ever indeed, but of the regal type. He standeth not daily offering over and over again the same sacrifices; He offered Himself once for all, and then sat down on a celestial throne. He who on earth was as one that serveth is now ministered unto; He that humbled Himself is exalted. His work too, however arduous and painful, was not like that of a criminal in the treadmill, but rather like that of a warrior in a campaign. He had His battle, and then His victory; He had His cross, and then His crown "of full, and everlasting, and passionless renown."

How it came about that Christ got done with His

priestly work, so far as sacrifice was concerned, and in due course entered into glory is thus explained: "For by one offering [1] He hath perfected for ever them that are sanctified" (ver. 14). His one offering serves all the purposes of all the sacrifices under the law: sanctifies, i.e. places men in covenant relations with God, like the "blood of the covenant" inaugurated at Sinai; perfects, i.e. keeps those covenant relations intact, maintains uninterrupted fellowship with God, the end which all Levitical sacrifices, offered daily, monthly, or yearly, vainly sought to effect. Surely a sufficient reason for the cessation of Christ's priestly work, in so far as it was servile! If the one sacrifice secured all that was wanted, why offer more? Why work for working's sake? The earnest man does no work aimlessly. He will spare no pains to accomplish a desired end; but that done, he will rest from his labours. One can indeed conceive a man of heroic spirit heaving a sigh when the toil and struggle are past. There was such an elevation of mind, such a buoyancy of spirit, such a blessed satisfaction of conscience connected therewith,

---

[1] μία προσφορά might be taken as nominative to the verb, which would give us this contrast: all the Levitical sacrifices together were never able to take away sin; Christ's one sacrifice, on the contrary, hath perfected for ever those whom it sanctifies. No recent commentator, so far as I have observed, takes προσφορά as a nominative. Westcott remarks: "It is significant that Christ Himself is said to perfect 'by the offering'; it is not said that 'the offering' perfects. His action is personal in the application of His own work. The importance of this form of expression appears from the language used of the Law: vii. 16, οὐδὲν ἐτελείωσεν ὁ νόμος. Comp. ix. 9, x. 1. In the case of Levitical institutions, the action of the appointed ministers fell into the background."

that, despite the drudgery and the strain upon the powers of endurance, he could almost wish he had the same work to do over again. "All things that are, are with more spirit chased than enjoyed." Yet, if inactivity be distasteful to the moral hero, not less so is an idle, aimless busybodyism. And then it is to be remembered that, though the particular task be ended, there may be other work to do. The case is so with men on earth; but how is it, it may be asked, with Christ in heaven? What new work is there for Him to do? Does not His whole occupation now consist in sitting on a throne? and is not that, to speak with reverence, as monotonous as the mechanical, never-ending routine of the Levitical service? Can we imagine the eager, adventurous, enthusiastic spirit of Jesus content with that passive existence in heavenly glory? Surely He must remember almost with regret that sublime career on earth, and be tempted to wish that He were back again in the arena of conflict, to go through His course of suffering once more!

Such thoughts, though bold, are not impious, for they do homage to the heart of Christ; yet, while natural, they are not well founded. For Christ's celestial state is not so passive as at first it seems. He too has new work to do, which occupies His mind, and shuts out regret that the old work is at an end. "He ever liveth to make intercession." He watches the progress of the world's history and the development of His kingdom. He uses His power to promote the triumph of good over evil. From the invisible heights of heaven, whence all below is in full view to the eye of His "eternal spirit,"

He not only surveys, but conducts the fight between the kingdom of light and the kingdom of darkness. And up yonder His breast heaves with the varied emotions naturally awakened by the chequered course of the battle. By sympathy with His friends He fights His own battles over again with His own old foes, superstition, hypocrisy, unbelief, unrighteousness. No need therefore to look back to the long distant, ever-receding past, as if all the interest of His eternal existence were wrapped up in those memorable thirty-three years. The present is full of thrilling interest for Him, the present, I mean, of this world's history. His eyes see, His ears hear, His heart is interested in the things of earth. Earth is a very minute object seen from the skies; but the omniscient eye of Christ is a telescope of unlimited magnifying power, which can make the earth to His view just what it is to ours, a large world, full of exciting grand dramas going through their several acts, and filling His breast with strong emotions, such as we feel when we read of battles fought, of barbaric empires perishing, of slavery and other iniquities receiving their death-doom. And the future of the world is a source of intense interest to the King on the throne, not less than the present. He watches with eager, expectant eye the progress of that great struggle between good and evil, whose final issue shall be the triumph of the good over the evil. He has great expectations as well as great recollections, pleasures of hope as well as pleasures of memory. The final issues of things, whereof the beginnings were in His own earthly life, rising there like a mighty river in an untracked mountain region, are in His view; and He looks for them with patient yet unflagging confidence, waiting for the end, for the final victory of the Divine kingdom: "expecting till His enemies be made His footstool." He has had longer to wait than it entered into the mind of the writer of this Epistle to imagine; but hope deferred maketh not *His* heart sick.

The picture of the sacerdotal drudge and the Priest on the throne would have made a most impressive close to the discourse on the priestly office of Christ. One may be inclined to say, After that, not another word. Yet there is another word, intended to substantiate the statement, that by His one offering Christ perfected for ever the sanctified, bringing them nigh and keeping them nigh to God. There was no logical necessity for this being done, for the position has been proved over and over again, and one is tempted to wonder that a writer of such consummate tact should spoil the artistic effect of that fine picture by requoting Jeremiah's oracle of the new covenant, and pointing its moral anew. But he is writing for Hebrew Christians, not for us, and he is more concerned about convincing them than about the artistic finish of his discourse. He fears lest, after all he has said, Levitical rites should still hold possession of their minds, and he makes one last effort to break the spell, at the risk of being thought tedious. It is one of very many indications, that have been pointed out as we came upon them, in how benighted a condition were the first readers as to the whole subject of Christ's priesthood and the claims of Christianity to be the final religion. And, of course, if the elaborate argument going before failed to convince them, this last touch would not succeed. It would be so easy to raise objections. The argument is: The oracle promises complete pardon of sin, but where such pardon is there is no longer offering for sin. To which two objections might be taken. First, the oracle makes no mention of a sin-offering as the ground of forgiveness: why should not its meaning be—an amnesty for the guilty past, the heart regenerated, therefore no more sin done, therefore no further interruption of the friendly relation subsisting between the covenant people and their God? Abolition of Levitical sacrifice may possibly be involved, but what indication is there that another kind of sacrifice was to take its place? Next, is not the promise of perpetual forgiveness too strictly interpreted? Perpetual forgiveness, sin remembered no more: is this not an ideal? Will there not in reality under the new covenant, as under the old, be new sin committed even by men who have the law written on their heart, therefore need for new acts of forgiveness, and therefore naturally for new offerings for sin? So we have the dilemma: either the new covenant points to no new kind of offering, or it does not preclude a plurality of sacrifices. How difficult for men living in different worlds of thought to convince one another by argument! The spiritual guides of a transition time have a difficult and comparatively thankless task to perform. They are compelled by the necessities of their position to use old forms of thought as the vehicle of new ideas; and their reward is, that the new element in their teaching makes it unacceptable to their contemporaries attached to the past, while the old element, on the other hand, makes it uninviting and obscure to men of later generations.

We have made small progress indeed in the understanding of this Epistle if we have not discovered in it, under its Levitical forms of thought, many great moral and religious truths. But much more than this is involved in a thorough insight into its meaning. Some of the most important truths it teaches have grown through long familiarity trite. The "new covenant" is a commonplace in theology. That Christ's offering of Himself had a value that could not belong to the sacrifice of a beast is now a truism. That Christianity is "better," presents a higher type of religion, than Leviticalism is at this date axiomatically clear. Understanding of this Epistle means power to realise that none of these now familiar truths were commonplaces for its author. It was the vivid perception of this fact that many years ago opened my eyes to the thrilling interest and abiding value of this New Testament writing, and awakened in me a desire to unfold its significance to others. I do not think that one who makes it his specific aim to interpret the *spirit* of the book undertakes a superfluous task. Many men of greater learning by far than I lay claim to have applied their powers to the elucidation of its text, and have done much to make the meaning of every word and phrase clear. But, while the work of verbal exegesis has been almost brought to perfection, the interpretation of the spirit is far from complete. Too many learned commentators write as if the ideas of a new covenant, atonement through self-sacrifice, a forerunner, etc., had been as familiar to the writer and his first readers as they are to themselves and as if the doctrine that Christianity was the religion of good hope, because it for the first time brought men nigh to God, was a matter of course to all parties. Even the pregnant remark, that "that which decayeth and waxeth old is ready to vanish away," is lightly passed over, as if its applicability to the ancient constitution of Israel and the venerable Levitical priesthood were called in question by no one. Even Bleek, still our foremost commentator on the Epistle, often disappoints in connection with the interpretation of its spirit.

This leads me to remark, at the close of my exposition of the doctrinal part of the Epistle, what I have again and again remarked in its course, that successful interpretation of the spirit of this sacred writing depends, above all, on a right conception of the religious situation of the first readers. Was it that of men who had no real insight into the nature and worth of Christianity as the final, perennial religion, and into its characteristic truths? or was it that of men who, while fairly well-grounded in the Christian faith, were sorely tempted to apostasy by outward trial, and disappointment as to the second advent, and stood in need of aids to steadfastness, including among these a restatement of familiar Christian doctrines, such as that of our Lord's priesthood? I have gone on the supposition that the former of these alternatives is the true one, and conceived the attitude of the first readers towards Levitical rites to have been similar to that of the Judaists, with whom Paul contended, towards circumcision. The view we take on this question affects, not only our interpretation of many texts, but still more our idea of the man who wrote the texts. On it depends whether we conceive of him as a theologian or as a prophet, as a doctor or as an apostle, as a philosophic student or as a moral hero. If my view of the situation be right, then he belonged to the nobler categories, and was a man like-minded with Paul, the vindicator of the independence of Christianity against legalists, who assailed it. He was one who, with prophetic boldness and apostolic inspiration, asserted the antiquation of the old covenant and worship against men holding on desperately to these, and dared to apply the maxim, "the decadent old must pass away," to institutions that had lasted more than a thousand years, writing to men who probably regarded his views as little short of blasphemy.

It requires an effort of historical imagination to realise the situation which called forth this great Epistle. It greatly helps one when he himself lives in a transition time and is in sympathy with the changes it brings. One can then divine the spirit in which the Epistle was written, understand the attitude of its author towards the past, and his enthusiasm for the new in the present, and appreciate the heroic moral basis of his religious character. Learning can do much for the interpretation of the letter; but when spiritual affinity is lacking, learned labour may end in a scholastic commentary on a biblical writing from which the soul has fled.

The task I undertook was to expound the doctrinal part of the Epistle with reference to its central theological idea and the apologetic occasion. I have come to the end of that task. Exposition of the remaining portion of the Epistle (chiefly hortatory in its character), on the same scale, might tend rather to fatigue the reader than to throw additional light on the aim of the writing. The general purpose of this book will be best served by a hasty sketch of the drift of the hortatory section following. Such a sketch is offered in the next two chapters under the suggestive titles, "Draw near!" "Be not of them that draw back." A final chapter will endeavour to summarise the theological import of the Epistle in the light of the foregoing exposition.

CHAPTER XIX

DRAW NEAR!

CHAP. x. 19-31

IN what I have to say on the remainder of the Epistle my object will be simply to notice those passages which touch and lend support to the leading idea of the doctrinal part—Christianity, the religion of unrestricted fellowship with God. In this connection the exhortation which begins at ver. 19 of the tenth chapter claims special attention. It rests on and is expressed in terms of the central truth. "Christ has made it possible to have perfect fellowship with God; that is the objective significance of the Christian era. Therefore draw near, realise your privilege subjectively."

Draw near! that is the appropriate application of the whole foregoing argument, the goal to which the long train of thought has been leading up. Readers who have felt the force of the theoretical statement can do nothing else than come into the presence of God with filial trust and holy joy. They do not merely hope for free access as a future good. They consciously enjoy it now as a present possession. For that is implied in the exhortation $\pi\rho o\sigma\epsilon\rho\chi\omega\mu\epsilon\theta a$, "let us draw near." The thing is to be done now, the privilege can be enjoyed at once; if it be not, it is our own fault. There is thus a noteworthy advance at this point on the teaching in the sixth chapter, where the *summum bonum*, nearness to God, appears as a boon in store for us in the future— Christ has gone within the veil as our Forerunner, and we shall follow Him by and by; but meantime we only cast into that sacred region the anchor of our hope. Now, not hope, but full assurance of faith, making the future present, is the watchword. The increased boldness of tone befits the close of the argument intended to show that Christianity is the perfect religion. And yet we are not to conceive of this boldness as something to which the writer has gradually worked himself up. It is but a return to his manner of speaking, when he was on the threshold of his great demonstration, that in Jesus Christ we have the true ideal Priest over the house of God (chap. iv. 16).

The exhortation to draw near is enforced by the two reasons, that there is an open way, and a powerful friend at court (vers. 20, 21). The terms in which the way of access is described are worthy of note. It is called *new* ($\pi\rho\acute{o}\sigma\phi\alpha\tau\text{o}\nu$ [1]) and *living* ($\zeta\tilde{\omega}\sigma\alpha\nu$). With reference to the former of these two epithets, one has occasion to repeat the observation already more than once made in the course of our study of the Epistle: how boldly the writer puts in the forefront just those features of the

---

[1] This word meant originally "newly slain" ($\pi\rho\acute{o}s$, $\phi\acute{e}\nu\omega$), and one is tempted to find in it here a reference to the sacrifice by which the way was opened up. But in later usage the word means simply "new," without thought of any connection with sacrifice.

Christian religion which a timid prudence would take care to conceal! To the conservative mind of Hebrew readers, enamoured of the ancient Levitical system, the novelty of the way might seem the reverse of a recommendation. Nevertheless, the teacher hesitates not to proclaim with emphasis the fact that the way is new. And his boldness was never more completely justified. For in this case the contrast is not between a new, unfrequented path, and an old one, familiar and well-trodden; but rather between a new way and no way at all. While the veil existed, dividing the tabernacle into a Holy place and an inaccessible most Holy place, the way into God's presence was not opened up. Men were kept at a distance in fear, not daring to go beyond the door of the tent, or at farthest, in the case of ordinary priests, the screen which separated the outer from the inner compartment. To call the way new was simply to pronounce on Leviticalism a verdict of incompetence.

In the expression a "*living* way" we have an exhibition of boldness under another form. The writer not only dares to emphasise an unpopular aspect of the Christian religion by the use of the term new, but has the courage in its praise to create what on the surface appears an incongruous combination of ideas. For such courage all the New Testament writers had need. A "living way," "living stones": such expressions bear witness to the inadequacy of ordinary language to convey the truth concerning the good that came to the world by Jesus Christ. Bible writers laboured in expression, throwing out words and phrases with a certain sublime helplessness at an object passing human comprehension. And yet the meaning here is plain enough. The epithet "living" implies that God's presence is not now, as of old, restricted to any particular place. To be near Him we do not need to pass locally from one point in space to another. We draw nigh to God by right thoughts of His character, and by loving, trustful affections. When we think of Him as revealed to us in Christ, when we trust Him implicitly, as one who for Christ's sake forgiveth our sin, we are in His very presence. The way is living because it is spiritual, a way which we tread, not by the feet, but by the mind and the heart, as is hinted in ver. 22, where it is said, "Let us draw near with true heart and with full assurance of faith." The way is Christ Himself, the Revealer and the Reconciler, and we come to God through Him when we trust Him in both capacities.

Of the new and living way it is further affirmed that it has been consecrated for us by Jesus through the veil. It has been consecrated for us by being first used, trodden by Him. The expression, "through the veil" (διὰ τοῦ καταπετάσματος), suggests a double contrast. First, between the old and the new dispensations in respect of access to God. Under the Levitical system there was a veil which barred the way, so that beyond it no man but the high priest might go. Under the new economy there is no bar—the way lies right through the veil to the very presence of God. But, secondly, there is a contrast between Christ and Christians not less than between the two dispensations. There is no veil for us, but there was a veil for our great High Priest. He opened up the way for us through the veil, pushing it aside, never again to be drawn across the entrance. What this means is explained in the words, "that is to say, His flesh." The thought of the writer seems to be that the veil through which Jesus had to pass, by the pushing aside of which He opened up an entrance into the Divine presence, was His mortal flesh. That is to say, in unfigurative terms, the truth taught is, that we owe our liberty Godwards to the fact that Christ took a body and passed with it into glory through a course of humiliation and suffering. There was a veil for Him, inasmuch as it behoved Him to suffer in the flesh, and so pass into glory; there is no veil for us, because the Just One suffered for the unjust, that He might bring them nigh to God. This conception of Christ's flesh as a veil is beautiful as a passing, poetic thought, but care must be taken not to press it too far. It "cannot, of course, be made part of a consistent and complete typology. It is not meant for this. But as the veil stood locally before the holiest in the Mosaic tabernacle, the way into which lay through it, so Christ's life in the flesh stood between Him and His entrance before God, and His flesh had to be rent ere He could enter."[1] The one truth to be laid to heart is, that our liberty of access cost Christ much. The making of the new way was no light matter for Him.

[1] Professor A. B. Davidson, p. 211. Bishop Westcott points out the difficulties connected with the view that the veil means Christ's flesh, which he thinks so serious as to justify a departure from the universal exegetical tradition, to the effect of identifying Christ's flesh, not with the *veil*, but with the *way*. He renders: "the entrance which He inaugurated for us, even a fresh and living way through the veil, that is to say, a way of His flesh."

Having stated the grounds of the exhortation to draw near, the writer next describes the appropriate manner of approach: "With a true heart, in full assurance of faith, having our hearts sprinkled from an evil conscience, and our bodies washed with pure water" (ver. 22). These four particulars are to be regarded, not in the light of legal requirements necessary to an acceptable approach, but rather as together indicating the state of mind which is congruous to the privileged position of Christians. "Come thus; in our happy circumstances we can come so; it is fitting and easy"—so we are to take the exhortation. A parallel suggests itself between this text in our Epistle and Romans v. 1–11, where Paul expatiates on the privileges of the justified man. "Being therefore," exclaims the apostle, "justified by faith, let us have peace with God; and let us joy in hope of a blessed future, yea, even in present tribulation, and, above all, in God Himself." He means to say that, the method of justification being by faith, and not by legal works, such a bright, buoyant, joyous mood is within the reach of all believers; life need not be a thing of gloom, sadness, and uncertainty. Even so here. We must be careful not to read this verse as if it meant, Take heed how ye draw near to the presence of God; see that ye come in a right frame of mind and heart. It means rather, Think of the open way and of the powerful friend at court, and come boldly, gladly, assured of your welcome. All the phrases which indicate the manner of approach must be interpreted in this spirit.

With a true heart. This is commonly taken as equivalent to "in sincerity." I object to this rendering as too narrow, and moreover as leaning to legalism, making the expression point to requirement rather than to privilege. Literally translated, the words mean: "With a heart answering to the ideal" ($ἀληθινῆς$); that is to say, in the excellent words of Bishop Westcott, "a heart which fulfils the ideal office of the heart, the seat of the individual character, towards God."[1] The question thus comes to be, What sort of heart is that which realises the ideal of worship, offering eloquent worship, blessing God with all that is within? An undivided, sincere heart, doubtless, but also something more. Besides sincerity there must be gladness, the gladness that is possible when men worship a God whom they can utterly trust and love. Along with this gladness begotten of faith go enthusiasm, generous self-abandonment, spontaneous service, rendered not slavishly, in mechanical compliance with rigid rules, but in the free spirit of sonship, the heart obeying no law but its own devoted impulses. In short, the direction, "with a true heart," must be analysed into two: with *heart*, as opposed to heartlessly; with a *true* heart, as opposed to half-heartedly or insincerely. I am persuaded that the writer of our Epistle had in view the former not less, rather more, than the latter. It was not his purpose to insist so much on the subjective, ethical condition of an acceptable approach to God, as on the objective, religious condition of an approach which shall be real, involving actual, conscious fellowship with God. There is a latent contrast between the glad-heartedness in worship which

---

[1] *Commentary*, p. 322. Weiss' comment is, "a heart as it ought to be" (*wie es sein soll*).

is possible to one who worships the Father whom Jesus revealed, and the depression and gloom inseparable from all religion that has for its object a God who hides Himself, and keeps His votaries far off. It would be false to say that the religion of Israel was joyless; on the contrary, in comparison with ethnic religions, it was bright and happy. Witness the 100th Psalm, beginning, "Make a joyful noise unto the Lord, all ye lands," and ending with that noble confession of faith which reveals the secret of the gladness: "For the Lord is good; His mercy is everlasting; and His truth endureth to all generations."[1] But Israel's religion was joyous in spite of the peculiarities of the Levitical system of worship. Its many rules and restrictions, with penalties attached for transgression, its jealous arrangements for protecting the majesty of God, all tended to engender an oppressive sense of solemnity, and a chilling feeling of fear. The spirit of the system was sombre and awe-inspiring.

Even if sincerity were the thing primarily intended by the requirement, "with true heart," it would still be necessary to interpret it widely, so as to include the gladness inspired by faith. For sincerity and gladness are closely allied: to have a sincere heart you must have a glad heart as well. Insincerity has two sources, the moral state of a corrupt heart, and the fear of a timid true heart. A religion of fear makes the best men hypocrites, feigning sentiments which they do not feel.

---

[1] We must remember here what is stated in Chapter ii. p. 31, about two types of piety in the Old Testament, some portions of the literature being legal, others evangelic in tone. Now we are under the shadow of Sinai, anon on the bright hilltop of Zion.

The formalism of such a religion tends to aggravate the evil. There is so much routine duty, that worshippers almost inevitably get into a way of putting exact compliance with the rubric in the place of worship " in spirit and in truth." Indeed, it may be affirmed that the votaries of crude cults have no conception of worshipping in spirit or in truth. The very notion of sincerity is possible only when God is conceived of as good and as Spirit: His goodness drawing out the heart into eloquent utterance of adoration, trust, and love, His spirituality emancipating the conscience from bondage to form.

In the light of these remarks, we comprehend why our author, having said " with true heart," goes on next to say " in full assurance of faith." He simply indicates by this second expression that which makes the glad, sincere heart possible: absolute, unqualified confidence, without any doubt of a gracious reception. It is implied that such confidence is justified by the facts mentioned in the preamble to the exhortation.

In the first two specifications spiritual truth is expressed in spiritual language. The third and fourth, on the other hand, are stated in typological terms, suggested by the Levitical rules of purification by blood and water to be observed by the priests. When Aaron and his sons were consecrated to the priesthood, they were sprinkled with the blood of sacrifices. They were also washed with water.[1] It was, further, the duty of the priests to wash their hands and feet in the brazen laver every time they entered the tabernacle or approached the altar.[2] How, then, are we to understand these two

[1] Ex. xxix. 4.   [2] Ex. xxx. 19-21.

last clauses in the directory for Christian worship? Are we to find in them nothing more than a graceful allusion to Levitical ritual? or shall we extract from them merely the general idea that Christians have all the privilege and standing of priests, yea, of high priests coming into the very presence of God? There can be little doubt that the writer does intend to suggest that idea. He says in effect: "Draw near priest-like, for priests indeed you *are*." But it is reasonable to suppose that he also means to indicate in what priest-likeness consists; in other words, that he attaches some definite, practical sense to the specifications, "having our hearts sprinkled from an evil conscience, and our bodies washed with pure water."

It is not difficult to determine to what the former points. The heart sprinkled from an evil conscience is synonymous with the conscience purged from dead works (ix. 14). The state described is that of a heart or a conscience which has experienced the full effect of Christ's sacrifice, taken in all the latitude assigned to it in a previous chapter, as embracing the pardon of sin, moral renewal, and deliverance from the dominion of a legal spirit.[1] It is not so easy to decide what precisely is signified by the body "washed with pure water." The meaning is plain in reference to the Levitical type, but what is the corresponding fact in the spiritual sphere? The common reply to the question is, Christian baptism. The suggestion is tempting, and even not altogether destitute of probability; and yet one cannot help feeling that, if baptism had been in the writer's mind, it would

[1] Chapter xvi. pp. 349–354.

have been easy and natural for him to have indicated his thought by the addition of a word. I doubt if this final specification serves any purpose beyond expressing the thoroughness of the cleansing process undergone by a Christian man who surrenders himself completely to the redeeming influence of Christ. The whole man, body, soul, and spirit, becomes purified, consecrated, transfigured, a veritable king and priest of God. The two clauses express together one thought. "The rhetorical balance of parts must not be made a doctrinal distinction of effects."[1]

Such, then, is the ideal state and standing of the Christian worshipper, the manner of approach to God possible and real for one who understands and appreciates his position as living in the era of the better hope through which we draw nigh to God. He can and does come into the Divine presence with gladness and sincerity, with heart and with the whole heart, having no doubt at all of his welcome, and untroubled by the thought of his sin, being assured of forgiveness and conscious of Christ's renovating power; he comes in the evangelic, filial spirit of thankfulness, not in the legal spirit of a slave; asking, not, How may I satisfy the exacting demands of an austere Deity? but, "What

---

[1] Professor A. B. Davidson, *The Epistle to the Hebrews*, p. 213. Most recent commentators find in the last clause of ver. 22 a reference to baptism. Vaughan says: "The reference to baptism is clear." Is it? It would have been if the writer had said, "and your bodies washed with the pure water of baptism." Wishes count for much in the interpretation of such texts. A reference to baptism in such a connection of thought would imply an importance assigned to sacraments which I should accept only on very clear evidence.

shall I render unto the Lord for all His benefits?" This is the type of Christian piety which prevails at all times when the intuition of God's grace in Christ is restored. It was pre-eminently the prevailing type in the apostolic age among all who understood the epoch-making significance of Christ's work, and the extent to which He made all things new. But, alas! the difficulty is to remain up in that sunny region, or, indeed, ever to get up to it, away out of the low-lying, unhealthy valleys of legalism, filled with mist and gloom.

The Hebrew Church, to which our Epistle was addressed, had never been up there, or, at least, had been unable for any time to remain there; and hence the glowing description of the ideal Christian worship, which we have been considering, is followed by a most depressing picture of the actual situation in that unhappy community (vers. 23–25). What we find in these verses formally, indeed, is but an exhortation which might with more or less point be addressed to any Christian community. Yet it is not to be taken as a commonplace admonition, but as a counsel urgently called for by a state of things presenting a sad contrast to the bright ideal previously depicted. Each clause in the exhortation suggests an evil not imaginary, but imminent. "Let us hold fast the profession of our hope without wavering," hints at a more than possible apostasy. "Let us consider one another to provoke unto love and to good works," implies the chilling of the religious affections. "Not forsaking the assembling of ourselves together," indicates a tendency to isolation, involving forfeiture of all the benefits that come from association in religion. That is to say, the Hebrews were letting their faith go, allowing their love to grow cold, neglecting social worship and all means of keeping one another in heart, so that they were becoming like a demoralised army with its discipline broken, a mere disorderly mob, a sure prey to the foe.

For this sad state of matters there is but one radical cure: clear vision of the ideal, vivid realisation of the grace wherein believers in Jesus stand, insight into the incomparable value of the Christian faith. Given this, the faith would be dearer than life; cold, selfish isolation would cease; a close brotherhood would be established, inspired by the sense of a common possession of something worth living and dying for. It was the knowledge of this that moved the writer of our Epistle to make a great effort to expound the nature and show the glory of the New Testament religion. He believed that the best of all antidotes to apostasy was intelligent conviction. In the course of his work he plies his readers with every conceivable aid to constancy, calling up old memories, appealing alternately to hope and fear, pointing, on the one hand, to historic examples of the fate of unbelief, and, on the other, to lives made sublime by the power of faith. But his main trust is in instruction. If he can only get them to understand the religion they profess, all will be well, everything else will follow of course.

The teacher has done his best, but at the end of his great effort he seems to be depressed with the sense of failure. Witness the ominous passage following, concerning the doom of apostates (vers. 26–31). I have drawn a parallel between Hebrews x. 19-22 and Romans v. 1–11, but I must here note a contrast. There is nothing in the Epistle to the Romans corresponding to this sombre picture of judgment without mercy. Paul allows no shadow to fall on the sunny landscape of the justified man's privileges. The summer mood lasts till we come to the ninth chapter, when there is a sudden change. The explanation of the difference is, that in Paul's case the causes of gloom are without the Church, in the spiritual state of unbelieving Israel. Here, on the contrary, they are within the Church, among Christians who are in danger of joining the ranks of their unbelieving countrymen, the question of the hour being whether they are to remain Christian, or to renounce the Christian name.

It was a solemn question for the Hebrew Church *on the eve of Israel's judgment day.* For such is the situation suggested by the words, "and so much the more, as ye see the day approaching" (ver. 25). This is one of the passages in the Epistle which help us to fix the time when it was written, as falling within the fateful period of the Jewish war, which in 70 A.D. issued in the destruction of the holy city. The "day" is that predicted by Jesus as He sat on the Mount of Olives, looking sorrowfully down upon the temple, and said: "Verily I say unto you, There shall not be left here one stone upon another that shall not be thrown down." If, as is not improbable, our author was acquainted with our Lord's prophecy, we cannot be surprised at the tragic style in which he depicts the horrors of that day, winding up with the reflection, "It is a fearful thing to fall into the hands of the living God." It was a fearful thing, indeed, for Israel in those years. And it would be a fearful thing for the Hebrew Christians also, if they apostatised; for then they would inevitably share the fate of the guilty nation. And surely most righteously! For how great would be their guilt!—greater than that of men who in ancient times transgressed Moses' law, greater than that of their contemporaries who had never believed in Jesus; the greatest guilt possible. For what greater crime can be conceived than to tread underfoot the Son of God, to treat the precious blood of Christ shed for man's redemption as a common thing, and to do outrage to the Spirit of grace? Of all this, it is rightly held, he is guilty who, having once believed, apostatises. He once worshipped Jesus as the Son of God, and now he curses Him; he once believed that Jesus died, the Just for the unjust: now he thinks of Christ's death as that of a common man, or even of a criminal; he once was a partaker of the Holy Ghost, and now he laughs at his former religious experience as a hallucination.

Two points in this sombre passage, of exegetic interest for one who is mainly concerned with the theology of the Epistle, may now be noticed. One is the combination here, as in chapter ix. 14, of blood with spirit. The "blood of the covenant," the "Spirit of grace." Here they appear as distinct sources of sanctification. But in the writer's mind, as in truth, they are closely allied. The blood is the blood of Christ, the Spirit is the spirit of Christ. He is the

Spirit through whose inspiration Christ shed His blood, and He is the Spirit who passes into the hearts of all that believe in Christ, and thus becomes a renewing influence. The other point is the unique title for the Spirit—the Spirit of *grace*. The question arises, How is the designation to be understood? Does it mean the Spirit who imparts grace, or the Spirit who is Himself the gift of God's grace? Formally distinct, the two meanings run into each other. The Spirit's presence is felt as an energy, producing effects through which God's grace is manifested. The more important question is, What is the nature of the effects? Are they *ethical*, or merely *charismatical*? Does the grace of which the Spirit is the vehicle consist in the power to speak with tongues and to do other supernatural acts, or in the power to live holy lives? In the former case, we should have to recognise a difference between the doctrine of the Spirit taught in our Epistle and that contained in Paul's Epistles, according to which the Holy Spirit, while the source of miraculous charisms, is, before all things, the immanent ground of Christian sanctity. I do not think any such difference exists. I believe that the writer of this Epistle, if not a disciple of Paul, is at least in sympathy with Paul in his conception of the Spirit's work. As was meet in one who had so enlightened a view as to the absolute worth of the good that came to the world through Jesus Christ, he uses repeatedly the word "grace," and in most instances he employs it in an ethical sense: as in the expression, "the throne of grace";[1] in the saying, "it

[1] Chap. iv. 16.

is a good thing that the heart be established with grace"; [1] and in the concluding prayer, "grace be with you all." [2] There is little reason to doubt that he uses it in the same sense here. It has been remarked that the author of the Epistle to the Hebrews does not speak of the Spirit's influence among Christians in so lively a way as Paul. [3] That may be; but the explanation of the fact is probably to be found, not in any supposed abatement of the Spirit's influence in the subapostolic generation, [4] but in the circumstance that the Pauline doctrine of the Spirit had become, when our Epistle was written, the common possession of the Church. [5]

[1] Chap. xiii. 9.   [2] Chap. xiii. 25.
[3] *Vide* Ewald, *Die Lehre der Bibel von Gott.*, iii. 400.
[4] So Ewald, who seems to regard the doctrine of the Spirit in our Epistle as essentially Pauline.
[5] Westcott takes the gen. in the phrase τὸ πνεῦμα τῆς χάριτος as = "the Spirit through whom the grace of God is manifested"; Vaughan as = the Spirit who is all grace.

CHAPTER XX

BE NOT OF THEM THAT DRAW BACK

CHAP. X. 32—CHAP. XII. 29

"DRAW near," the teacher had said, in a tone of cheerful emphasis. "Draw not back," he now says in a tone of deep solemnity. "Draw not back" is virtually the burden of all that follows from this point onwards to the end of the twelfth chapter. The friend of the Hebrew Church fears the deprecated result, and puts forth a great final effort to avert it. In spite of his inward fear, he assumes a tone of confidence, and says, "We (you and I) are not of them who draw back unto perdition : but of them that believe to the saving of the soul" (chap. x. 39). But he means: "Be ye not, ye must not be, it is not to be thought of, such a disastrous issue is intolerable." What he dreads is mean, ignoble, dastardly slinking from Christian standing and responsibility, through an abject desire for safety, which defeats itself, and brings on the moral coward the very evil he seeks to shun; what he commends is the heroic spirit of faith, which enables a man to live a true, just, godly life, preferring duty to safety: so, while willing to lose life, really gaining it, as Jesus had taught His disciples.

In laconic phrase he offers as the watchword for times of trial, "not men of shrinking, but men of faith" (οὐχ ὑποστολῆς,[1] ἀλλὰ πίστεως).

To insure that the Hebrews shall so behave as to merit this description, the writer brings to bear on them a variety of stimulating influences: their own past memories (chap. x. 32–36), the heroic career of the men of faith of former times (chap. xi.), the example of Jesus (chap. xii. 2, 3), the uses of affliction (chap. xii. 5–13), the solemn responsibilities lying on the privileged recipients of a final revelation (chap. xii. 14–29). With reference to the first, he bids them in effect conduct themselves at the end of their Christian life in a manner worthy of its beginning, when they both bravely endured hardships on account of the faith, and generously sympathised with brethren exposed to trial. Why should they cast away that old boldness, which, persevered in to the end (now not far off), must have worthy recompense? What a pity to lose heart, when patience only for a little longer will bring the promised reward!

2. The second line of thought is worked out with great elaboration. This magnificent discourse on faith may conceivably have been prepared for and used on other occasions, and afterwards embodied in our Epistle as well fitted to serve the purpose in hand, to help waverers to be men of faith by showing them what

---

[1] ὑποστολή is used here only in the New Testament, and little used at all in the sense it bears here. The verb is used not only in the previous verse, but in a very expressive way in Gal. ii. 12, in reference to the behaviour of Peter on the arrival of the bigots from Jerusalem: ὑπέστελλεν = he stealthily and sneakingly slunk away.

faith had done for others. The opening sentence, containing what looks like a scholastic definition of faith, might suggest that the leading aim of the discourse had originally been to illustrate the nature of faith as there defined to be the substance or assurance of things hoped for, and the evidence or proof of things not seen, whether past, present, or future. The first example of faith's action taken from the creation of the world appears to bear out this view, as it serves merely to explain the nature of faith and the vast range of its action as a principle in the human mind. It is not an instance of the faith by which the elders obtained a good report, but only the first case in the Old Testament history in which an opportunity occurs for showing the psychological nature of faith as the evidence of things not seen; that by which we apprehend the visible world to be the product of an invisible creative word of God. The same desire to illustrate the abstract nature of faith and the range of its action seems to come out in ver. 6, where it is argued that pleasing God necessarily involves faith (and not merely good conduct), inasmuch as he who seeks to please God, *ipso facto*, believes that God is, and that He rewards well-doing, the one act of faith exemplifying its nature as evidence of the unseen, the other as the assurance of things hoped for.

Whatever truth there may be in the foregoing conjecture, there can be no doubt that the main purpose of the discourse as it here stands is to show, not the abstract nature of faith, but its moral power: how it enables men to live noble lives and so gain a good report. The writer's interest in the psychology of faith lies chiefly in the fact that it furnishes the key to faith's wonderful practical virtue. The connection of thought is to this effect: "Be ye men of faith, my Hebrew brethren, for faith is a mighty thing: it makes one as sure of the future as if it were present, and brings the invisible within view. Through these its marvellous properties the good men of olden time were enabled so to live as to deserve the testimony that they were 'righteous' (ver. 4), that they 'pleased God' (ver. 5), that they were men of whom God was not ashamed (ver. 16), and 'of whom the world was not worthy' (ver. 38)." Such is the writer's argument, and in the sequel of his discourse he makes good his position. The examples cited are all relevant as instances of the action of faith as defined; in all faith was the working power. The actions specified are important, having a foremost place in the *memorabilia* of Old Testament story. The actors are all worthy of honourable mention. Their characters bear the heroic stamp due in every case to their faith, even the least worthy, *e.g.* "the harlot Rahab," rising above moral commonplace into the lofty region of heroism through the redeeming power of a faith that could rightly interpret past events and shrewdly forecast the future.

The eloquent preacher makes good his case, yet in the end of his discourse he is constrained to make an important admission. "These all being witnessed to (μαρτυρηθέντες) through faith, (yet) received not the promises." That is to say, faith, as the assurance of things hoped for and the proof of things not seen, helped them to live well, so that God and discerning men could give them a certificate of nobility; but that of which faith assured them, the things hoped for, they did not obtain. They got their certificate of character, and—nothing more. Does this not look like saying that faith entices men into a heroic, arduous career that will win for them a barren renown, by promises of a future which in the form these assume to the imagination will never be realised? It does; and the fact is even so, and it is a great fact in human experience, this "illusiveness of life"—a bitter fact till it is understood and accepted as an essential element in the Divine discipline of character. The writer of our Epistle would not conceal the truth from his readers, even though it might tend to defeat his purpose to inspire them with the spirit of fortitude, by suggesting depressing, pessimistic thoughts and dark questions, whether it was worth while living nobly if the end was to be disappointment. But he skilfully contrives, while admitting the fact, to put such a construction on the disappointing experience of Old Testament saints that it shall encourage rather than depress: "God providing something better concerning us, that they without us should not be made perfect" (ver. 40). That is to say: first, our experience is not to be as theirs, in our case the promise shall be fulfilled; second, even in their case the disappointment was not final and absolute, it was only a case of deferred fulfilment, that we and they might, by the fulfilment of our common hopes, be perfected together. The author conceives of the end of the world as at hand, and of the age of fulfilment as approaching, bringing with it the realisation of all religious ideals—the perfect pardon of sin, the heavenly country, the city which hath the foundations, whose architect and builder is God; bringing these alike to the "elders" and to those on whom the ends of the world are come, doubled in value to all by common participation.

The witnessed or certificated ones ($\mu\alpha\rho\tau\upsilon\rho\eta\theta\acute{\epsilon}\nu\tau\epsilon\varsigma$, xi. 39) next become a great cloud of *witnesses* ($\nu\acute{\epsilon}\phi o \varsigma$ $\mu\alpha\rho\tau\acute{\upsilon}\rho\omega\nu$, xii. 1), gathered around the men now undergoing trial on earth, the spectators in imagination, if not in literal fact, of their behaviour, and bearing testimony by their recorded lives to the power of faith, and by their faithfulness even unto death encouraging their suffering brethren to play the man and to run their appointed race strenuously and persistently till they have reached the goal. It is a spirit-stirring scene that is thus by a few felicitous phrases brought before our view; but the eye is not allowed to rest on it. For among the cloud of witnesses that constitute the ideal spectatorship of the race One stands out conspicuous above all the rest—JESUS, the Captain and Perfecter of faith, the Man who first perfectly realised the idea of living by faith, and who thereby became the Model and Leader of all the faithful, to whom they look as their pattern, and from whose heroic behaviour they draw their inspiration. Therefore our author, having suggested the idea of a cloud of witnesses, consisting of all in past ages who have a fair and honourable record, hastens to point out the great central Personality, and ask his readers to fix their attention on Him, saying in effect: "Conscious of that imposing crowd, run your race; but before all, run it, if you would run well, looking unto Jesus." What will they see there? One who undauntedly endured the bitter suffering of the cross, and who despised the ignominy of it, sustained by a faith that so vividly realised coming joy and glory as to obliterate the consciousness of present pain and shame; One, moreover, in whose case it is clearly seen that faith is no deceiver, making promises that will never be fulfilled; for, behold, the crucified One is now set down on the right hand of the throne of God! "Consider Him," continues the preacher, with eloquent urgency. "Compare His experience with your own, and your own with His, and extract from the comparison consolatory lessons. Realise first of all that the experiences are comparable, that they belong to the same category of the trial and triumph of faith, that Jesus and you have been brothers in tribulation, and may be brothers in bliss. Then, having mastered the truth that the experiences of the Leader and the led are analogous,[1] note further that the experience of the Leader differs from that of the led, though not in kind, yet in degree. He was by far the greater sufferer. What humiliating contradiction of sinners,[2] by word and deed, in life and

---

[1] ἀναλογίσασθε, ver. 3.

[2] The reading, "sinners against themselves" (εἰς ἑαυτούς), becomes credible if, with Westcott and Vaughan, we find in the phrase an allusion to the rebellion of Korah and his companions, who, in Num. xvi. 38, are described as "sinners against their own souls." Von Soden adopts the reading εἰς ἑαυτούς, holding that with the usual reading εἰς ἑαυτόν neither the term ἀντιλογίαν, nor the emphatic ὑπὸ τῶν ἁμαρτωλῶν, can be explained. With εἰς ἑαυτούς the passage points to "the tragic fact that Jesus was the victim, not of a contradiction against Him, but of a portentous violent contradiction of

in death, He endured! what blasphemies against the Son of man—'drunkard, glutton, boon companion of publicans and sinners'!—what ribald indignities, before and during the crucifixion! Ye have not endured anything like that. Ye have not been crucified; ye know little of the hatred, contempt, and reviling, that are worse than violent death."

From this topic, the example of Jesus, fertile in consolation, the writer easily passes to another, also fruitful of instruction, the uses of affliction (xii. 5–13). Here the chief feature of didactic interest is the manner in which the writer brings the hard experiences of life under the view-point of man's filial relation to God. This mention of the fatherhood of God, just after referring to the earthly trials of Christ, suggests the thought that our author has present to his mind Christ's habit of calling God His Father, and the comfort and peace He derived from that name. He cites indeed, not the Gospels, but the Book of Proverbs; it is possible nevertheless that he draws his inspiration, not from Solomon, but from Jesus. One cannot help feeling that under such expressions as the "contradiction of sinners," "the Father of spirits," there lurks a familiar acquaintance with the evangelic tradition of the life of the Son of man, and with His doctrine of God and man, and their mutual relations. The teacher of the Hebrews under-

men against themselves, against their better selves and their true interest; a contradiction by which they showed themselves emphatically as sinners, and which for them as such was so irrational and so fatal. How hard was that for Him! He would save them, but they were their own worst foes." He refers to Matt. xxiii. 37 and Phil. i. 28, as illustrative texts.

27

stands the filial consciousness of Jesus as it found expression in the prayer, "I thank Thee, O Father, Lord of heaven and earth," and knows that it meant for Him loyal submission, perfect trust, intimate, joyful fellowship, and absolute independence in His attitude toward the world; and it is his desire that those to whom he writes may attain unto the same filial consciousness, with all its spiritual blessedness. It would have been gratifying had this part of his exhortation contained a single distinct allusion to the gospel records of Christ's sayings. But, alas! the Hebrew Christians were so far below the breezy, bracing heights of sonship in the dank, misty hollows of legalism, that their teacher is constrained to extract for their benefit the elements of the doctrine of a paternal providence from Old Testament texts; these truths, namely: that God does regard men as His children; that sorrowful experiences reveal His fatherly love, are the chastisement He administers to those He counts sons; that the aim of all His discipline is to make men partakers of His holiness—an end worthy of Him, and supremely important for them.

This end — holiness — next becomes the subject of discourse. That you should be truly holy is God's great purpose in all His dealings with you: make it your own great business to be God-consecrated men; guard sedulously against moral stains; remissness here may be fatal; holiness becometh Christians in view of their position and privileges—such is the drift of the following section (xii. 12–29). We notice here for the first time a distinct reference to evil conduct as a possible source of danger: "Lest there be any fornicator, or profane person, as Esau, who for one meal sold his own birthright" (ver. 16). The word πόρνος is not to be spiritualised; we ought rather to find in it a hint that in the Hebrew Church, besides defective insight into and appreciation of the Christian religion, and a timid, unheroic temper, there was a third evil influence at work exposing them to shipwreck, a tendency to vulgar immorality, sensualism in diverse forms—a base, ignoble, Esau-like preference of immediate enjoyment, present gratification of animal appetite, to the honourable vocation and destiny of sons of God, a state of mind well deserving to be stigmatised as "profane" (βέβηλος). To what extent this tendency prevailed we can only conjecture; but it may be assumed that a writer characterised by a delicate reserve would not have mentioned the topic at all, unless it had been urgent; and the emphasis and iteration of his admonition, "looking to it that there be no one falling from the grace of God, no root of bitterness springing up *in gall*,[1] no fornicator or profane person," is very ominous. Then all history tells that a transition time in religion, when an old faith is passing away and a new one is coming in, is apt to be a time characterised by a dissolution of morals. Such

---

[1] Ἐνοχλῇ, ver. 15, is the undisputed reading; but there is probability in the suggestion that the two letters οχ had been at an early date transposed in transcription, and that the original reading was ἐν χολῇ, as in Deuteronomy xxix. 18, which the writer has in his mind and here quotes. Rendall adopts this reading, and Westcott more cautiously simply alludes to it in a bracketed remark: "The strange coincidence of letters between ΕΝΟΧΛΗ and ΕΝΧΟΛΗ of Deut. xxix. 18 cannot escape notice." The rendering given above assumes that ἐν χολῇ is the true text. Ἐνοχλῇ demands the rendering of the A.V.: "Springing up *trouble you.*"

an age presents startling contrasts: here, fanatical attachment to the past; there heroic devotion to the new revelation; in a third class, unsettlement in opinion, scepticism, licentiousness. This bad leaven of doubt accompanied by moral laxity seems to have been at work in the Hebrew Church, and in proportion as it was it made the chance of success in an effort to bring them to a better mind infinitesimally small. The profane person who prefers the mess of pottage to the heavenly calling is doomed. There is no place of repentance for him; he does not even, like Esau, desire it: he habitually despises his birthright. And such a man is a curse to the community in which he lives. He is a plant whose root sucks poison from the soil, and which bears fruit death-bringing to all who partake of it.

But charity hopeth all things; therefore, in spite of the presence among them of the Esau-spirit, the friend of the Hebrew Christians persists in pressing on their attention their heavenly birthright, and in a passage of majestic eloquence brings before their minds all the august, sacred realities of the new dispensation, each and all enforcing the admonition, Be holy. To make the argument more impressive it is put in the form of a contrast between the awe-inspiring phenomena of the law-giving and the still more solemn, while also more genial, surroundings of one whose lot is cast in the Christian era: "Ye have not come to Sinai; ye have come to Zion." The argument is *à fortiori*: Your fathers, when they approached the mount of lawgiving, had to prepare themselves and make themselves technically holy;[1] how

[1] Ex. xix. 14–25.

much more ought ye to be holy "in all manner of conversation"—ye who are surrounded by things of a higher order: not sensible, but spiritual; not transient, but abiding; not inspiring mere abject terror, but the higher, godly fear of reverence!

For detailed exegesis this eloquent passage, forming the splendid finale to the exhortation to steadfastness, commencing at chapter x. 19, presents a variety of difficult problems relating to the text,[1] the bearing of individual expressions,[2] and the scope of the whole. For a general survey like the present the last of these topics is alone of importance. It has been disputed whether we are to find in the contrast between the two dispensations a single or a double antithesis: that between the sensible and supersensible, physical and spiritual alone; or also one between the terrifying character of the earlier dispensation and the gracious, winsome character of the later. In favour of the former view are the facts that the immediate aim of the contrast is to present an incitement to holiness, that fear is regarded by the writer as an element in the New Testament religion not less than in the Old (ver. 28), and that God is referred to, not as the Father, as one would expect in an attempt to describe the grace of the New Testament, but as the Judge

---

[1] It is doubtful whether ὄρει belongs to the text in ver. 18. If it be omitted we get the sense, "Ye are not come unto a palpable and burning fire," or "a material and kindled fire," as Westcott renders it.

[2] It is disputed whether "the general assembly and Church of the first-born" refer to angels, or form a distinct class of citizens; namely, Christian men on earth, whose names are written in heaven.

(ver. 23), and is even declared in the sequel to be a consuming fire (ver. 29). In view of these facts, it might seem as if the gracious aspect of some of the things enumerated, as in the clauses referring to "Jesus, the Mediator of the new covenant," and to "the blood of sprinkling that speaketh better things than that of Abel," were accidental to the aim of the writer, or not present to his view at all. But the holiness and the fear of the Christian are different from those of Israel at Sinai. They are such as are producible, not by material fire, but by association with the spiritual commonwealth of which God is the head. They are the holiness and the fear of those who are themselves citizens. The grace lies in admission to citizenship, and privilege is the source of obligation. The moral is: Be thankful for membership in such an august society, and strive to be worthy of it. In the writer's own words: "We, receiving a kingdom which cannot be moved, let us be thankful,[1] and in the spirit of thankfulness serve God acceptably with godly fear and awe."

The designation "kingdom," here used for the good that came to the world through Jesus Christ, suggests that at this point, as in his doctrine of God's paternal providence, the writer may have had present to his mind the teaching of our Lord as recorded in the Synoptical Gospels. But here, as in the other instance, the express allusion is not to the evangelic tradition, but to the Hebrew Scriptures. The train of thought commencing

---

[1] Ἔχωμεν χάριν. Westcott remarks: "The use of the phrase χάριν ἔχειν elsewhere in the New Testament is strongly in favour of the sense, '*let us feel* and show *thankfulness* to God.'"

with "see that ye refuse not Him that speaketh" (ver. 25), and ending with the words just quoted (ver. 28), is suggested, and in expression coloured, by an oracle of the prophet Haggai, intended to encourage the people of Israel, returned from exile, in the work of rebuilding the temple, by assuring them that the second house should be greater than the first, and that the kingdom of Judah should again be established, though it should be necessary to shake the heavens and the earth, and to overturn all other kingdoms, in order to achieve the result (Hag. ii.). This prophecy the writer regards as Messianic, and from it he takes occasion to draw what we may call a supplementary contrast between the Sinaitic and the Christian revelations, so as still further to deepen the sense of responsibility in those who are the recipients of the latter. In both cases God spoke to men; by what agents, whether angels, Moses, or Christ, is here left out of account. But in the earlier revelation He spake "on earth" ($\dot{\epsilon}\pi\grave{\iota}\ \gamma\hat{\eta}s$, ver. 25), in the later "from heaven" ($\dot{a}\pi'\ o\dot{v}\rho a\nu\hat{\omega}\nu$, ver. 25): earth meaning the place of shadows, heaven the place of realities. In the first case God's voice shook the earth, not the whole earth, but Mount Sinai and its environment: "the whole mount quaked greatly" (Ex. xix. 18); in the second, the Divine voice, according to the prophetic oracle, was to shake, "not the earth only, but also heaven" (ver. 26), the whole universe of being—a statement implying the universal character of Christianity: God's voice in Christ concerns the whole world. And the shaking produced by this voice, presumably, though the fact is not expressly indicated, is of a different nature from that which took place at Sinai—a moral, not a physical earthquake. In the mind of the writer probably, as in our Lord's apocalyptic discourse, as recorded in the Gospels, the material and the spiritual aspects are mixed up, the shaking affecting the frame of nature, the fortunes of nations, the minds of men, causing stars, thrones, city walls, temples, effete religions, to tumble down into one vast mass of ruin. Lastly, God's first voice, being a voice spoken on earth, like all things earthly, is transient; God's second voice, spoken from heaven, is final and, with all that it creates, eternal. The transiency of the first voice, with the system of things it belongs to, is implied in the prophetic expression, "yet once more" (ἔτι ἅπαξ, ver. 26). It implies that the order of things to which the first voice belonged was not satisfactory or fitted to abide. It implies further that the order of things to be ushered in by the second voice will remain. For God is to speak only this one time more—once for all. Thus the voice of God uttered in the end of the days through His Son signifies, on the one hand, the removal of all things capable of being shaken because "made," material, earthly; and, on the other, the establishment of an order that shall be permanent, unshakable, because not "made" after the fashion of the sensible world, spiritual, heavenly—the bringing in, in power and glory, of the kingdom of heaven.

With what sublime serenity the author of our Epistle contemplates the destruction of the old world and the birth-pangs of the new, albeit the process involves much that is disastrous, tragic, awful to think of, for the people to which his readers belong! It is the calm of faith: of one who understands what is going on, who knows that, whatever may perish, there is always something of priceless worth that remains; that, though the earth be removed, and though the mountains be carried into the midst of the sea, and the waters thereof roar and be troubled, there is a river of life, a strong refuge, a city of God, a "kingdom which cannot be moved." One who has this faith passes quietly and peacefully through the perils of a transition time, when the hearts of those who do not understand and believe fail them for fear, and for looking after those things which are coming on the earth.

The long exhortation to Christian steadfastness is ended. What remains of the Epistle, chapter xiii., is an epilogue, containing, in addition to sundry ethical precepts (vers. 1–6), a passage bearing on the main theme, which lets us see how difficult the writer found it to take final leave of his subject, doubtless due to a fear that, after all he had written, he had failed to accomplish his purpose (vers. 7–14). The drift of this postscript is: "Cleave to Christ and the Christian faith by all means and at all hazards. Be moved to do so by the memory of deceased apostolic teachers; contemplating the issue of their life, their death in faith, some of them in martyrdom, imitate these believing, faithful men. Be moved also and above all by the consideration that in the great Object of our faith we have One that can satisfy all spiritual needs. Jesus Christ is yesterday, and to-day, the same, and for ever. What He was to your departed instructors He can still be to you. Cling to Him as your sympathetic Brother, Captain, and High Priest. Be not carried away from Him by Judaistic teachings in reference to meats,[1] etc., foreign to the genius of the Christian faith, and valueless to one whose heart is established with grace. Break finally with Judaism, forsake the synagogue, go forth "without the camp," bearing cheerfully any reproach in fidelity to Him who "suffered without the gate." Ye must make your choice between Christianity and Judaism. Ye cannot amalgamate the two. As the victim slain for sin on the day of atonement was not eaten by the priests, but removed without the camp and burned, so those who cling to the Levitical system can have no part in the great Christian sacrifice which was offered up on Calvary outside the gate of Jerusalem. To share in the benefit of that sacrifice you also must go outside, no matter what it may cost." Here once more we note the affinity between the writer of our Epistle and the Apostle Paul in pressing on half-hearted Christians, prone to compromise, the inexorable "either—or." "Either the law, or faith," said Paul; "Either the Levitical ritual, or the one sacrifice of Christ, offered through the eternal Spirit," says the unknown inspired man who wrote this remarkable book.

It is worthy of note that the closing benediction contains the solitary reference to be found in the Epistle to

---

[1] In the depreciation of marriage (supposed to be referred to in xiii. 4), angelolatry, and sacrificial meals (ver. 9), Rendall sees traces of *Essene* influence. *Vide* Appendix to *The Epistle to the Hebrews*, pp. 86-92.

the resurrection of our Lord: "The God of peace *who brought again from the dead* our Lord Jesus" (ver. 20). It looks almost like an endeavour to compensate for a defect in the body of the writing. A reference so explicit and unequivocal supplies conclusive evidence that the writer was acquainted with the evangelic tradition concerning that momentous event, and unhesitatingly accepted it as true. Still, the fact remains that that event, as distinct from the ascension, possesses no special theological significance, and has no place assigned to it in the theoretic structure. In this respect the Epistle to the Hebrews presents a striking contrast to the Epistles of Paul.

CHAPTER XXI

THE THEOLOGICAL IMPORT OF THE EPISTLE

THE grand distinction and merit of the Christian religion, for the writer of the Epistle, is that it brings men near to God. It is the religion of free access and intimate fellowship.

The value of this peculiarity is heightened by contrast with the antecedent Levitical religion, which is shown to have been a religion that failed to render this supreme service to worshippers. It did not bring the Israelite nigh to God; it kept him in fear at a distance. It had a sanctuary into which none might enter but priests; its sanctuary was divided into two compartments by a veil, beyond which, into the place called most holy, no one might go save the chief priest, and he only on one day in the year, and with due precautions. The effect was to make God for the common mind an unapproachable being dwelling in isolation and darkness.

This radical difference between the two religions implies and rests on a difference in their respective provisions for dealing with human sin. For sin is the great separator. It creates a gulf between man and God. The sinner is afraid to come near to the Holy One. The penitent sinner even trembles at the thought of entering into the Divine Presence. He needs to be assured of his welcome; means for overcoming his suspicion and dread must be provided. Judged by this test, Leviticalism is held to have failed. It did not perfect the worshipper as to conscience. It did not give him adequate assurance that his sin was forgiven and that God was gracious. Christianity, on the other hand, satisfies all requirements. It thoroughly cleanses the conscience, and gives boldness to come into the presence of God.

The verdict of incompetency to solve the problem of sin pronounced upon Leviticalism implies thorough dissatisfaction with its sacrificial and sacerdotal system. This dissatisfaction finds vigorous, unqualified expression in the Epistle. Both the victims offered and the offering priests are condemned as inadequate to the ends for which they existed. The blood of bulls and goats could not take away sin. The officiating priests were themselves sinners, who had to offer for their own sins before offering for the sins of the people. Such men offering such sacrifices were engaged in a vain work, offering oftentimes the same victims which, however often offered, could never take away sin.

Such a sweeping verdict on Leviticalism imposes on the writer an imperative obligation to show that Christianity is not liable to the same imputation of incompetency. It must be proved that its sacrificial and sacerdotal provisions for dealing with sin meet all requirements. The keen critic of the ancient Hebrew ritual is fully alive to the task he creates for himself, and does not shirk it. The priesthood of Christ and the sacrifice of Christ occupy a very prominent place in his system of

Christian thought. He knows only of one Priest and one Sacrifice; it is one of the excellences of Christianity, in his judgment, that it needs, and admits of, no more; and he puts forth all his exegetic and philosophic strength to do their transcendent worth full justice.

The doctrine of Christ's priesthood is a theological specialty of our Epistle. Practically it is the only book of the New Testament in which that doctrine finds any, or at least adequate, recognition.

The prominence given to that theme is, of course, due in part to the apologetic aim. One whose purpose was to wean Hebrew Christians from undue attachment to Levitical institutions would have to show, if possible, that Christianity was not without its priesthood and means of propitiation; that, on the contrary, it had the substance whereof the Levitical ritual was but the rude shadow. Not otherwise could he hope to make his readers content with the new faith. And it is apparent to the intelligent student of his writing that his whole manner of treating the subject is controlled by the exigencies of the apologetic situation. But this is not the whole truth. The writer could not honestly pursue such a line of argument to produce conviction in the minds of others unless what he said represented a sincere conviction of his own mind. The apologist is most successful when he offers to others as aids to faith thoughts which have first helped himself. Therefore it may be taken for granted that the priesthood of Christ was a religious reality for our author, apart altogether from the apologetic use to which it was turned.

Priestly functions are simply a special aspect or form

of salvation by *mediation*. That the salvation of men should be achieved on this method probably presented itself to the mind of our author as an axiom. If not the only possible method, and therefore necessary if men were to be saved at all, it seemed to him at least a natural, reasonable, and God-worthy method. It became God, the first cause and last end of all, to communicate to men the blessings of His grace through a Mediator, whether called a *Captain*, a *Sanctifier*, a *Priest*, a *Surety*, or a *Shepherd*. The use of this method is not conceived as belonging exclusively to the rudimentary forms of religion; it is regarded as a feature of the final form, a characteristic of the absolute perfect religion. That religion demands, not discontinuance of mediation, but a Mediator worthy of the position and adequate to the vocation. The final religion, therefore, will have its Priest; but the vital question is, What shall be the manner of the Man who under the perfect state of things shall transact for men in things pertaining to God?

The Epistle to the Hebrews gives a distinct, definite answer to this question: but, owing to the exigencies of the situation, in a very roundabout way. The writer had to deal with readers who could not conceive how Jesus could be a priest, if only because He did not, as they learned from the evangelic tradition, belong to the sacerdotal tribe. Hence his employment of *Melchisedec* as an apologetic medium. By the use of that historic figure he could show that a man might be a priest without belonging to the tribe of Levi, and not a priest of an irregular or inferior kind, but such as an inspired Psalmist could invest with all the august dignity of a sacerdotal ideal. A priest after the order of Melchisedec, according to the Psalmist, was one in whom the ideal of priesthood was realised. This being the chosen line of approach to the pre-eminent priesthood of Christ, of course the "order of Melchisedec" had to be determined, its characteristic notes had to be ascertained. This, accordingly, is done in the seventh chapter of the Epistle by a hermeneutical method which, whatever its merits, would raise no scruples in the minds of the first readers. But it may very readily raise doubts in the minds of modern Christians. Even the value attached to the oracle in the Psalm may appear to many excessive. It may seem a case of straining the didactic significance of what is in truth a very obscure, mysterious utterance. These doubts and hesitations of moderns may possess little intrinsic weight, but they cannot be disregarded. It would be a serious thing if doubt as to the validity of the proof carried along with it doubt as to the reality of the thing proved. It is therefore desirable, if possible, to make the priesthood of Christ independent of a line of evidence which at this date appears, to at least some minds, subtle and artificial. It can be done, and the Epistle itself supplies pregnant hints which help us in the task.

What are the essential elements in the case? What are the facts in the history of Jesus out of which a thoughtful man might now, unaware that the attempt had ever been made before, construct for himself a priestly theory as to the significance of our Lord's earthly life? It would be easy to state the grounds on which an intelligent reader of the Gospels might readily feel justified in conceiving of Jesus as a great religious Teacher, or Hebrew Prophet. It is enough to point to the Sermon on the Mount, and the many searching words of criticism on the religion of the time. But what features of the wonderful ministry might suggest the idea of investing with sacerdotal robes One who was the sworn foe of priestcraft, and an object of deadly enmity to temple officials? They are not so obvious; they do not lie on the surface; but they are there. Two things fix the attention of one who thoroughly understands the earthly career of Jesus: *self-sacrifice* and *solidarity with sinners*. Are not these the essential elements of priestliness? One might, it is true, note these things in Jesus and yet not think of calling Him a priest. But that might be due more to the fact of the priest, as we know him, falling far below the ideal constituted by these characteristics, than to the intrinsic inapplicability of the term to one in whose character they were the conspicuous features. If you want a name for one who is uniquely self-devoted, and endowed with unparalleled sympathy with sinful men, what better can you find than *Priest*? This Man has His sacrifice, and He offers it for others. His offering is Himself, His life; and He lays it down "a ransom for the many."

The two things above noted as the fact-basis of a priestly construction of our Lord's earthly life find, as we have seen, prominent recognition in our Epistle. The principle of solidarity receives happy expression in the words, "Sanctifier and sanctified all one" (ii. 11); and that Jesus gave His life for the salvation of men is again and again proclaimed (ii. 9, vii. 27, ix. 14). These two positions are stated independently of the *theologoumenon* concerning the Melchisedec priesthood. The former is enunciated as an axiom involved in the relation spoken of. The relation demands solidarity, and solidarity constitutes the relation. One man cannot sanctify others unless he be one with them, and wherever a holy being is indeed one with unholy beings, he is *ipso facto* a priestly sanctifier. As for the latter, the self-sacrifice of Christ, it is not presented by the writer as included in any known type of priesthood recognised in Hebrew history; not even in the Melchisedec type, so far as appears on the surface of the argument. The writer makes no attempt to deduce it as a note of that type; there is nothing to show that he even thought such a thing possible. At most Christ's self-sacrifice is connected with the Melchisedec excursus by a very slender logical thread, thus: The story of Melchisedec, with the relative Messianic oracle in the Psalm, shows that there is a priesthood for the Christ independent of the Levitical order. Therefore Jesus as the Christ is a Priest. But if He be a Priest, He must have something to offer. That something can be nothing else than Himself; there is nothing else to point to. That the act of Jesus in surrendering His life *was* sacrificial in its character, and that it exemplified the highest form of sacrifice, are propositions for which no proof is offered: they rest on their own self-evidence.

It thus appears that for the writer, as for us, the ultimate basis for the priestly conception of Christ's work was supplied by the two facts above specified. If now we ask, How did he know these facts? I presume the answer must be: Much in the same way as we know them, namely, through the evangelic tradition, in either a written or an unwritten form. That was certainly the source of his knowledge that Jesus endured death in the form of crucifixion (xii. 2). That it was likewise the source of his knowledge of the other cardinal fact, solidarity, may appear more doubtful. That the Sanctifier was not ashamed to call unsanctified men His brethren is presented rather as an inference from certain Messianic texts, than as an induction based on the solid facts of the gospel history. What a feeble impression these texts make compared with a single gospel fact, say the meeting of Jesus with the publicans and sinners of Capernaum! Who, in view of that one fact, could for a moment doubt that the Sinless One was not ashamed to call sinners His brethren! Assuredly the fact proves the thesis well—*too well* for Hebrew Christian readers. They could not appreciate such facts; they would regard them rather as an integral part of that strange state of humiliation which was one of the stumbling-blocks for their faith. Hence, however well he knew the evangelic tradition, the writer had to deny himself the pleasure of drawing on it for illustration of Messiah's solidarity with sinners. He must content himself with establishing that solidarity by Messianic citations, and then using it to explain gospel facts viewed as *problems*, not as proofs; such facts as that Christ was born, tempted, subject to death. Of these he knew from the evangelic tradition, and doubtless from the same source he knew of many other significant experiences of Jesus, His eating and drinking with publicans and sinners included.

In connection with the doctrine of Christ's priesthood, and the sacrificial construction put upon His death, one has occasion to note the mental versatility of our author. He is not a man of one idea, the slave of a formula, incapable of regarding a great subject from more than a single favourite point of view. He firmly believes in the sacrificial character of Christ's death; it is a cardinal tenet of his theology. But that is not the only aspect under which he views the event. He handles the topic with great freedom, presenting it under five phases adapted to varying connections of thought and argumentative exigencies. Beginning with the lowest and most elementary view, and rising gradually to the highest, they are as follows:—

1. Jesus died once, and once only, as it is appointed unto all men once to die (ix. 27). On this view Christ's death is simply an instance of the common lot.

2. Jesus died as a testator who, by a will, bequeaths an inheritance (ix. 16). From this point of view His death might have taken place in any manner, by disease or by accident. All that is necessary is that the testator be, and be known to be, dead, as the condition of the will coming into effect.

3. The death of Jesus was the culminating point of a varied experience of suffering through which He was qualified for His office as Captain of salvation. Crucifixion, with all that went before it, was a discipline for Him, not a sacrifice for others (ii. 10).

4. The death of Jesus, as a sinless Man, broke the connection between sin and death as its penalty, and so delivered sinful men from the fear of death as penal (ii. 14, 15). On this view the idea is not that the Sinless One dies instead of the sinful, but that the Sinless One, though sinless, dies; nor does any emphasis lie on the manner of His death.

5. The death of Jesus was a *priestly act of self-sacrifice* whereby He " perfected for ever them that are sanctified" (x. 14).

All those five views of the same event possessed for the time real, though not equal, *apologetic* value. They helped Hebrew Christians to see, in one way or another, why it behoved Jesus to die. Dogmatic theology has made little or no use of any but the last. It is, of course, by far the most important, but a theological system is self-impoverished which finds no place under its categories for the third aspect, which presents Christ's death in a light at once eminently human and eminently natural. From this point of view the earthly career of Jesus, with its tragic experience of suffering, is invested with the unique ethical interest of a heroic life lived under the hardest conditions. Then from the same point of view the whole suffering experience of Jesus, including His death, is seen to be the natural result of His moral fidelity. The cross came to Him because He cared supremely for the Divine interest and for duty. It is not a matter of minor moment whether Christians know and confess these things or ignore them. That Socinians make everything of this aspect of Christ's sufferings is no reason why we should make nothing of it.

One thing more must be said of Christ's priestly function. It has been said again and again in the exposition but it needs repetition. Christ's sacrifice is not on the same level with Levitical sacrifice. A recent writer on the theology of our Epistle, comparing Christianity with Leviticalism, has remarked: "The religious and theological idea has not varied.... It is the ritual notion of bloody sacrifice."[1] The statement is true in form only, not in substance. Blood, as such, is not the important matter in the sacrifice of Christ, as conceived by our writer. Blood, death, has value only as revealing will, spirit. It is the eternal spirit of holy love, the righteous will fulfilling all righteousness, that gives the sacrifice of Jesus transcendent worth, and makes it differ *toto cœlo* from the ritual sacrifices of Leviticalism. Till that truth is clearly seen, and firmly grasped, we have not escaped from the religion of shadows.

When spirit, as distinct from flesh and blood, has taken its due place in Christian thought, there will be no desire to leave behind the conception of Christ as a Priest, as unworthy of the final religion. Jesus Christ will be trusted and adored as the great High Priest of humanity. But the religion of the spirit will acknowledge no other priest beside Him. Priestcraft, sacerdotalism, sacraments turned into magic sources of spiritual benefit, have no place in true Christianity. They are a lapse back to the era of shadows, a lapse only too intelligible and explicable, nevertheless lamentable. There

[1] Ménégoz, p. 255.

is nothing to encourage such a lapse in our Epistle. It has been truly said that "no writing, apparently, is less favourable to the establishment of a human priesthood than the treatise in which it is proved that Christ has put an end to the Levitical priesthood, substituting for the terrestrial high priests and material sacrifices of the old covenant the celestial sacrifice, unique, supreme, final, in which He combines the functions of Priest and Victim. Henceforth no more need of new priests and new sacrifices."[1] Yet the same writer contends that the doctrinal premises of this conception are such as necessarily lead to the reconstruction of a new sacerdotal order, and even finds in the ἡγούμενοι of chapter xiii., as the regular intermediaries of the work of salvation, the rudiments of such an order. This is simply a plausible error. Doubtless the parallelism run between Levitical priests and Christ might lead Christian readers to assimilate Christian pastors to Levitical priests, till at length sacerdotal conceptions of the Christian ministry took full possession of men's minds. But this would be only an instance of the abuse of Scripture by persons who, while conversant with the letter, failed to penetrate its spirit. As for the ἡγούμενοι or "leaders," no functions are ascribed to them save such as the most orthodox Protestant might ascribe to his pastor. All pastors "watch for souls," and there was much need for such watchers in a Church which was in imminent danger of dissolution through the cowardice and disloyalty of its members.

The priestly vocation of Christ implies a lofty conception of His *Person*. He whose function it is to bring

[1] Reville, *Les Origines de L'Episcopat*, pp. 391, 392.

men nigh to God, the great end of religion, must be Himself very near to God in character and in nature. So accordingly Christ appears in our Epistle. He is represented as near to God in character—" without sin " (iv. 15). The very title " Sanctifier " implies such moral nearness to the Divine Being. The solidarity between Sanctifier and sanctified is subject to this limitation, that while the latter are sinners the former is not. A sanctifier, from the nature of the case, must be holy in some sense, ritually at least, or by comparison with those he sanctifies—as a saint is holy compared with ordinary men. The ideal sanctifier, possessing the highest qualifications for his function, will be really not ritually holy, holy absolutely, not relatively. The type of priesthood exemplified in Christ guarantees rare, if not unique, absolute, moral excellence. It is a type in which Priest and Victim are combined in the same person. Its sacrifice is self-sacrifice. Jesus sanctified sinners by giving Himself in life and in death for them. Such self-devotion is possible only for one whose spirit is pure, noble, heroic.

Christ is also represented as very near to God in *nature*. He is called " the Son," a name which seems to place Him at once within the sphere of the Divine. It has been maintained that it is not the intention of the writer to ascribe Deity in the strict sense to the Son. In answer to this it may be affirmed that it was the interest of the writer, as the eulogist of Christ's priesthood, to charge His Sonship with the greatest possible fulness of meaning. The greater the condescension the greater the merit of the self-sacrifice, and the higher the dignity the greater the condescension. The condescension reaches a maximum when the self-devoted One stoops down from a position of Divine Majesty. The same interest, that of magnifying the sacrifice, requires the Sonship to be of older date than the life on earth. Self-consecration within the limits of a human life is great, but greater is a devoted mind whose first act is to enter humanity, in order therein to exhibit in life and death the "*eternal spirit*" of self-sacrifice. From yet another point of view the Deity of Christ may be said to be a postulate of the system of thought embodied in our Epistle. Its great doctrine is the absolute, perfect, and therefore final nature of the Christian religion. But Christianity cannot be the absolute religion unless Jesus, the Author and Finisher of faith, the object of Christian trust and reverence, have for faith the religious value of God. The Son and the Father must be one.

The Divine dignity of the Son is asserted in the Epistle in no stinted terms, but that does not prevent the author from doing equal justice to the *earthly state of humiliation*. The dignity is asserted with emphasis to enhance the greatness of the sacrifice, not to eclipse it. The writer was therefore only consistent with himself in not allowing the sacrifice to be eclipsed. He was under no temptation to cast a veil over the humiliation, because, as was pointed out in the exposition, there was for his mind no incompatibility between the dignity and the apparent degradation. The Son on the throne and the Son wearing human garb and suffering mortal pain was the same in spirit—a priest for ever in His heart. He left glory behind when He came into our world, but only to find therein a new glory—that of a Captain leading a host through the hardships of the wilderness to the promised land. A new glory, yet not altogether new, for the glory of the Son had from of old been that of One who in purpose was a Lamb slain.

The thoughtful student of our Epistle feels that the writer speaks of the humiliation state not by constraint but willingly, as one charmed by its unique pathos. No theme was more welcome to his mind. He could, one imagines, have sympathised with the sentiment of Anselm when he said, " I know not how it is that Thou art far sweeter in the heart of one who loves Thee in that Thou art flesh, than in that Thou art the Word; sweeter in Thy humility than in Thy exaltation." [1]

The humiliation of Christ is described as realistically as is possible without concrete detail such as could not easily find a place within the limits of an epistle. The Son became man, like other men, through birth; subject therefore to the law of physical and mental growth. On arriving at maturity, He experienced temptation under all the variety of forms with which life makes other men acquainted. Ever loyal to the right amid these moral trials, He encountered the troubles which overtake all who are animated by the passion for righteousness. He endured the " contradiction of sinners "—was misunderstood, maligned, hated, put to death, by men who were very religious and yet the most malignant enemies of God

---

[1] " Et certe nescio, quia nec plene comprehendere valeo, unde hoc est, quod longe dulcior es in corde diligentis te in eo quod caro es, quam in eo quod verbum : dulcior in eo quod humilis, quam in eo quod sublimis." Meditatio xii., *De Humanitate Christi*, near the beginning.

and all real good. All this He bravely bore, yet not without shrinking, and even, at the last crisis, deadly overmastering fear, revealing very human though innocent infirmity. To this infirmity, in the garden, He gave unrestrained utterance "with strong crying and tears." Finally, He was subject to the law of growth even in the moral sphere, reaching perfection only by a process of development, as in the case of ordinary men; learning trust, sympathy, obedience by testing experience. The Gospels supply the data for verifying the truth of this picture, but nowhere else in the New Testament are the earthly lot and human behaviour of Jesus depicted in such vivid and lifelike colours. Not even all the Gospels (not Luke, *e.g.*) show us Jesus in the weakness of His flesh side by side with the purity of His spirit, as He is exhibited here. We are so accustomed to one-sidedness in human thought, even in the case of philosophers, that we hardly expect one whose delight it was to contemplate the Divine dignity of the Son to display such masterliness in the treatment of His lowliness. Think of Philo with his Logos invested with the most dazzling attributes, but never allowed to become incarnate or to touch the ground! What a barren, wearisome splendour it all is, for lack of a decided contrast! If our author had ever been a disciple of Philo, he must have taken lessons in a very different school before he wrote this Epistle with its Christ so truly human while divine.

This vivid presentation of the humiliation of Christ lends itself to the hortatory purposes of the Epistle. The more Christ endured in the way of temptation, suffering, and indignity, the greater His capacity to sympathise with Christians subject to similar experiences. It is one of the aims of the writer to insist on this sympathy, regarding it as he does as a powerful aid to Christian fidelity. Hence the strong negative assertion that "we have not an High Priest who cannot be touched with the feeling of our infirmities" (iv. 15), and the positive exhortation to "look unto Jesus the Leader in the life of faith and the perfect pattern of faith, who braved death and shame in loyalty to God and duty" (xii. 2). But the sympathy could not be effectively asserted if the humiliation were thrown into the shade. It must be ostentatiously proclaimed, not timidly slurred over. This accordingly is done with the thoroughness which may be looked for when a task of delicate nature is performed at once from personal liking, and with a sense of its utility to others.

There is nothing on the surface of the Epistle very distinctive in its way of speaking concerning *God*. One's first impression might even be that its dominant idea of God was that of the Old Testament, wherein God is chiefly viewed as a moral Governor rendering to every man according to his work, with special emphasis on the punitive aspect of Divine Providence. God is described as "a rewarder of them that diligently seek Him" (xi. 6), and with stern emphasis as "a consuming fire." A very different conception this from that suggested by the genial saying of the Great Teacher on the Mount concerning the Father in heaven, "who maketh His sun to rise on the evil and on the good, and sendeth rain on the just and on the unjust,"—benignity, not strict retributive justice, His conspicuous attribute! The paternal aspect of the Divine character does find recognition, however, though chiefly in the final hortatory section. There God is called "the Father of spirits" (xii. 9), and it is set forth as His supreme aim in all His dealings with His children to make them "partakers of His holiness" (xii. 10). The expression "Father of spirits" seems to suggest a paternal relation of God to men as such, co-extensive with the human family, or rather, inclusive of the human family, embracing it in a larger category, the world of spirits, including men living in the flesh but having a spirit, the spirits of just men made perfect, and angels. In the theoretic part of the Epistle the Father-hood is implied rather than expressed, and chiefly though not exclusively in reference to Christ. God is by implication the Father of "the Son," and also of the many sons whom the Son, as Captain of salvation, conducts to glory.

That the distinctively Christian conception of God as Father is comparatively in the background, so far as formal statement is concerned, may be ascribed to the exigencies of the apologetic argument rather than to the imperfectly Christianised condition of the writer's theology. That Old and New Testament conceptions should mingle in the idea of God cherished by one living in a transition time, on the border-line between an old and a new world, is in itself not surprising. But the presence of what may be called the pre-Christian element is due mainly to the fact that the author has to do with readers who belong to the old world rather than to the new. Then the historic situation in which the Epistle in all probability was written—the destruction of Jerusalem and of the Jewish State impending—fully accounts for the sombre side of the Divine character, as depicted in it, represented by the repellent phrase, "a consuming fire." There is a sombre side even in Christ's presentation of God, due to the same cause—the ruin of the Jewish people foreseen as a certainty. In the moral order of the world, God does show Himself at times very really as a consuming fire. Prophets knew this, Jesus knew it, apostles knew it; and however firmly they believed in and asserted the loving-kindness of God, it was without prejudice to their belief in, and, when needful, their earnest proclamation of, the darker aspect of Divine action as manifested in Providence. It was the unwelcome task of those whose lot was cast in evil times to give this aspect special prominence. Hence the deep shadow resting on the countenance of God in our Epistle.

Yet the writer believed with all his heart in the Father-God of Jesus. How could he help doing so, holding such a view as he teaches concerning Christianity as the religion of free access to God? This central conception covers the whole ground. A religion of unrestricted access is, must be, a religion of sonship in relation to God as Father. Its spirit is *filial*, not *legal*: it brings its votaries to Mount Zion, not to Mount Sinai. That is possible only because God is eminently *accessible*— above all things gracious—the generous, bountiful giver of all good, a Being who loves not to dwell in darkness, apart, but welcomes to His presence even the sinful, confessing their sin, and treats them as if they had never sinned, as set forth in the Parable of the Prodigal.

In a religion of free access to a gracious God, *faith* must necessarily occupy a prominent place. Faith in man answers to grace in God. We draw near to our Father in heaven by trust. A gracious God is a Giver of all good, and men are humble, thankful receivers, and receiving is faith. The religious function of faith in trusting God's good will, and accepting His grace, finds due recognition in our Epistle, as in the exhortations to come boldly, confidently, unto the throne of grace (iv. 16), and to draw near in full assurance of faith (x. 19), the purpose of the coming being to receive the blessings of salvation, to obtain mercy and find grace for seasonable succour. This is Paul's doctrine of justification by faith, stripped of its theological technicality. Paul's doctrine of faith as an energetic principle making for personal righteousness (Gal. v. 6) also reappears in our Epistle, but with a noteworthy change in the form under which it is presented. The action of faith, in Paul's handling of the topic, is confined to the moral and religious sphere. The sole question in which he is interested is the tendency of faith to promote Christian goodness, to show that faith alone is competent to all the requirements of the spiritual life, able at once to "justify" and to "sanctify." The writer of our Epistle takes a wider view of faith's activity, viewing it as a principle which enters into and is the secret spring of all great heroic conduct, of all remarkable historical characters, from Enoch the saint to Rahab the harlot, enabling men to subdue kingdoms and stop the mouths of lions, as well as to work righteousness. Nothing great done in this world, in any sphere, without faith—

such is the comprehensive thesis of our author, though it must be observed that his chief interest also is in the action of faith within the religious sphere, and that most of his instances lie within that region. Still, the wide universal outlook is there, and it is worth noting as a mark of the *philosophic* thinker as distinct from the purely religious thinker exemplified in Paul. Corresponding to the wide range of faith's activity is the motive power which lends it the needful force. In Paul's presentation faith works by *love*; in our Epistle faith derives its virtue from its psychological character as a faculty of the human mind, whereby it can make the future present and the unseen visible. This faculty is not, as such, ethical or religious; it is a natural endowment of man. It was by faith that Columbus persevered in his voyage of discovery, quite as much as it was by faith that Abraham set out in quest of the land of promise, not knowing whither he went. In both cases, faith's nature, as able to make the future present and the unseen visible, was signally exemplified. It is not to be supposed, however, that one man's faith is in all respects the same as another's. A differentiating principle comes into play in connection with the *kind of invisibles which faith makes visible*. It may be a great trans-Atlantic western continent, or it may be a heavenly country, a city whose builder and maker is God. For the heavenly realities which the philosophic vision of our author descried, the faith of some men has no eye, the range of its vision being restricted to this present life and the tangible interests of time. It is the faith which sees God, the world above, the life beyond the veil, which, in the view of our Epistle, emphatically saves.

Such faith, it is therein taught, does indeed *save*. Witness the description of the men who persevere in Christian belief as the men of faith *unto the winning of the soul* (chap. x. 39).[1] This winning of the soul, as our author conceives it, is a great affair. His idea of salvation is not partial and fragmentary, but full, many-sided. It does not mean merely pardon of sin, though it embraces that, and in a very ample sense. It includes nearness to God in life, "holiness, without which no man shall see the Lord" (xii. 14), loyal obedience to Jesus Christ the Lord (v. 9), a priestly life of thanksgiving and beneficence (xiii. 15, 16). It means great good in store for the faithful in another and better world — lordship in the world to come, a Sabbatic rest, citizenship in the heavenly Jerusalem. But the *summum bonum* is not exclusively other-worldly. The felicity of the other world is the reward of an unworldly life here and now, which forms an essential ingredient of the state of salvation. The "saved" man is a moral hero in this present world, and takes his place among the ranks of the glorious company who have gained the diploma of righteousness. He wins his soul

---

[1] εἰς περιποίησιν ψυχῆς. Vaughan's note here is instructive. "The verb περιποιεῖν (*to make to be over and above*) carries the two ideas of *survival* and *surplus*. The former predominates in the active voice, *to save* (a *life*, etc.), the latter in the middle, *to acquire*. . . . The noun in its New Testament use takes its colour from the middle, *acquisition*. Thus here the thought is that of the ψυχή being in this life *the stake of the contest*, to be won or lost in the great day."

by being willing to lose life for the sake of truth and duty. So the Master taught, and the author of this Epistle understood and earnestly re-echoed His teaching.

In the foregoing rapid sketch we have seen how the author's theological system springs genetically out of the radical conception of the Christian religion as the religion of free access to God. The system in all its ramifications rises naturally and easily out of the religious consciousness of a thoroughly Christianised man. It has not been necessary to take into account the philosophy of the author, as furnishing the only key to his views on any topic of cardinal importance, though the philosopher does appear now and then, as in the manner of describing the Son (chap. i. 1—3) and of defining faith (chap. xi.). At one point only is it necessary to lay his philosophy under requisition with a view to the full understanding of his theology. I refer, of course, to his final utterance on the subject of Christ's self-sacrifice. It repays us to keep in mind, at this point, his conception of heaven as the locus of realities, and of earth as the place of shadows. The distinction is not one belonging so much to the category of space, as to that of spiritual value. Hence the thesis: heaven the place of the real, is convertible: the real is the heavenly. Heaven is wherever reality is: earth is a synonym for the shadowy. Therefore the death of Christ, though occurring in this visible world on a hill called Calvary, essentially belongs to the heavenlies. As an act of the Spirit, it was and is a sacrifice performed in the heavenly sanctuary. As an act of an Eternal Spirit, it has no exclusive connection with a certain point of time in human history. It is eternal, and, like Christ Himself, is the same yesterday, to-day, and for ever. Levitical sacrifices, on the other hand, had nothing either of the heavenly or of the eternal in them. Devoid of spirit, they belonged exclusively to the region of shadows, and their effect was momentary and purely conventional. To this extent a speculative element must be recognised in the Epistle, and for the charm it lends to the work, and the aid it brings to the interpreter at a crucial point in the train of thought, we owe a debt of gratitude to the writer. Philosophy has not always rendered good service, unmixed with evil, to theology. But in the case before us the benefit is real, and there is no drawback.

THE END

www.ingramcontent.com/pod-product-compliance
Lightning Source LLC
Chambersburg PA
CBHW032002300426
44117CB00008B/875